AF383180

# Conversations about Sculpture

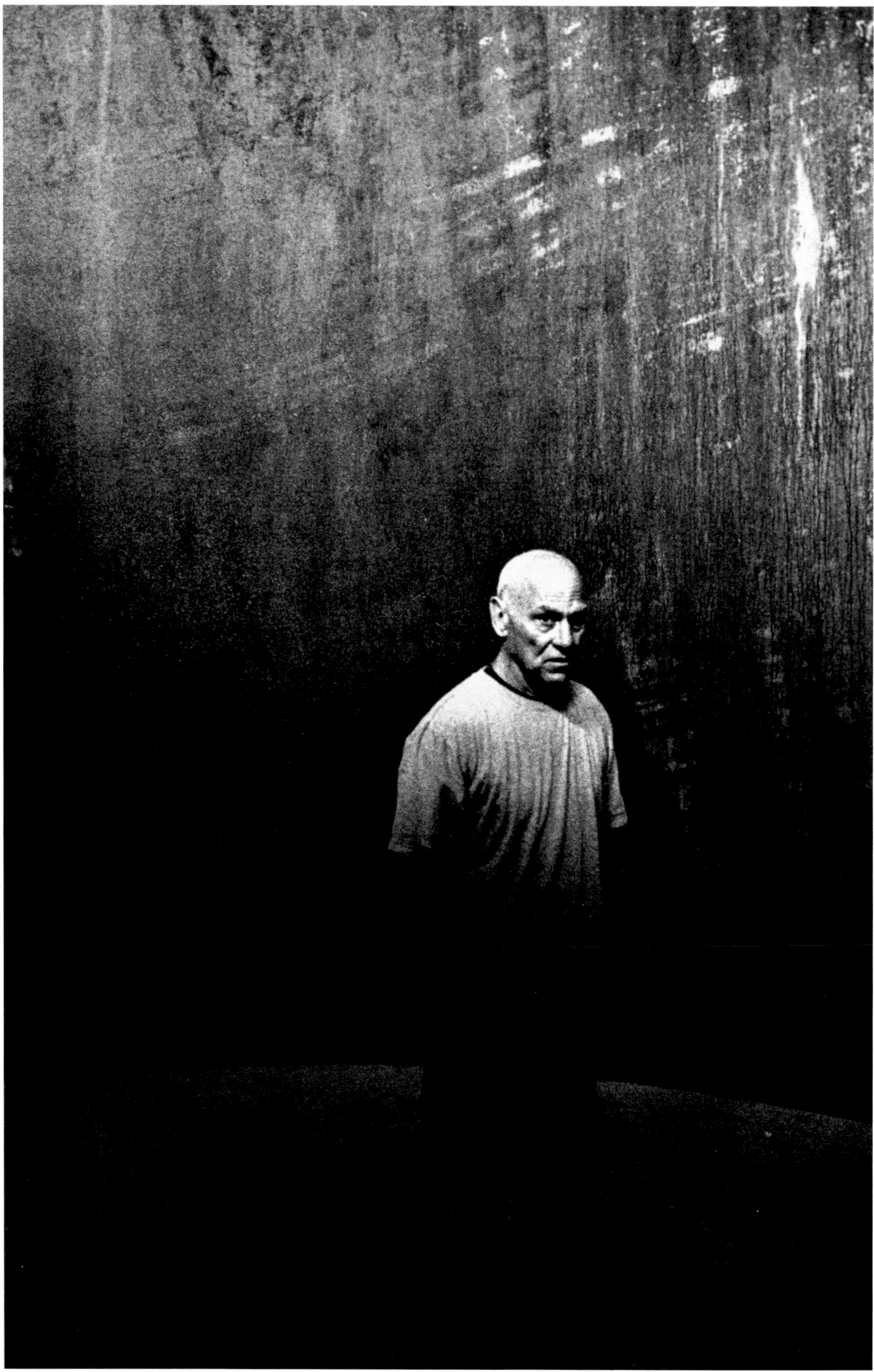

# RICHARD SERRA
# HAL FOSTER

## Conversations about Sculpture

**Yale University Press** New Haven and London

This publication is made possible in part by a grant from the Barr Ferree Foundation
Publication Fund, Department of Art and Archaeology, Princeton University.



Unless otherwise noted, all works are by Richard Serra.

yalebooks.com/art

Designed by McCall Associates, New York
Set in type by Mark Nelson
Printed in Italy by Verona Libri

Library of Congress Control Number: 2018932956
ISBN 978-0-300-23596-8

A catalogue record for this book is available from the British Library.

This paper meets the requirements of ANSI/NISO Z 39.48–1992 (Permanence of Paper).

10 9 8 7 6 5 4 3 2 1

Cover illustration: Richard Serra, *Splashing*, 1968 (see page 53)
Frontispiece: Robert Frank, *Richard Serra,* 2002. © Robert Frank;
courtesy Pace/MacGill Gallery, New York.

CONTENTS

# Preface

Richard Serra and I met at the Odeon in Lower Manhattan in the early 1980s, back when that restaurant was still a hangout for artists and writers who lived in the neighborhood. I was in my late twenties, Serra only in his mid-forties, but he was well known, and I was intimidated. His reputation as a forceful debater also put me on guard. At the same time, I was struck that he wanted to engage a young critic, and to do so late into the night. (It was always late at the Odeon, yet the soft halo of the pastel clock over the long bar somehow made the hour seem beside the point.)

During that period Serra had begun to produce large steel pieces in situ, most notably *Tilted Arc* (1981), which was only a few blocks away, and they had already attracted the attention of architects like Frank Gehry, who was with Serra that night. We talked about this latest development in his sculpture, but he also wanted to know about a group of artists then on the rise, "Pictures" artists such as Cindy Sherman and Louise Lawler, most of whom were my friends. What innovation did they bring? Given its fascination with media images, was this art anything more than Pop come again? Although his critical suspicion was hardly free of the competitive streak that runs deep in his personality (as the reader will see, not even the dead are safe from his challenges), his desire to understand the new work was genuine. For all his commitment to his sculpture, Serra remains inquisitive about other practices. This curiosity is fully on display in the conversations that follow.

A few years after our first meeting, the controversy around *Tilted Arc* broke, and Serra was the object of attack in the press and on the street (we discuss the case in "Controversies"). When the General Services Administration, the federal agency that commissioned the sculpture, staged a skewed hearing about its removal, I testified on his behalf, but not with the passion that he required, and we fell out of touch after the destruction of *Tilted Arc* in 1989. Like the economy at large, the art market experienced both a boom and a bust during the Reagan-Bush years, and galleries and museums expanded further in the 1990s. None of these structural changes in the art system appeared to faze Serra, who continued to elaborate his sculptural language on his own terms. In fact, he did not adapt to the changed scale of the art world (richer patrons, grander galleries, bigger museums) so much as he bent it to his will. I followed this development closely, and gradually we fell back into conversation.

Serra has always sought the resistance of another voice. Philip Glass fulfilled that role early on; then there was Robert Smithson, whose dialogue with Serra was cut short by his premature death. Critics and curators like Rosalind Krauss, David Sylvester, and Kirk Varnedoe also stepped up over the years, and for decades he has had an essential interlocutor in his wife, Clara Weyergraf-Serra, who participates in some of the conversations here. Serra turned back to me because, even though I was influenced by his generation,

I am not part of it: I speak a similar language but have a different perspective. We know how to agree just enough so that when we disagree the differences count.

If any artist disproves the old F. Scott Fitzgerald line that there are no second acts in American lives, that artist is Serra. The acclaim that greeted his *Torqued Ellipses,* which emerged in the mid-1990s, was equal to the abuse heaped on *Tilted Arc* a decade before. The torqued sculptures are that rare thing, a radical innovation in art that people outside the art world also appreciate deeply. To come to terms with this invention and to convey its import to others, we started to have regular discussions. In the early 2000s we did a few public talks, and a little later I began to record our private conversations. Although I was sometimes on the defensive in our initial sessions, I soon learned to push back, not only for the sake of the debate but also for the elucidation of the work. I remain largely a foil in this dialogue, yet I get my touches in as we move along. That said, as I test Serra, he calls  me into question, and some of my assumptions are laid bare in the process. Although I could have pressed him harder at times, my aim was to prompt, not to provoke— and not to let the conversation falter.

This was tricky when it came to accounts I had heard before. Most artists have stories that assist in the retrospective positing of an origin or the narrative shaping of a career; such set pieces render moments of inspiration or innovation dramatic. And Serra has excellent ones to tell, such as his witnessing a massive ship launched in San Francisco Bay as a little boy or his coming upon a pod of whales beached several years later—powerful intimations of great weight buoyed and great weight grounded. Perhaps, like many origin stories, they become partly fictive in the telling, but it was not my role to probe them too much: I am not a biographer, much less an analyst, and often memories are memories, not screens. In any case, what makes these anecdotes effective is that they transform private moments into public explications, as when Serra recounts his mistaking of the ellipses of the Borromini church San Carlo alle Quattro Fontane as torqued (in "Torqued Shapes"); or they turn everyday experiences into fresh insights, as when he reflects on how the world seems to rotate when we reverse directions along a beach (in "Symbolic Forms"). One of the subcurrents of this dialogue is his ambivalent relation to psychological read-ings, which is both specific to Serra and general to his cohort (he names Smithson, Eva Hesse, and Bruce Nauman, in particular). Yet his insistence on the phenomenological experience of art is not necessarily a resistance to its unconscious dimension.

Personally, I am most interested in exchanges in which we either collide or glide by each other, as when we take up the distinction between site and context (in "Specific Sites"), the difference between a critical approach from within an art form and one from outside it (in "Prime Objects"), the role of symbolism in sculpture (in "Symbolic Forms"), the nature of materialism in art (in "Sculpture Hadn't Dealt with Steel"), and the changed valence of

industrial production in society (in "Controversies"). Even more than I, Serra wanted
to avoid moments of agreement, though he provides a key instance in our discussion of
political commitment in art: "I don't direct my work toward engagement, but I think part
of its autonomy includes engagement. Why can't it be both?" This resistance to reconcili-
ation makes for reflections of great honesty—Serra is open about the role of mortality
in his late style—as well as expressions of real modesty: "Duchamp said that you're lucky
if you get thirty or forty years. . . . Warhol said all we get is fifteen minutes. Who knows?
The fact is you can't know." An undergraduate student put it to me best: "Serra often speaks
in a manner that is filled with passionate imagination while at the same time stubbornly
simple and averse to ostentation."

Our conversation begins with his childhood in San Francisco and his work in steel
mills as a young man, then moves to his encounter with painting in college (the Mexican
muralists were most important) and his graduate training at Yale (at a time when Josef
Albers was still influential). Serra recounts his sojourn in Paris, where he was immersed
in the sculpture of Constantin Brancusi and Alberto Giacometti, as well as his contact
with Arte Povera in Rome. On his return to New York he first experimented with rubber
and lead, which leads him to distinguish the "dirty" Minimalism of his cohort from the
"shiny" version of Donald Judd and Dan Flavin. Here, too, we discuss his affinities with
the Minimalist music of Philip Glass and Steve Reich, as well as his admiration for the
Judson Church dance of Yvonne Rainer, Trisha Brown, and Simone Forti, whose matter
of-fact choreography supported his own commitment to basic actions performed on non-
art materials. Critical of the Duchampian readymade, Serra used gravity to free sculpture
from its traditional supports, and process to break up its integral forms. His next move
was to turn to steel construction, which allowed him first to vector sculpture into space
and then to delineate a field in a manner partly inspired by Japanese gardens. Thus began
his long engagement with the framing of sites and the gathering of people, whether in a
gallery, a city, or a landscape.

His torqued ellipses and spirals marked another transformation in his sculpture,
and from the mid-1990s onward Serra elaborated this language of complex spaces and fast
surfaces, which often disconnect inside and outside and disorient the viewer radically.
During this fertile period he also explored other geometrical sections (such as the torus)
and other spatial intervals (such as offset grids of straight plates at different heights),
which test our ability to see and to think on our feet in different ways. At the same time
Serra insisted on the weighty concentration of his forged rounds and blocks as a counter
to the light thrust of his curvilinear pieces—and continues to do so to this day.

At moments we pause the narrative of his sculpture to discuss fundamental issues
that exceed any one practice: How does an artist enter into the history of his or her medium?

How might he or she break with given forms and innovate new types? How might these prime objects return in different guises in the course of a career? Serra also fields questions slightly outside his comfort zone, such as on the role of symbolic forms like stelae and sarcophagi and psychological icons like towers and bridges in his work. More than once we take a run at the difficult issue of monumentality, about which Serra remains conflicted.

This inquiry leads us into an expanded field of art where we discuss his fascination with prehistoric figures, Etruscan sculptures, and Cambodian pots, as well as with unusual works by canonical artists like Donatello and Michelangelo, all of which he takes as so many "triggers for thought." Crucially, this expanded field includes architecture: Serra describes the importance of his visits over the years to sites such as Luxor and the Hagia Sophia, Machu Picchu and the Mozarabic buildings near Madrid. In all these experiences structure is as important as place: to a great extent Serra has refashioned sculpture through an emphasis on tectonics—hence his deep interest in certain engineers and architects of the modern period, especially Robert Maillart, Mies van der Rohe, late Le Corbusier, late Frank Lloyd Wright, Louis Kahn, Hans Scharoun, and Jørn Utzon, all of whom he comments on here. (We also speculate on the significance of his sculpture for contemporary designers.) In part his turn to architecture was driven by his dissatisfaction with avant-gardist paradigms of the readymade and the assemblage, as well as with immediate precedents in welded sculpture and "specific objects" (David Smith and Donald Judd).

The book includes a frank discussion of accidents and controversies in his career, such as the death of a rigger in Minneapolis in 1971, the fight over a tower in West Germany in 1977, the abandonment of one public commission in Washington in 1978 and another in Berlin in 2005, and of course the destruction of *Tilted Arc* in 1989. By way of conclusion I ask Serra about other tensions in his art, such as the public address of most of his sculpture versus the private setting of many of its presentations, or his identification with industrial labor in the midst of a plutocratic art world. Sometimes our conversation is heated, but one of his mottos is to work through contradictions, and I admire his commitment to do so. I also respect his double insistence that innovation comes through critique and that critique begins at home.

Although we use terms such as "prime objects" and "symbolic forms" that might not be familiar, we do our best to define them when they appear. However, one keyword should be parsed here. *Gestalt* (German for "shape") is a term once used in experimental psychology to convey how the mind organizes a unified perception out of discrepant stimuli. One of its famous slogans—"the whole is other than the sum of the parts"— captures its thrust for Serra, for whom gestalt readings resolve a complex sculpture too readily into a simple form. "The gestalt is a great limitation, a pictorial limitation," he argues. "The viewer can complete the image of an object by looking at one part only."

This resistance to gestalt accounts runs throughout his work, and it is overdetermined. Not only is Serra averse to imagistic kinds of art such as Surrealism or Pop that, focused on literary or media content, tend to devalue expressive form and embodied experience, but, as suggested in the anecdotes mentioned above, he is also committed to a phenomenological orientation to the world that refuses to frame it as a picture. Finally, this critique has a target close by: "Most Minimalists are stuck with gestalt readings," Serra avers. "They don't truly open the space; for the most part their constructions remain objects."

I stress this resistance to imagistic accounts because it helps to explain his insistence on material and process. With this emphasis Serra aims, in good modernist fashion, to break with convention in order to refresh perception, but he is also wary of preconception (this is behind his suspicion, also voiced here, of Conceptual art). In fact, Serra often points to moments when he is inspired, not stymied, by his own puzzlement before a new work ("I couldn't have anticipated that" is a repeated refrain). He trusts in his experience to correct what he thinks and to change how he works. Such is his version of materialism: practice before theory but not against it; drawing after sculpture to learn from it rather than to predetermine it; "work comes out of work."[1] There is an ethical lesson to extract from this belief: "With most art, if you're patient, you can find a way into the language, and it will give you some feedback. It's probably true with most people too." And a political implication too: questions are best pursued in the open, with others if possible, in conflict if need be.

Certainly Serra finds his strength in the material language of his sculpture, insisting on the category when others abandon it or stretch it beyond recognition. In this way he keeps faith with the great art of the past; at the same time he insists on the present of our own experience. Such is the first and last criterion for him: How does the work engage us, and how do we engage it, right here, right now? This suggests that our experience is never prescribed, that, however private, it is also public, and that, however intense, it is also testable. This is why, though the seeds of his work are European, its roots are American. "I'm a person who wants to deal with his own experience," Serra says early on, "and the things I want to know I want to know myself." This statement aligns him not only with transcendentalists like Ralph Waldo Emerson but also with pragmatists like John Dewey (my first title for this book was "Sculpture as Experience"), as well as with materialists like Albers, who brought his "learning by doing" approach from the Bauhaus first to Black Mountain College and then to Yale.[2]

"A lot of people downtown were involved with making and doing, only everybody was making and doing different things," Serra tells us about his initial milieu in New York. "Everybody was just making something, and everybody was everybody else's audience." He captures a spirit of collaboration across art forms, and acknowledges the generosity of older artists like Jasper Johns as well. Yet, in the midst of such cooperation there is also rivalry, both sibling and Oedipal, fired by a group insistence on individual innovation. "I was trying to find a way to assert my own way of making, of confronting the artists in front of me, and offering an initial proposition of what sculpture could be," Serra says of his first years in New York. In one instance he points to how his early work, *Plinths* (1967), takes up a columnar piece by Barnett Newman titled *Here I* (1950), and this exchange follows:

> **RS**: I think the subtext was "How can I attack Barney?"
> You see, I loved his work.
>
> **HF**: You loved it so you attacked it?
>
> **RS**: That's a familiar dynamic. Harold Bloom discusses
> it in *The Anxiety of Influence*—it's about how you go about
> trumping the precursor.[3]

Even though Serra avows that art moves forward by critique, he insists elsewhere that "artists don't replace one another." For me this is one of the great provocations in this dialogue: to think through the apparent contradiction between a history that is agonistic in the short term, a pitched battle between artists, and a "history that doesn't go away" in the long run, an open source for all artists. Somehow Serra inscribes this double temporality in his spatial art: he focuses on the next step within his own development in a contested field on the one hand, and looks back into the deep past of sculpture, in the West and across cultures, on the other.

At one point I ask Serra what motivated the acerbic intelligence of his friend Robert Smithson, and he replies directly: "A need to overcome Catholicism through nihilism—he and Warhol both." What drives the fierce intelligence of Richard Serra? I hope this dialogue provides enough clues for readers to formulate their own answers, and that it prompts further questions about this essential artist and his extraordinary generation, about modern sculpture and its connection to architecture and landscape, about contemporary art and its relation to culture and politics, and much more besides.

**HAL FOSTER**

# Sand Dunes and Steel Mills

**HF**: Let's begin at the beginning. Tell me about your formation.

**RS**: When I was very young we moved to an undeveloped area that fronted San Francisco's Ocean Beach. It was quite large, a mile and a half by two miles, an expanse of sand dunes, no blacktop roads. I had a limited concept of the outer world; even going downtown was a major event. Reading and my stamp collection were my only means to explore other places. So I learned to value my own experience. Growing up in an isolated place threw me back on my own resources. I learned early on to be self-reliant.

**HF**: No early exposure to art?

**RS**: No. I'd never seen a Cézanne until I came to the East Coast. I'd seen a couple of Matisses at the San Francisco Museum, but I had little background in European art and little background in art in general.

**HF**: You began to draw at an early age, though, and more insistently than most children do. Why?

**RS**: I was born into a household with a very intelligent brother who had the affection of our parents (my mother was Russian Jewish, my father was Spanish, in background). It was difficult for me to compete with my brother, who was four years older, except for the fact that I could draw. That captured the imagination of my parents, who were totally supportive, so every night, after dinner, I would draw. We had rolls of butcher paper, and I'd draw everything just to please them—the view out the window, the dunes, the fishing boats. The zoo was about a half a mile away, and I'd go there and draw the animals. In fact, I drew all the things that kids usually draw. I remember in the third grade my teacher invited my mother to school one day, and she had put up my drawings all around the room. Drawing for me was a way to find a language of my own—and to be doted on by my parents.

Sometimes my father would go down to the garage with my brother to work on the car. I thought that was a bore, but I'd follow along and draw all the engine parts. That stymied them: they were intent on putting the engine back together, while I was analyzing the parts. Drawing was something I could always do, and I've always relied on it.

**HF**: But you weren't an artist at school, right?

**RS**: No. I did sports—baseball, track, football—and eventually I got a scholarship to go to the University of California, Berkeley. The first year I broke my back playing football, and it was a blessing in disguise. Having looked at the art department at Berkeley, I saw there was nothing there for me, so I decided to transfer to UC Santa Barbara, where

I majored in English. There was a whole world of reading and writing I was interested in, and at that point Santa Barbara was a hotbed of intellectual activity. Who wouldn't want to take a sabbatical by the sea? Reinhold Niebuhr, Aldous Huxley, Margaret Mead, Christopher Isherwood, Walter Ong—they were all there.

Rico Lebrun and Howard Warshaw were in the art department at Santa Barbara; they were great draftsmen, and they took me under their wing. Both were muralists, and they were very interested in the Mexican painters, especially José Orozco and David Siqueiros. During my second year at Santa Barbara I hitchhiked down to Guadalajara and later on to Mexico City. I was deeply impressed by what Orozco had done at the Hospicio Cabañas in Guadalajara—the sheer strength of the work, the way it wrapped around the interior and punched holes in the architecture. The power of his murals completely reconfigured the space. His cupola depicts an enormous red fireball with men stretched around its circumference; it creates the illusion of a deep hole in the ceiling, altering the perception of the architecture drastically. The walls that surround the chapel are almost demolished in a similar manner. The architecture crumbles under the weight of death and destruction.

**HF**: That certainly suggests an early interest in how art might engage architecture aggressively. Did the connection of the muralists to their communities impress you as well?

**RS**: Yes. Their work had social and political implications as well as expressive and architectural ones. It had enormous aspirations. In comparison, the paintings I was studying and seeing in magazines seemed too contained by their frame—so much picture-making, so much "How To Paint a Painting." The Mexican work was a step in another direction, and it struck me that there might be ways to make art outside the dictates of the time. But when you're young, you don't know which step will lead to another.

**HF**: I assume this was 1959 or so. You hadn't seen a Jackson Pollock at this point?

**RS**: I didn't know who he was.

**HF**: How else did the muralists influence you?

**RS**: At the time, Lebrun and Warshaw were working on a mural in the courtyard of the library at the Santa Barbara Museum. They had divided the wall in half, and one was working on one side and one on the other, each responding to the other. I went every day to watch the mural develop. Here again I saw that painting could relate to architecture and didn't simply have to be an object for exchange. In the same museum I used to look at the Wright Ludington collection of European modernism, which included a large number of Picasso drawings. So I had a vague idea of what modernism was about as well.

**HF**: Yet you majored in literature at Santa Barbara. What writers struck you the most?

**RS**: I was very involved with existentialism; I wrote my senior thesis on Camus's *The Stranger,* and *The Myth of Sisyphus* was also an important text for me. What existentialism does is bring you back to the intensity of where you are at that exact time and place, which is not like any other time and place, and how meaningful that can be. It makes you focus on your relationship to time and its passage, your relationship to your own necessities. And that became a subtext of the way I've led my life.

**HF**: You were also taken by the American transcendentalists.

**RS**: After Camus, Emerson became my Bible. The whole idea of self-reliance was very important to me. Vico said the only things we really understand are the things we have made ourselves, which aren't too many. I think that's true: the things you do yourself are the things you understand. All of us have things that we do individually, by ourselves, that give us internal feedback. If you want to make art, those are the things you have to hang on to, even if everyone else disapproves of them; those are the things you have to reinforce. Yes, the transcendentalists were big for me, not only Emerson but also Thoreau. Later on I read Hawthorne, Melville, and Whitman.

**HF**: Your stress on the transparency of your work—its exposure of its material, process, structure, and site—has a democratic aspiration that is in line with that American tradition. Did that aspect of your art derive, in part, from your reading?

**RS**: When you're eighteen or nineteen years old, you don't know how influences will be processed. More important was my experience in steel mills catching red-hot rivets and sticking them between flanges.

**HF**: How old were you?

**RS**: Same age.

**HF**: You worked during the summers?

**RS**: Yes. The Crown Zellerbach Building was being built in San Francisco, and I was working at Bethlehem Steel in Alameda where large sections of trusses were fitted together and trucked to the city. I'd go to the city on the weekends and see things I had put together being hoisted up and set in place. I was born into a working-class family, and I took pride in the work I did in the steel mill. I identified with it.

**HF**: The question of labor in your work is a large one; we'll need to come back to it. So even then you had a sense of the importance of industrial materials and structures for you—that materials should be exposed and structures self-supporting?

**RS**: Not explicitly. You don't say that to yourself, but you have an idea that it's important.

**HF**: That it be evident, that it make sense, that it be logical.

**RS**: That you're putting something together that's going to stand, and it's something that's modern. At the time the Crown Zellerbach was the most modern building in San Francisco.

**HF**: Did that sense of the modern thrill you?

**RS**: Yes, it did.

**HF**: Might it be that your commitment to construction comes through these experiences first, and the art-historical precedents are secondary?

**RS**: When you're eighteen or nineteen, you don't know, but it certainly affected me. I suspect people who build bridges have that same reverence for their work. They say, "I was part of building that bridge." That's a great kind of internal nourishment. But at the time I didn't know what to do with myself—go to law school, grad school, I didn't know—but I kept taking drawing courses. My teachers, Warshaw in particular, recognized that I had a facility for it. He was really my mentor at Santa Barbara.

**HF**: Did he suggest you go to Yale?

**RS**: No. I took a printmaking course with an artist who had taught at Yale, and he suggested I apply. The Yale faculty said they'd give me a grant on the basis of my grade-point average and twelve drawings; they said they could teach me something! Yale required that I get their undergraduate art history degree, so I stayed three years (1961–64) rather than the normal two for the MFA degree.

**HF**: What was your experience at Yale like?

**RS**: Yale changed my life. Up till that point I had coasted along in school, but at Yale there was intense competition among the students. I had confidence in my ability to draw but little idea of how to go about painting, and I was mortified during my first year. Some students were more developed—like Brice Marden, who had gone to art school in Boston, or Chuck Close, who had made constructions, or Rackstraw Downs, who was a proficient hard-edge painter even then. They were all in my class, and Robert Mangold was a year ahead.

So there were people who, in terms of knowing the procedures of art, of painting in particular, were more advanced than I was.

**HF**: Were they informed about events in New York?

**RS**: Jasper Johns already permeated Yale.

**HF**: So the shift away from Abstract Expressionist protocols had occurred in the school?

**RS**: No. Abstract Expressionism was still the dominant language among painters who were a year or two ahead of me at Yale. They were still slashing around, and so was I. But the discourse had changed somewhat, because even then Johns and Robert Rauschenberg were considered pivotal figures, and Pop was creeping in. What was great about Yale were the visitors they invited: Rauschenberg, Philip Guston, Ad Reinhardt, Frank Stella… It was a rotating door for artists from New York.

**HF**: Were you left to figure out these different artists, to parse their various positions, on your own?

**RS**: That occurred during the second and third years. The first year was fairly disciplined: you had to take drawing and design. The design courses stemmed from the Bauhaus teaching tradition of using a cork or a potato as a tool to make dots—basically figure-ground problems to do with shape, field, scanning, and mapping. The courses were set up to emphasize that every mark counted, and we spent hours, days, even weeks on dot problems. Then there were color courses, and we had to take calligraphy too. I wasn't very good at it, and I remember the teacher telling me it didn't really matter.

**HF**: Why?

**RS**: He said there were many different ways to make marks, and thousands of people in the history of art had made drawings of trees, so there weren't any rules. You didn't have to make straight lines absolutely straight, or diagonal lines perfectly diagonal, as long as you understood pulse, beat, spacing, and rhythm. He told me not to worry too much about the exactitude of the mark. That was comforting.

**HF**: Were the design courses still inflected by Josef Albers? Is there a way in which you opted for Albers over Duchamp, so to speak, in your own relation to found material?

**RS**: Yes. Albers's was the best course taught there, even though people like Brice and Chuck didn't take it. Albers had just retired, but his spirit was everywhere at Yale. When I graduated, he asked me to help him proof his book *The Interaction of Color* (1963) at Yale University Press because I had taught the color course in my last year. I spent the summer proofing the book, and we'd go over it together. If you taught his course you developed an eye for things besides color saturation, tone, equivalence, and so on. You understood subjective qualities like "wet" and "dry" colors. Your eyes became attuned to seeing minute variations.

**HF:** But color isn't pronounced in your work—except for your film *Color Aid* (1971), which was inspired by *The Interaction of Color.*

**RS:** It is if you think black is a color! Then it's very pronounced in my work.

**HF:** Black as in all colors rather than none at all?

**RS:** I've always thought of black as a color and used it as such. It's limited, but it's also very definite.

**HF:** You privilege the final dark grey of your steel plates, presenting black-and-white photos only. Yet often viewers are struck by the rich oranges and reds of your steel plates when they're new. Why not acknowledge that manifestation too?

**RS:** Because next week it'll change.

**HF:** Can you simply bracket the experience of the sculpture's different colors? It's one that sticks with many people.

**RS:** It's transitional to me. Color's not my problem. On the other hand, it presented a tremendous challenge for postwar American painters. Barnett Newman, Ellsworth Kelly, Andy Warhol, Stella, pretty much any painter I can think of, had to confront Matisse more than Albers, and they didn't advance beyond his structuring with color. Nobody has structured the field through color, using all its force, like Matisse. Nobody has advanced the use of color more than Matisse.

**HF:** How about Dan Flavin?

**RS:** Well, that's a different ball of wax; that's projecting color into space. And it probably owes more to Impressionism than to Matisse. But if anyone did find a way around the dominance of Matisse in color, it was Flavin.

**HF:** How did you negotiate the figures who visited Yale, with all their different materials, mediums, and protocols in the studio? Apart from Albers, you had Rauschenberg, Johns, and Stella as well as Guston and Reinhardt.

**RS:** Reinhardt was very influential. He gave university-wide lectures, not just to art and architecture students. His "Twelve Rules for a New Academy" (1953) and his manifestoes were impressive, especially the way he approached a position through negation. But you had to digest all the visitors as best you could. Also, twice a day at Yale I passed Mondrian's *Foxtrot;* Duchamp's *Tu m'* was upstairs, and Brancusi's *Yellow Bird* was in the hall.

We were in school not to break ground but to work our way from Cézanne to Pollock, de Kooning, or Johns. That's what students did at the time. Some imitated the New York scene immediately in front of them, but if that was all you were doing, you were already rearguard, and everybody knew it. I ended up painting knock-off Pollock–de Koonings.

**HF**: Was Russian Constructivism in the mix for you then? Camilla Gray's book, *The Great Experiment: Russian Art 1863–1922,* was published in 1962, and it was immediately important for Carl Andre, Sol LeWitt, and Flavin.

**RS**: I wasn't interested in Constructivism at the time. I was a painter, trying to figure out what that meant, and whether I wanted to continue painting. Yale awards a traveling fellowship; I was fortunate enough to get one, so I had a year in Europe. I went to Paris, and that changed my whole grounding.

**HF**: Why? I know you went to the Cinemathèque Française regularly, and that the Brancusi studio was important to you, but how did Paris change your entire orientation?

**RS**: I hadn't looked at much sculpture before. I was going to the Académie de la Grande Chaumière to draw every day, but that seemed, well, academic. I saw as many shows as I could; the big ones involved well-established artists: Magritte, Francis Bacon, Giacometti, artists of that generation. They were mythical figures, empowering, but there was no new scene in Paris. Ileanna Sonnabend had a gallery that showed Edward Higgins and Lee Bontecou, yet Rauschenberg wasn't there. In fact, the American scene hadn't entered Paris much, and the abstract scene—the École de Paris with artists like Hans Hartung— was boring. I found my way to Brancusi's reconstructed studio in the Musée National d'Art Moderne, and I began to draw. I can't tell you why, but something just clicked. Drawing has a lot to do with how a volume hits an edge, how it cuts into space, and it was enormously helpful for me to work there. Maybe the studio had an aura that attracted me too; maybe it smelled like art.

**HF**: Did Brancusi equal sculpture for you then? Or did you see a tradition—before him, after him—that you could draw on?

**RS**: No. I knew very little about Brancusi, very little about sculpture. But if you're young and want a foothold in sculpture—whether to go into figuration and content or into abstraction and space—Brancusi is an encyclopedia. He's very pure, authoritative, convincing.

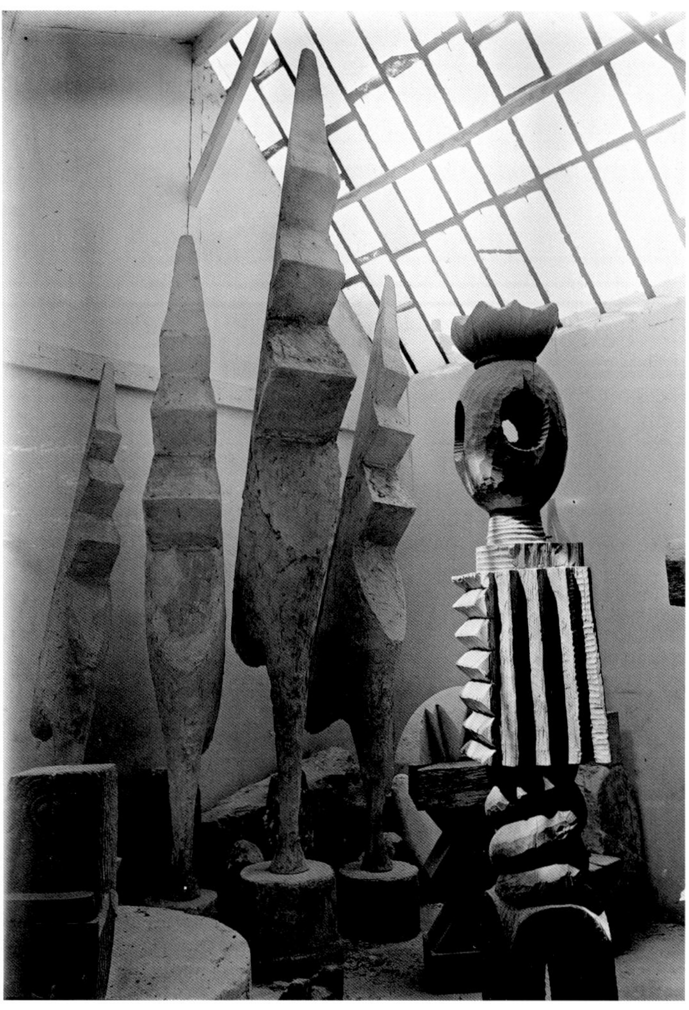

Constantin Brancusi, *View of His Studio,* c. 1945–46. Shown are
*The Kiss* (c. 1940), *The Cocks I–IV* (1924?, 1930, c. 1930–34, 1941–44),
*The King of Kings* (1938?), and *Maïastra* (c. 1923–40). Silver gelatin dry glass
plate negative, 7 $\frac{1}{16}$ × 5 $\frac{1}{8}$ in. (18 × 13 cm). Centre Georges Pompidou,
Musée National d'Art Moderne, Paris.

There was the New Wave in Paris, and I was going to the Cinemathèque to see
Truffaut, Godard, Resnais, and Bresson. I was aware that I was watching a new idiom
in the making. By comparison the French painting scene wasn't interesting, with the
exception of the artist who painted under the influence of mescaline…

**HF**: Henri Michaux.

**RS**: Yes, I saw a show of his and never forgot it; it was one of the most interesting events
in my year in Paris. I had a fairly good sense of Pollock by then, and that show—in terms
of marking a field—suggested a similar nonanalytical way out. It certainly had nothing
to do with Brancusi: he was about a reduction to form, volume, shape. Michaux, like
Pollock, opened up the field.

**HF**: Nonanalytical as in not fully calculated? No apparent intention that preceded the
actual marks?

**RS**: Yes, there was nothing prescribed about it, and that interested me. I had done mescaline in Santa Barbara, but I didn't understand how anyone could make art in that state.
In my last year in college I had read Michel Butor as well as Camus. Butor's spareness
of language influenced me: the clarity in his descriptions and his concrete relation to
experience. Later I discovered that Roland Barthes had the same clarity of language.
Again, between Santa Barbara, Yale, and Paris a lot was coming at me: Camus, Michaux,
Brancusi, film…I didn't know how all those things would come together.

**HF**: The work you began to do then—objects, assemblages…

**RS**: That was the next year, in 1966, when I went to Florence on a Fulbright. I had read
John Cage's *Silence* (1961); Phil Glass and I read it to each other in Paris. Cage collaged his
lectures from different conventions and disciplines, and he did it in a very roll-the-dice
way. With its antecedents in Dada, it was too much like unrestrained poetry, and that
didn't interest me. I was involved in language, with its specificity—whether in Americans
like Faulkner or Steinbeck, or Russians like Dostoevsky, Pushkin, or Gogol, or the French
like Stendhal, Camus, or Butor—and Cage's permissive poetry didn't have enough
structure for me.

**HF**: It was a dead end for you—unlike for many in the generation ahead of you in
New York.

**RS**: Yes. In Florence I started painting grids with arbitrary colors, covering each square in
a minute or so. Then I went to the American library, saw a recent issue of *Artnews* that
included a grid painting by Kelly with random colors, and it looked like what I had just done.

I thought if Cage was going to lead me to become a formalist Kelly, I couldn't go on, so I dropped Cage as well as Kelly. Then I made a trip to Spain, and seeing Velázquez was very important. That ended it for me.

**HF**: *Las Meninas* in particular? Ended what exactly? There seemed to be nothing left to do with the fundamental problems of painting?

**RS**: I realized there was a split between the interior illusion of space and the projected space I was standing in, and that I was the subject of the painting and Velázquez was looking at me. That really bothered me—that I was the subject of the painting—because I didn't think I could make a painting in which the viewer was its subject. I wasn't interested in mirrors. I knew what the Dutch had done, and Velázquez had done it better. I was flabbergasted.

**HF**: Why? You make sculpture whose subject is the viewer—why not painting? It's interesting that your encounter with *Las Meninas* occurred just about when Foucault took it up as the paragon of classical representation in *The Order of Things* (1966). And he says much the same thing—that the painting makes the viewer its subject.

**RS**: *Las Meninas* made me see that my way of dealing with painting was limited to looking at something inside a frame. Living in Florence, I had come to love the Florentine painters—Fra Angelico, Uccello, all of them. But I thought, "Jesus, I'm up to the same thing. I might as well be looking out the window. All I'm doing is looking at painting inside a frame." It's then that I decided to make cages, to stuff them with material, to use live animals, to do anything to get away from my education, from all of it.

**HF**: To get away from pictorial space?

**RS**: Yes. In the Museo della Specola in Florence there are stuffed cadavers by Clemente Susini made of wax, slit from scrotum to throat, and opened up so you can see the splayed intestines. They're extraordinarily beautiful and also perverse and sexual. Nancy Graves and I (we were together then) used to go look at them. At the same time I became interested in zoos (Florence had the first zoos). So I got the idea of stuffing animals and presenting assemblages, and I used cages, stacking them one on top of the other à la Brancusi. Again, I wanted to do something I wasn't taught or had seen before, something that dealt with different materials. I took stuff from junk shops, thrift stores, and off the street, just threw it together, and tried to make some metaphor out of what was stuffed and what was alive, illusion and reality. It was barnyard-assemblage-Surrealism, very much student work.

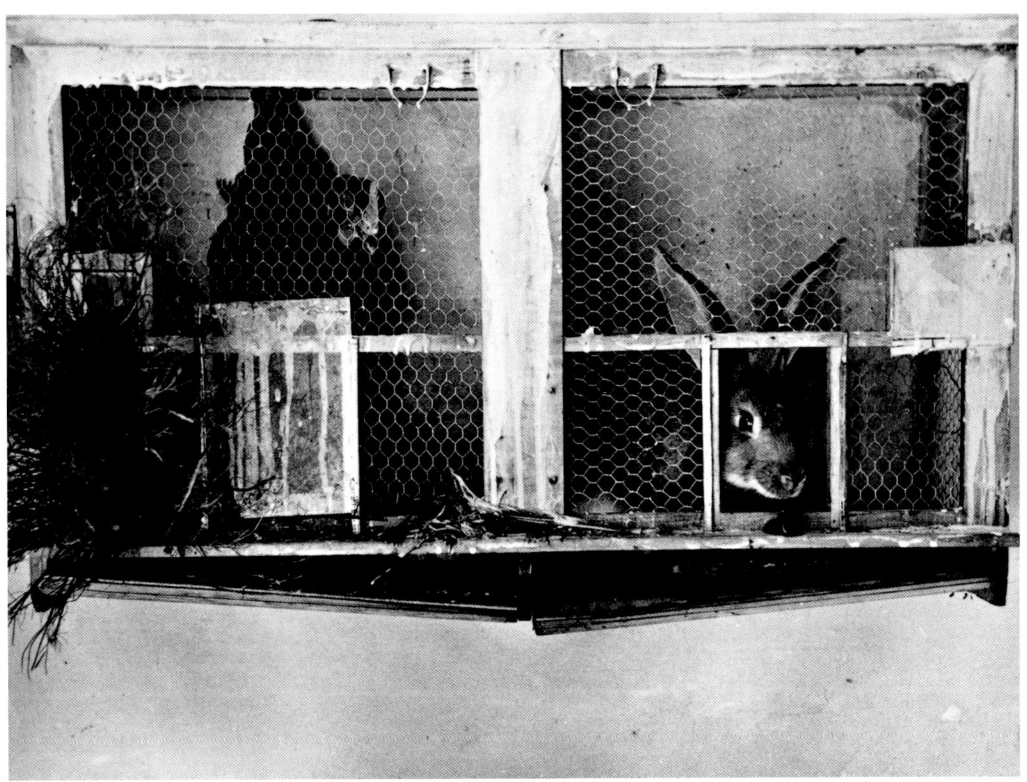

*Live Animal Habitat,* 1965–66. Mixed media, c. 16 × 45 × 10 in.
(40.6 × 114.3 × 25.4 cm). Temporary installation in the exhibition
*Richard Serra,* Galleria La Salita, Rome, 1966.

**HF**: Was there any sense of the beginnings of Arte Povera then?

**RS**: When I went to Rome I had a show that caused an enormous uproar.

**HF**: This is still 1966?

**RS**: Yes. The police closed down the show because of the live animals, so we got an injunction to reopen it. All the people from the Tartaruga gallery came to see it (Tartaruga exhibited Cy Twombly and Piero Manzoni, as well as Jannis Kounellis and others who would later form Arte Povera). A lot of things were in the air: Rauschenberg, Lucas Samaras, Ed Kienholz, many others dealing with assemblage. Three years later Kounellis lined up his twelve horses in that gallery. So my work was inadvertently connected to Arte Povera.

**HF**: But you didn't elaborate on that line of work.

**RS**: I didn't know what it was. We were isolated. We thought we were up to no good, but we didn't know whether no good was good, or whether anyone would be interested.

# Down and Dirty Minimalism

**HF**: When did you return to New York from Europe?

**RS**: In late 1966. When I came back, I knew I wouldn't continue the assemblages with animals I had done in Italy. They were experiments, and their metaphors seemed too easy. I was trying to move away from painting in the most absurd way possible. However, the fallout was that I became interested in all kinds of materials. One day in New York a rubber warehouse emptied its contents onto the street at Thomas and West Broadway, around the corner from my studio. I asked the company for some of the rubber, and they said I could take as much as I could haul away. I asked Chuck Close, Phil Glass, and a few other friends to help me cart away several truckloads. We filled my loft with tons of rubber.

**HF**: What was it about the rubber that interested you?

**RS**: It was as if I were given an assignment, "Here's material, it's yours to deal with," and I thought, "I can use this." It had the feel of the barnyard scrap I'd been using, but it also had an industrial look, and I understood its flexibility. At Yale when I was assigned a design problem, I was also given a way of dealing with the material, a set of procedures. I had a lot of rubber; the challenge was to discover its potential.

**HF**: Did you think that this might amount to an intervention in sculpture?

**RS**: No. I had no idea of making either sculpture or painting at the time. But I had looked at Pollock, especially in my last year at Yale, and there was a painting he did for Peggy Guggenheim, *Mural* (1943), that develops horizontally over nineteen feet as a series of vertical loops. It's probably the beginning of serialization within abstraction, although no one saw it that way at the time; it also recalled the Mexican muralists. That interested me, and so when I began to use rubber I cut it into belts and hung them using Pollock's painting as a subtext. The idea of hanging was influenced by Oldenburg, too—not by what he was making but by how he was using gravity as a force, as a forming device.

**HF**: For you, gravity was about forming or structuring; for others it was about deforming or destructuring. Wasn't the use of gravity already clear in Pollock?

**RS**: Maybe, but you'd have to have the analytical sense to recognize Pollock's drips as a result of gravity. When you're a student looking at reproductions in a magazine, it's hard to figure that the paint was dripped down onto the canvas on the floor.

**HF**: What about Hans Namuth's photographs or his film of Pollock working?

**RS**: I didn't see the film until twenty years later; probably not many people did. Pollock was an enormous figure, but not because of his use of gravity. It was because he did exactly

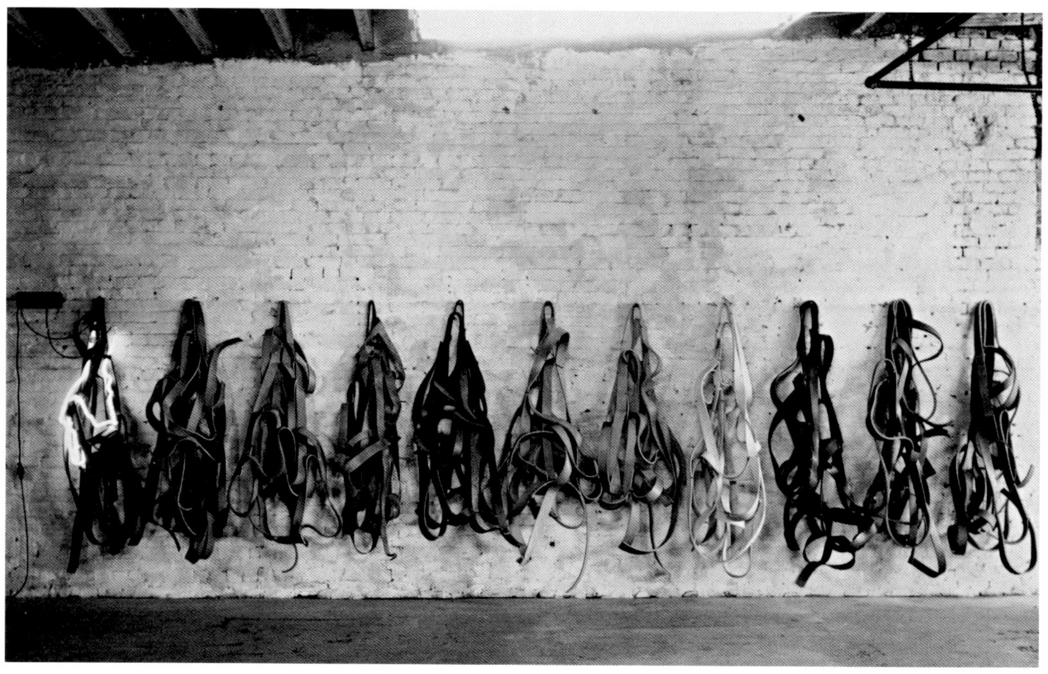

*Belts*, 1966–67. Vulcanized rubber and blue neon tubing, nine belts, c. 6 ft. × 25 ft. × 20 in.
(1.8 m × 7.6 m × 50.8 cm). Solomon R. Guggenheim Museum, New York. Panza Collection.
Photo Peter Moore.

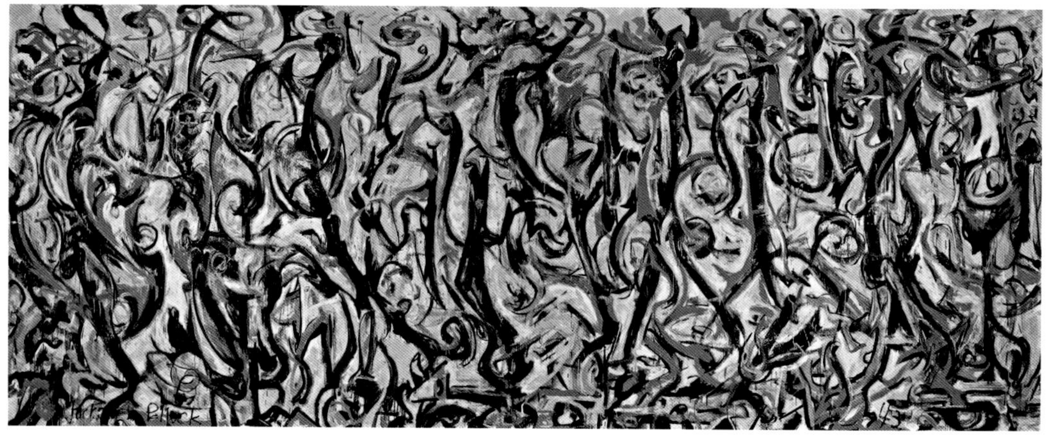

Jackson Pollock, *Mural,* 1943. Oil and casein on canvas, 7 ft. 11 in. × 19 ft. 10 in. (2.4 m × 6 m).
University of Iowa Museum of Art. Gift of Peggy Guggenheim, 1959.

what your teachers said you couldn't do: he dripped. It was like telling the academy to screw itself; that was very empowering. It was the same with Stan Brakhage, who was the cinematic counterpart of Pollock. And then Warhol came along being completely subversive in a mockingly stupid sort of way. His deadpan movies where nothing happened really stayed with me. Those early films were as empowering in terms of freedom as Pollock's drip had been.

**HF**: Warhol didn't displace your interest in Pollock?

**RS**: History would have you believe that people replace people and genres replace genres. I don't think anything replaces anything: there's Cézanne, Matisse, Picasso, Pollock; there's Johns, Warhol, Bruce Nauman. . . . Artists don't replace one another. Cézanne didn't replace Giotto.

**HF**: But the prewar artists you mention, not to mention the postwar ones, still present different models of working. What about Barnett Newman? He was very important to Judd, Flavin, and others, but less so, it seems, to you.

**RS**: I couldn't see Newman at first. I had no way of understanding him until his show at the Guggenheim in 1966. That show absolutely floored me, but before that I didn't have a clue. There was a big show of Abstract Expressionism while I was still at Yale, and it was easy for me to read painters like Guston and de Kooning, but not Newman. You see what you want to see or what you can see. I didn't know how to look at Newman then.

**HF**: You got what you needed out of Pollock and Oldenburg.

**RS**: They were easier to understand. I wasn't interested in any dictate about how to make an autonomous object. I was interested in my ability to move in relation to material and have that material move me, bodily, in as open a field as possible. That's why Pollock and Oldenburg worked for me. Oldenburg's was the only show I saw at Green Gallery (it was in 1962); his big *Floor Burger* was there, and I thought it was really good. It was different from just looking at an object; it was more compelling and more unknowable.

**HF**: Unknowable?

**RS**: It was a hamburger that didn't make sense: a big, fluffy, obdurate thing, with one side nothing like the other, inflated and deflated at once. It was perverse, mimicking and mocking the commercial product, really messing with it. I thought it was radical in terms of scale, and it had a complete disregard for proper art materials.

One thing that differentiates my generation—Robert Smithson, Eva Hesse, Nauman, even Warhol—from the Minimalists is that Judd and Flavin were about a high-priest

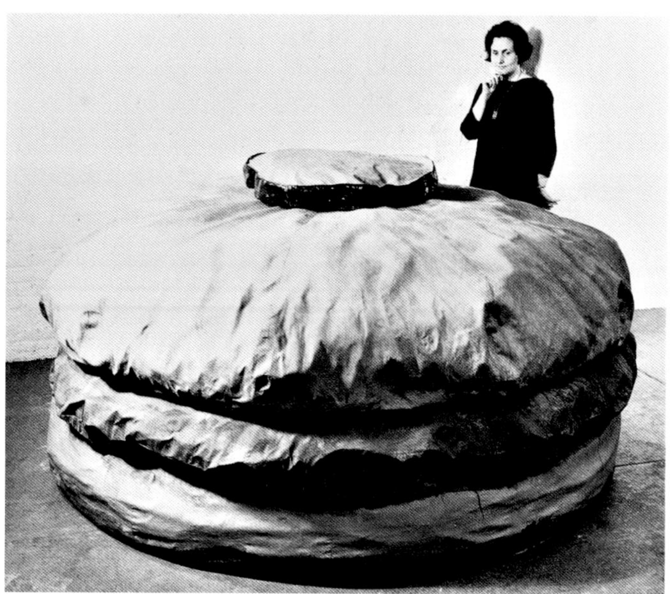

Claes Oldenburg, *Floor Burger,* 1962. Canvas filled with foam rubber and cardboard boxes, painted with latex and Liquitex, 4 ft. 4 in. × 7 ft. 7 in. (1.3 m × 2.1 m). Art Gallery of Ontario, Toronto, Purchase 1967.

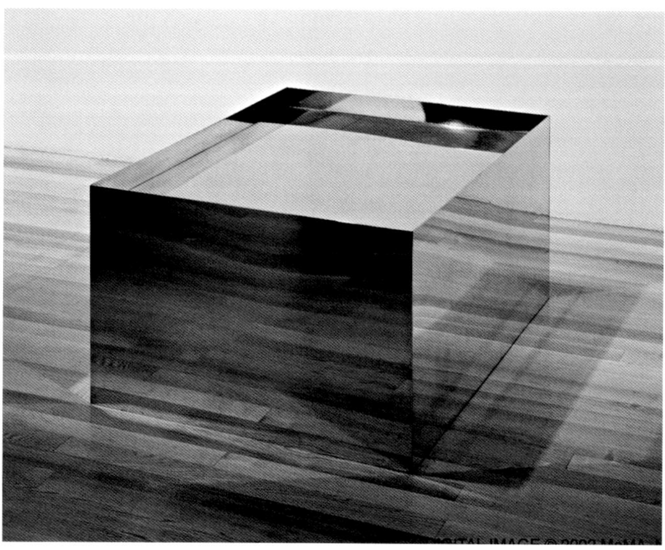

Donald Judd, *Untitled,* 1968. Brass, 22 × 48 ¼ × 36 in. (55.9 × 122.6 × 91.4 cm). The Museum of Modern Art, New York. Gift of Philip Johnson.

extension of modernism and we were not. Even if they broke with modernism they retained a Puritanical notion of the authority of the object, with a certain set of dos and don'ts: you polish your brass, you get the color just right, you finish your product to perfection. There was still an elitist notion of the product there.

**HF**: Judd wanted to trump the modernist line, not to break with it?

**RS**: Exactly. They wanted to have the shiniest, speediest object out there, and that's not what Warhol was up to. Take a grid of his silk-screened car crashes: the dot starts to blur after the fourth or fifth pass over the screen because the overlays are off register. They call up the idea of scanning that Anton Ehrenzweig developed in *The Hidden Order of Art* (1967), and that goes back to Pollock again: it's not about analyzing every part and particle, every detail.[1] Both Pollock and Warhol are contrary to Judd in that respect. It's about how you read before you analyze and recognize; it's about not differentiating between figure and ground, and it's not about the authority of shape.

The high-priest line of Minimalism includes Judd, and maybe Sol LeWitt more than Flavin. LeWitt's work left me cold; it seemed too scripted. He gives you the prescription, you fill in the narrative, and LeWitt says he doesn't care what it looks like. That seemed too didactic to me. When the Conceptualists were working on their manifesto at Max's Kansas City, they asked me to join them, but I didn't want any part of it. They said, "What's your intention? We saw your *House of Cards*—do you think you're making sculpture?" And I said, "If you want to propose definitions of sculpture, 'specific objects' or concepts, well, I don't know right now." So they called me a primitive, but then I thought they were a bunch of hall monitors. When I first splashed lead, one of them phoned up and told me I couldn't do that—he had already thrown silver paint out his window against a brick wall. I said, "I don't give a shit. I'm laying down a couple of tons of lead to cast off architecture." They thought that language was going to supplant the perception of the object.

**HF**: LeWitt famously proposed that "the idea becomes a machine that makes the art."[2] That dictum might supplant a lot—process, play, experiment…

**RS**: It cancels all that out. It seemed to me an enormous limitation, and I wasn't interested in intention being a work of art.

**HF**: Yet if you were suspicious of Conceptualism, which is also, I assume, to be skeptical of its reliance on language, what do you do with the fact that much of your early work issued directly from a list of words on a piece of paper—that is, from your "Verb List" (1967)?

"Verb List," 1967. Graphite on two sheets of paper, each 10 × 8 ½ in. (25.4 × 21.6 cm).
The Museum of Modern Art, New York. Gift of the artist in honor of Wynn Kramarsky.

**RS**: Those words don't give definition to a work; they give definition to a process. They're not conceptual in the same way. They lead to actions, not concepts or statements, and those actions bring in the properties of materials. In Conceptual art there's often no object, no construction, no need to make anything at all.

**Clara Weyergraf-Serra**: I have a simpler response. If Richard had left it as a list of verbs, that would've been a Conceptual piece, but the "Verb List" actually generated works.

**HF**: What about intention then? You say you weren't interested in "intention being a work of art," but you were included in "When Attitudes Become Form," the celebrated show of Post-Minimalist art in 1969. Didn't that draw you into the orbit of Conceptualism?[3]

**RS**: Yes, and dealers sold people's dreams on pieces of paper. That never interested me. I was more concerned with my own perception of the physical manifestation of things. Sure, there's intention in art, but as an artist and a viewer I want to interpret *my* experience, not anybody else's intention. I was mainly interested in space: How do you separate elements, how do you walk between them, through them, around them, how do you open up a field?

To me Flavin was the first to open up context, more so than Judd. When I first lived in New York, I thought he had his hands on the most formidable material. I saw his show at Kornblee Gallery in 1967: you walked into the room, and all you saw was green; a green light in a corner, one on the wall here, another over there, the entire room was green. And the windows where light flooded in from the outside were pink, the complementary color of green. It was one of the most amazing shows I've ever seen because you were standing in a space created by light as color, and he had done away with the object: the object wasn't the consideration, the field was, the context was. That's why, of all the artists I was looking at then, Flavin had the most powerful material going.

**HF**: Were you concerned that his colored light sometimes overwhelms the fixture and almost obliterates the space? Flavin doesn't always fasten down the effects of his light to his support.

**RS**: No, that didn't bother me. In fact, if the mechanical housing had disappeared, that would've been fine.

**HF**: Doesn't that contradict your own insistence on revealing material, structure, and space?

**RS**: Flavin's not only about the fixture. Maybe he is in his early "icons" and his *Monuments to Tatlin* (1964–69), but they have more to do with drawing. The pieces that resonated for me deal with context, even if that means evaporating the space. The other person in the

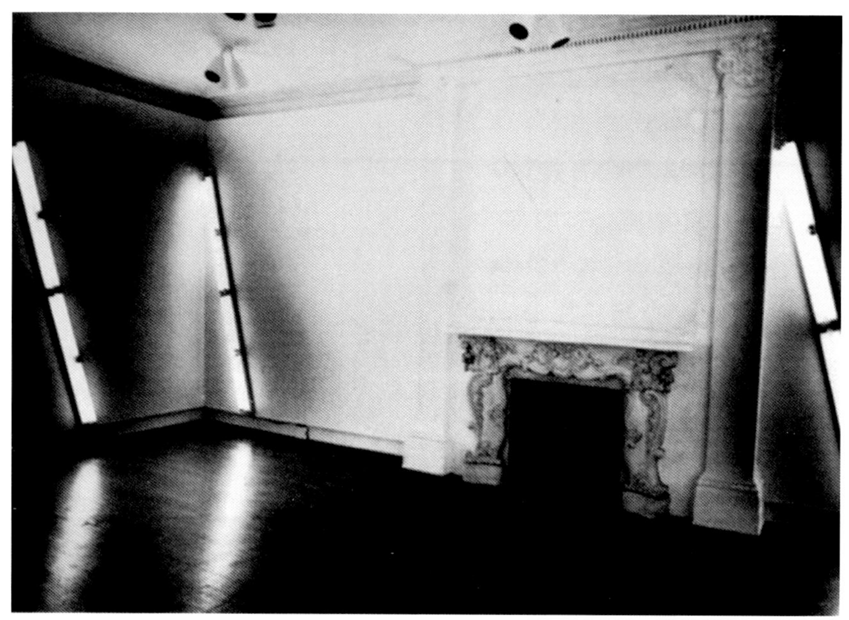

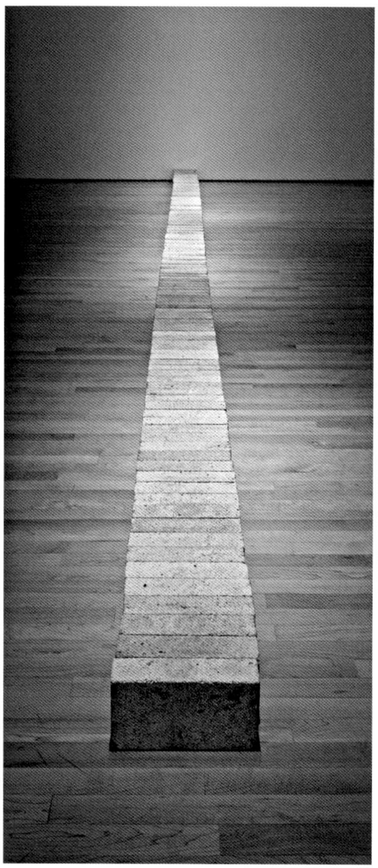

Installation view of Dan Flavin exhibition, Kornblee Gallery, New York, October 7–November 8, 1967.

Carl Andre, *Lever,* 1966. 137 firebricks, 4 ½ in. × 8 ⅞ in. × 29 ft. (11.4 cm × 22.5 cm × 8.8 m) installed; 4 ½ × 8 ⅞ × 2 ½ in. (11.4 × 22.5 × 6.4 cm) each brick. National Gallery of Canada, Ontario. Purchased 1969.

low-order line of Minimalism that interested me was Carl Andre, because he was involved in materiality, in the brick as a brick.

**HF**: In the brick as a unit too.

**RS**: Yes, that's true, but not entirely. When Andre spoke of the "uncarved block" of wood, it seemed wrong to me, a sort of shibboleth, because he had obviously sawn them or had them machine-cut. But Andre was interested in the nature of his materials—wood and brick, and lead, zinc, and copper plates. It wasn't just "Send me so many units." He was interested in the chemistry of materials (the Valence chart of the elements), whereas Judd was mostly interested in their effects. Andre was also involved in the baseness of his materials, and so were we—Smithson, Hesse, Nauman, myself, and even Warhol to some extent. We were all on the down and dirty end of Minimalism, pushing it into something else. We didn't think you could make advanced art using commodity strategies. We were hands on.

**HF**: How did Judd and Flavin use such strategies?

**RS**: By working in editions, for one thing: "Here's a stack of boxes, make four; here are some lights, make five." Despite Judd and Flavin saying that was a way to get away from the market, it played right into it. Markets will take as much as you give them. If someone sold out a show, we'd say, "Too bad," meaning that the work couldn't be too inventive if collectors understood it so easily.

**HF**: Minimalists and Conceptualists might have seen you as a wild card more than a primitive: you had a range of interests, and you weren't very dogmatic about them, at least not at the start. But you did share with them a suspicion of the pictorial. On the other hand, you came to be committed, like Andre, to sculpture in a way that Judd and Flavin were not—they wanted to work in a space apart from painting and sculpture alike.

**RS**: I never bought into the dictates of Judd's "Specific Objects" (1965), his neither-painting-nor-sculpture proposition. I understood that to substantiate his definition of the specific object he had to use Oldenburg, John Chamberlain, H. C. Westermann, and others around him. It allowed him to say, "These works differ from what sculpture has been and what painting now is," even though much of his own work had more to do with painting, bringing its flatness out into space, mostly coming out of Newman. "And if we call it 'the specific object' we don't have to worry too much about things that have come before; it'll be an autonomous category." I have enormous admiration for Judd (he was dealing with volume in a way that no one else had), but that definition seemed too limited to me— too authoritative and judgmental. Flavin seemed more radical, and Andre more abstract.

Coming out of Pollock and looking at Oldenburg, I was interested in how actual space functioned, not in any gestalt reading of pictorial space, and the specific object was still primarily about that. I was interested in the volume of space, in the entire context—what happened when you walked around, what happened to the rhythm of your body in motion. So I started going to dance concerts at the Judson Church (I was living with Joan Jonas then) to see how those performers were experimenting with the open field—Yvonne Rainer, Trisha Brown, and Simone Forti in particular.

**HF**: Can you talk specifically about the relation of your early pieces to what you experienced there?

**RS**: Yvonne, Trisha, Simone, Steve Paxton, and some others formed a group called Grand Union in 1970. They'd perform two or three times a week, and I'd go to all the performances. They'd use all kind of materials—ladders, boxes, a mattress on the floor, powder thrown in the air—and they'd jump on things. They'd also do a lot of holds where one performer would fall and another would catch her, or one would be off balance and another would stabilize her. I thought that kind of applied equilibrium had a relationship to my work.

**HF**: Did Judson Dance help you understand the dynamic play of forces in your prop pieces in particular?

**RS**: Yes. I saw things—in terms of movement and stasis, weight and support—that I could use in my sculpture. And I was faithful: I watched it all. So, yes, when I got into propping it was probably a direct result of looking at what Yvonne and Trisha were doing. In a sense all the early props have a relation to the body in terms of balance and counterbalance; they're an abstract reference to the body.

**HF**: What else in your early work was supported by what you saw in the dances?

**RS**: Body in relation to material, circulation in relation to material, force, also repetition. How one confronts an object—objects in space, objects moved in space. They were trying to produce dance in a way that heretofore hadn't been conceived of as dance, using found movement and material. The dancers at that time—again, Yvonne, Trisha, Simone, and others—were also performing in non-art spaces: on rooftops, streets, anywhere and everywhere. In terms of what I was looking at—painters, sculptors, musicians, or whomever—these women were the avant-garde, truly ahead of everything else being done.

I remember one performance called *Rose Fractions* (1969) in which Yvonne did an absolutely great thing. In the middle of the piece a wood grid dropped from the ceiling at the front of the stage. (It covered the stage width; in fact it was a stage flat.) It was

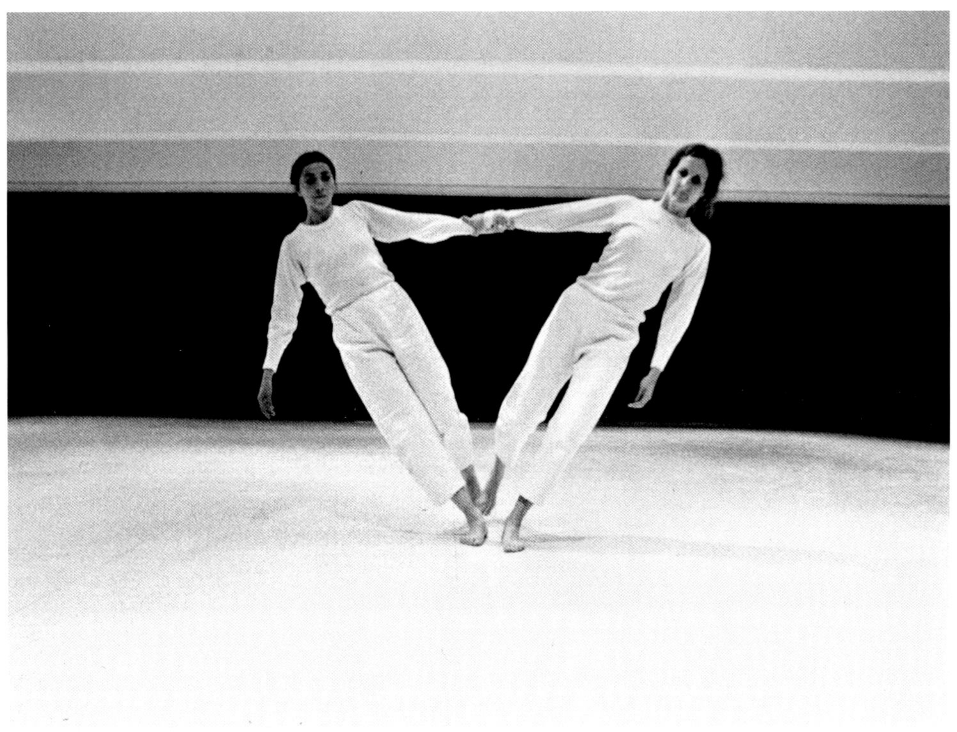

Trisha Brown, *Leaning Duets,* 1970. 10 minutes, sound: verbal instruction between dancers. Original cast: Jared Bark, Carmen Beuchat, Trisha Brown, Ben Dolphin, Caroline Goodden, Richard Nonas, Patsy Norvell, Lincoln Scott, Kei Takei. Photo, 1971.

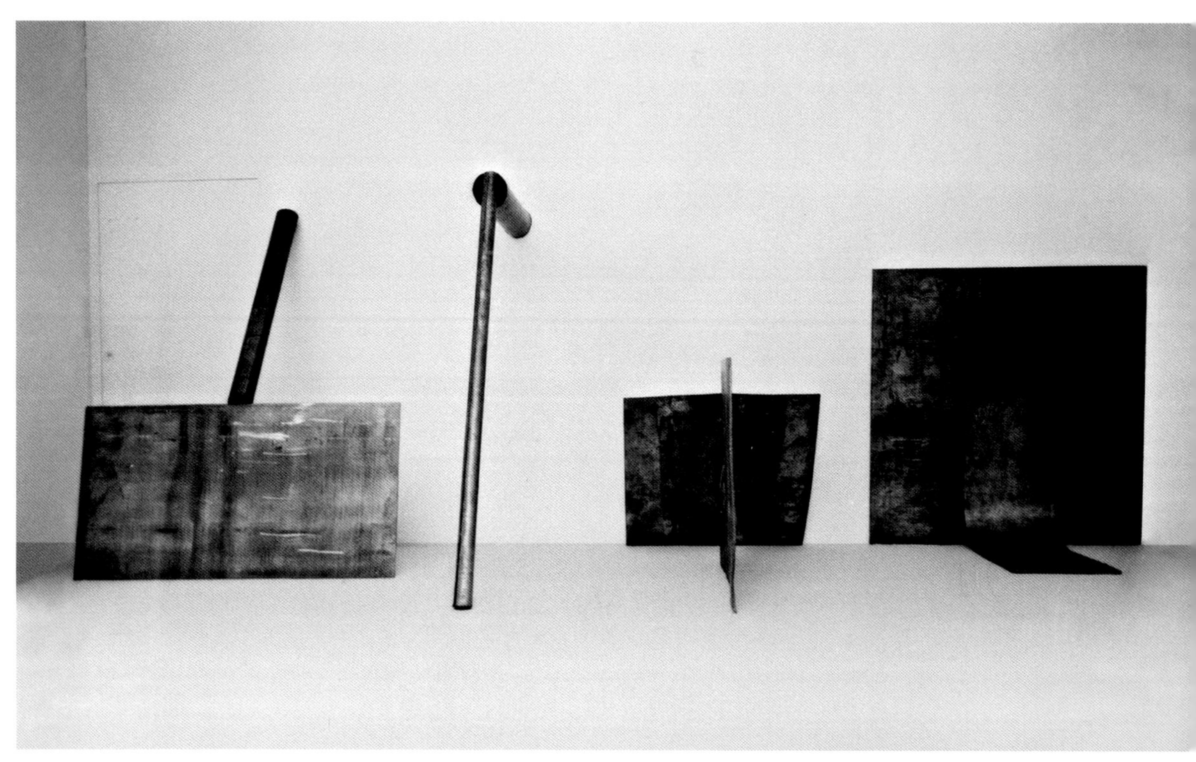

Installation view of seven prop pieces (all 1969). Lead, various dimensions.
Temporary installation in the exhibition *Nine Young Artists: Theodoron Awards,*
Solomon R. Guggenheim Museum, New York, 1969. Photo Peter Moore.

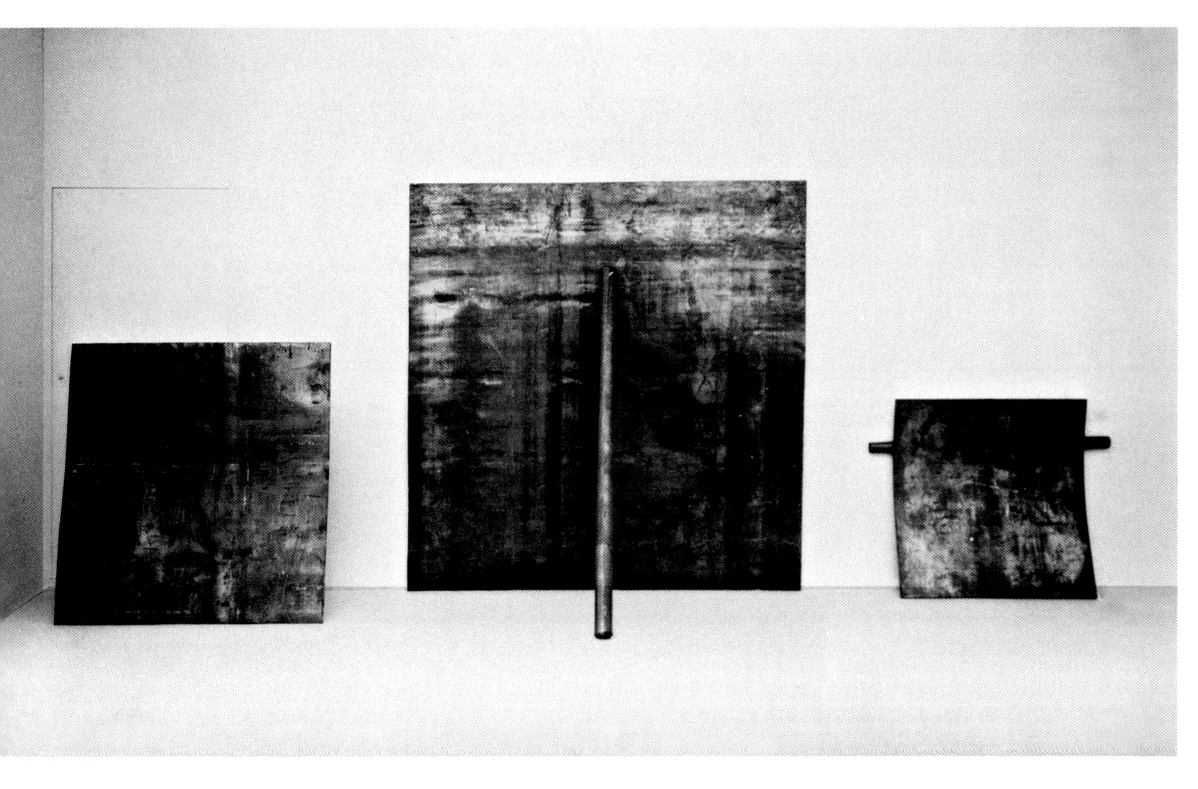

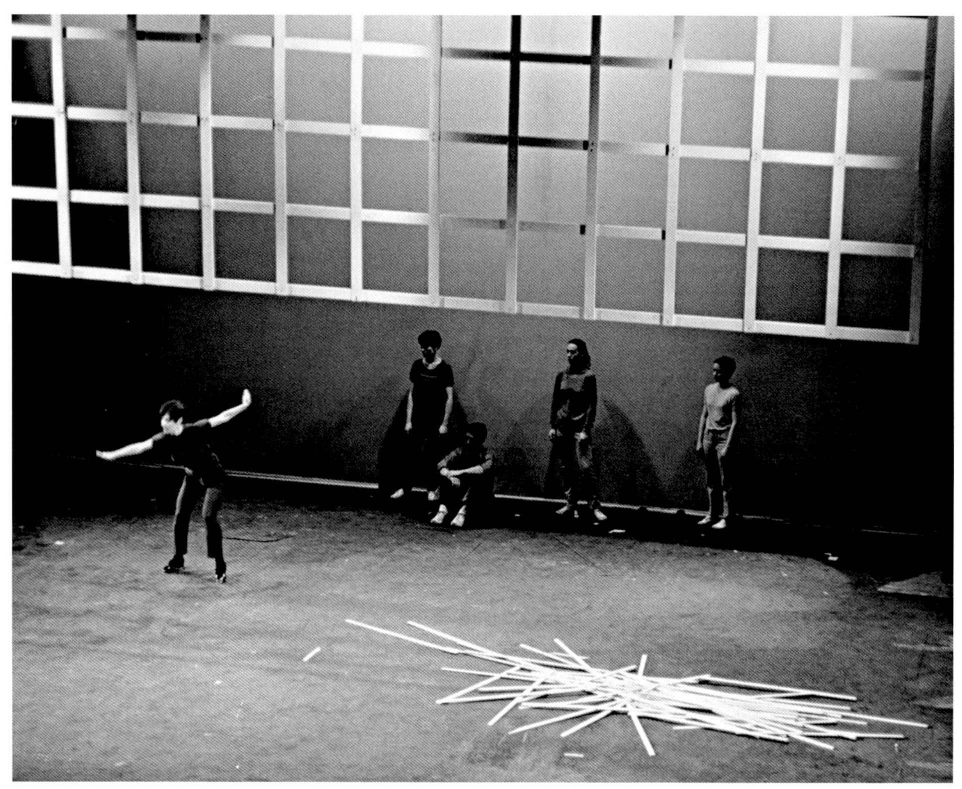

Peter Moore, Performance view of Yvonne Rainer's "Trio A" in *The Mind Is a Muscle.*
Anderson Theater, New York, April 11, 1968. Getty Research Institute, Los Angeles (2006.M.24).

there for about two minutes, then pulled back up. I thought, "That takes care of any grid I've ever seen." To do it that big, to do it only for a short time, not to use it as a set but to assert a grid in front of the field of performance, I thought, "That takes a lot of people into account right there and crystallizes viewing in relationship to space and time." I thought she brought Renaissance perspective right up to date.[4]

**HF**: Was Judson dance, the way they used everyday action, also in line with the simple tasks you laid out in the "Verb List"?

**RS**: Yes. For example, Trisha did a piece called *Accumulation* (1971) in which she did one movement, added another, and so on. It was just movement on top of movement.

But then a lot of people downtown were involved with making and doing, only everybody was making and doing different things. People didn't call themselves film-makers or composers or musicians or painters or sculptors. You didn't want to identify. Everybody was just making something, and everybody was everybody else's audience.

I remember when I first met Steve Reich; he lived right down the street from me. One day I asked him what he was up to, and he said he was working on tape music. It turns out he'd been in Harlem taping somebody, and he asked me if I wanted to listen. I thought, "Why not?" Steve had gone to a police precinct where a black kid had been thrown in the tank and severely beaten, and he didn't want to stay overnight. He figured he could get out by being transferred to a hospital. The kid said, "I had to open up the bruise and let some of the bruise blood come out to show them." Steve recorded that statement, then took it back to his studio and looped it to make *Come Out* (1966): "I had to open up the bruise and let some of the bruise blood come out to show them … to open up the bruise and let some of the bruise blood come out to show them … come out to show them come out to show them come out to show come out to show …" The statement was looped and overlaid in repetition, and as it went out of phase the words disintegrated into sounds. I thought, "Jesus, I just spent two years with Phil, and now here's Steve recording an actual person, and the result of looping, repetition, and phasing has a definite relationship to Phil's serial compositions."

And then Michael Snow—I met him in a coffee shop around the corner—showed me his *Wavelength* (1967), a film of an agonizingly slow pan across his studio space to the opposite wall, where the camera zoomed in on a photo of open water, of waves, hanging on the wall. We all had *doing* in common, we shared a language of practices and procedures, and we all became close friends.

**HF**: In 1981, Annette Michelson asked if you saw films like Snow's, or indeed your own, as somehow sculptural, and you rejected the notion.[5]

**RS**: I saw my films as separate investigations, and to say "sculptural film" is like saying "sculptural architecture"—it just doesn't ring true to me.

**HF**: But surely "sculptural architecture" exists; you mean "sculptural film" is just not true, in your terms, to either sculpture or film?

**RS**: Right. In film you have the materiality of the light, the celluloid, the projector, and the frame, and you need a black box to see the film. Those are the productive limitations of the medium. You might be able to find metaphorical analogues for them in sculpture, but that's all. Even though I think everything feeds into everything else, I don't think you investigate film to make sculpture or vice versa. That doesn't mean the investigations are entirely separate, but I've never thought they had that much to do with each other. On the other hand, I made *Hand Catching Lead* (1968) because someone said they wanted to do a film about the installation of *House of Cards,* and I thought *Hand Catching Lead* would be a better way of giving people an idea of propping a piece together: you either catch it or you don't, you either get the equilibrium right or you don't.[6] But I didn't think of the film as sculpture, nor did I think anyone would see the film in any relation to *House of Cards*. If everything that's not painting or photography has now come to fall under the rubric "sculpture," well, that's a different problem. In sculpture you can't get away from certain things: material, mass, weight, gravity, balance, place, light, time, movement. They're givens, and how you deal with them defines what you make.

**HF**: Right, but some of those qualities are shared by other mediums and practices.

**RS**: In film maybe light, maybe time, but very few.

**HF**: What other connections are there between your early work and Minimalist art, film, dance, and music? Your pieces are rarely serial, for example, like Minimalist music.

**RS**: Well, sometimes they're sequential. And my splashing and casting lead could be seen as serial. A lot of what I do in drawing comes out of being around Steve and Phil early on. In fact, I think my whole drawing practice is involved with repetition, knowing there's no possibility of repeating, knowing that it's going to yield something different every time.

**HF**: You talk about this group of artists as makers or doers, as if it didn't matter what the medium was. But at least from this moment on you insisted you were a sculptor—unlike others, such as Judd or Morris, who made "objects" or "installations." Why did you insist on the category of sculpture while others in your milieu resisted medium-specific definitions?

**RS**: I think I can tell you. I started making my props in 1968. How do you hold something up against the wall? How do you use something on the wall to hold up something coming

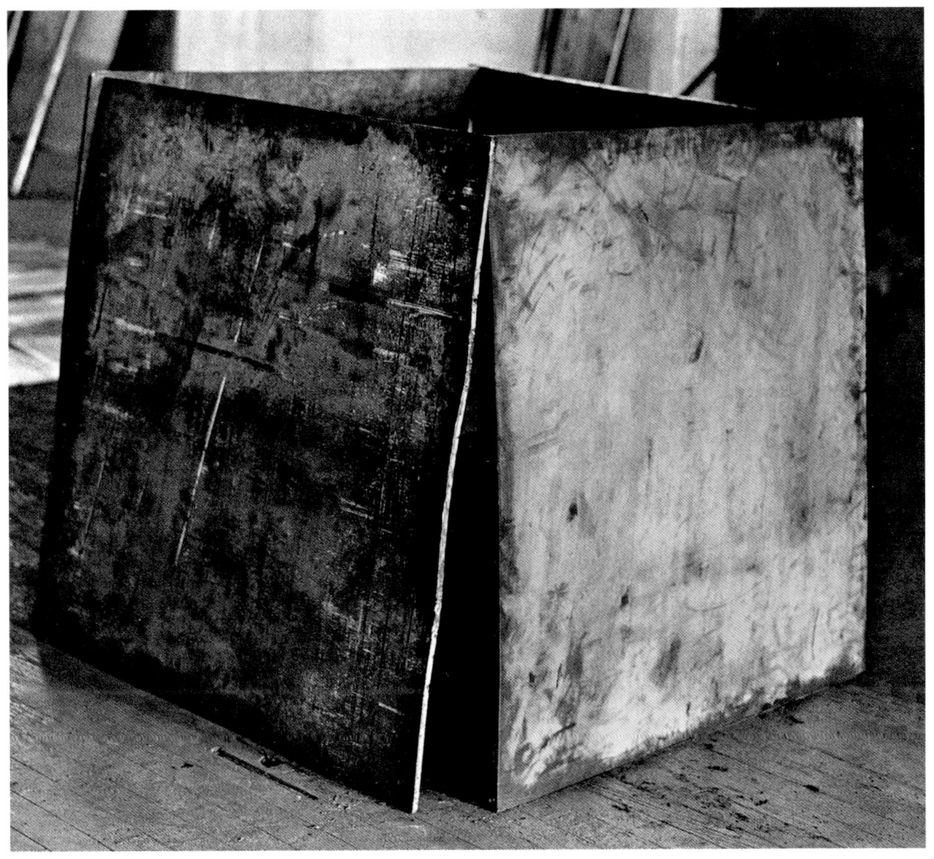

*One Ton Prop (House of Cards),* 1969. Lead, four plates, each 48 × 48 × 1 in. (121.9 × 121.9 × 2.5 cm).
The Museum of Modern Art, New York. Gift of the Grinstein Family, Los Angeles. Photo Peter Moore.

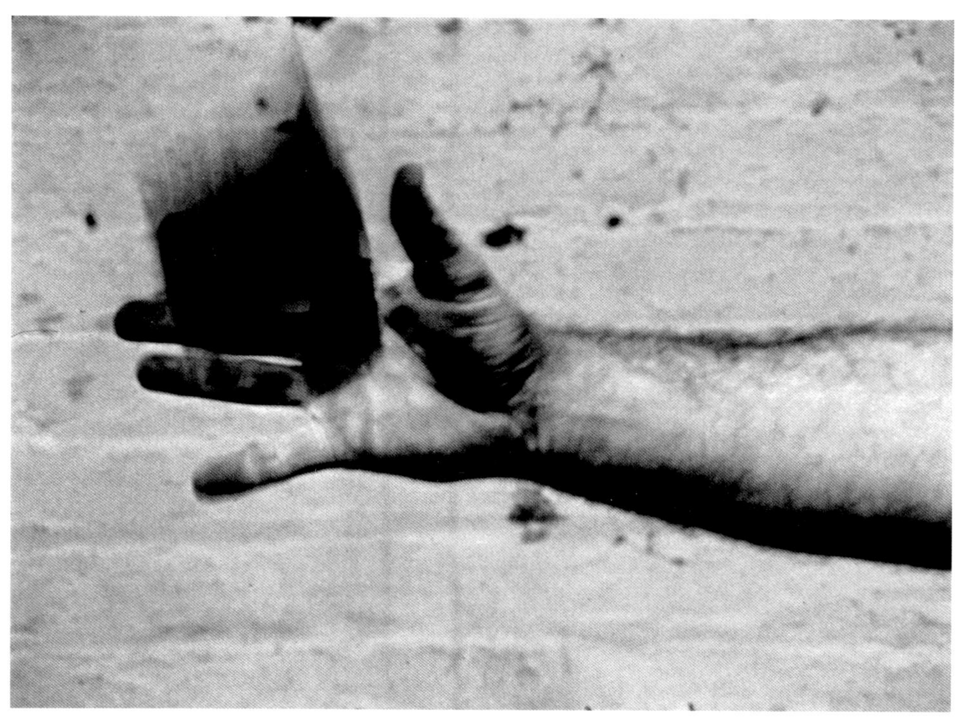

*Hand Catching Lead,* 1968. 16 mm film, black and white,
3 min. 30 sec. The Museum of Modern Art, New York.

off the floor? How do you lean a couple of elements together to make them free-stand? There weren't any precedents for the props; they didn't come out of the specific object. I had done rolls of lead on the floor; I understood I could take material, roll it up, and it'd still be an object even though it was primarily about its own making. Minimalism was completely divorced from process, whereas I was interested in manifestations of making, looking, and walking.

I was very interested in Andre because he always dealt with the physicality of matter. Different kinds of wood, different kinds of metal: he went through the whole chart— copper, lead, zinc, aluminum, magnesium. One day I said to Carl, "Look, somebody's got to get those plates up off the floor," and he looked at me, smiled, and said, "Don't worry, Richard. Somebody will." I thought, "Oh God, I better do it." So I took four lead plates— if you put the four of them together they weigh a ton—and dragged them up to my studio one at a time in the elevator. I thought by leaning them together and overlapping them at the top edge I could get them to free-stand, and when I did it looked like a house of cards. Even though it seemed it might collapse, in fact it stood up. You could see through it, look into it, walk around it, and I thought, "There's no getting around it, this is sculpture." Now, was it sculpture as sculpture had been heretofore known? No. But was I willing to stake my belief on what I was up to—on unattached lead plates propped against each other, weighing a ton, and always about to implode—to stake my belief on them being sculpture? Yes. Just as much as Andre was when he laid one brick after the other to make *Lever* (1966), and people yelled at him, "That's not art." The stakes were very serious and very high.

A lot of what we were doing downtown was experimental, but that doesn't mean we didn't know what the historical responsibilities were. I was thinking about Brancusi and Giacometti—I looked at them every day when I was in Paris. Closer to home I was thinking about Johns and a host of others. We knew what the odds were in terms of finding our own way of doing and making that was going to challenge what came before us. I think all of us felt that was what we needed to do—to make our own syntax, to define ourselves as artists. Not to make somebody else's work. To make our own.

I got divorced over *House of Cards*. Nancy Graves asked if I was going to show it as sculpture. I said yes, and she said she couldn't live with me anymore.

**HF:** That's what I mean by insistence! It's some indication of how fraught definitions were then.

**RS:** Look, I understood what my responsibilities were. If you say "I'm an artist" you can do lots of things; you don't have to pin yourself to any one tradition. I know that's a very conventional thing to do—to say "I'm a painter" or "I'm a sculptor." But I didn't sit in front of Giacometti every night at La Coupole in Paris, or go to Brancusi's studio every day, for nothing. I was empowered by them. And so after *House of Cards* I knew it was a sculpture, and I couldn't play around anymore. It wasn't a question of neither-nor.

**HF**: Did you feel that the sculptural tradition was not as strong, that it might give you more room to move than painting?

**RS**: Yes, I thought it was wide open. I didn't want to make sculpture as it was before, but having developed an understanding of tectonics, I thought I could make *my* sculpture.

**HF**: At least since the Renaissance sculpture has been subordinate to painting; certainly it is throughout modernism: the dominant models of art are articulated in relation to painting, even when it's antagonistic, as in Minimalism.

**RS**: It's still seen as secondary. I might just be the odd figure who has produced a big body of work. It might empower some other sculptors, but you don't know whether it'll lead to any resurgence of sculpture per se. I think if you want to make sculpture, you have to have a deep, internal belief in it. If you don't have it, don't do it.

# To Lift, To Splash, To Prop...

**HF**: Let's bear down on some key early works.

**RS**: I've already mentioned *Belts* (1966–67) and how it comes out of Pollock's *Mural* (1943), which is a serial sequence of figures. It's probably one of his breakthrough pieces. I wanted to try to reiterate its tangle of drawing in vulcanized rubber, off the wall, in a way that made clear that the line was looped and continuous. I was a painter at Yale, but after I returned from Europe I wanted to make a definite move away from painting. I had to get away especially from Pollock and Newman, who were enormous figures for me. *Belts* was my first attempt to deconstruct Pollock.

**HF**: Deconstruct him through a movement into different material and actual space?

**RS**: Yes, into literal space.

**HF**: Why the neon tube in the first skein on the left?

**RS**: It was intended to reinforce the linearity of the piece as a whole. When I was in my late teens I worked in steel mills where I either caught rivets or worked the reamer (that's a tool you drill holes with). At the end of the day when we put the reamers away, there'd be one with a light, and that's where all the reamers hung in a row. To put a light on the first object and have the others follow it seemed to me the simplest way of signifying repetition.

**HF**: To repeat is to order. So *Belts* is not an antiformal piece for you?

**RS**: I didn't think of it as such. I was trying to make a drawing and move into three dimensions at the same time. I ended up with a relief. Every time the rubber crosses itself I took a bent nail and attached it. So it's a continuous drawing with cut strips of rubber. I was trying to follow a built-in structural premise. I wanted to make the strips form a continuous progression by working right out of Pollock's figuration, although *Belts* doesn't look figurative.

**HF**: In addition to line, *Belts* is about gravity. In fact, the downward pull of the belts counters the suspension of the line.

**RS**: Yes. Unlike any other structural principle, gravity is a force. It's not something you can construct with easily, but you can use it to make an object attain its own position in space by reacting to its own load. Probably the only way to use it in construction is as a cantilever or in a keystone; there are very few other places where gravity is used in construction as a force. Early on it appealed to me because it wasn't codified in the history of sculpture; it was a force that sculpture was supposed to overcome, not to exploit.

**HF**: Were the *Doors* and *Troughs* (1966–67) also important in this respect?

*Doors,* 1966–67. Rubber and fiberglass, four parts, each 36 in. × 9 ft. × 2 in. (91.4 cm × 2.7 m × 5 cm). The Doris and Donald Fisher Collection at the San Francisco Museum of Modern Art and the San Francisco Museum of Modern Art. Photo Peter Moore.

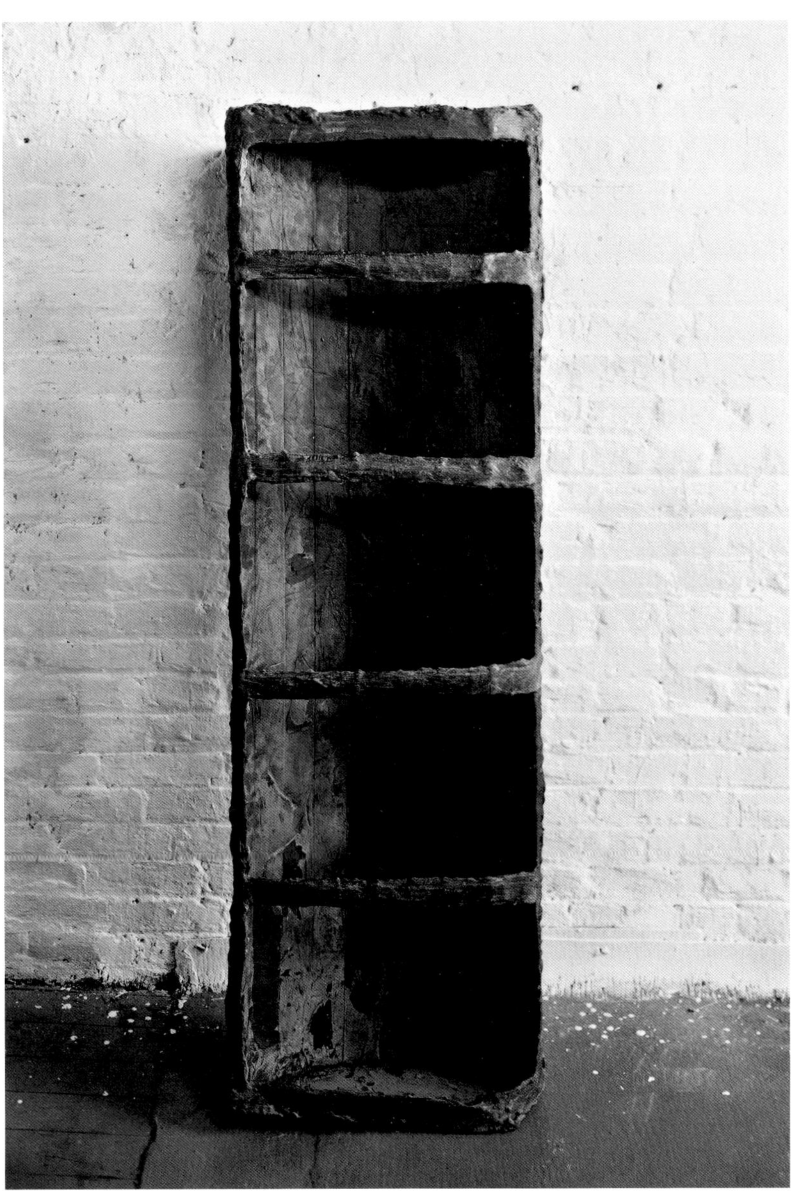

*Trough Pieces,* 1966–67 (detail). Rubber and fiberglass, 59 ½ × 18 ½ × 6 ¼ in.
(151.1 × 47 × 15.9 cm). Museum Ludwig, Cologne. Photo Peter Moore.

**RS**: Yes, and in this way in particular: The artists who were significant to me at the time were Judd, Flavin, and Andre, and most of them were a decade older. What they had done is take the work off the pedestal, thus putting the emphasis on the object. What they hadn't done was emphasize the making of the object itself. Most of their work looks mechanical, like outsourced products. With the exception of Andre, who was putting pieces on the floor that were not attached, Minimalism was basically a neo-Constructivist movement.

**HF**: In the sense of Naum Gabo and Antoine Pevsner, not Vladimir Tatlin and Alexander Rodchenko?

**RS**: Right. For the most part Minimalism is involved with a concept of construction, and I wanted to get away from that. Of course I also wanted to get away from modeling and casting. I definitely wanted to take the work off the pedestal. That's what my first meager attempts to deal with the making of a piece were about: "What do I have in front of me? How can I deal with it directly and get around the readymade of Duchamp as well?" And I thought, "Jasper Johns emphasizes making, the physicality of his material; he's not involved in mimicry." And it seemed I could do the same thing in the most intense way possible. I had no idea whether what I was doing would be art or not. So I made the *Doors,* which didn't look like doors at all, even though I cast them from rusty steel doors that I dragged off the pier right down in front of my studio.

**HF**: They are cast from actual doors?

**RS**: Yes, from shed doors that were part of the pier structure lining the Hudson River. I dragged the doors up about six flights, and then fiberglassed and rubberized them; the fiberglass is on the back, the rubber is on the front. When you look at them you don't have the sense I was trying to make a metal door. They don't look like metal at all.

**HF**: You also rotated a vertical thing to the horizontal—you laid the long edge of the *Doors* on the floor. And with the *Troughs* you turned a horizontal object into a vertical.

**RS**: Yes. I called them "troughs" because that's what they looked like, but the objects I cast were probably used as molds for cement casting. These were just things I was finding on the street that I thought I could use in some way, remaking them without the results looking like improved readymades.

**HF**: So these count as first works?

**RS**: In a way. I was trying to find a way to assert my own way of making, of confronting the artists who were in front of me and offering an initial proposition of what sculpture could be. I was also trying to deal with the Duchamp legacy, which I wanted to avoid at all costs.

**HF**: That's an interesting formulation—dealing with and avoiding at the same time. Do you mean taking on artists in order to get around or past them somehow? Did your "Verb List" come into play here?

**RS**: I didn't want to fall into the pitfalls of dealing with antecedents. That means you're pretty much out on your own trying to build your syntax. So I compiled a list of verbs and actions I thought I could perform in relation to matter and in relation to place. When you get involved with enacting a verb, it doesn't necessarily mean that the residue is going to have any aesthetic value.

I can give you an example. I was working with Phil Glass who was then earning a living as a plumber. We bought thirty-five feet of lead and unrolled it, and then we rolled it back up as tight as we could. Then we looked at it, and thought, "Could it be?" So we sat around, looked at it a little longer, and thought, "Maybe, maybe not." Then we did a double roll. And then we did something a little more adventurous: we rolled one sheet of lead on itself to make an internal curl, and then we rolled it back on top to produce a continuous triple roll.

At that point the art world was very small, and there wasn't any audience for this work. Dick Bellamy, whom I had met in Venice, was the first to show my sculpture. He ran the Green Gallery, where he exhibited a host of terrific artists. Dick was the most radical dealer on the scene, a kind of poet promoting the most experimental extensions of art. He became a witness to the making of these pieces, and he thought I should show them. That gave me a great deal of confidence because, when I first came to New York, I knew who the big figures were. They were taking their best shots, and I didn't want to get in the crossfire. But when Dick saw my pieces move from rubber into lead, he said, "Let's get these out into the world." He showed the belt pieces too.

**HF**: What about *To Lift* (1967)? That's another key early piece.

**RS**: *To Lift* embodies one of the verbs in the "Verb List." I took a piece of vulcanized rubber ten feet long, put it on its edge, lifted it up, looked at it, and again thought, "Maybe, maybe not." I was living in a loft with a mattress on the floor, running water but no heat. We would do these things, Glass and myself, leave them out, look at them, and try to figure out whether they held enough interest. The interest had to be intense for us.

**HF**: What does "interest" mean exactly? According to what criteria? Clement Greenberg insisted that a work had to have "quality," which was to be judged in relation to the best art of the past, whereas Judd said simply, "A work of art needs only to be interesting," that is, it only had to challenge conventions.[1] Your idea of "interest" seems to split this difference.

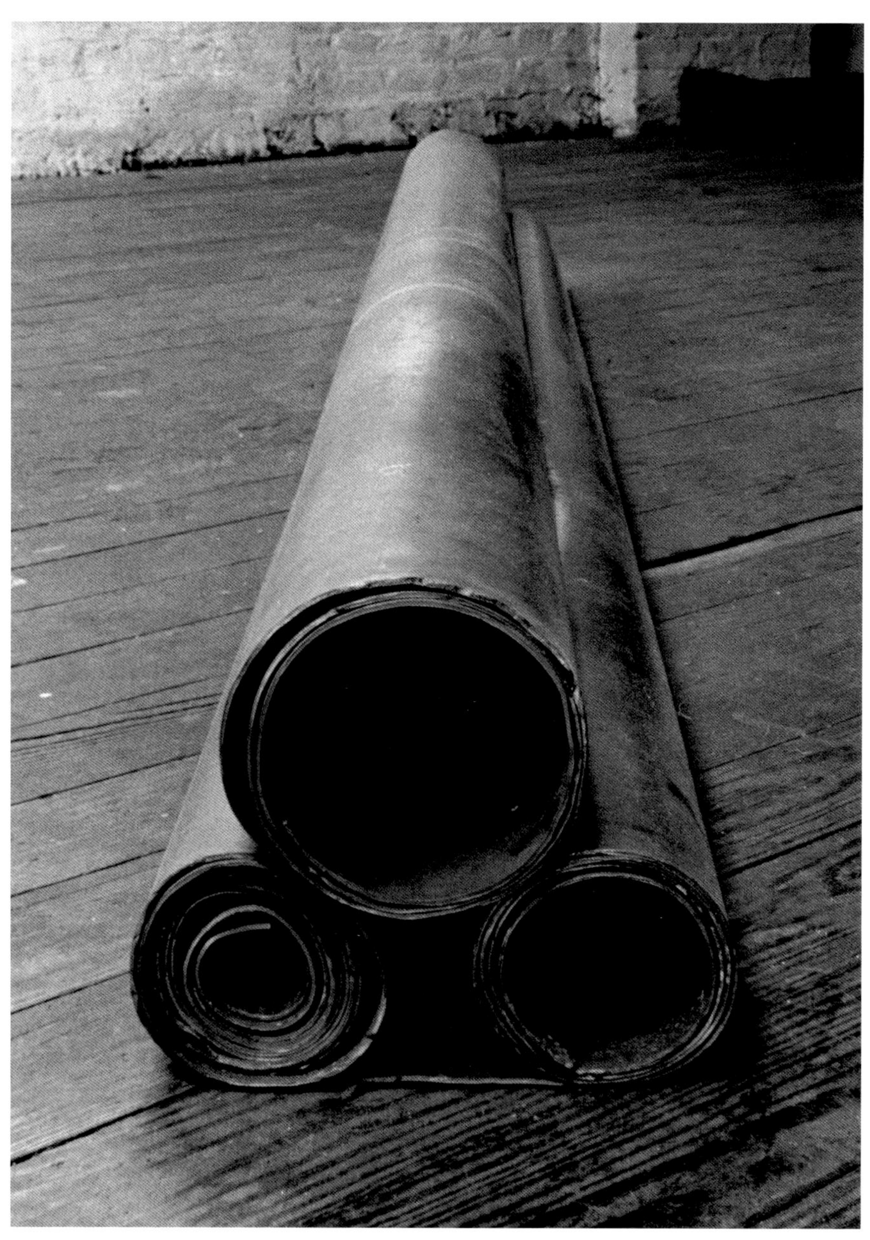

*Slow Roll: For Philip Glass,* 1968. Lead, overall 8 × 7 ¼ × 72 ¼ in.
(20.3 × 18.4 × 183.5 cm). Osaka City Museum of Modern Art, Japan.
Photo Peter Moore.

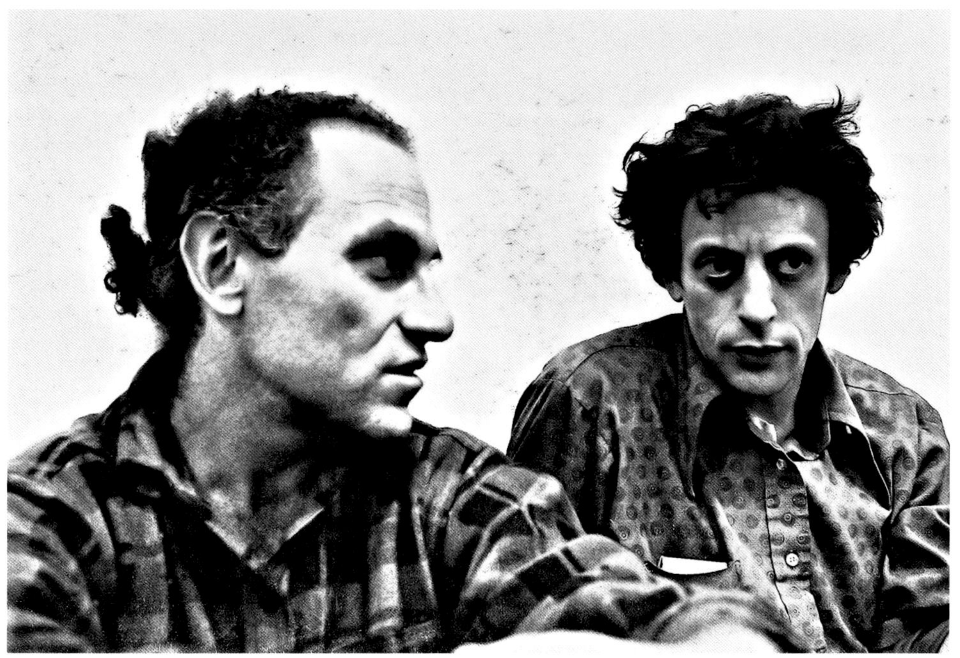

Richard Serra and Philip Glass, 1969.

**RS**: Phil and I used to play the pinball machines in Paris, and if you'd light up enough rotations on the bumpers you'd get a bonus. We used to talk about work in that same way: "Oh, that one looks like a bonus." We went through a lot of misses, but then there'd be a hit, a piece with internal necessity, and we'd say, "We lit one up." It's very important, especially when you're young, to find people who share a mindset with you, people you can play off, and Phil was a very interesting person for me to have a dialogue with.

**HF**: "Internal necessity" is a modernist criterion; it's a phrase Kandinsky used, for example, and it's all about aesthetic motivation—how to motivate the work of art after abstraction, after the guarantee of reference is no longer in place, how to keep it from becoming arbitrary. So what necessity did *To Lift* embody? What did it light up?

**RS**: It was a freestanding topological form that was continuous inside and outside. It didn't appear to me like any other sculpture, yet I couldn't deny it was three-dimensional— it was standing there on the floor. I'm not going to compare it to a Donatello, but as far as I was concerned, there it was. It had a claim. If I set it back down it wasn't anything, but if I lifted it up again it was the same thing representing itself as a problem, asking me if it could be perceived as sculpture. And I kept saying, "Why not? Why couldn't it be perceived as sculpture?"

**HF**: You said you asked Andre why he didn't lift his pieces off the floor. Was *To Lift,* in a sense, an action performed on Andre?

**RS**: No, we have to give that one to *House of Cards* (1969).

**HF**: What about *Chunk* (1967), the rough slab of rubber you simply leaned against the wall? That's an early piece that challenges preconceptions about sculpture too.

**RS**: I told you about the warehouse being emptied out on Thomas and West Broadway near my loft on Greenwich. A big front loader was taking all this discarded rubber off the street, putting it in trucks and hauling it away. So I got Glass, Steve Reich, Chuck Close, and Michael Snow, and we just loaded up my truck.

**HF**: Those guys were movers?

**RS**: Yes. In fact I started a little furniture moving company with Glass, Reich, Close, Snow, Spalding Gray, and Dickie Landry. We just loaded up the rubber and brought it upstairs to my loft. Again, it was like getting a grant of material: I had tons and tons of rubber to use. So I asked, "What kind of material is it?" It's very pliable; you can fold it. But you can also cut it, tangle it, and so on. There were a great many things to do with it. *Chunk* was one of the pieces that came out of my investigation into the potential of using rubber.

**HF**: What helped you think it could be a material for you? Who opened up that possibility?

**RS**: I think it goes back to a course I took at Yale taught by Neil Welliver. It was a design course handed down by Albers, and its premise was that matter informs form. Welliver would say, "Take any material you want and make something, then make something exactly like it in another material, and you'll see what the difference is." I got to the point where I was running cement through a meat grinder, making things that looked like cannoli. But it helped me understand that investigating the properties of a material can open up a whole host of ways of doing, making, and forming. It's like Louis Kahn asking, "What does a brick want to be?" I don't know if that's still relevant to young artists today, but I completely believed in understanding the readout of material properties. And it was almost irrelevant what the material was. So when I saw all that rubber, I thought, "I can use that."

**HF**: So material plus action equals a work that might have or might not have a bonus.

**RS**: That's right.

**HF**: Was Albers's insistence on material and process a way for you to get around the readymade and the great obsession with Duchamp at the time?

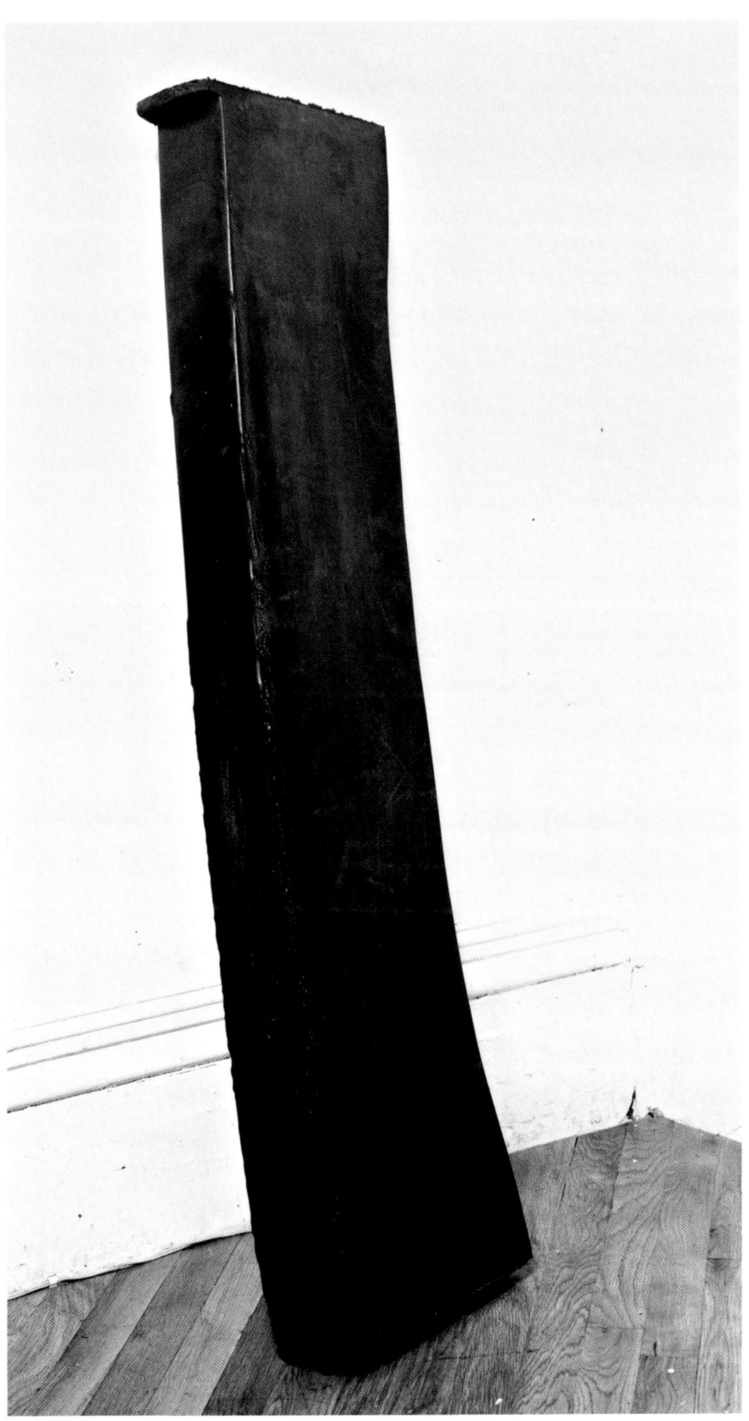

*Chunk,* 1967. Vulcanized rubber, 48 ½ × 18 × 19 ¾ in.
(123.2 × 45.7 × 50.2 cm) The Museum of Modern Art, New York.
Nina and Gordon Bunshaft Bequest (by exchange) and promised
gift of Emily Rauh Pulitzer and purchase. Photo Peter Moore.

**RS**: I was fine with other people using the readymade, but for me it was a trap. It seemed to be too wide-ranging in its permissiveness: you could put one thing next to another and get a poetic reading that led you back immediately to Kurt Schwitters. It was something about the ease in which it was being reformulated that made me uneasy. So I said to myself there are certain things I won't do: I'm not going to model or cast, I won't rely on an armature or place anything on a pedestal, and I'm not using readymades. Those are the conventions I wanted to avoid. When you decide to go with the negation of conventional ways of making sculpture, it leaves you out on the edge.

**HF**: But you proceeded analytically and constructively. With rubber you could fold it, cut it, tangle it, and so on. Where does negation come into play?

**RS**: My idea of negation came from having Reinhardt as a teacher for a while at Yale. Reinhardt was very definite about saying there are certain things you can do and certain things you can't do. And basically what you can't do is lean on others too much; it's really your mandate to invent, to invent your own poetics. I took that as a credo.

**HF**: So you made negation positive or at least productive. Reinhardt insisted on his "No."

**RS**: I think he made a great body of work out of his "No."

**HF**: I agree. My point is that you were interested in transformation as much as in negation: whatever you found you changed somehow. What about a thing he negated and you didn't— the body? What about bodiliness in your early work? Unlike the readymade, many of those pieces evoke or engage the body directly. It's one of the first moves you make.

**RS**: That was another way of getting away from Minimalism, which seemed devoid of the body in relation to material as well as activity. I wanted to bring back a do-it-yourself, hands-on way of making. The group of us who came after Minimalism were involved in this. It wasn't just me; it was Hesse, who had a beautiful touch, Nauman, and Smithson. We all resisted the mandates of Minimalism. That said, the people who were most interested in us were the Minimalists. Judd became like an older brother figure for me; he was very supportive. Robert Morris was interested too, figuring out what he could pick up on. And Johns couldn't have been more open, especially to Glass and myself. So it was a tight-knit community of younger and older figures. The older invited the younger in, and they encouraged us. I don't know if that situation still exists, but it was very much a part of the atmosphere of the 1960s in New York.

**HF**: In addition to the body, there's an allusion to architecture early on, at least to the space around the object, the space that the object impinges on, as in a piece like *Plinths* (1967).

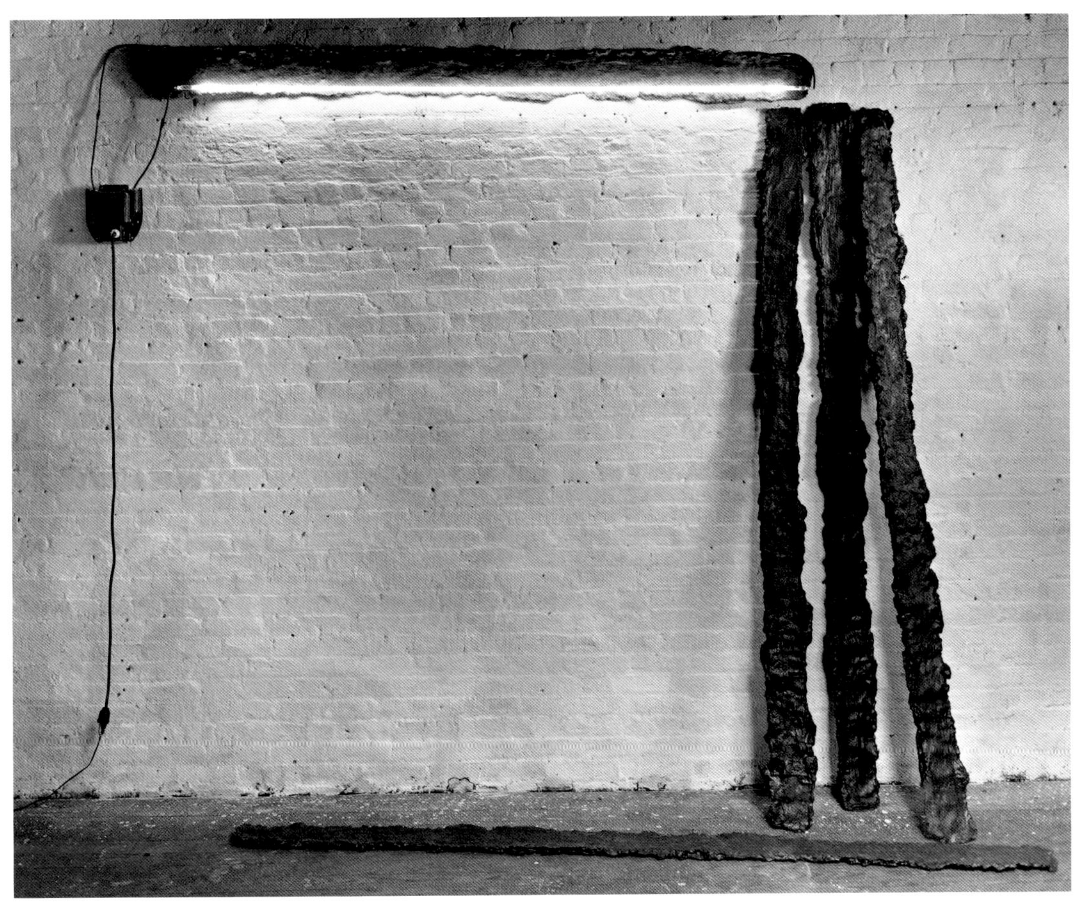

*Plinths*, 1967. Fiberglass, rubber, blue neon tubing; five pieces of rubber,
each 93 ¼ × 6 ¾ × 1 in. (237 × 17 × 2.5 cm), neon 6 ft. 6 ¾ in. (2 m). Centre Georges
Pompidou, Musée National d'Art Moderne, Paris. Photo Peter Moore.

**RS**: More than architecture, *Plinths* refers to Newman's *Here I* (1950), which is a vertical column first made of plaster and set on a milk crate. Rather than trying to make a vertical, freestanding, formal, didactic statement, I thought I'd just make these forms and arrange them—either lean them against the wall or disperse them on the floor. The arrangement was very casual and open, but I think the subtext was "How can I attack Barney?" You see, I loved his work.

**HF**: You loved it so you attacked it?

**RS**: That's a familiar dynamic. Harold Bloom discusses it in *The Anxiety of Influence* (1973)— it's about how you go about trumping your precursors.

**HF**: Bloom talks about productive misreadings and critical swerves, not outright attacks. That book was important to me too, but doesn't it limit literary history, or here art history, to a set of preoccupations that are finally too Oedipal, too boy-oriented?

**RS**: I'm not preoccupied with Freud and the Oedipal complex.

**HF**: Well, the Bloom model is an adaptation of that model, and you subscribe to it. But let's get back to the bodiliness of your early work. What about *Template* and *Slant Step Folded* (both 1967), two rubber pieces that evoke the body, or at least posture and gesture, in different ways?

**RS**: *Template* came out of a handbook I found on Delancey Street, a manual for cutting patterns for coats and dresses. I thought, "This is a useful kind of drawing." I just took one pattern, ripped it out, and made a bad copy. It was in two parts, so I clipped them together and hung them on the wall. It has a vague relationship to Oldenburg. Bellamy gave me Oldenburg's *Cash Register* (1961) to store. It's more a lumpy form than a cash register, painted silver, red, and blue. I didn't want to do Oldenburgs, but it was interesting having it there every day in my studio: it presented the rawness of a physical object in the room. Oldenburg was always in the back of my mind, a player I had to contend with. He was one of the first people to use gravity, particularly when he got to his soft pieces.

**HF**: What about Oldenburg's move into space—the way that, through manipulations of scale, he opens up and controls a space. Was that important to you?

**RS**: When I first came down from Yale, I saw Oldenburg's *Floor Burger* and thought it was phenomenal. The scale was just outrageous. You could push your hand into the kapok and it would take a different form—it was silly and stupid and wonderful at the same time. I thought it challenged Judd in a very perverse way. Just taking the idea of representation and turning it on its head—this enormous hamburger had nothing to do with replicating

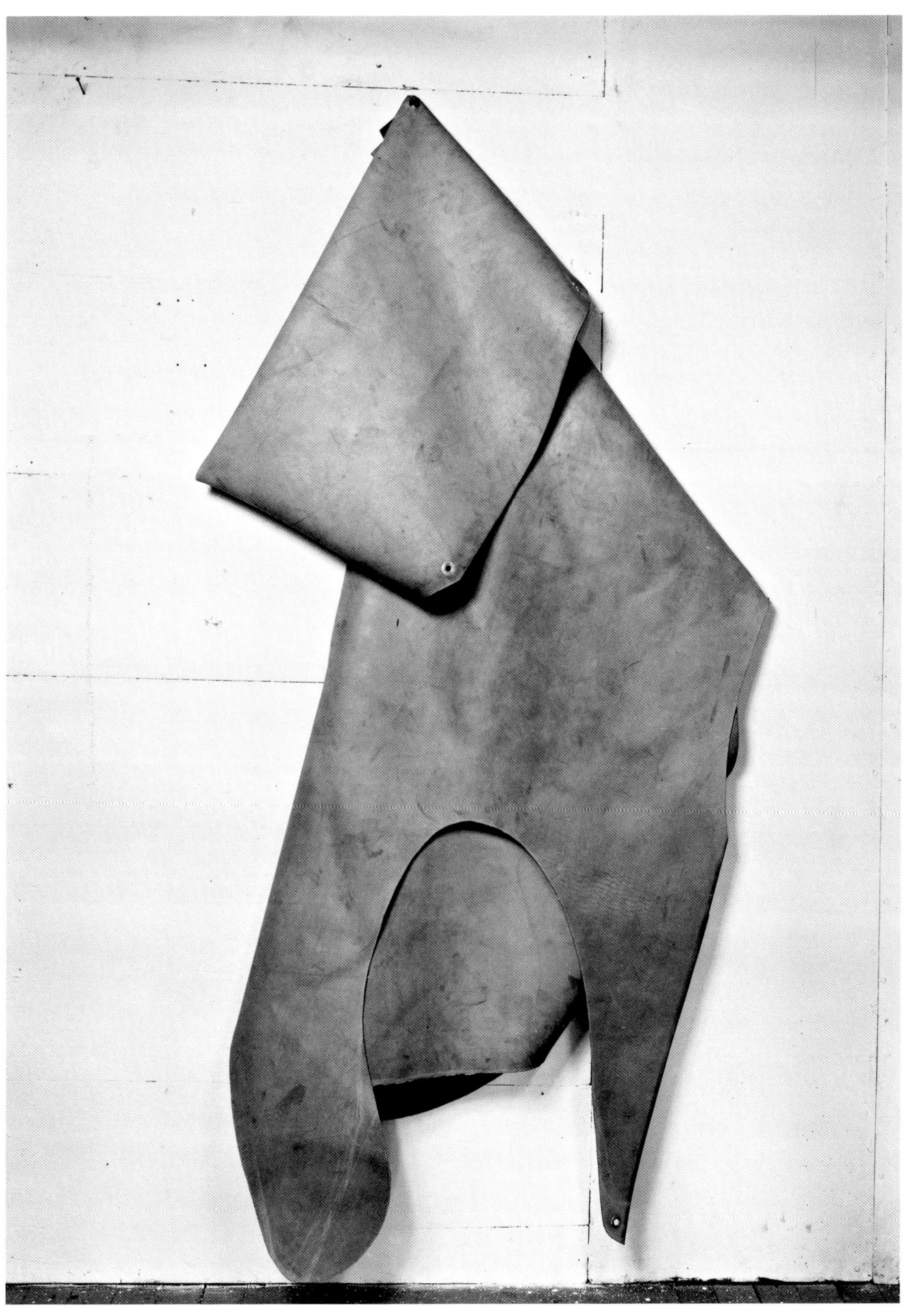

*Template,* 1967. Vulcanized rubber, c. 7 ft. 9 in. × 39 in. × 8 in. (2.4 m × 99.1 cm × 20.3 cm).
Solomon R. Guggenheim Museum, New York. Panza Collection. Photo Peter Moore.

a hamburger. I became a very big advocate. I think Oldenburg has been underrated; he's a marvelous sculptor.

**HF**: I totally agree. Oldenburg also engages the body in an entirely new way: some of his *Store* objects are like estranged pieces of our own bodies or, conversely, everyday things that we have somehow ingested and crapped out. They're absolutely wild—like nothing else before. But back to the opening on to space in your work: what else helped you get there?

**RS**: Sometimes just working, just doing, can push you along and open things up. Take *Splashing* (1968), the first splash piece against the wall: liquefying the lead, then making it solid again—that really attacked the whole problem of modeling and casting, and it immediately brought the context, the architecture, into play. One of the limitations of Minimalism was that it didn't deal with context. The perception of a Minimalist object is mostly limited to a gestalt reading in a room: you read one side and then fill in the others in your head. That doesn't take in the consideration of time in relation to place, the whole subject-object relationship. The object is content to present itself in its own specificity. Like Smithson, Hesse, and Nauman, I wanted to find a way around that limitation.

**HF**: And casting pieces first showed you a way to do so?

**RS**: Yes. At first I just took a ladle of lead, laid it down along the wall, took another ladle of lead, laid it down, and so on. The repetition was the important thing. I was amassing a couple of tons of lead against the wall so that it looked like a continuous splash, but actually it took about eight hours, so it wasn't a continuous splash at all. After we did it I thought, "Why don't we just uncork it? Turn it over and see the wall and the floor it was cast from?" We did the first lead splash at the Castelli Warehouse; then I was invited to participate in the Whitney Annual. That show was called "Anti-Illusion: Procedures/ Materials" (1969), and it included the whole group of us from downtown—Reich, Glass, Hesse, all of us. And that piece was in that show.

    I built *Splash Piece: Casting* (1969–70) for Johns. Phil and I were heating the lead scraps, but there was one rectangular plate too large to melt, so I set it in the corner, and I thought, "Look, it free-stands." Soon after I went out and got a big plate. I had to hire a rigger, which I'd never done before. That move got me out of the studio and into a whole new world of engagement. I just shoved the plate right into the corner, knowing that the junction with the wall would hold it up, that nothing else was needed to support it other than the architecture.

**HF**: That piece was *Strike* (1969–71). I get how the splash pieces register context, but was *Strike* the key work in your move into space?

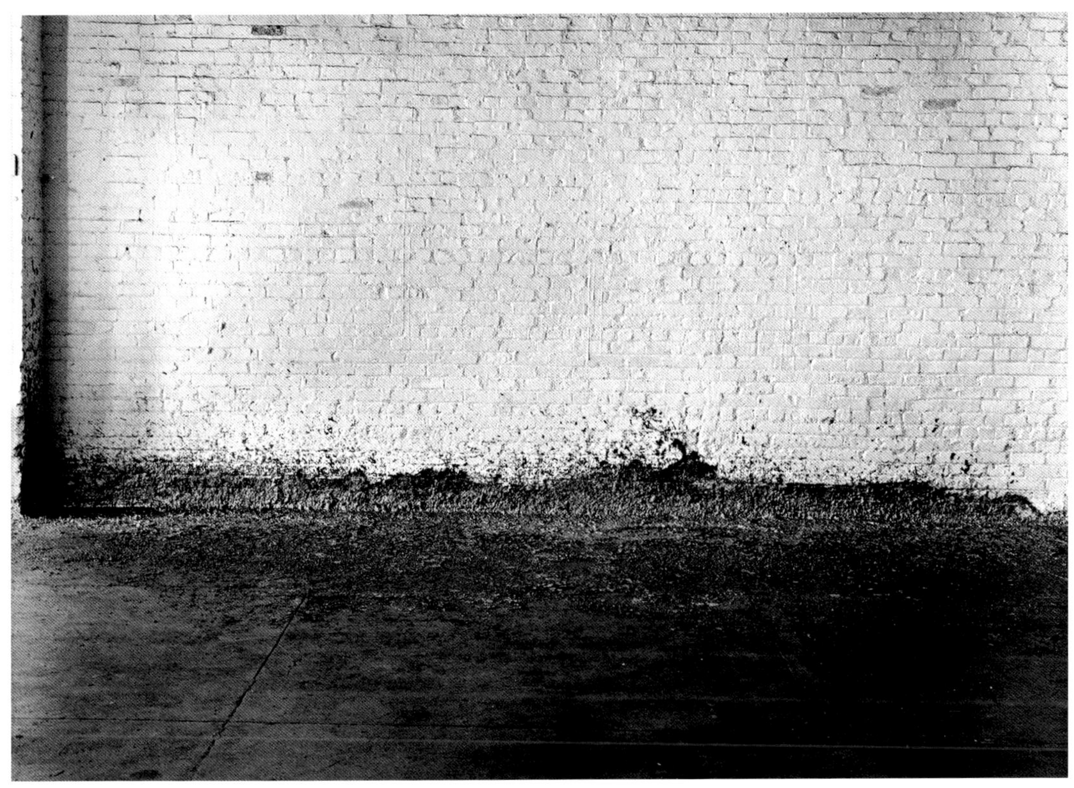

*Splashing,* 1968. Lead, c. 18 in. × 26 ft. (45.7 cm × 7.9 m). Temporary, site-specific installation in the exhibition "Nine at Castelli," Castelli Warehouse, New York, 1968.

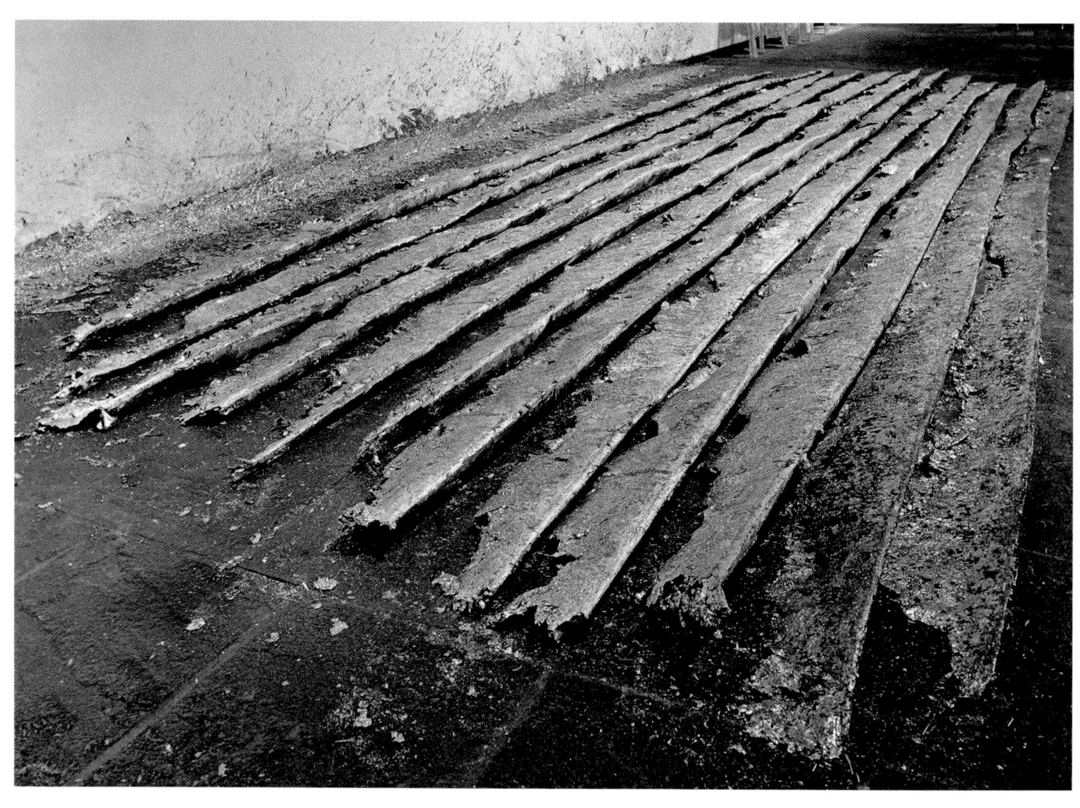

*Casting*, 1969. Lead, c. 4 in. × 25 ft. × 15 ft. (10.2 cm × 7.6 m × 4.6 m). Temporary, site-specific installation in the exhibition "Anti-Illusion: Procedures/Materials," Whitney Museum of American Art, New York, 1969. Photo Peter Moore.

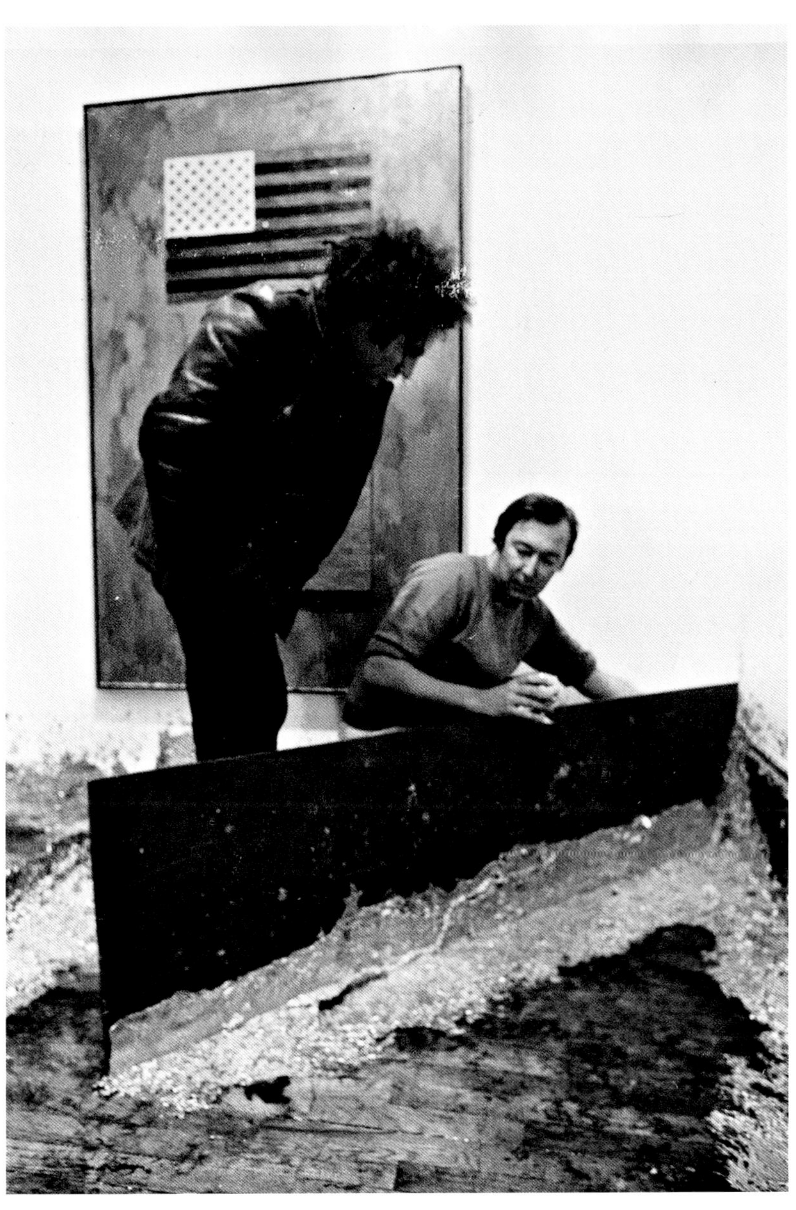

Richard Serra and Jasper Johns with *Splash Piece: Casting,*
1969–70, in Johns's studio, New York, 1969.

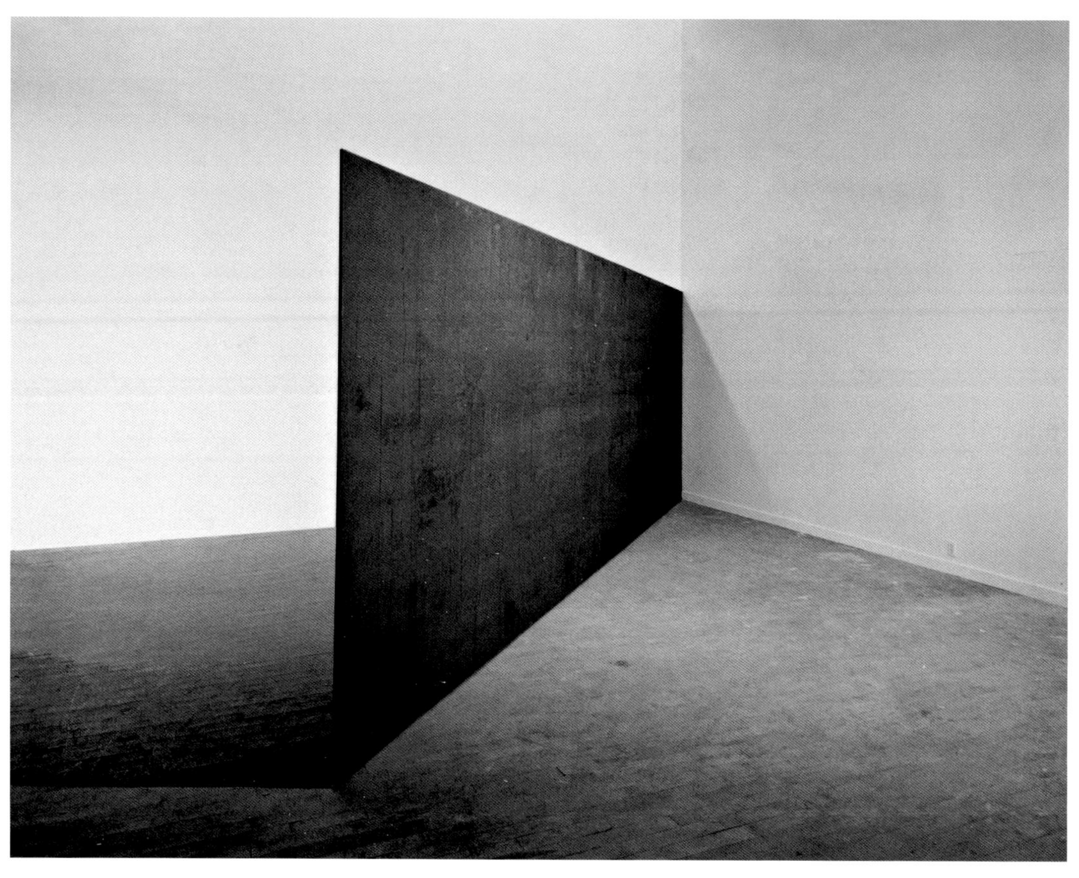

*Strike: To Roberta and Rudy*, 1969–71. Hot-rolled steel, 8 ft. 1 in. × 24 ft. × 1 ½ in. (2.5 m × 7.3 m × 3.8 cm). Solomon R. Guggenheim Museum, New York. Panza Collection. Photo Peter Moore.

**RS**: Yes. *Strike* was my break into space. I realized if I wedged a plate into the corner, it would be freestanding. So I got a plate eight by twenty-four feet, and that was *Strike*. It declared the whole space in dividing it, and I realized I could hold the room the way Flavin did, only do it with my own material. But it took me a couple of years to catch up to that implication.

**HF**: What is extraordinary is that your claiming of sculpture—your move of picking up the Andre, as it were, and activating the ambient space—was also potentially a dissolving of sculpture into that space, into a field of process, movement, and time. It is as though the recovery of the sculptural activates the field, and that in turn scatters the sculptural— at least as understood in the traditional sense of the object alone.

**RS**: *Cutting Device: Base Plate Measure* (1969) speaks to that problem. Phil and I were debating whether it'd be possible to use more than one material in relation to process and how the residue might avoid the pitfalls of composition, collage, assemblage, and poetic metaphor. We placed a long sheet of steel—we called it the "base plate"—on the floor and stacked different materials horizontally across it in a way that overhung the edges of the steel. We then cut with a circular saw through those materials along both edges of the base plate, which became the underlying measure for the cut. As we were sawing we pushed the material aside. The act of cutting simultaneously separated and joined those scattered elements; it was the cutting that was the focus, not the arrangement of the different elements. But once you get the sculpture off the ground and freestanding you want to open up the field. And, again, that took me a couple of more years.

**HF**: You said you were frustrated by the Minimalists—that, even as some opened up the space of the work to the gallery, the object was still the focus, and even then it was partially occluded. How has your relation to ambient space, to physical site, changed since that first incursion in *Strike*.

**RS**: Once I got into a larger context, I had to deal with how the space functions. Where's the door? How do people enter? Where does the light come from? What's the weight load? And then other contexts, other settings, opened up. The move into the landscape, which happened with *Shift* (1970) and *Pulitzer Piece: Stepped Elevation* (1969–71), was huge, and that raised other questions in turn. What's the elevation? How do you deal with its shifts? I was still involved with making and doing, but in a way my hand was extended by other people, by the riggers and their tools.

How do you deal with a space in a way that will bring a sculptural resolution to all its indices? How do you take a field that is undifferentiated or heterogeneous and turn it into a homogeneous sculptural place that anybody can recognize the moment they walk

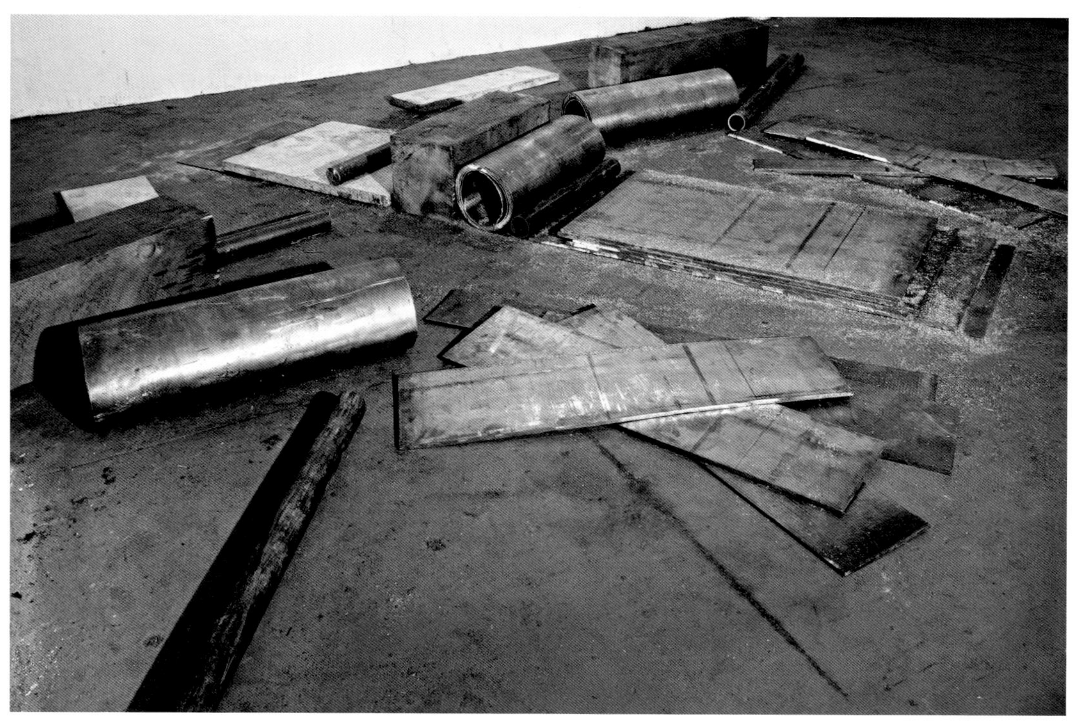

Above: *Cutting Device: Base Plate Measure,* 1969. Lead, wood, stone, steel, c. 12 in. × 18 ft. × 15 ft. 7 ¾ in. (30.5 cm × 5.5 m × 4.8 m). The Museum of Modern Art, New York. Gift of Philip Johnson. Photo Peter Moore.

Opposite: *Shift,* 1970–72. Concrete, six sections: 60 in. × 90 ft. × 8 in. (152.4 cm × 27.4 m × 20.3 cm), 60 in. × 240 ft. × 8 in. (152.4 cm × 73.1 m × 20.3 cm), 60 in. × 150 ft. × 8 in. (152.4 cm × 45.7 m × 20.3 cm), 60 in. × 120 ft. × 8 in. (152.4 cm × 36.6 m × 20.3 cm), 60 in. × 110 ft. × 8 in. (152.4 cm × 33.5 m × 20.3 cm), 60 in. × 105 ft. × 8 in. (152.4 cm × 32 m × 20.3 cm), installed at King City, Ontario, Canada. Collection Great Gulf Homes, Toronto. (The Municipality of King Township designated *Shift* as a Heritage Landscape under the Ontario Heritage Act, 2013.)

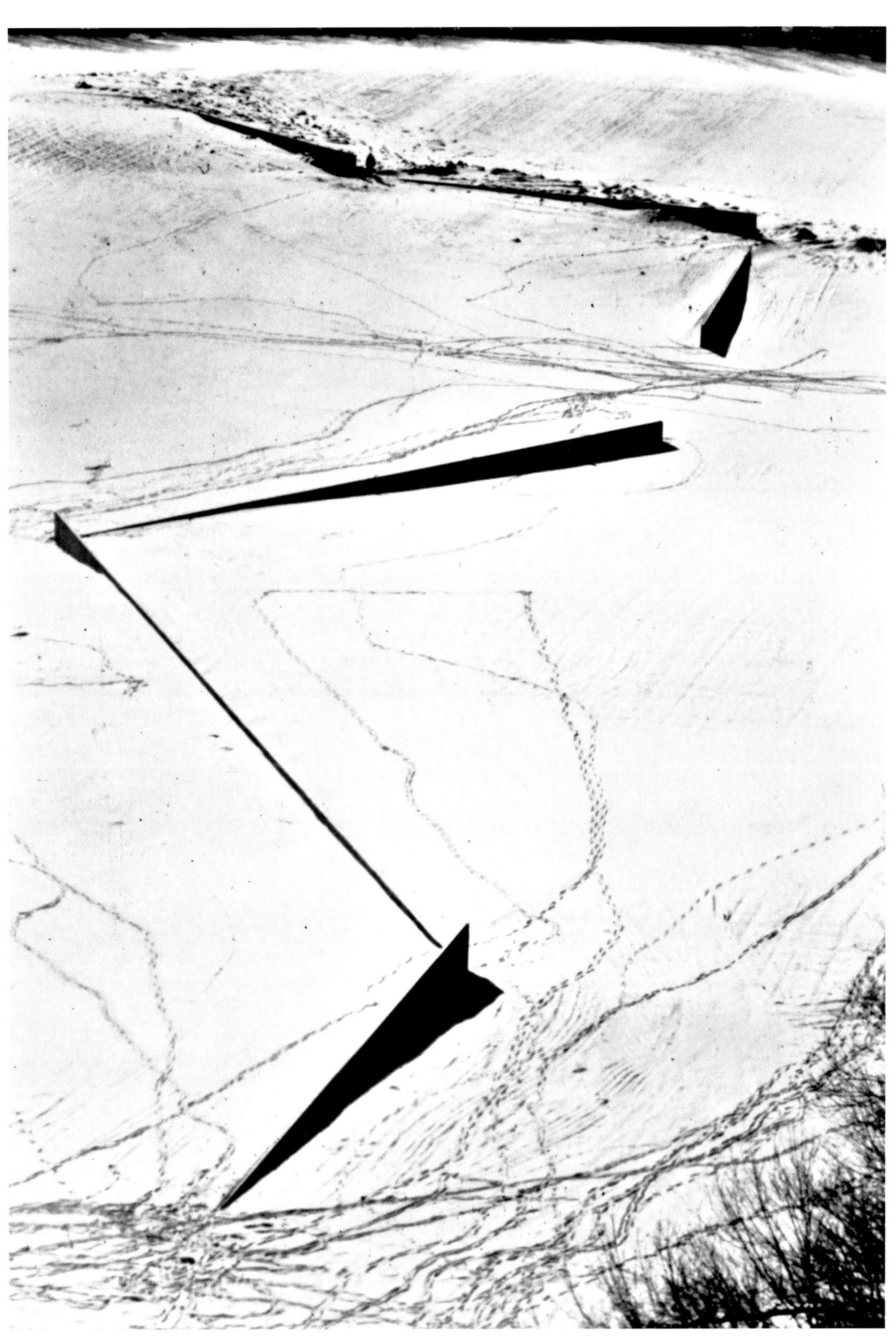

into it? If you enter a room and there are four plates coming out of the four corners—
that's *Circuit* (1972)—you immediately realize you're in a sculptural place. How do you
do that in other contexts? How do you challenge those spaces, changing them into places
that deal with volume in a way that hadn't been done before? Basically what I try to do
is articulate space.

**HF**: Always in relation to the body—that emphasis is already there in your early work.

**RS**: Yes, to the body and its movement. And the relationship of both to time. Also in
relationship to labor, to the effort of production, to how the things come into being.
Not hiding labor and production in the manifestation of the work. It's very important to
me to bring the fabricator and the rigger into the process of making and have that be
registered in the work. That goes back to my working in steel mills as a kid. It's just something I ethically need to do for myself.

**HF**: Here's an invitation to be immodest. From a distance of fifty years, where do you
see your early work in the history of sculpture?

**RS**: If you ask me what counts, I think you don't know—you can't know. You make work,
you look at work, you analyze work, and you have to come back to your work over and
over again to see if there's any resolution. Sometimes an old problem kicks you off in
another direction because the solution you thought you were looking for engenders a whole
different set of problems.

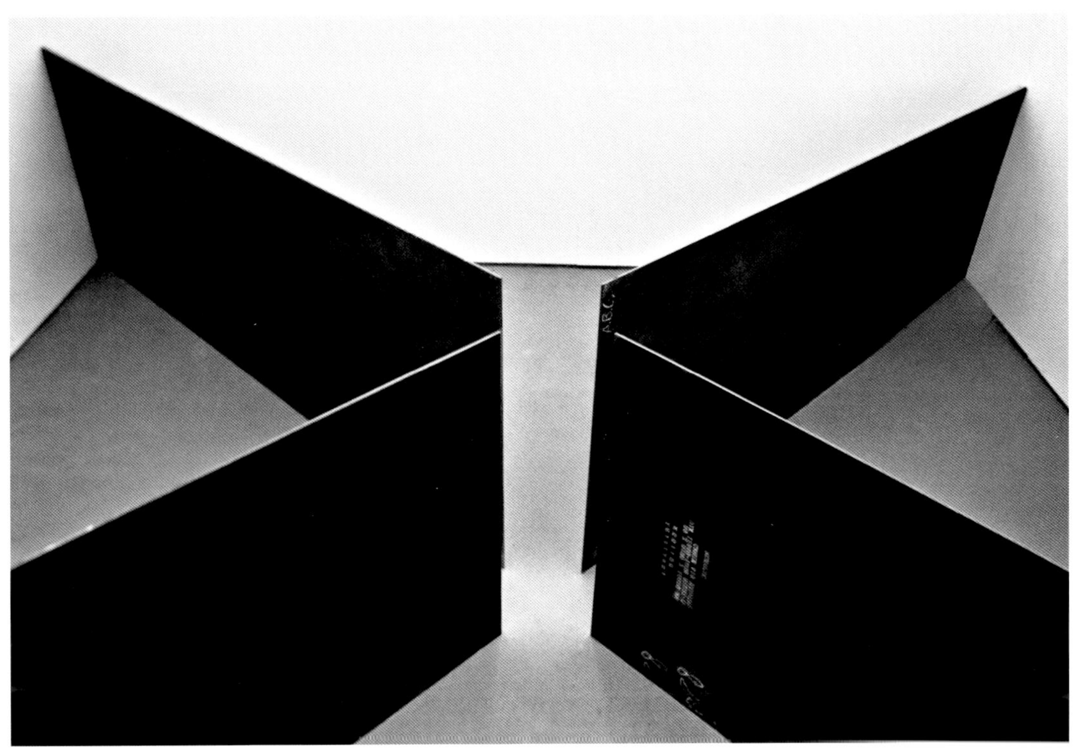

*Circuit,* 1972. Hot-rolled steel, four plates, each 8 ft. × 24 ft. × 1 in. (2.4 m × 7.3 m × 2.5 cm). The Museum of Modern Art, New York. Gift of the artist in honor of Harald Szeemann.

# Specific Sites

**HF**: Was there an internal necessity, once you pulled your sculpture up in the prop pieces, to pull it apart as well?

**RS**: Not at first. When I lifted the plates off the ground, I realized it was also a limitation, and that there was a need to separate them, but at the time I didn't know how. The move into space happened with *Strike* (1969–71). *Strike* cut, divided, and declared the room as context.

**HF**: Is this where your trip to Japan in 1970 and your encounter with Zen gardens comes into play?

**RS**: No. The small lead plate I shoved into the corner when I was working on *Splash Piece: Casting* for Johns was the origin of *Strike,* but the experience of the Japanese gardens was enormously important for my first landscape pieces. The gardens opened up a perceptual world; they made me rethink the undifferentiated field of Pollock and the writings of Anton Ehrenzweig. What is essential is the time of experiencing the gardens as you move through them: it's a physical time. Time is compressed or protracted, but it's always articulated. Perception narrows to details, but always returns to the field in its entirety.

**HF**: How did you process your experience in Japan? Clearly your work was headed in that direction; you were also looking at the first earthworks—Michael Heizer's *Double Negative* (1969–70) and Robert Smithson's *Spiral Jetty* (1970). How did all these different interests come together to make for your specific intervention into space—opening up a sculptural field and delineating it with the body moving in time?

**RS**: The most consequential move into the landscape was *Pulitzer Piece: Stepped Elevation* (1970–71), followed by *Shift* (1970–72) and *Spin Out (for Bob Smithson)* (1972–73). They were all crucial for me because they took concerns I had worked out in interior spaces and tested them in exterior settings. *Pulitzer Piece* was my first big step into the landscape. That was after going to Japan, which changed my way of seeing space in relation to time. The stakes were very high. I was up against the Pulitzer collection—Monet, Matisse, Picasso, you name it. It took a couple of years to finish.

**HF**: What was the next moment in the development of your ideas about site?

**RS**: When Heizer and Smithson began doing earthworks, they asked me to join them. I was interested in their work, but it wasn't for me. I saw Heizer as extending Judd's volumes into the landscape, and I saw Smithson as dealing with his own peculiar iconography of geology, crystallography, and all the rest. I helped him lay out *Spiral Jetty,* and after he died I worked with others to finish *Amarillo Ramp* (1973).

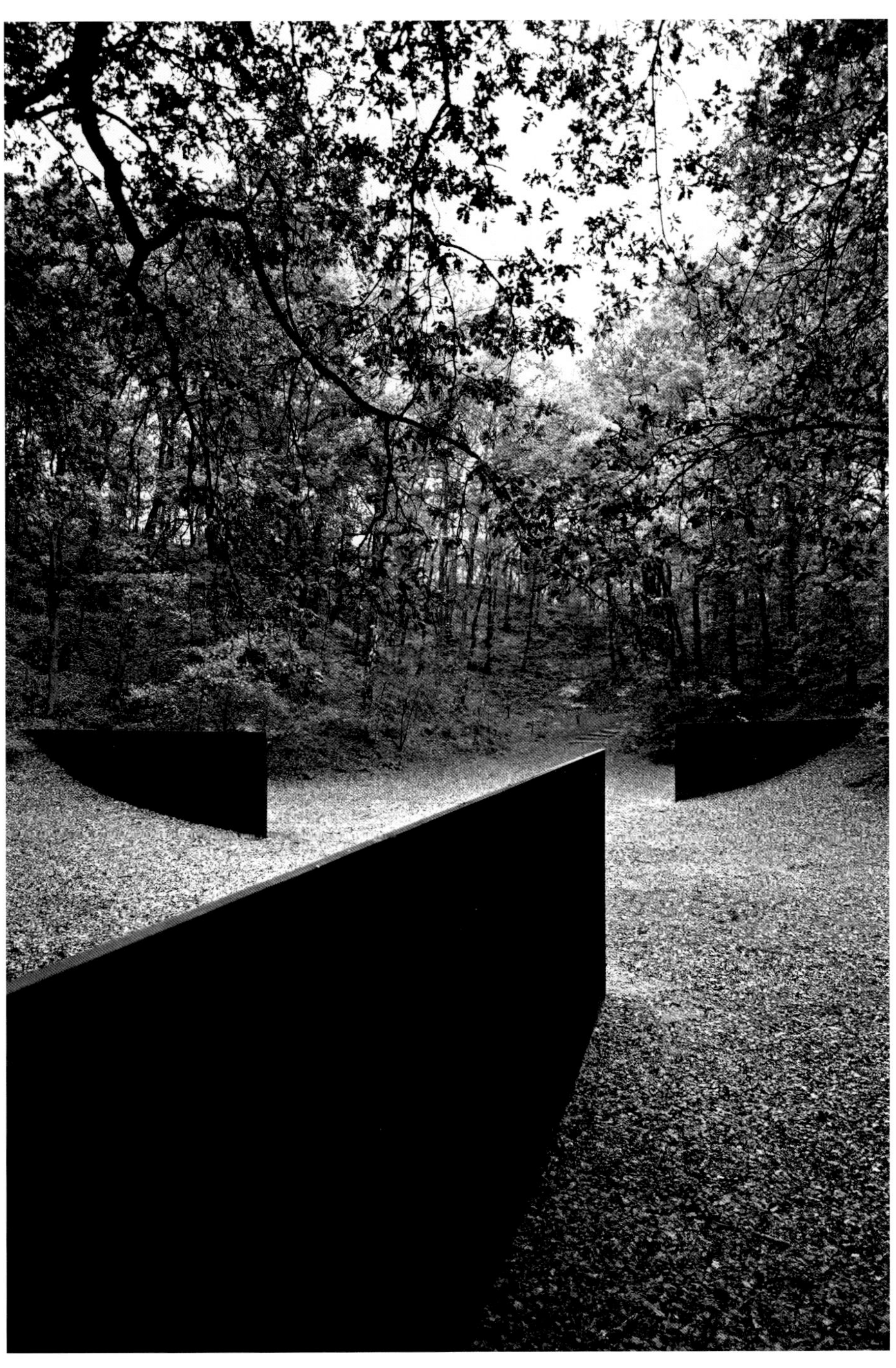

*Spin Out (For Bob Smithson),* 1972–73. Weatherproof steel, three plates, each 10 ft. × 40 ft. × 1 ½ in. (3 m × 12.2 m × 3.8 cm). Kröller-Müller Museum, Otterlo, The Netherlands.

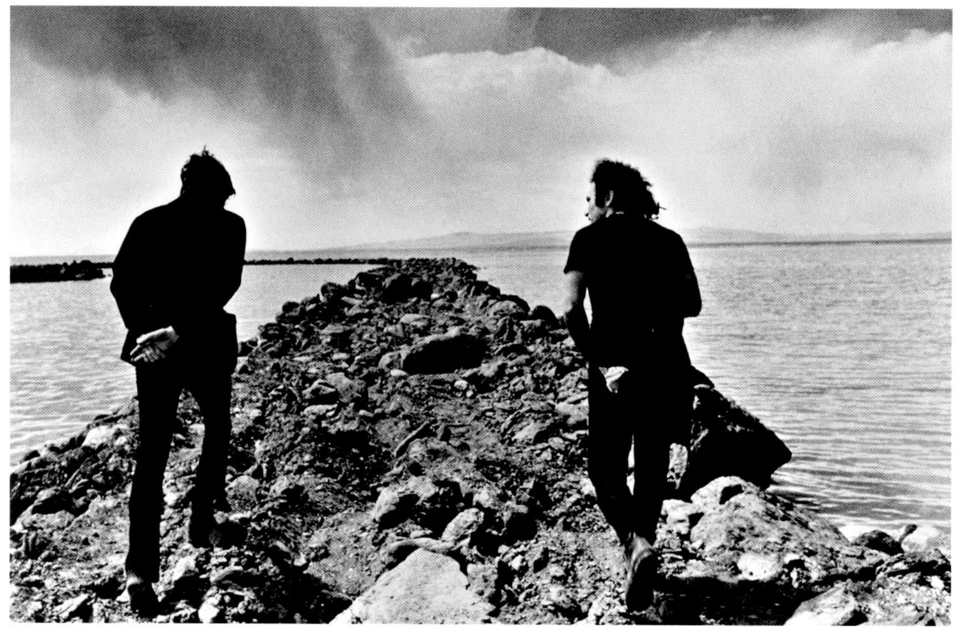

Robert Smithson and Richard Serra at *Spiral Jetty,* Great Salt Lake, Utah, 1970.

**HF**: What was your relationship with him like?

**RS**: Dan Graham introduced us when I moved to New York, and we became close friends: we saw each other several times a week and talked every night. Smithson was a great critical voice, always pestering and mocking. He was ironic and humorous in a nasty sort of way. I loved playing off his intelligence; it was perverse, diverse, broad, and serious. He put many different thoughts into play—low and high culture, science, art, astrology, fiction, film, anything you could think of—and he melded those ideas into bizarre combinations. Smithson was a visionary, but he was also pretty weird. People say his writing was the most important contribution other than his earthworks—maybe— but he was just as important as a person on the scene who challenged people. He was a catalyst for all of us. I was friendly with Judd, who was supportive of my work. Initially Smithson supported Judd's work, but that was short-lived, and they had a falling out. They were enormously competitive, each with his original way of thinking. Smithson was competitive with everyone with the exception of Warhol and Andre. It was easy to be seduced by Smithson. His notions about material and entropy always interested me.

**HF**: What drove his acerbic intelligence?

**RS**: I think a need to overcome Catholicism through nihilism—he and Warhol both. I grew up with a lot of Irish kids, so I understood that kind of enraged Catholic. But Smithson was really wonderful too, and when he died I was very angry. I'd lost a true friend.

**HF**: In an early text, "Play It Again, Sam" (1970), you're skeptical of scatter installations (despite doing a few yourself); you call them a "lateral spread of materials" on the floor. Your complaint is that they reinscribe a "landscape mode," one that doesn't avoid "arrangement qua figure ground: the pictorial convention." Further, you say, "Lateral extension in this case allows sculpture to be viewed pictorially—that is, as if the floor were the canvas plane. It is no coincidence that most earthworks are photographed from the air."[1]

**RS**: Yes, for the most part earthworks are graphic ideas imposed on the landscape. I was interested in a different penetration into the land, one that would open up the field and bring you into it bodily through movement, not just draw you in visually. The rhythm of the body moving through space has been the motivating source of most of my work.

**HF**: In a conversation a decade later you talk about how earthworks came to the public mostly in the form of documents: "I have never found that satisfying. I would rather have the actual experience of work at urban scale."[2] You also assert that photographs destroy the "temporal experience" of earthworks, that the photos become a way to consume them.

**RS**: It's a virtual market device. I saw that early on and didn't want any part of it.

**HF**: Did that aversion lead to any testy exchanges with Smithson or Heizer as to the limits of documentation or indeed of the site/non-site idea?[3]

**RS**: No. Artists have their own ways of doing things, and you can't be putting them down. I see documentation as an attribute, just as I see language as an attribute. The non-sites ended up being a road show, without commitment to any specific place. The concept of the non-site is a theoretical justification for homeless objects.

**HF**: You see them as secondary.

**RS**: Yes. They are artifices that lead you in other directions. A photograph of an earthwork reduces it, flattens it, frames it. It changes its color, takes away its tactility, has nothing to do with its three-dimensionality, nothing to do with its context, nothing to do with its space. It's virtual reality.

**HF**: So you were never interested in how the non-site idea could render the work of art textual and so open it up to other forms, formats, sources, and meanings.

RS: I thought that textuality was a departure from the physical realities of the world we live in. I had the same problem with some of the "Pictures" artists.

HF: "Pictures" artists like Cindy Sherman and Louise Lawler showed us how mass media have transformed the world we live in. That was their intention, and their textualization of the art work helped them realize it. They turned what was a problem for you into an advantage for them. But back to your site pieces.

RS: I didn't want to make a sign or a symbol in the landscape as earthworks do; I wanted to work with its topography. How do you make walking and looking the content of your work? What happens to your body when the elevation is constantly shifting and there's no horizon to orient you, no flat plane? How do you cut into the land, gather it in a volume, and hold that volume?

HF: That interest has persisted, and you've developed a language to articulate those volumes in different sites. Yet already in 1980, even as you continued with landscape projects, you said you preferred urban settings. What do the two kinds of intervention share, and how do they diverge? Also in 1980 you remarked, "In the landscape pieces the redefinition of the site becomes the content of the work."[4] Isn't that true of your urban pieces as well?

RS: Take Splashing, the first lead splash at the Castelli warehouse: not only is it built into the space directly, but it changes the architecture totally.

HF: I understand that's your initial instance of site-specificity, but it's interior and architectural. My question is about sites that are exterior and urban.

RS: Urban sites are much more difficult. You have more contingencies with more attributes, and you must push back with your own sculptural invention against a host of narratives, many of which are ideological. You have to gather the volumes that are already there, the circulation patterns, whatever, in fact all that goes into how the site is defined and perceived. I want to reclaim the site for sculpture.

HF: Is there more gathering to do in the urban pieces than in the landscape pieces?

RS: Landscape sites are easier for me to deal with because there's less interference.

Clara Weyergraf-Serra: What do you mean by "gathering"?

HF: I think it has to do with the way a piece picks up on aspects of its surroundings and pulls them into itself as part of its content. Do you feel more compelled to do this gathering in the urban sites with all their contingencies?

**RS**: You're presented with different kinds of sites, and you have to work with what's given in those sites. Landscape sites are easier to work with than urban sites for the reasons I just mentioned.

**HF**: What other similarities and dissimilarities obtain in the two types of site? At least initially, most of your landscape projects favored a horizontal extension across a site, as in a cut, while most of your city projects privileged a vertical marking of a site, as with a tower. The early urban arcs, such as *St. John's Rotary Arc* (1980) and *Tilted Arc* (1981), both in lower Manhattan, were obvious exceptions, but they were positioned in particular spaces—a "leftover site" (as you called it) in the first instance, the exit of the Holland Tunnel, and a plaza space in the second, near the courthouses—which they marked in distinctive ways. Maybe your arcs mediate between the horizontal landscape pieces and the vertical urban ones. How do you decide, then, when to propose, in an urban context, a tower like *Sight Point* (1972–75) or an arc like *St. John's Rotary Arc*?

**RS**: Again, for the most part the sites are given; you don't choose them, though with *Sight Point,* which is at the Stedelijk in Amsterdam, I was able to select the site, and I decided to build a tower.

**HF**: It sounds as though the distinctions are not hard and fast, that some aspects of the landscape pieces can be carried over to the urban pieces and vice versa.

**RS**: I haven't found a seamless way of moving from one to the other. Actually, I don't think it can be seamless, and maybe it shouldn't be.

**HF**: A commonality between the two types of work is that both are opposed to gestalt readings.[5]

**RS**: That's true. The gestalt is a great limitation, a pictorial limitation: the viewer can complete the image of an object by looking at one part only. Most Minimalists are stuck with gestalt readings. They don't truly open the space; for the most part their constructions remain objects.

**HF**: The resistance to gestalt readings is already present in your early work. It was important to you to carry forward that critique in your sited works?

**RS**: Yes, absolutely.

**HF**: Let me point to another distinction between the two types, an opposition even, and ask if it still holds. In 1983 you said, "In the landscape, even if I go through the same process of site analysis, the sculptures have more to do with movement than with location.

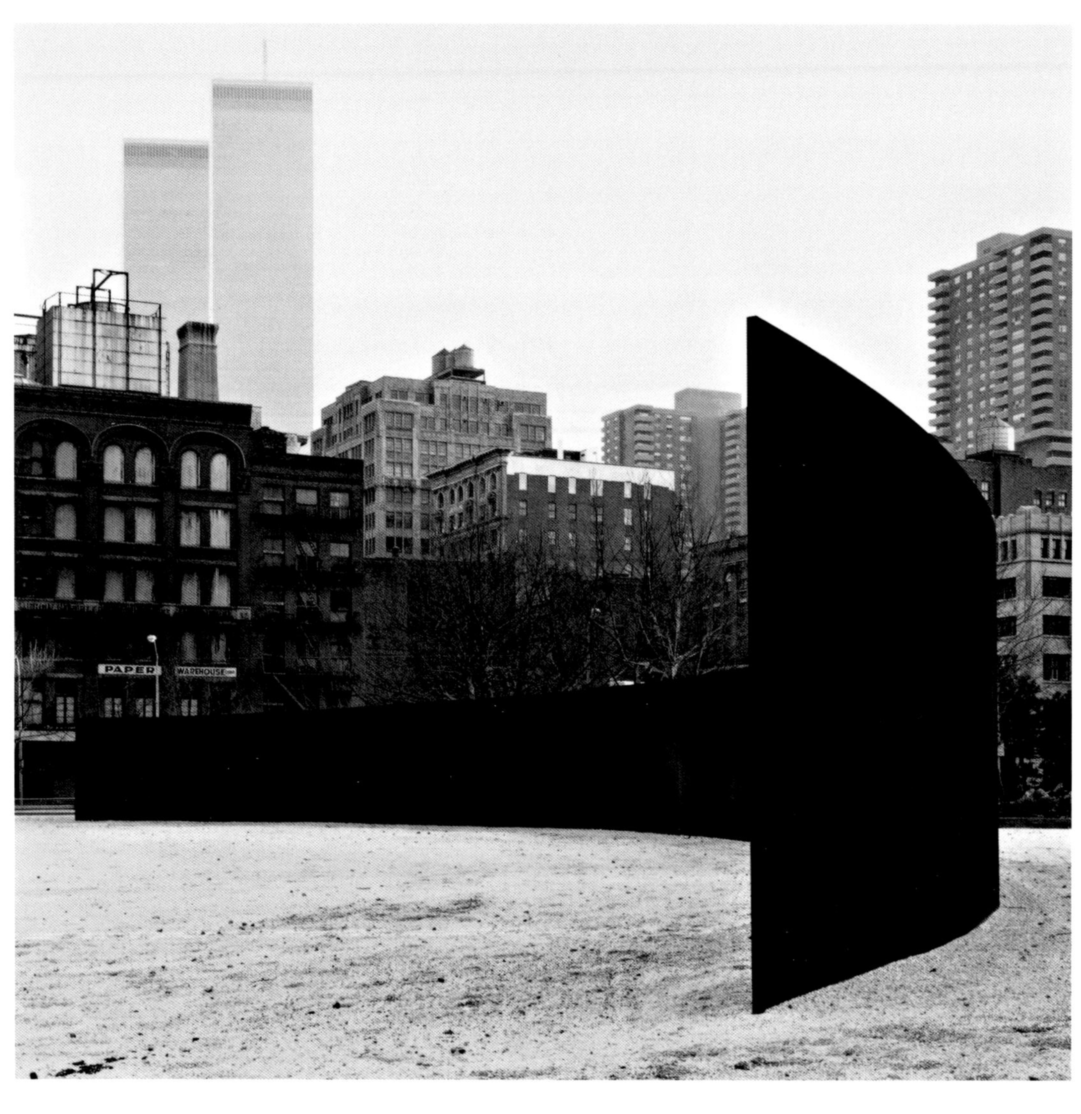

*St. John's Rotary Arc,* 1980. Weatherproof steel, cylindrical section 12 ft. × 180 ft. × 2 ½ in. (3.6 m × 54.9 m × 6.4 cm). As installed at Holland Tunnel exit, New York, 1980–88.

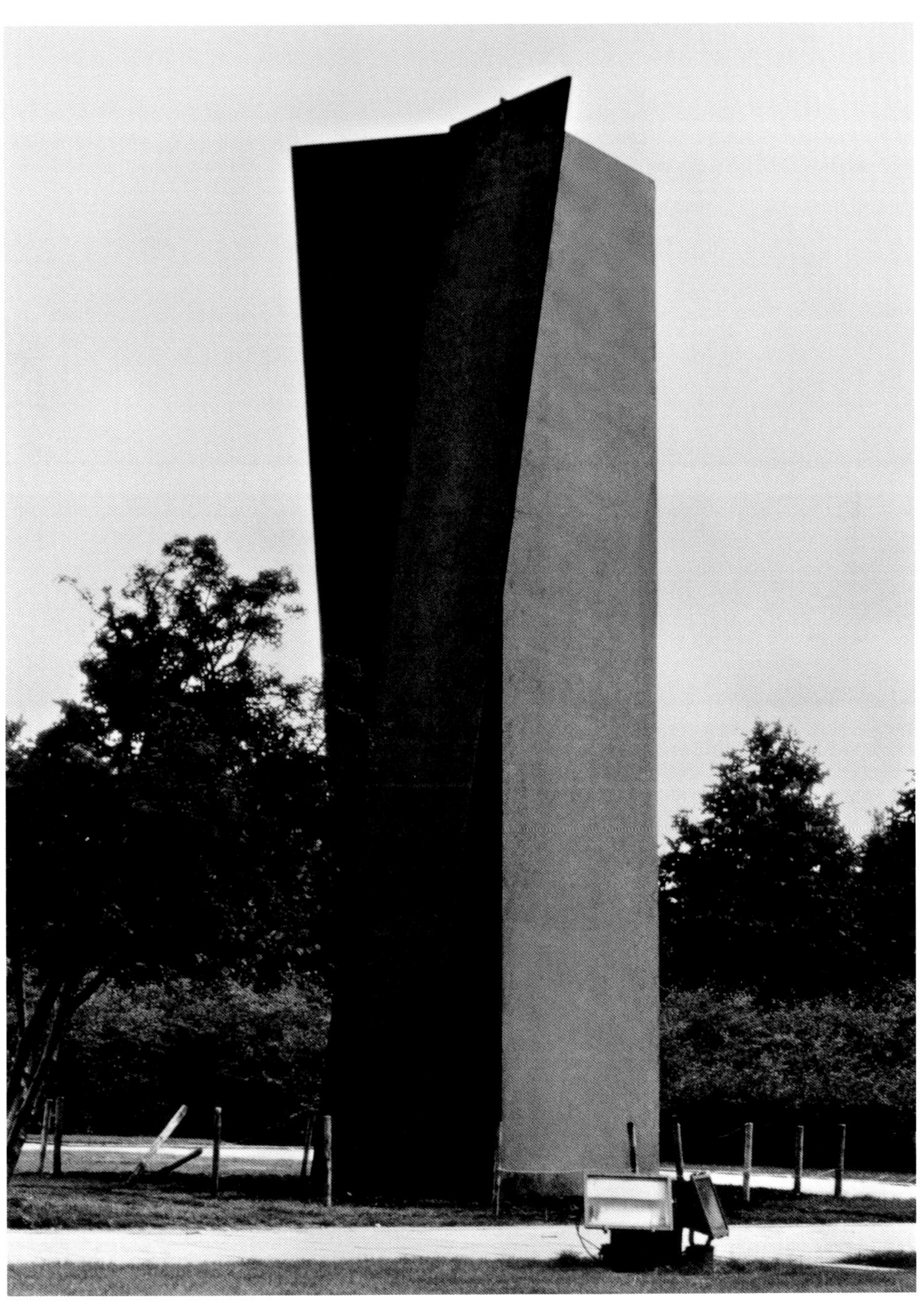

*Sight Point,* 1972–75. Weatherproof steel, three plates, each 40 ft. × 10 ft. × 2 ½ in. (12.2 m × 3 m × 6.4 cm).
Stedelijk Museum, Amsterdam, The Netherlands. Reinstallation in 2012 supported by Irene and Rijkman Groenink.

The landscape pieces are usually open, the urban pieces generally closed. . . . You enter in the structure, which is a space that breaks with the surroundings."[6] Does this open-closed binary still obtain?

**RS**: That statement is mostly about the towers.

**HF**: So the arcs do have more in common with the landscape pieces, and you can use that part of your landscape language in the city if the site allowed it. Which do permit it?

**RS**: Plazas, traffic rotaries, and university campuses, to name a few.

**HF**: Like the serpentine piece at Princeton, *The Hedgehog and the Fox* (1998).

**RS**: Yes, but then there's the piece at Yale, *Stacks* (1990), which is neither an arc nor a serpentine. It was moved from an interior site and repositioned in a courtyard fronting the museum. It's open like a landscape piece, but it also reads vertically. Its two plates are centered on each other and set a good distance apart, each one tilted into the ground. *Stacks* is another piece that breaks with the landscape-urban opposition.

**HF**: What about the opposition between open and closed structures you noted in 1983?

**RS**: Well, up to that point that was probably true.

**HF**: So you began with certain oppositions, such as horizontal-vertical and open-closed, and you moved to complicate them.

**CW-S**: Where would you place *Clara-Clara* (1983)?[7]

**RS**: Typologically speaking, *Clara-Clara* is a landscape piece.

**HF**: It's in a pretty famous urban setting! But then the park mediates between the landscape and the city.

**CW-S**: I think *Clara-Clara* is an urban piece through and through.

**HF**: Certainly it wants to be in that particular setting. I identify it with the Tuileries axis so much that I imagine it there to this day. It might be another instance of a work that is both-and. There's a further distinction between your landscape and urban pieces: you talk about "redefinition" in relation to the former and "contradiction," even "subversion," in relation to the latter. Does that difference still hold?

**RS**: I think so. When you're in an urban setting, you're up against your surroundings, the architecture above all, most of which is mediocre or worse. You can't avoid it; you have to acknowledge it.

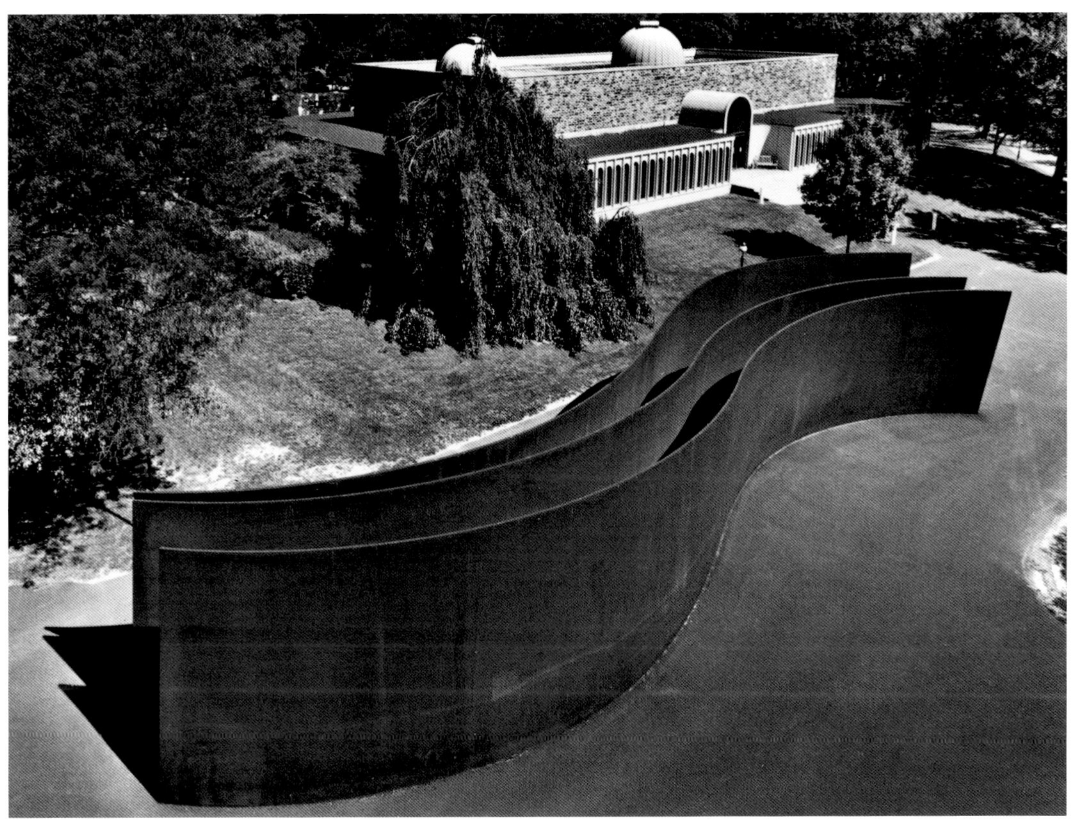

*The Hedgehog and the Fox,* 1998. Weatherproof steel, three parts, each comprising two identical conical/elliptical sections inverted relative to each other, 15 ft. 6 in. × 91 ft. 6 in. × 24 ft. 6 in. (4.7 × 27.9 × 7.5 m) overall, plates 2 in. (5 cm) thick. Princeton University, New Jersey. Gift of The Peter T. Joseph Foundation, 1998.

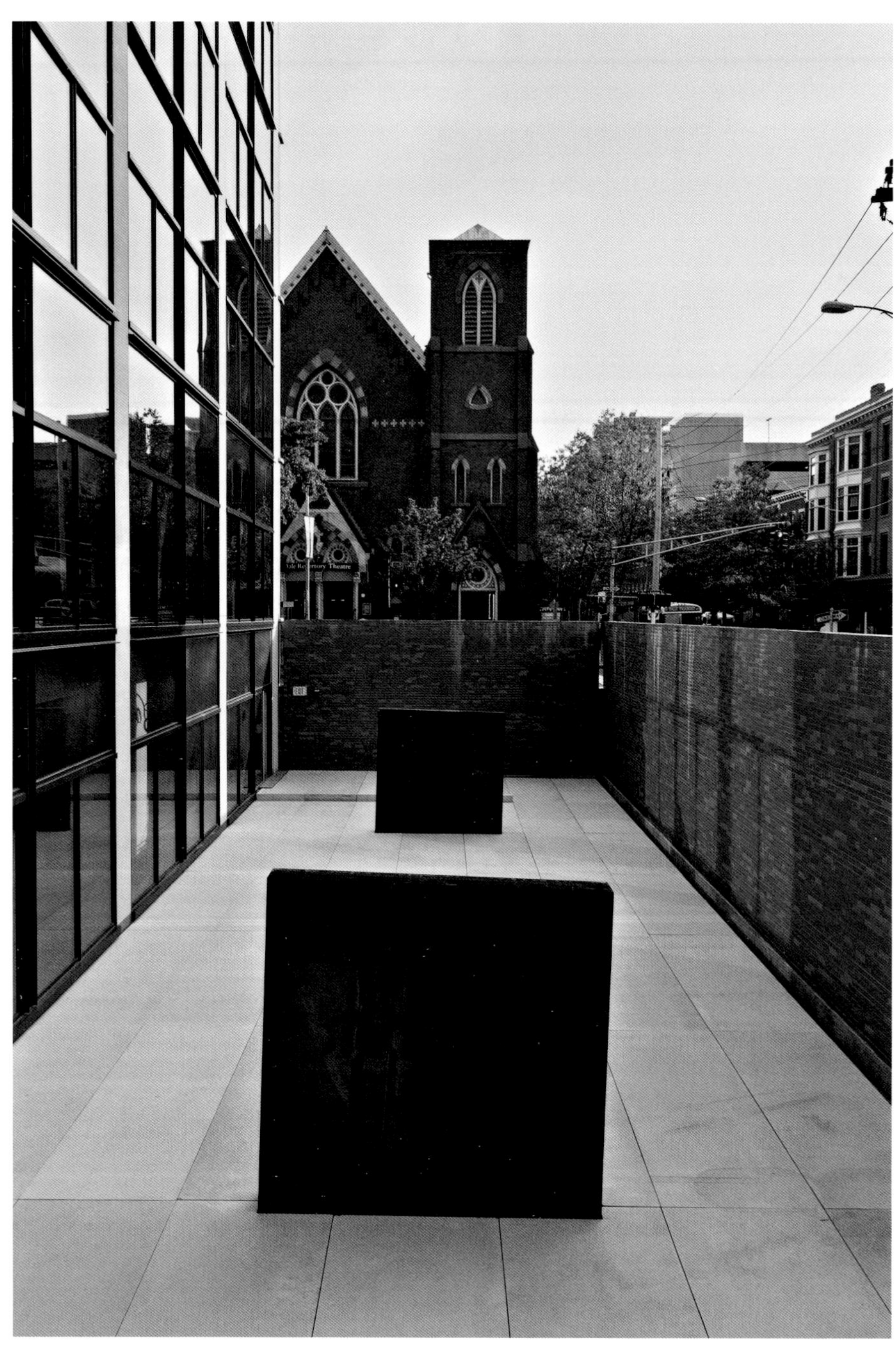

*Stacks,* 1990. Hot-rolled steel, two slabs, each 8 ft. × 8 ft. × 10 in. (2.4 m × 2.4 m × 25.4 cm). Yale University Art Gallery, New Haven. Katherine Ordway Fund.

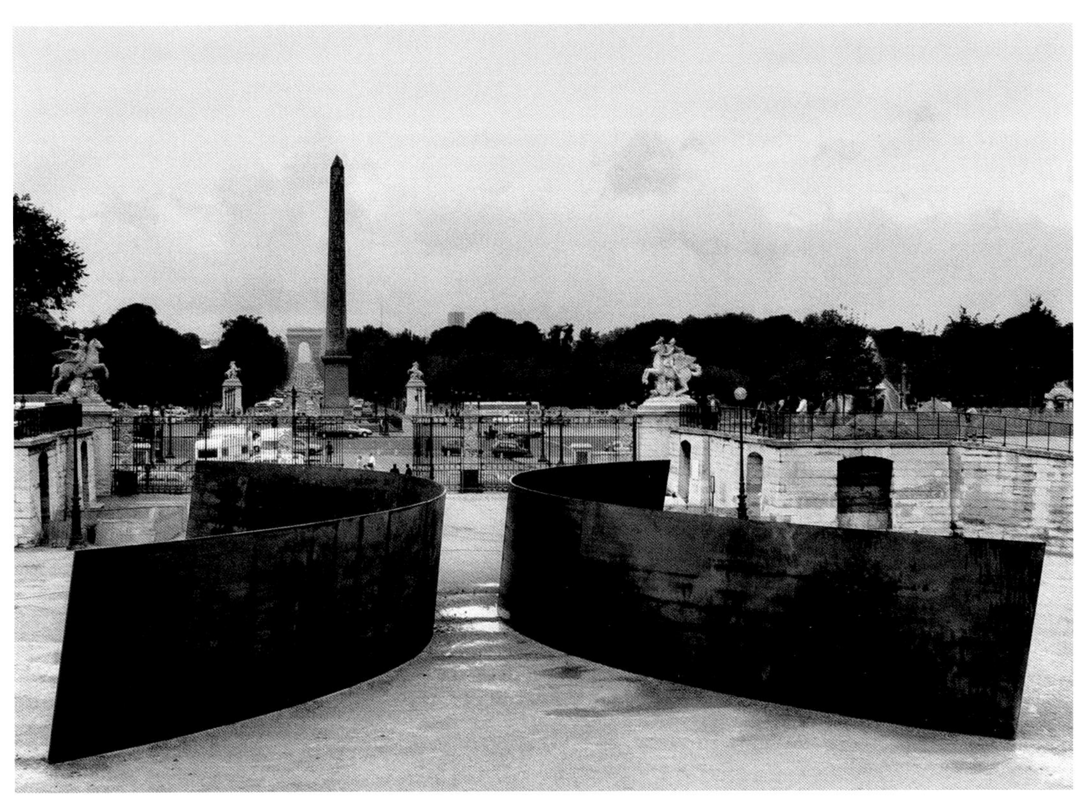

*Clara-Clara*, 1983. Weatherproof steel, two near-identical conical sections inverted relative to each other, 12 ft. × 109 ft. × 2 in. (3.7 m × 33.2 m × 5 cm), 12 ft. × 107 ft. 10 in. × 2 in. (3.7 m × 32.8 m × 5 cm). Collection City of Paris.

**HF**: So is the primary motive to claim a sculptural place or to critique the architecture?

**RS**: Both at once.

**HF**: Are those different gestures, or are they bound up with each other?

**RS**: They're bound up with each other. I'm using one language, sculpture, to critique another, architecture; they're at once different and comparable—that's what makes it work. I approach landscape in a different way. I'm not up against impinging surroundings. I want to reveal the topography of the site.

**HF**: This need to contradict . . .

**RS**: For me it goes back to the Mexican muralists, to the way Orozco punched virtual holes in the walls and ceilings in the Hospicio in Guadalajara. My urban sculptures link up with that ambition. Le Corbusier once wrote a letter supporting the altering of architecture through painting. That's one reason for doing it.

**HF**: To enrage the architects?

**RS**: To critique the architecture. Le Corbusier actually said it was acceptable to destroy the architecture. That's not my intention. I'm not out to enrage architects.[8]

**HF**: As an architect and a painter-muralist, he was on both sides of that argument.

**RS**: I bring up Corb because his position anticipates your question. And those Mexican murals are not only social but also political.

**HF**: In your 1985 text on *Sight Point* you write: "I am interested in work where the artist is a maker of an 'anti-environment' which takes its own place or makes its own situation." "Anti-environment" sounds even stronger than "contradiction." You continue: "Every site has its boundary, and it is in relation to that boundary that scale becomes the issue. Sculpture built in the studio has studio scale."[9] Did this insistence on scale get you out of the studio and to the site—that is, to a notion of site-specificity that's not only about materials and processes in situ?

**RS**: It was certainly one factor. As for "anti-environments," most of the towers qualify as such because they coalesce a site in a new way that's specific and different from the original intentions of the space.

**HF**: To what extent is your confrontation with mediocre architecture and to what extent is it with bad urban planning? I asked you a related question in 1986, and you responded: "We cannot repeal the industrial revolution, which is the cause of the urban glut. We can only work with the junk pile. Postmodernist megastructures are a glib solution to refurbish the garbage."[10] You also commented, in relation to plazas, parks, corporate offices, and public buildings, that "it's difficult to subvert those sites. That's why you have so many corporate baubles."[11] Why did those settings prove to be especially difficult?

**RS**: A park is already an artificial site. Corporate buildings pose a similar dilemma. You become part of an overriding ideological program, which is to extend the corporation into public space. In that respect my greatest disappointment occurred when I worked for the Gap in San Francisco. My sculpture was supposed to be outside in the street, but fearing adverse reaction from the public the Gap people decided to move it inside. The sculpture was erected as the building was constructed around it. They said they'd leave the enormous front entrance open for the public, but they never did, and now you have to get permission to see the sculpture. I was coopted by the corporation.

**HF**: Let's go back to *Clara-Clara,* which is one of my favorite pieces. Positioned in the Tuileries, it articulated the park; it didn't contradict it, much less subvert it. But it still worked beautifully as an urban piece.

**RS**: Yes, due to its placement. Because it was positioned at the western entrance of the Tuileries, *Clara-Clara* didn't really take on the attributes of a piece in a park. It was more of a link between the Champs Élysées, the Place de la Concorde, and the Tuileries.

**HF**: But it still framed the park; in fact it framed the entire axis at that point. This leads me to your resistance to the picturesque, which is also a kind of framing. Is there a contradiction here? "When Smithson went to see *Shift,*" you commented in 1980, "he spoke of its picturesque quality, and I wasn't sure what he was talking about." But a few years later you did know and you didn't like it: "If you use the word 'frame' in referring to the landscape, you imply a notion of the picturesque, I have never really found the notion of framing parts of the landscape particularly interesting in terms of its potential for sculpture."[12]

**RS**: I'm interested in framing, but not if it's overarticulated, as in "You must look through this frame, and remain stationary as you do." Not framing as with a camera, seeking out just one image. That's one of the reasons I gave up filmmaking.

**HF**: But your films are all about framing.

**RS**: Well, there's one called *Frame* (1969).

**HF**: In which you measure with a ruler, and frame with a camera, a window in a loft— or rather you try to do those things but fail to do them very accurately. The failure of measuring and framing seems to be the point. But some of your other films are also

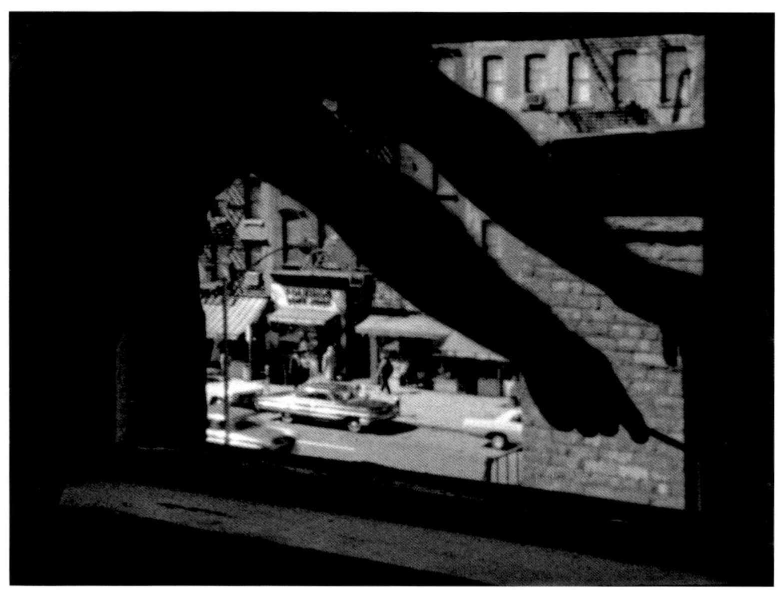

*Frame,* 1969. 16 mm film, black and white, sound, 22 min.
The Museum of Modern Art, New York.

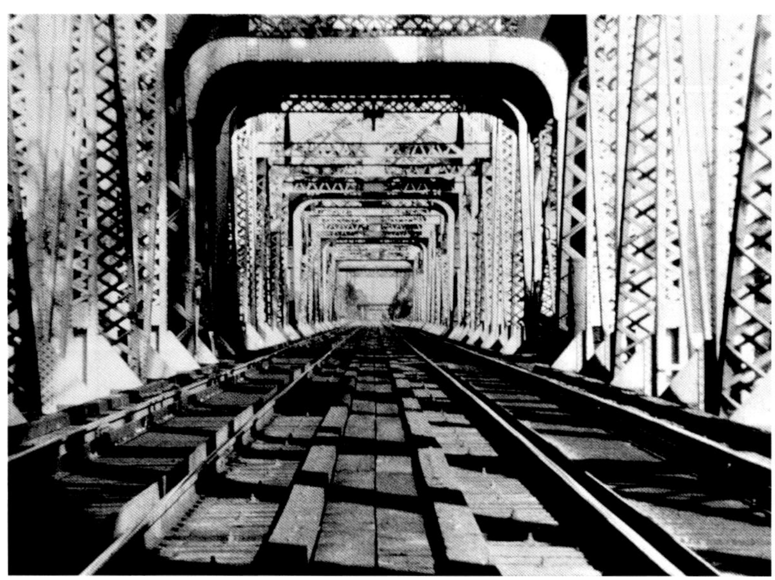

*Railroad Turnbridge,* 1976. 16 mm film, black and white, 19 min.
The Museum of Modern Art, New York.

about framing: trying to keep your hand in the frame as you grab for falling scraps of lead in *Hand Catching Lead* (1968), or trying to keep your arm up while holding bigger chunks of lead in *Hand Lead Fulcrum* (1968). And *Railroad Turnbridge* (1976) uses the bridge to frame the landscape.

**RS**: Yes, those films are about the limitations of the frame. I gave up filmmaking when it became apparent there was no way to get outside the constraints of the frame.

**HF**: That's the reason you gave for abandoning painting too—the limitations of the frame. In any case, you don't see your sculpture as picturesque, that is, you don't see it as a sequence of pictures.

**RS**: Framing can be a subtext, but it wasn't the impetus behind my initial move into space.

**HF**: So there's a clear distinction for you between "gathering" and "framing."

**RS**: Framing is always secondary. It leads to image-making.

**HF**: You also object to the idea of "sculptural film," but, to take up the inverse, you've spoken of some site works, such as *St. John's Rotary Arc,* in cinematic terms.

**RS**: I used those terms in relation to that piece because it was primarily seen from the viewpoint of people in cars driving around the rotary during a passage of time.

**HF**: Are there other works that are cinematic in that sense?

**RS**: There's the vertical piece in Luxembourg, *Exchange* (1996). That's also viewed most often from a car.

**HF**: Let me ask you again about your predilection for "leftover sites." I wonder if that condition reflects a time in the life of cities in the late 1970s and early 1980s when industrial production had largely moved out of urban centers. You saw an advantage for your work in that transformation, which at the time looked like dereliction. Although you wrote in 1985 that "every context has its frame and ideological overtones," you also suggested that "one way of avoiding ideological cooptation is to choose leftover sites which cannot be the object of ideological misinterpretation."[13] Are you still sure about that last part? Why would a "leftover site" be any less ideologically charged than a public plaza?

**RS**: Some sites are deemed useless, but they're not to me.

**HF**: Like the rotary outside Holland Tunnel?

**RS**: Yes, that was a leftover site. Another was 183rd Street in the Bronx, a dead end where I placed *To Encircle Base Plate Hexagram, Right Angle Inverted* (1970).

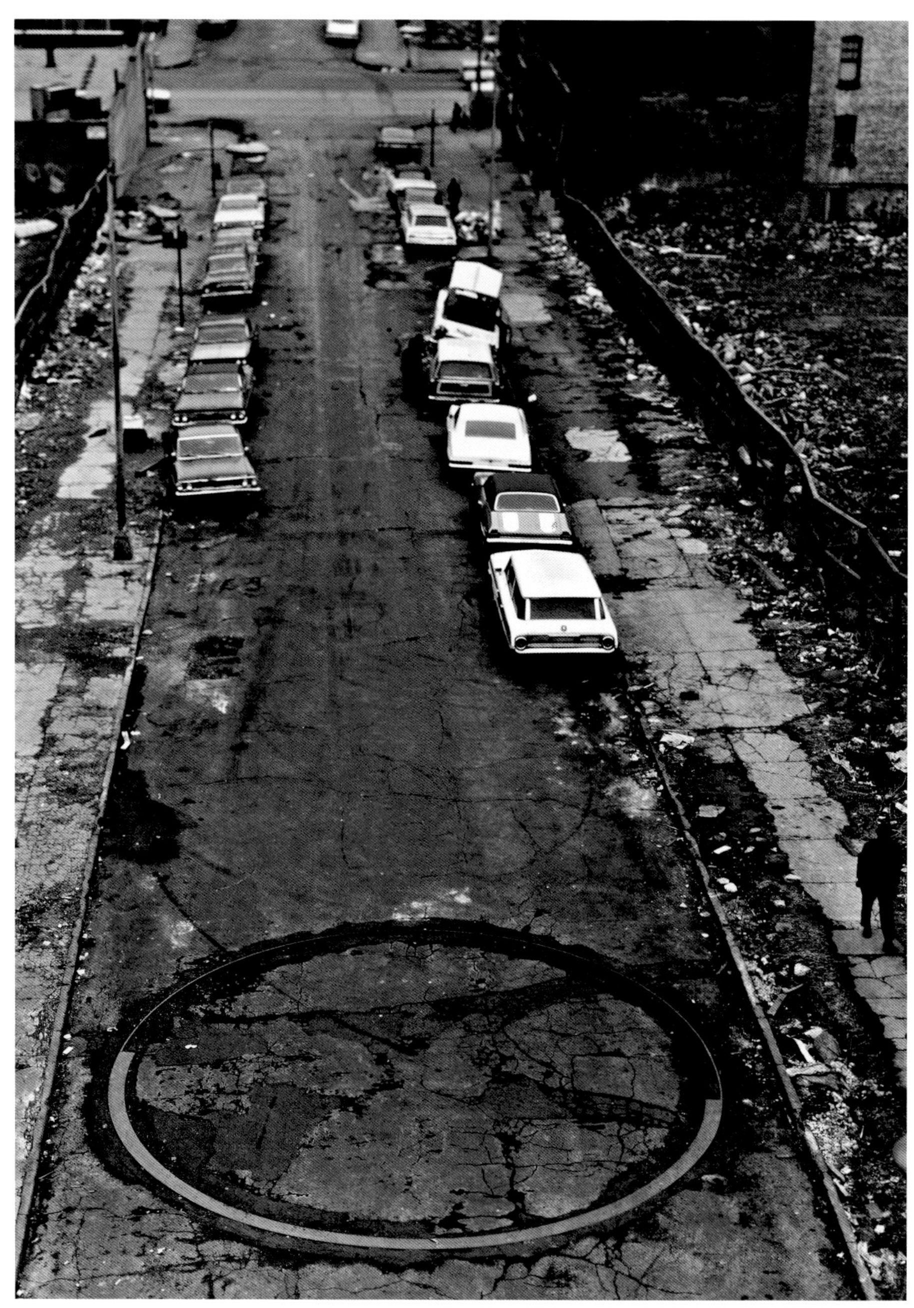

*To Encircle Base Plate Hexagram, Right Angles Inverted,* 1970. Hot-rolled steel, 25 ft. 4 in. diameter ×
8 in. rim (7.7 m × 20.3 cm), as installed at 183rd Street and Webster Avenue in "Annual Exhibition of
Contemporary American Sculpture," Whitney Museum of American Art, New York, 1970. Saint Louis Art
Museum, Missouri. Gift of Mr. and Mrs. K. Ronald Greenberg. Photo Peter Moore.

**HF**: The Bronx piece gets us to the problem of "ideological misinterpretation" and the difference between "site" and "context." Might one person's leftover site be another person's neighborhood? Or, to put it less glibly, might your move to make a sculptural place out of a leftover site declare it defunct as a social space too definitively? Or, if we grant that it is truly derelict, might making a sculptural place out of an anomic site end up redeeming it somehow—redeeming it less for a local community than for city authorities who are otherwise indifferent to the place or indeed to the community?[14]

**RS**: Redeeming it? I think a sculpture can specify a place, can make it relevant when you'd otherwise pass it by. Leftover sites aren't articulated architectural spaces. That's where sculpture can come into play. No one paid any attention to my piece in the Bronx; the community had no idea that it was a work of art.

**HF**: "That's where sculpture can come into play": Is there a danger of rehabilitation there?

**RS**: Like I'm working for the Boy Scouts?

**HF**: I don't think anyone would accuse you of that.

**RS**: Or supporting urban renewal? You have to understand that the dead end in the Bronx was used for removing parts from stolen cars and then torching what was left.

**HF**: I'm also thinking of Smithson's insistence, with respect to earthworks, on entropy as opposed to amelioration, on breakdown as opposed to reclamation, on "the sites of time" as opposed to "the gardens of history."[15] Your work is neither the one nor the other.

**CW-S**: There's a vertical plate piece called *Bramme für das Ruhrgebiet* (1998). It's sited on a slag heap in the most industrial region of Germany.

**RS**: We moved thousands upon thousands of tons of coal and slag to shape the topography of an immense hill as a reversed curve, and planted a plate on top.

**CW-S**: No one knew what to do with the enormous slag heaps.

**HF**: Isn't that a kind of rehabilitation?

**RS**: Or a kind of burial mound: we were burying the coal industry.

**HF**: Here's another potential problem. Also in 1985 you wrote: "I do not necessarily worry about the indigenous community. I am not going to concern myself with what 'they' consider to be adequate, appropriate solutions."[16] You made that statement before artists had done much to develop the social aspects of site-specificity. Still, it reads provocatively today.

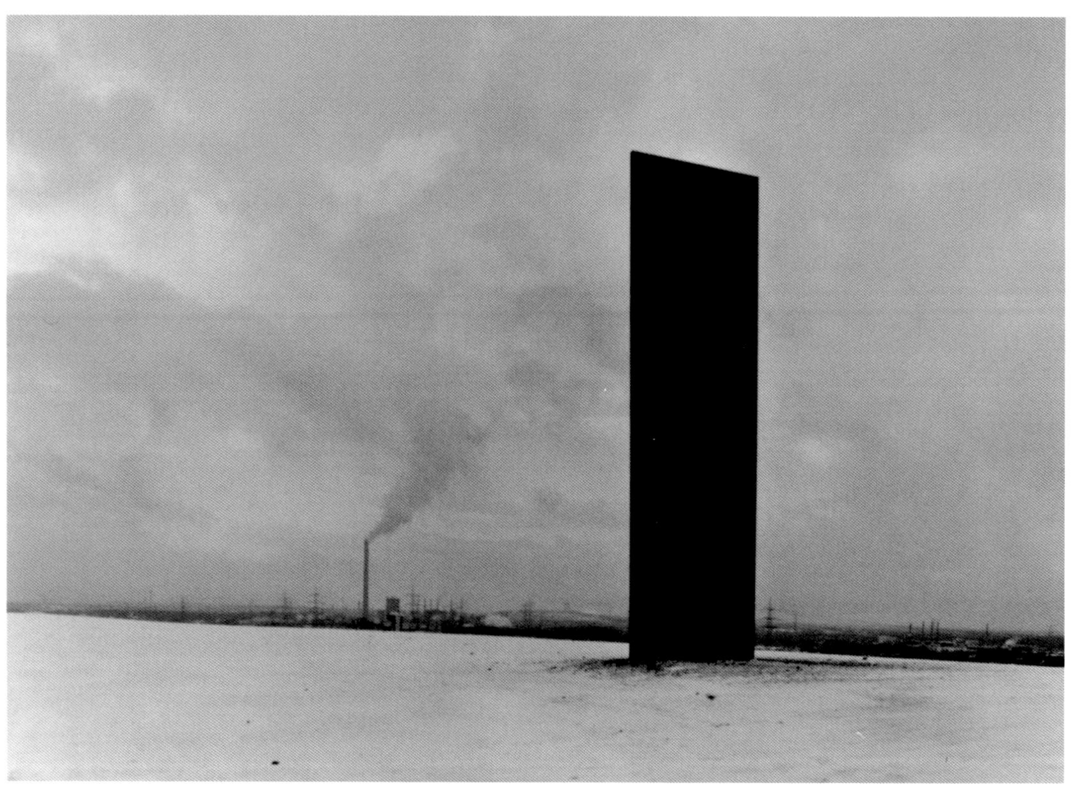

*Bramme für das Ruhrgebiet,* 1998. Weatherproof steel, 47 ft. 7 in. × 13 ft. 11 ½ in. × 5 in.
(14.5 m × 4.2 m × 12.7 cm). Schürenbachhalde, Emscher Park, Gelsenkirchen.
Collection Internationale Bauausstellung Emscher, Gelsenkirchen, Germany.

**RS**: I'll stand by that one even if it pisses a lot of people off.

**HF**: It also allows you to avoid the problems that attend art conceived in terms of social work.

**RS**: You mean bad sculpture done by community committee? For me the whole idea that art's democratic is nonsense. I've gotten a lot of flak for that position. If you cater to the demographics of a given context, you risk serving ever-fluctuating political positions. You become a pawn in shifting ideological arguments.

**HF**: Might it be that you're so inside your language, so attuned to its nuances, that you're not always alert to conditions that are already there, embedded in the context—conditions that are social, economic, and political? Does your very insistence on the formal, structural, and phenomenological aspects of your sculpture end up being a way, inadvertently, to deflect certain realities of urban life, even though you say the experience of those realities is a primary concern of your work?

**RS**: I'll restate what I previously said. If you go into a community to make a work, and you try to follow the demands of the local people, which are never homogenous anyway, you end up serving their interests more than your own. And usually their interests are transitory. Most of those communities change over time; the demographics shift. Politics change, political representatives change. So you have to hold fast to your work.

**HF**: But don't you then divide site from context, treating site as primarily physical and context as primarily social, privileging the former and bracketing the latter?

**RS**: No. I'm dealing with context; I'm just not treating the community as the preeminent arbiter of context—that's the difference.

**HF**: But why assume the community isn't the preeminent arbiter?

**CW-S**: I don't think Richard falls into the trap of autonomous art. When he puts a piece in an urban context it's an intervention. The sheer scale alone forces people to consider their relationship with the context.

**HF**: So the context is already there; it's just not articulated. That's the work of the piece, and that's part of the gathering that it performs. Is that the reasoning? At the Gap in San Francisco, say, you can't help but think of the architecture and what it does, the corporation and what it does, and so on. Maybe your polemical formulation about site, then, simplifies the situation, and doesn't do justice to what the work actually does.

**CW-S**: Language tends to simplify, and statements can change as the work develops and changes.

**HF**: Discourse is site-specific too.

**CW-S**: Yet one thing Richard has always maintained is that there's no preformulated content, that content is what the viewers provide.

**HF**: Let me ask you another version of the question about site versus context, now in relation to your landscape pieces, many of which are produced for super-rich collectors. This is a touchy subject too, but here goes. Could it be argued that you're so focused on topography and elevation that you treat the settings as physical only, and that context is thereby bracketed—context here in the sense that these sites are usually on estates founded on massive inequality of wealth, one of the great problems that bedevil this country?

**RS**: I don't pay much attention to collectors as long as they don't interfere. Sometimes they're helpful.

**HF**: That's not my question. Do these pieces ask the viewers, even if those viewers are only the patrons, to reflect on the preconditions of the context—to reflect on what allows these estates to exist in the first place? Is there any critical dimension to these pieces, a reflexivity that reflects, so to speak, on their own socioeconomic frame?

**RS**: In that sense there's a critical dimension to these pieces only if they alter the landscape in a way that makes you think about the land differently—as property, say.

**CW-S**: In the landscape pieces, such as *Snake Eyes and Boxcars* (1993) in Sonoma County or *Te Tuhirangi Contour* (2000–2002) in New Zealand, it's very important to Richard that they be seen by the public. *Snake Eyes* is on Oliver Ranch, which Steve Oliver has given to the state of California, while the collector in New Zealand opens his space to the public on a regular basis.

**HF**: Do you think they're led by the work somehow to make it public?

**CW-S**: It's not a prerequisite, but most clients who commission landscape pieces intend to give the public access to the work.

**RS**: Right now we're constructing a piece for a large site near Cleveland, which the client is going to donate to a public entity. It's one of the largest interventions in the landscape I've attempted. In your article on *East-West/West-East,* my piece in the desert in Qatar, you suggested that no one would go out to visit the site. The implication was that it was an elitist incursion into a place that had no audience. Not true. I believe your prejudice determined your prediction.[17]

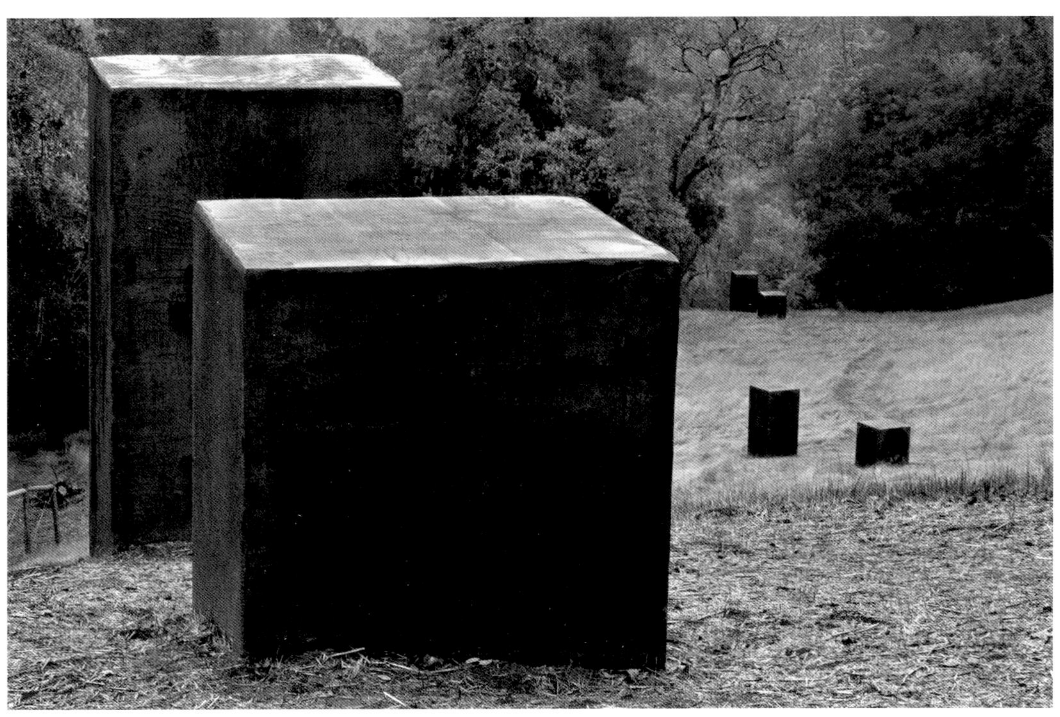

*Snake Eyes and Boxcars,* 1993. Forged steel, twelve blocks, six 8 ft. 1 in. × 41 in. × 41 in.
(2.1 m × 104.1 × 104.1 cm), six 48 × 41 × 41 in. (121.9 × 104.1 × 104.1 cm). Collection Nancy
and Steven Oliver, Alexander Valley, California.

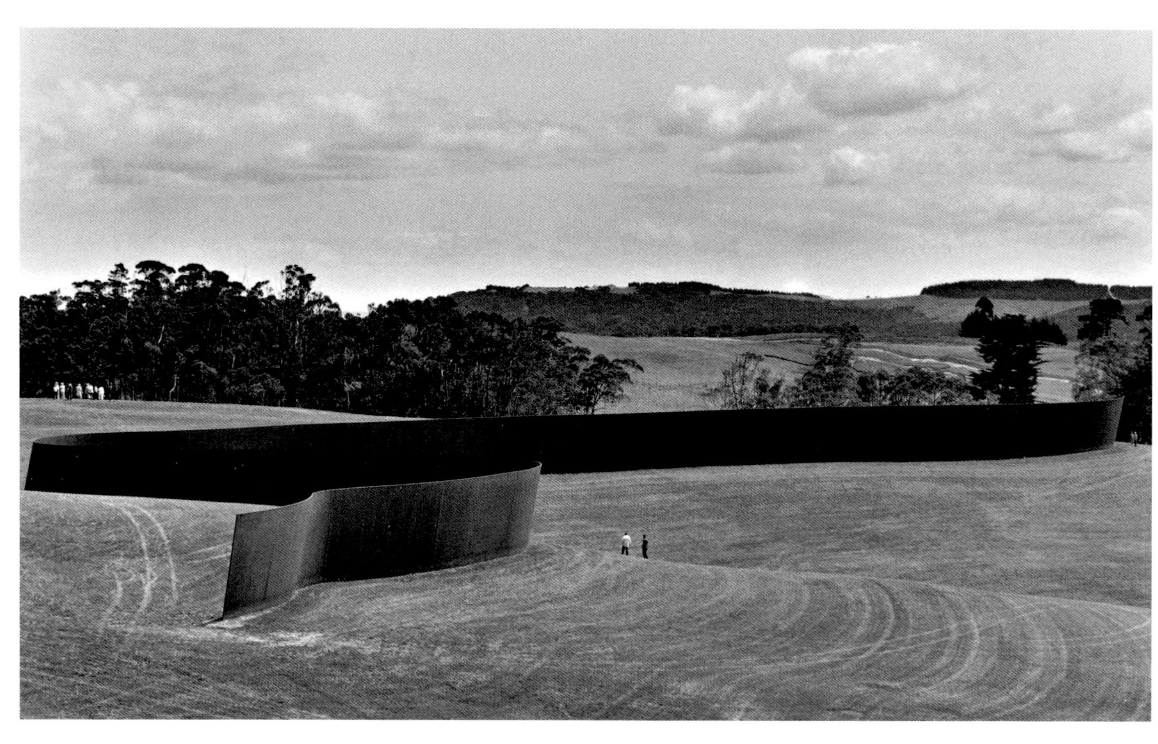

*Te Tuhirangi Contour,* 2000–2002. Weatherproof steel, 19 ft. 8 in. × 843 ft. 2 in. × 2 in.
(6 m × 257 m × 5 cm). The Farm, Kaipara, North Island, New Zealand.

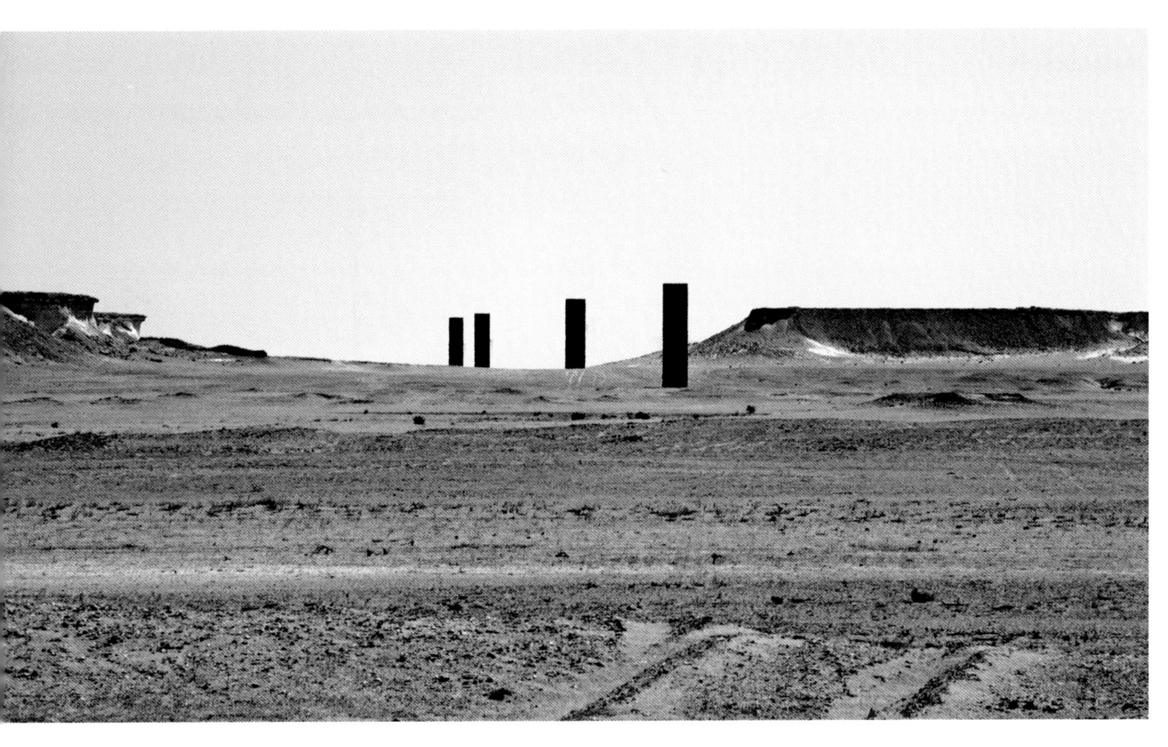

*East-West/West-East*, 2014. Weatherproof steel, four plates, two 54 ft. 9 ½ in. × 13 ft. 1 ½ in. × 5 ¼ in. (16.7 m × 4 m × 13.3 cm), two 48 ft. 2 ¾ in. × 13 ft. 1 ½ in. × 5 ¼ in. (14.7 m × 4 m × 13.3 cm). Brouq Nature Reserve, Qatar. Qatar Museums Authority, Doha.

**HF:** I didn't say no one, and I'm happy to revise that part of my argument if need be, but my principal question about *East-West/West-East* is different. It's a question at once particular to you and general to art history: To what extent can we query an artist who helps to establish a discourse—in this case site-specificity—but doesn't pursue it in the ways subsequent artists have done? To what extent can we turn around on the original artist and question him or her according to criteria that were developed later, thereby implying a limitation to his or her position? It's a methodological conundrum, even an epistemological one, but it bears importantly on your work.

**RS:** How can you hold me responsible for what artists who come after me did? You're faulting me in light of a position taken by a subsequent generation. How can you blame me for what you see as a shortcoming from the perspective of present-day institution critique, which is what you're holding up as a foil here? I'm very conflicted about institution critique.

**HF:** Why?

**RS:** Institution critique occurs in every facet of our culture.

**HF:** What do you mean?

**RS:** There's always a debate about reform, whether it's about cultural, social, or political institutions. Is the criterion the greatest good for the greatest number, or going along with capitalist anarchy, or what? If you're talking about the institution critique of culture, you're talking about just one facet of institution critique, and I've always thought it had a subtext that smacks of nostalgic Marxism.

**HF:** You mean its Leftism is partly a posture, that it knows its critique to be limited, that it might even be compensatory somehow?

**RS:** Yes. And it has propagated artists who seem to be radical in their attack on the art institution, but I wonder whether they'll appear radical in the long run. I wonder how much historical shelf life the work will have. Take Michael Asher: it's not that his work is too site-specific; it's too time-based, too tied to the specificities of a particular moment. And it was supported by critics who wanted to constitute an insurgent movement against the art institution. All very well and good, but it doesn't match up to what the women's movement or the multicultural movement was able to achieve in terms of the advocacy of art by women or people of color.

**HF:** Why oppose the two, or judge one in terms of the other? When you say "shelf life" you mean it hasn't developed a language that can stand the test of time?

**RS**: Yes, and why not judge one against the other? We're talking about effectiveness.

**HF**: "Shelf life" is an idealist framework, one those artists might refuse. And as for "effectiveness," that's site-specific or institution-specific as well. Another way to think about effectiveness is in terms of changes within institutions prompted by institution critique. And another way to think about posterity is in terms of influence. Certainly artists like Asher, Hans Haacke, Daniel Buren, and Marcel Broodthaers have been very influential.

**RS**: You can say the same thing about Pop art. You can say it was institution critique too.

**HF**: That's a stretch. Except for moments in Warhol, Oldenburg, and a few others, it was more celebratory of consumerism than critical. The same question greeted the "Pictures" artists: To what degree are they critical of mass culture, and to what degree are they complicit with it?

**RS**: Pop art was not originally received as a celebration of consumerism, nor do I think it was conceived as such. And if you admit that Warhol and Oldenburg were exceptions, well, they were the two main figures in Pop. But back to my question: Is institution critique complicit?

**HF**: This is a place where a methodological question becomes a political one, and here's the difference as I see it between your position and theirs. You often refer to a postulate you associate with Bertrand Russell—that one can't critique a language from within that same language, that another language is required to do that. That's not the stance that institution critique takes up. It assumes you have to be on the inside in order to change the inside; you have to risk complicity. It's a deconstructive posture.

**RS**: I understand. But what if I say Cindy Sherman uses photography to deconstruct old movies in her *Untitled Film Stills,* or to deconstruct a traditional genre of painting in her *History Portraits*? Then she's closer to my approach. To critique the stereotyping of women she's not replicating a movie still or a history painting; she's using photography.

**HF**: We can bat that back and forth till the end of time.

**RS**: It's not even a contradiction. Otherwise you imply that institution critique is a second-order movement represented by the likes of Picabia.

**HF**: Picabia as institution critique? I don't think so. Picabia as dandy nihilist? For sure. But then deconstruction is not destruction. I see institution critique as closer, in strategy as well as in time, to Derrida and Foucault than to Picabia and Duchamp. Are the former "second-order"? Technically yes, in that they work within the languages, the philosophies, that they critique; they don't project an outside. But they're not second-order in terms of importance or influence. In any case, it's a different posture from your stated stance. You say you need another language, a sculptural language, to critique the languages of painting and architecture. But I think your predilection for the Russell line obscures one thrust of your work, which is indeed deconstructive. Still, you're saying that one position is better than the other, that one will last and the other might not.

**RS**: I'm not saying one's better than the other; I'm saying one's dependent and the other's not. If you take Asher and Buren, they rely on internal hand-me-downs. I don't think I do, and neither does Cindy Sherman.

**HF**: They can't be dismissed so easily. In terms of shelf life, we'll see. In terms of relevance or salience, that work has produced institutional changes and generated artistic practices. The results are already in as far as that goes.

**RS**: Yes, we have a whole postmodernist movement.

**HF**: And you're prepared to dismiss it all?

**RS**: No, I'm just not enthusiastic; I don't see too much of interest there. It comes down to the difference between exploitation and exploration.

**HF**: We won't be reconciled on that one, so let's go back to elaborations of the idea of site. You helped to establish it in formal, structural, and phenomenological terms, and then Asher, Buren, and Haacke developed it in institutional and socioeconomic terms. Subsequent artists made site discursive, so that, by the 1990s, homelessness could be a site, say, or homosexual desire.[18] You don't want to acknowledge those practices either as part of the geneaology of site work?

**RS**: Sure, I see the connections, but the work doesn't concern me much.

**CW-S**: The main difference between Richard and Asher, Buren, and Haacke is that Richard's interested in the invention of form.

**RS**: And they're not.

**CW-S**: His intervention is also critical, but he's more interested in the object that remains. I see Asher and Buren, at least from the late 1960s through the 1970s, more as performers.

**HF**: Performers?

**RS**: They're performing social commentary.

**CW-S**: Not that I would diminish that. I worked with Buren when he showed in Mönchen-gladbach, Germany. But that was a particular period, and his work lost its political edge.

**RS**: It became decorative.

**HF**: But surely Asher, Buren, and Haacke have developed languages of their own.

**CW-S**: A language, yes, but it's one that's most interesting at the time it's spoken, not so much the day after.

**RS**: That's what I mean by "shelf life."

**HF**: You see it as an intervention in the limited sense.

**CW-S**: Yes, but it's not less interesting for that reason. My position is different from Richard's, and I wouldn't criticize that work as he does.

**HF**: Let's go back to your resistance to the textualization of site advanced by Smithson with his notion of non-site and other sorts of documentation. He complicated the idea of site early on, allowing for different interests, different languages, to enter into his work. In a way he anticipated not only institution critique—the threading of the artist through the apparatus, as he once put—but also the idea of site as a matter of discourse, of art work almost as cultural studies. Dan Graham did a similar thing.

**RS**: The problem with Smithson is that after he textualized the work he could pick it up and move it to another site.

**HF**: So for you his "text" displaced or even forgot his "site."

**RS**: He used the non-site as a form of critical irony, but basically it allowed him to forgo concretizing his work in any one place. Then he used language as a way to negate site altogether. The difference is that my site pieces permanently alter the site because they're built into its very structure. Smithson wanted to have his cake and eat it too.

**HF**: Or, to put it negatively, as you did in your famous definition of site-specific work vis-à-vis *Tilted Arc,* to move the sculpture is to destroy it.

**RS**: Yes, and I think that qualifies *Tilted Arc* as institution critique.

**HF**: For many artists who work out of this history, sites are also textual because they can no longer be understood as fixed to physical settings, and so they follow Smithson's and Graham's lead rather than yours. In a world given over to digital transmission, financial networks, social media, and all the rest, they think it's almost nostalgic to see site as strictly physical.

**RS**: Benjamin Buchloh thought that the Conceptual artists were at the forefront of the neo–avant-garde back then because they replaced object and site with language. What's new? The artists you refer to allow capitalism to define the direction of their invention.

**HF**: If they see you as nostalgic, you see them as complicit?

**RS**: Yes. They're involved with the capitalist anarchy at large.

**HF**: "All that is solid melts into air"? We seem to be back to the distinction between practices that want to work deconstructively and practices that seek to be semiautonomous. I don't see those aims as opposed in your work, while you claim the one and question the other.

**RS**: I'd like to conclude by simply restating that my main concern is the invention of form.

# Prime Objects

**HF**: Let's talk about the prime objects in your work.

**RS**: First we need to agree on what the concept means. It comes from George Kubler, who in *The Shape of Time* (1962) defines a prime object as a break in a tradition, a historical event without precedent, one that disrupts what he calls the sequence of replicas. It establishes a new order, one of change.[1] In my case the breaks have come with pieces that engage gravity, space, and location.

**HF**: *The Shape of Time* was also taken up by some of your friends, like Robert Smithson. How was the book important to you in particular?

**RS**: Primarily for the proposition that, if you make sculpture, you have to find an entrance into its history, and you have to invent something that's not anticipated. I first related the prime object to my "Verb List." A notion I took from Bertrand Russell—that you can't criticize a language within that same language—was also important to me. Along with the prime object, that idea opened up the possibility of a critique of sculpture that didn't rely on antecedents. That's when I started performing the activities in the "Verb List," which took me outside the formulas of previous sculpture. No modeling, casting, armature, or pedestal: I considered them all to be conventions, and I didn't want to deal with any of them. That allowed me to enter an area of doing and making that was unprecedented, at least in my judgment. I don't know if my peers would agree.

**HF**: One thing Kubler did, as a historian of pre-Columbian art, was to expand the discipline of art history, and certainly he broke with the idea—which was strong, in different ways, in figures as diverse as Heinrich Wölfflin, E. H. Gombrich, and Clement Greenberg—that the history of art has a telos.

**RS**: Yes, he broke with the constriction of reading art history as a linear development. He also argued that every made thing could be, even should be, considered. Every object, all manmade things, not just art.

**HF**: A lot that Kubler dealt with in his own field was anonymous. He had to adjust his methodology because the artists were simply not known. But what about your prime objects? You suggested to me once that several works might qualify as such: *To Lift* (1967), vis-à-vis all your sculptures concerned with topology; *House of Cards* (1969), vis-à-vis all the prop pieces; *Strike: To Roberta and Rudy* (1969–71), vis-à-vis all the straight plate works; and *To Encircle Base Plate Hexagram, Right Angles Inverted* (1970), vis-à-vis the works embedded in a place.

**RS**: I'd start with the "Verb List," when I began to enact verbs on materials. That's how *To Lift* came to be, the inside and outside of which form a continuous topological surface.

Also, it's provisional: you lift it up, but it can fall back to the floor. So every time you put it up, you reenact its potential to stand. It's not a fixed form. And as with any prime object, *To Lift* can be reactivated.

**HF**: You mean you can return to the sequence it opened up at any time?

**RS**: Right. I didn't know that creating a topological surface by lifting a piece of rubber would reappear in my work, but it does—it returns in the torqued sculptures. So there can be a gap in time between the initial proposition and its elaboration in a whole other body of work (I don't know how many years in that case, maybe thirty). Any past problem is capable of reactivation under a new condition. Did I know I'd revisit topology? No. I stayed with flat plates for a long time. But exploring curves brought back the notion of a topological form with a surface that's continuous from inside to outside.

**HF**: Does that mean that the first *Torqued Ellipse* (1996) isn't a prime object in its own right?

**RS**: The first one might also constitute a prime object.

**HF**: Isn't there just one prime object in a sequence?

**RS**: The prime object opens a sequence and may reassert itself in a different form later in that sequence. No sequence is ever closed.

**HF**: And in that way becomes a prime object in its own right?

**RS**: In my definition, if not in Kubler's. I don't think anybody else would see the relationship between *To Lift* and the *Torqued Ellipses*. In fact, people said they hadn't seen anything quite like the *Ellipses* before. What the *Ellipses* do that *To Lift* doesn't is to allow you to enter into the space of the sculpture. Walking from outside to inside, you become the subject of the experience, whereas *To Lift* remains an object.

**Clara Weyergraf-Serra**: Is there a similar connection between *House of Cards* and your vertical pieces?

**RS**: *House of Cards* opened up the idea of building structures that are freestanding, where every part is interdependent on every other part, and that got me into making towers. Unlike the topological forms, there wasn't a big jump in time or conception between *House of Cards* and the first tower, *Sight Point* (1972–75), at the Stedelijk Museum in Amsterdam. But then *House of Cards* isn't fixed and the vertical pieces are, so they're more like constructions.

**CW-S**: But don't they function according to the principles of propping?

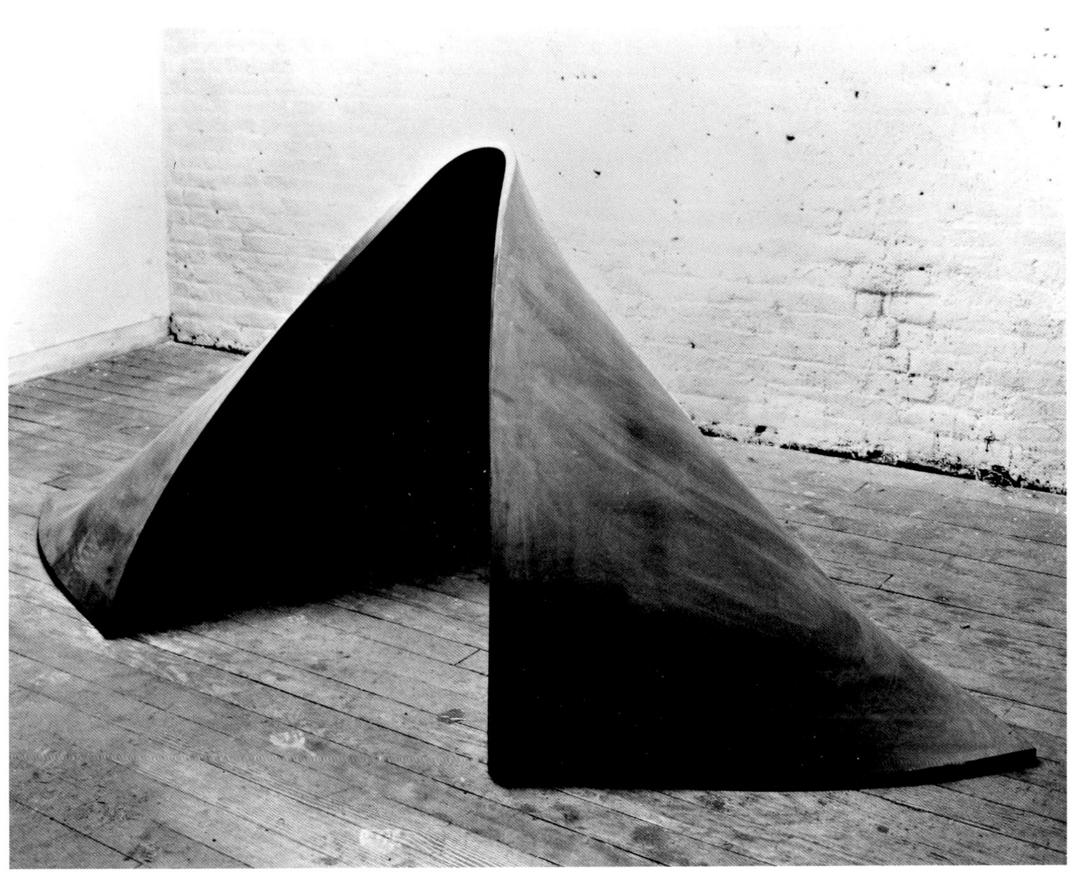

*To Lift,* 1967. Vulcanized rubber, 36 × 80 × 60 in. (91.4 × 203.2 × 152.4 cm).
The Museum of Modern Art, New York. Gift of the artist. Photo Peter Moore.

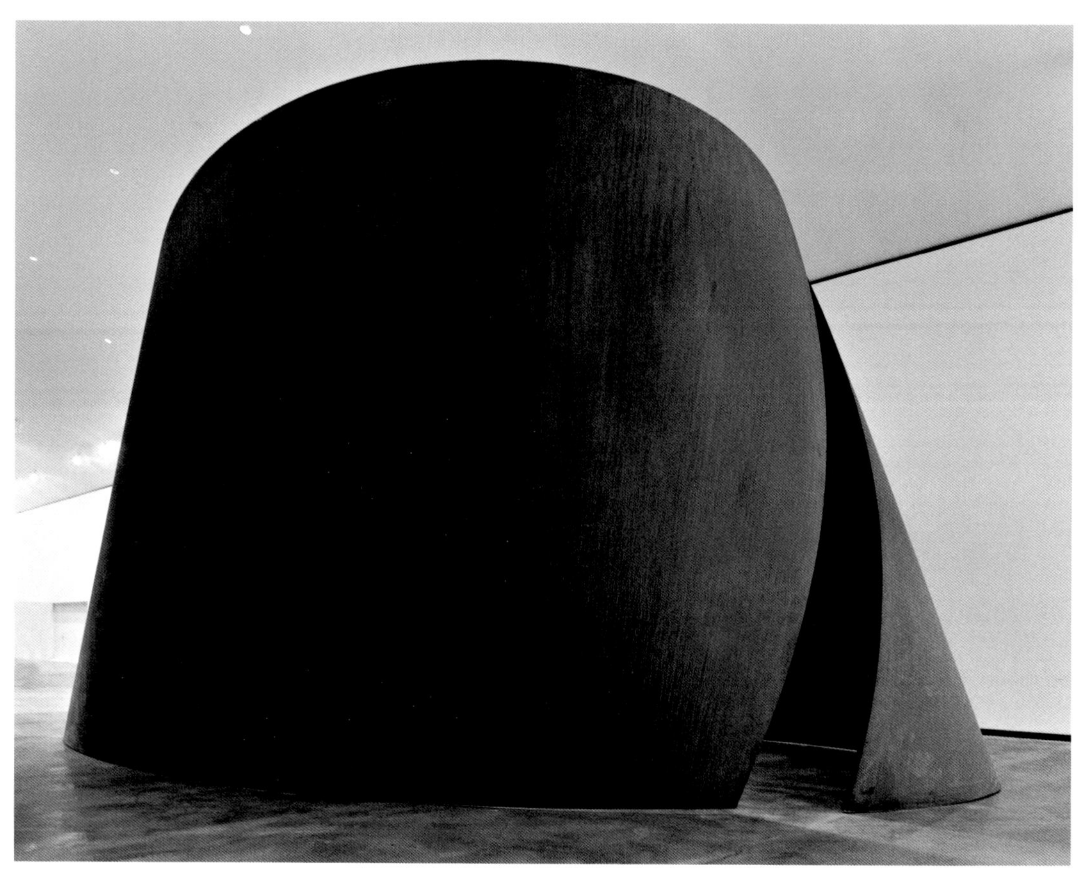

*Torqued Ellipse V,* 1998–99. Weatherproof steel, 13 ft. 8 ½ in. × 33 ft. 5 ½ in. × 19 ft. 8 ¼ in × 2 in.
(4.2 m × 10.2 m × 6 m × 5 cm), as installed in the exhibition "Richard Serra Sculpture"
at the Museo Guggenheim Bilbao, Spain, 1999.

**RS**: Yes, but in order to allay concerns about them overturning and to comply with building codes, I couldn't build them in public spaces without anchoring them.

**CW-S**: I'm not talking about the restrictions of building codes but about the principles of propping.

**RS**: The vertical pieces are fixed by necessity, and that pulls them back into constructed sculpture. *House of Cards* isn't related to any kind of Constructivism.

**CW-S**: Yet the vertical pieces wouldn't be possible without *House of Cards*.

**RS**: That's true, but, again, they're constructions, while *House of Cards* is of a different order.

**HF**: What about when you return to the prop pieces in the mid-1980s and again in the mid-2010s? Does that set up a new sequence?

**RS**: You mean the steel plate props? They're also of a different order, and I don't think they're prime objects. They're a kind of mutation.

**HF**: So exactly what sequence did *House of Cards* open up?

**RS**: Well, it opened up the sequences of all the lead props and steel towers. But more importantly it set up the idea that sculpture no longer needed to be welded. In fact, *House of Cards* set up the proposition that everything I do, in and of itself, could be freestanding.

**CW-S**: I want to come back to your vertical pieces because, when you build models for those pieces in the sandbox, they're freestanding.

**RS**: Yes and no, because the sandbox acts as a fulcrum to hold them. When they're erected outside, you can't prop the plates and shove them into the ground. You need foundations to conform to building codes and wind load. But in principle they're freestanding.

**HF**: Does anchoring them in this way qualify your commitment to structural transparency, to exposing how each piece works tectonically? We don't see the footing in, say, *Promenade* (2008) or *East-West/West-East* (2015). Might a purist see that as a perilous step down the slippery slope of concealing the structural setup totally, the way James Turrell usually does, for effect?

**RS**: Take *East-West/West-East*. If I had made its plates longer and sunk them deeper into the ground, I wouldn't have needed anchors. It all comes out of working in a sandbox. I could've just stuck them deeper in the desert sand.

**CW-S**: Actually *Promenade* wasn't anchored. Each plate simply slipped into a shoe set into the ground a little below grade.

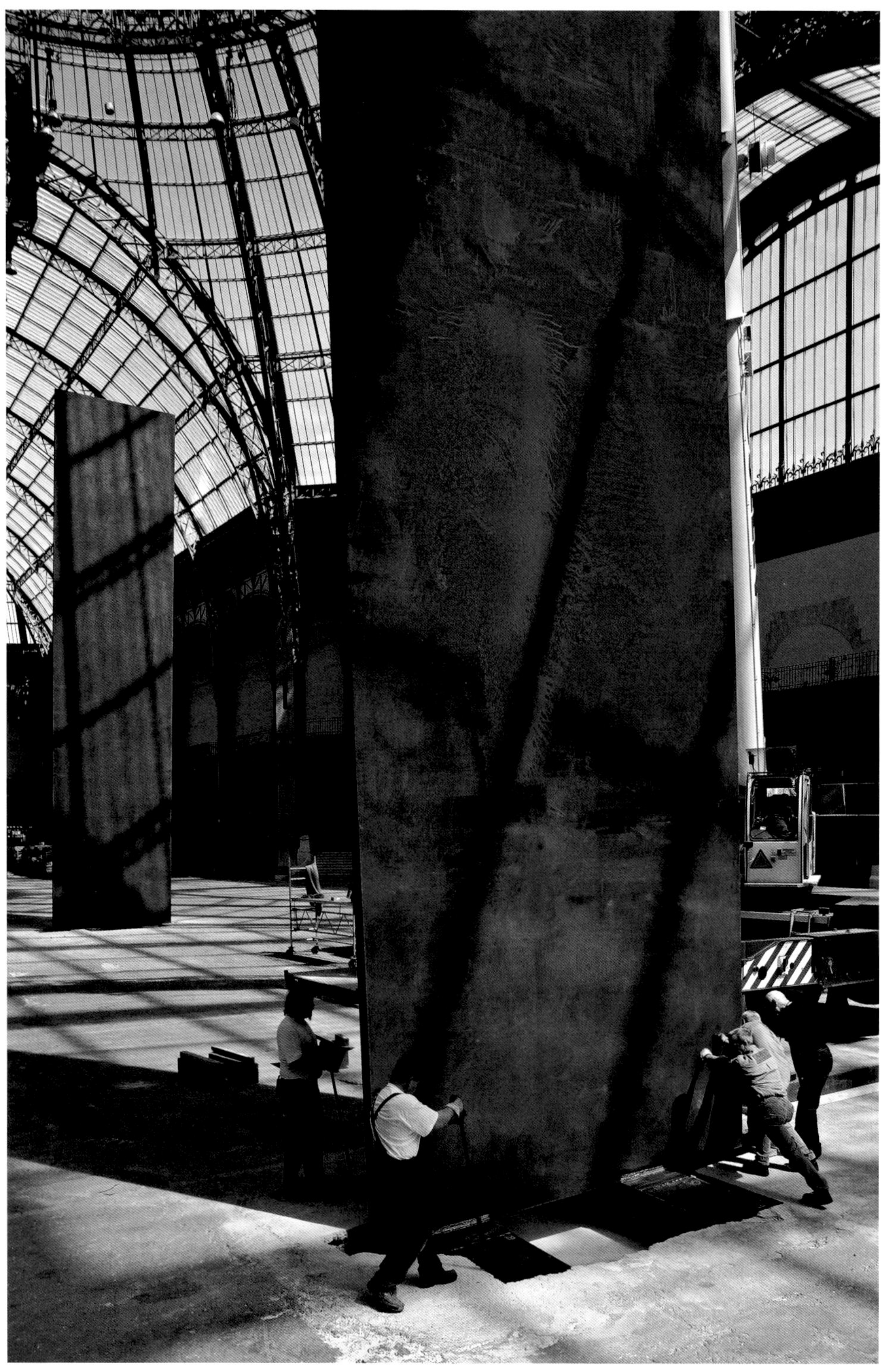

Installing *Promenade* at the Grand Palais, Paris, 2008.

**HF**: The only pieces that are truly anchored then are the towers?

**RS**: Yes. According to the local codes.

**HF**: Okay, back to the prime object. So it isn't necessarily a formal proposition or a typological category?

**RS**: No, it's a didactic proposition.

**HF**: About procedure.

**RS**: About a method that responds to the potential for a break in a continuum. It's a way of making an entrance into sculpture that has no antecedents. It's an invention or an innovation, but it doesn't necessarily have value as a work of art in itself.

**HF**: What do you mean exactly?

**RS**: Well, some things have value because they engender other work by you or other people. If you're trying to establish a new order, there's no guarantee people will assume your proposition is valid.

**HF**: Do you have examples of didactic pieces that aren't generative?

**RS**: The splash piece built into the Castelli Warehouse in 1968. It dealt with gravity and entropy, altered the architecture, and existed only in situ. That piece was didactic in that it was built in a place that it became part of, and it existed in that place only while it was available to the public or until it was destroyed. Everybody else at the time who said they did site-specific pieces—from Carl Andre to Smithson—always moved them. That's not site-specific.

**HF**: Is one difference between a prime object and a didactic work that the former is generative and the latter isn't necessarily so—because it's primarily a demonstration, like that splash piece, because it mostly instantiates a proposition?

**RS**: Prime objects might not fulfill the aesthetic criteria of a complex work, but in their didacticism they assert a theoretical proposition, which can be either a singular state-ment or a first move in a whole sequence of permutations. The important difference is not so much between prime object and didactic work as it is between prime object and replica. Often a prime object is made anonymously, and then it's reproduced. By and large replicas constitute the canons of art history, and they often obliterate the prime objects by their sheer number—and by all the conventions they put in place. We're in a heyday of replicas now.

**HF**: Is that why it's important for you, at times, to go back and retrieve a prime object? Lately your work has become more recursive. You return to certain pieces, prime or otherwise, as with your recent steel props and forged rounds and blocks.

**RS**: I can do that in relation to my work, but it's not a typical move in the history of sculpture. That's why we're still stuck with the conventions of armature, modeling, casting, and all the rest. Those are replicas of prime objects that have become conventional. The obvious example in our time is Duchamp's urinal. The fact that people keep remaking it is preposterous. Duchamp produced a prime object, and others replicate it ad nauseam.

**HF**: Sometimes it's not repeated so much as elaborated on—extended, repurposed.

**RS**: Unless you break with the conventions you're only doing replicas. Most contemporary paintings are replicas on stretcher bars and canvas.

**HF**: Kubler talks about entrances, as do you, but what's at stake here is departures, not entrances. And to make a departure, don't you need conventions in place—like modeling and casting—to serve as a foil? What marks the departure otherwise? And, if that's so, what happens when that foil is lost—when we have nothing but departures and no homeport? Wasn't that, in a way, the condition of sculpture by the end of the 1960s?

**RS**: My understanding of Kubler's prime object is that it is sui generis, that by definition it doesn't have a foil. Artists worthy of the name need to invent and to innovate; you have to find a way of differentiating from tradition. I happened to start with the "Verb List" performing activities in relation to material. Other people have done it in other ways. I think anyone who has made a change in the continuum of sculpture understands the necessity of the prime object. Andre, for example, was focused on prime objects.

**HF**: How so?

**RS**: *Lever* (1966) seems to me to be a prime object for him—maybe not consciously— as much as an open box was for Judd or a fluorescent tube for Flavin.

**HF**: The next prime object you mentioned to me is *Strike,* a long steel plate wedged into a corner that juts out into a gallery, an intervention into a space that divides it or declares it, to use your term. It set up the possibility of other straight plate pieces—and later of curvilinear ones too.

**RS**: Most immediately it opened up the possibility of *Circuit* (1972), four plates protruding out of the four corners of a room toward the center. More generally it opened up the possibility of entering into a space and making that space the sculpture, so that when you enter the room you become part of the work. The other interesting thing about *Strike* is that, in all its simplicity, the form moves from line to plane to volume; it opens the space and fans out into the field as you walk it. It declares the entire room as its content. At the same time it appears almost weightless.

**HF**: Not in my experience.

**RS**: You don't sense its gravitational load. You perceive it projecting into the room but not its downwardness. In that respect it differs from a piece like *Gravity* (1991) in the Holocaust Museum in D.C. It's not impaled in the ground as *Gravity* is. It doesn't really deal with the surface of the floor as much as it deals with the lateral extension into the room.

**HF**: If *Strike* is your initial opening into a field, is it your key prime object? You seem to regard that move as your most important one.

**RS**: There are several prime objects in my early work. My splash pieces and *Strike* are significant for the same reason—both alter the architectural context—but *Strike* also anticipates *Pulitzer Piece: Stepped Elevation* (1970–71), which is a landscape work.

**HF**: So is *Pulitzer Piece* the first you thought about explicitly in terms of field?

**RS**: No, in retrospect it's actually *Strike,* though there is a piece that came before, a lesser-known work at the Pasadena Museum called *Base Plate Deflection: In It, On It* (1970). I pushed a very thin flat steel plate halfway into the sloping ground; because of its thinness, it deflects. In a way it's my first curved piece, since the plate bends under its own weight. Andre saw it and said I had closed off a whole body of work for him. That's the first piece that explores impaling sculpture in the ground.

The next piece where plates are partially impaled into the ground is *Pulitzer Piece.* There the location of the plates responds to the elevational fall of the land over a given distance. The length of each of the three plates is determined by marking a five-foot drop in elevation from plate to plate. Starting at a plate height of five feet above ground, how far down does the plate have to go, following the slope, to arrive at the next contour line five feet down in elevation? The primary thinking behind pieces of that kind occurred in Pasadena, even though at the time I thought it was a one-off.

**HF**: Isn't the opening to field implicit in *Strike*?

**RS**: *Strike* is a plane in a room, a straight vertical elevation. As soon as you impale a plane in the slope of a landscape following a set drop in elevation, you're making a horizontal move into the field, with the top edge of each plate functioning as a surrogate horizon in the landscape.

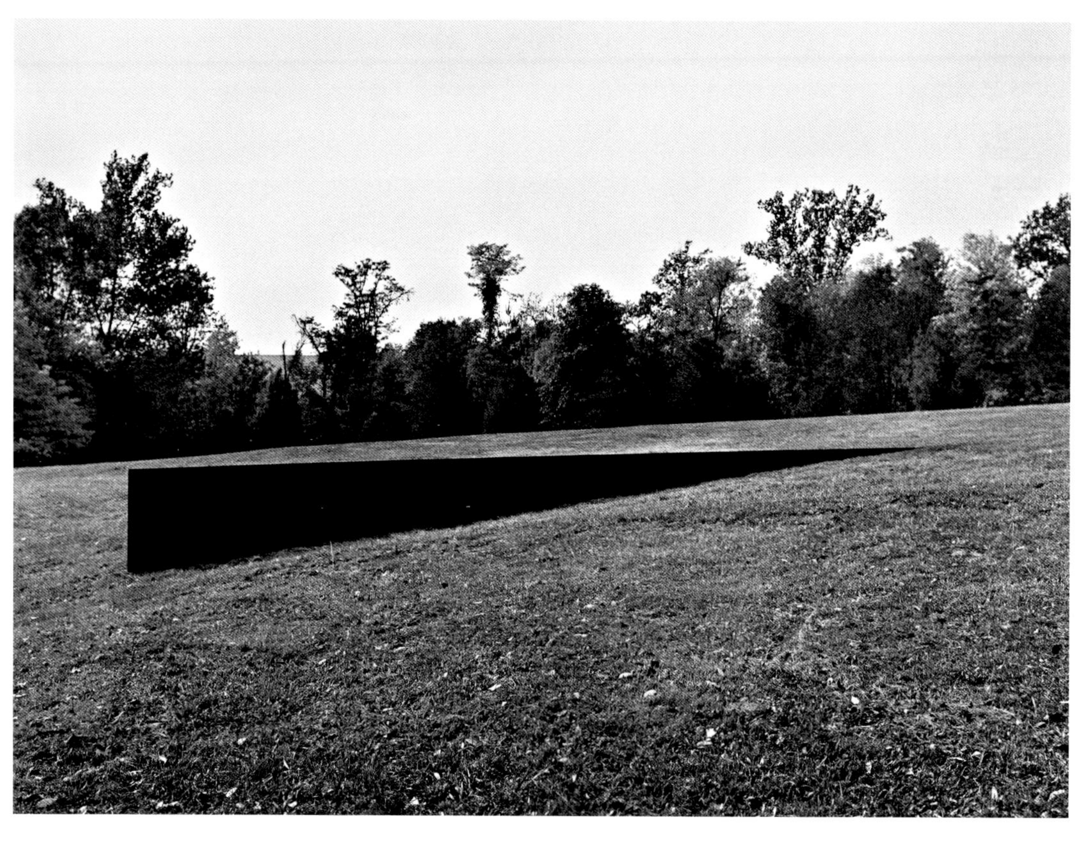

*Pulitzer Piece: Stepped Elevation,* 1970–71 (detail). Weatherproof steel; three plates, 60 in. × 40 ft. 3 in. × 2 in. (152.4 cm × 12.3 m × 5 cm), 60 in. × 45 ft. 11 in. × 2 in. (152.4 cm × 14 m × 5 cm), 60 in. × 50 ft. 7 in. × 2 in. (152.4 cm × 15.4 m × 5 cm). Pulitzer Residence, Saint Louis. Emily Rauh Pulitzer.

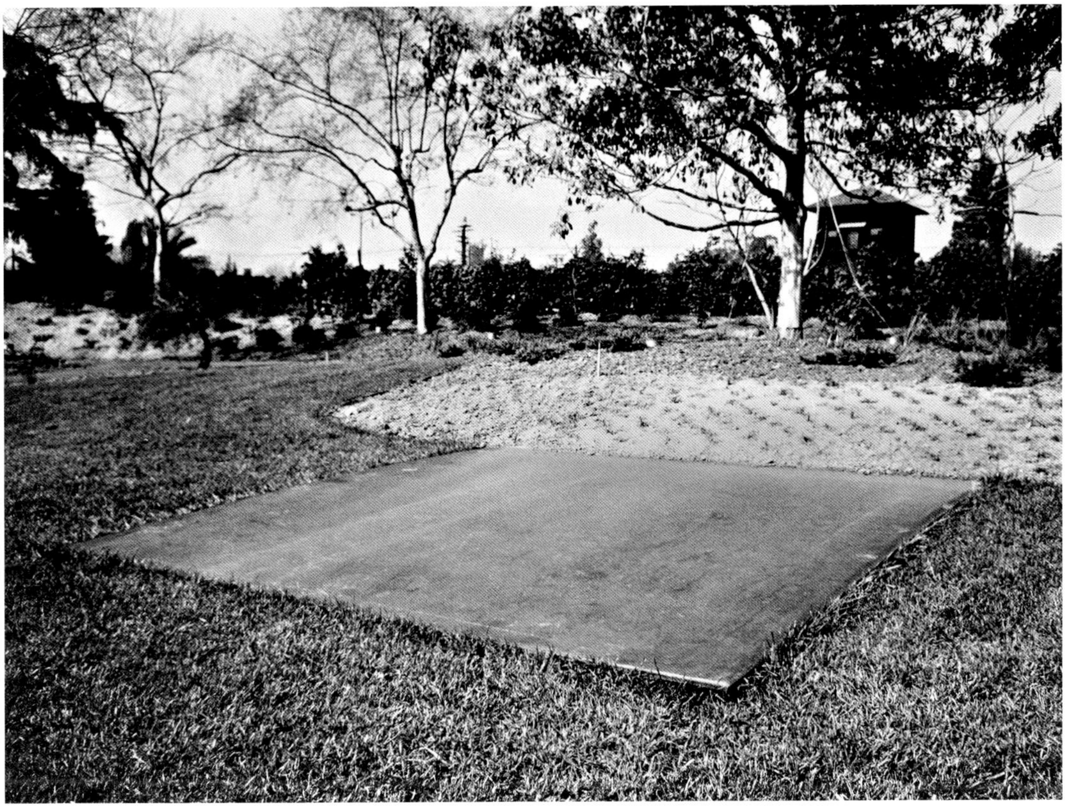

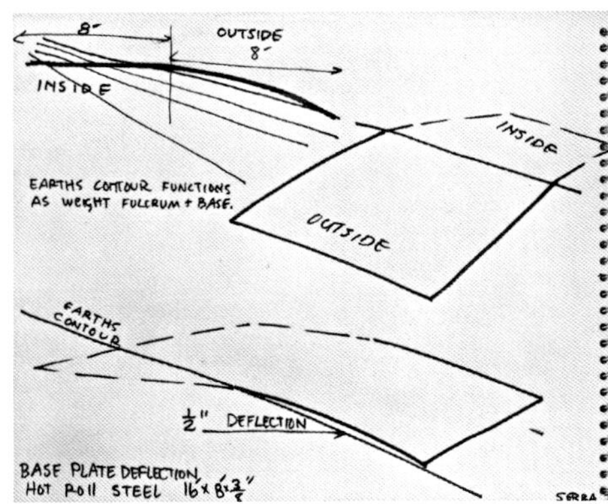


*Base Plate Deflection: In It, On It,* 1970. Hot-rolled steel, ⅜ in. × 8 ft. × 16 ft. (1 cm × 2.4 m × 4.9 m), insertion 8 ft. (2.4 m), deflection ½ in. (1.3 cm). Norton Simon Museum of Art, Pasadena, California.

Diagram of *Base Plate Deflection: In It, On It.*

**HF:** I take it that prime objects are known only in retrospect because they become prime by what they generate. Does that mean *Strike* is the first opening to a field experience in your work?

**RS:** I've never thought about it, but most likely, yes. Do you see it as a field piece? I don't usually think of it as such because I think of field pieces in terms of a horizontal movement in space. But I think you're right. That's not true of *Circuit.*

**HF:** In a way *Circuit* is a construction out of Tatlin. Could it be that a prime object, in your definition, opens up more than one sequence?

**RS:** Yes.

**HF:** Because *Strike* leads to *Circuit,* but it also leads to your field pieces, and those are two different paths.

**RS:** Right.

**HF:** What about *To Encircle,* your steel circle embedded in the Bronx?

**RS:** You called it a prime object, but I'm not sure it is. It's planted flush in the ground, and I don't consider it as generative as the pieces we've talked about. I've never revisited the Bronx piece to expand on its potential for generating a sequence.

**HF:** But isn't it the first piece that's absolutely site-specific—that is, in your definition of site-specificity, that "to move the work is to destroy it"?

**RS:** The first site-specific work is the splash piece in the Castelli Warehouse.

**HF:** But there the site was temporary and the work was ephemeral. What about one that remains in situ?

**RS:** Well, then we'd have to go back to *Base Plate Deflection* in Pasadena, which still exists.

**HF:** We've recovered that piece then. You would privilege it, in terms of site-specificity, over the Bronx piece?

**RS:** I think so, yes, because it deals with the deflection of the plate in relationship to its insertion in the land.

**HF:** What other prime objects would you propose?

**RS:** I don't know if it's a prime object, but if I asked you what form *Tilted Arc* (1981) is, what would you say—what geometry?

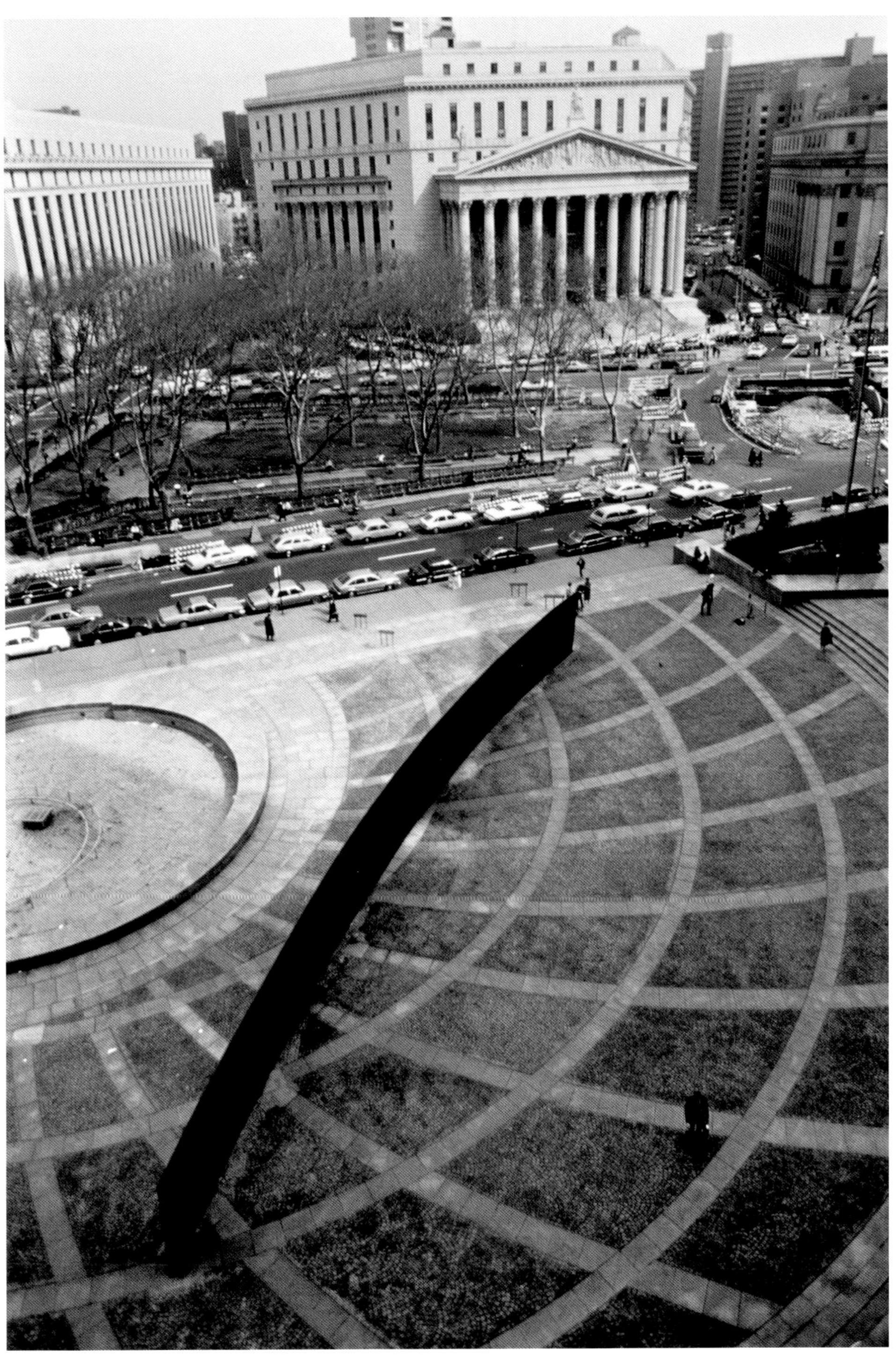

*Tilted Arc*, 1981. Weatherproof steel, cylindrical section 12 ft. × 120 ft. × 2 ½ in. (3.7 m × 36.6 m × 6.4 cm).
Federal Plaza, New York. Collection U.S. General Services Administration, Washington, D.C.
Destroyed by the United States Government, March 15, 1989.

**HF**: Is that a trick question? An arc?

**RS**: *Tilted Arc* was site-specific because it was impaled in the ground as a section of a cylinder. While the center of the plate touched the ground, the two ends were embedded in order to effect the tilt, which meant that the center rose higher than either end. The rise of the arc was never understood; in fact, it was never mentioned. That's part of the reason why it was site-specific. If it were just a section of a cone, you could've picked it up and moved it.

**CW-S**: But you read it as a conical section.

**RS**: No, you didn't! The top edge of the center of the piece was higher than the ends; the center of the piece rode on the ground. *Tilted Arc* was 120 feet long, so it was hard to see this variation, but it got lower in height as the curve starting at the center was impaled in the ground. No one ever noticed that it was a tilted section of a cylinder. Everyone thought that it was just a conical section that you could pick up and move. It was similar, in a way, to *Berlin Block (For Charlie Chaplin)* (1977) in front of the Neue Nationalgalerie. *Berlin Block* is also impaled in its plaza.

**HF**: Again, the prime object is not morphological but procedural. Things don't necessarily have to look alike. They are affined because they share a didactic method.

**RS**: That's right.

**HF**: What other prime objects are there?

**RS**: Apart from the ones we've mentioned, I'd say *Splashing* as an opening to the sequence of splash pieces, and *Pulitzer Piece* in Saint Louis.

**CW-S**: *Pulitzer Piece* isn't really a prime object because, as Hal pointed out, *Strike* is the opening to all the field pieces.

**RS**: Yes, but *Pulitzer Piece* was determined by the elevation and topology of the landscape, and that was new. I didn't make the connection to *Strike* when I did *Pulitzer Piece*. I was primarily concerned with finding a logic for setting plates into the land, and a large series of landscape pieces are generated by *Pulitzer Piece*. I think *Pulitzer Piece* is just as much a prime object as *Strike*.

**HF**: What about the Pasadena piece? Did you make that before or after you went to Japan?

**RS**: I made it right before, but I didn't think much about it at the time.

**HF**: What other proposals have been, if not prime, at least generative? What about the blocks and the rounds—how did they come to be?

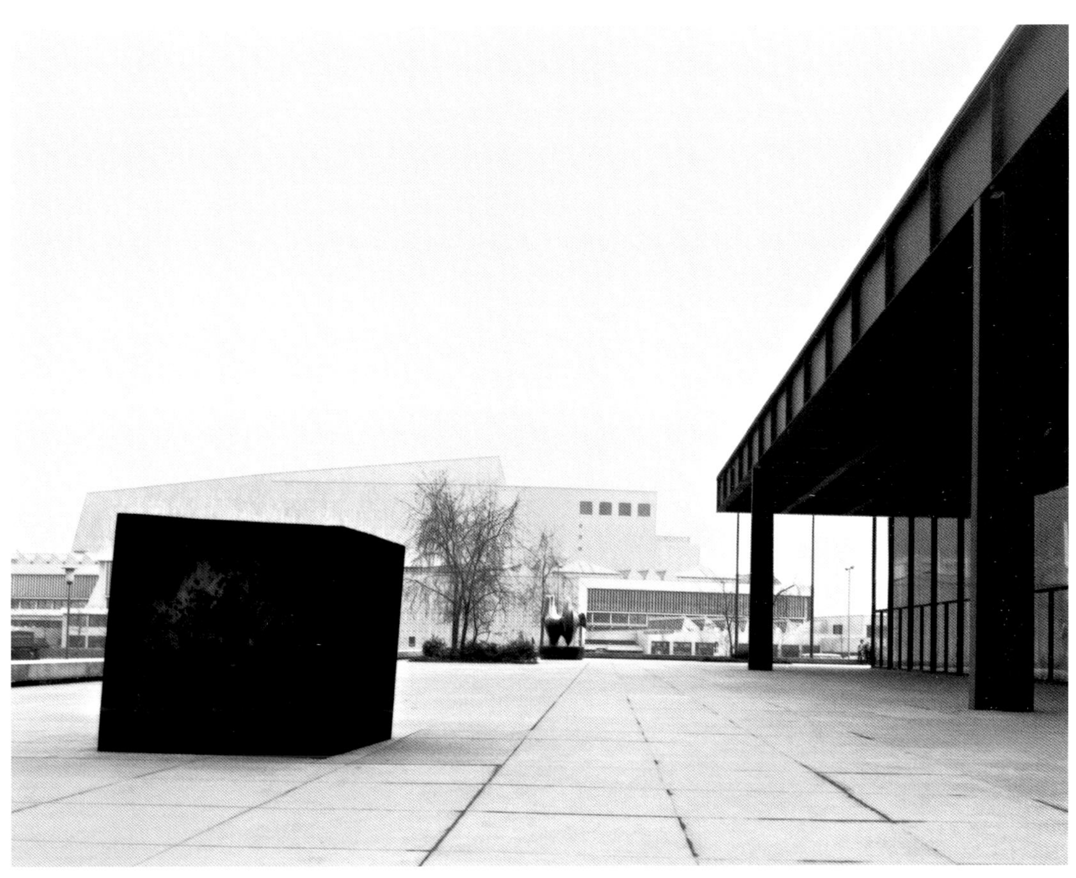

*Berlin Block (For Charlie Chaplin)*, 1977. Forged steel, 6 ft. 3 in. × 6 ft. 3 in. × 6 ft. 3 in. (1.90 × 1.9 × 1.9 m).
Permanent installation at the Neue Nationalgalerie, Berlin. Staatliche Museen zu Berlin, Preußischer
Kulturbesitz; purchased by Verein der Freunde der Nationalgalerie, 1979.

**RS**: *Berlin Block* is the first one. The idea of condensing a mass that's heavier by a third than anything that's cast really appealed to me. What's interesting about *Berlin Block,* other than its weight and density, is that its molecular structure is also cubic. It was very satisfying to have an internal order that's reiterated in the external shape. *Berlin Block* is the largest forged block I've ever done; it weighs seventy-seven tons.

**HF**: Was it your first forged piece?

**RS**: No, it followed *Consequence* (1977), a much smaller two-part forged piece. Alexander von Berswordt-Wallrabe, a dealer in Germany, had access to a steel mill through his relationship with its owners. Once I saw the forge—it's a machine about eighty feet high— I jumped into it whole hog. To forge a seventy-seven-ton block was unheard of; it was out of bounds. Outfitted in an asbestos suit, I was able to eyeball the piece as it was being made. They let me control the forging of the edges and measure the piece with a right angle.

**HF**: And that initiated a whole sequence of works. Again, a procedure is at the beginning of things.

**RS**: Technology can lead to invention. I was always involved with weight, but that really upped the ante. When you talk about prime objects—about entrances—one thing that distinguishes my work is that I've always considered weight to be a grounding principle: weight or the absence of weight.

**HF**: So much sculpture wants to get rid of weight, to sublimate mass. You often go against the traditional tendency to lift and to lighten—you press down, you condense.

**RS**: Everything is gravity-bound, and not to acknowledge that is to misunderstand one's relationship to how the world is perceived and how we interact with it. So all those pieces are concerned with weight and location.

**HF**: All the blocks and the rounds?

**RS**: Yes. *Berlin Block* can't move. If I had my druthers, nothing would be moved.

**HF**: So *Berlin Block* exists as a convergence of two sequences, because you relate it both to works that are impaled and to works that stress weight through forging.

**RS**: *Berlin Block* is different from *Pulitzer Piece* and *Strike.* They're involved with lateral movement, with cutting into the field, whereas *Berlin Block* deals with gravity, location, and displacement. It's positioned so that it offsets the rectilinear grid of the plaza.

**HF**: My point is that there are works that occupy more than one sequence, and they might be generative in different ways for different sequences.

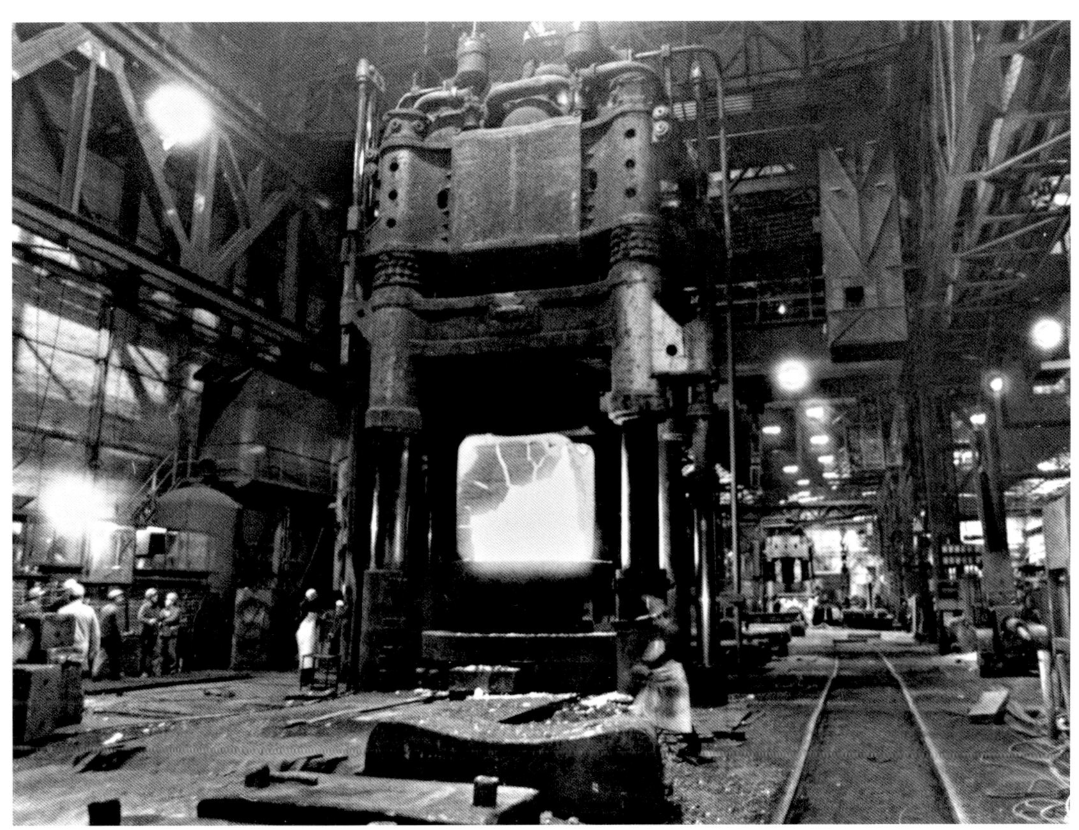

Forging of *Berlin Block (For Charlie Chaplin)* at Henrichshütte Hattingen, Germany, 1977.

**RS**: Yes, but you never know that in advance.

**HF**: I mentioned that you've returned to certain types of work such as the forged rounds and blocks, as in *Four Rounds: Equal Weight, Unequal Measure* and *Into and Across* (both 2017). Why these types in particular? They're mostly presented in galleries. Why this return to works that concern weight and measure in an otherwise abstract space?

**RS**: It's not a return; I've always gone back and forth between gallery installations and permanent sites. I use the gallery as a kind of laboratory to test ideas. Site-specific installations don't occur frequently, but I still want to continue to work and investigate different propositions.

To see and understand *Four Rounds* requires a sensory judgement that's not quite the same as weighing and measuring. I suspect that some visitors intuit the equivalence in mass without the aid of the title, but most don't, so this work tests their visceral reaction to the fact that the weights of the different rounds are equal. To understand *Four Rounds* demands sustained attention—that you twist and turn and rotate as you observe the work from the center and around each element. You sense that the four rounds might be identical in weight from afar, but you must walk up close to them to understand how they relate to the architecture and to each other, which they do in very different ways. You feel the mass of your own body as compared to the mass of each round.

All of my work relates to human scale. This is just as true of *Into and Across,* an installation of two forged sixty-inch cubes set in opposite corners of the same wall. One block is set flush into the corner and has two visible sides. The other block crosses the corner and has three visible sides, but you have to walk up close and peer around the frontal plane of the cube to discover the other two sides. In this work equals appear unequal: the blocks appear non-identical even though you intuit that they are identical. There's a tension between the two blocks as one pushes into the corner and one crosses the corner: they seem to be pulling toward each other.

**HF**: This sounds like weighing and measuring to me, only as operations relocated in the body. In any case, you invite us to gauge these different objects. Why is this important for you—for us—to do now? The art historian Michael Baxandall once argued that Italian Renaissance painters like Piero della Francesca played on the visual skills of their patrons—skills, involving mathematics and proportion, that, however conceptual, were essential to everyday life in the marketplace. "It is an important fact of art history," Baxandall writes, "that commodities have come regularly in standard-sized containers only since the nineteenth century: previously a container—a barrel, sack or bale—was unique, and calculating its volume quickly and accurately was a condition of business."

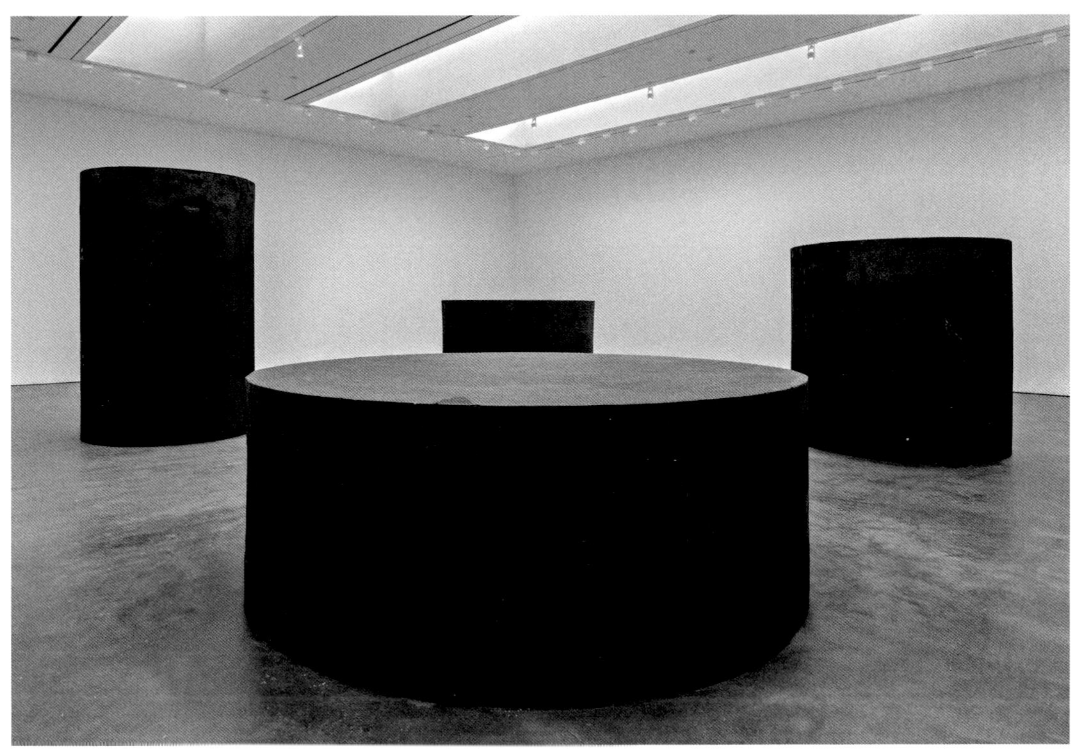

*Four Rounds: Equal Weight, Unequal Measure,* 2017. Forged steel, 10 ft. × 6 ft. 3 in. diameter
(3 × 1.9 m), 7 ft. 3 ½ × 7 ft. 7 in. diameter (2.2 × 2.3 m), 45 ¾ in. × 10 ft. 7 ¼ in. diameter (1.1 × 3.2 m),
64 ¼ in. × 9 ft. 2 in. diameter (1.6 × 2.8 m). Private Collection.

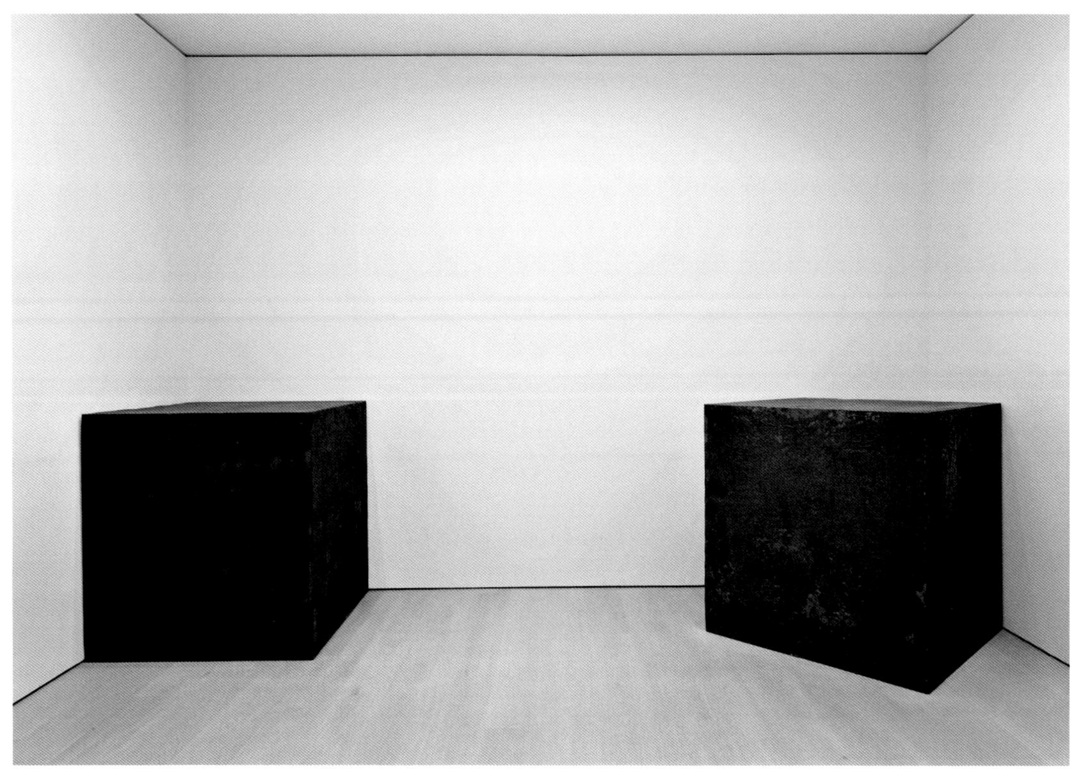

*Into and Across,* 2017. Forged steel, two blocks, each 60 × 60 × 60 in. (152.4 × 152.4 × 152.4 cm).

Painters like Piero drew on this "mercantile geometry," Baxandall claims; "the cognitive style" of the time was, in part, their medium. And like those patrons then, we viewers now, he asserts, "enjoy our own exercise of skill, and we particularly enjoy the playful exercise of skills which we use in normal life very earnestly."[2] Does this argument resonate at all with the gauging solicited by pieces like *Four Rounds* and *Into and Across*? If so, why do you invite this gauging? Is it, in part, to offer an aesthetic experience that doubles as remedial work in the art of assessing volume and weight, a skill that isn't everyday anymore? In fact, at a time when so much of our mediated experience, from the pixel to financial markets, is either below or beyond human scale, this skill in gauging might be mostly lost.

**RS**: I read that passage in Baxandall years ago, and my takeaway was that comparisons of weights were determining factors in the pricing of goods: the price of a sack of potatoes was different from that of a sack of wool, as determined by labor, transport, and storage. (It's true, though, that after I installed *Four Rounds* I thought about Uccello's *Battle of San Romano* [1432], in which the depicted elements on the ground, including helmets, lances, and armor, emphasize static, dead weight, held in place by gravitational load.) *Four Rounds* isn't concerned with weighing and measuring in the way Baxandall describes. Each round is singular, and all the rounds have different diameters and heights—they aren't permutations of an identical module (as is the case with other recent pieces like *Equal*). The rounds register as weight, weight, weight, weight, and only secondarily as measure.

**HF**: In that sense both the rounds and the blocks seem like countertypes to the torqued pieces. Let's take them up next.

# Torqued Shapes

**HF**: How did the *Torqued Ellipses* come about?

**RS**: After I made the first *Torqued Ellipse* in 1996, I wanted to develop the concept into a body of work, even though I wasn't certain of the parameters. They became clear as I built more. I became aware of the effects of different angles of incline, different lengths of passage, different closures, turnings, and so on. I could construct relationships between major and minor axes, and control the degree of rotation of the bottom ellipse to the top ellipse (it varies from ninety to sixty to thirty degrees). There was a new set of problems and variables to consider.

**HF**: What other factors guided this phase of your sculptural practice?

**RS**: I think your internal sense of time becomes more important in these pieces, more so than in *St. John's Rotary Arc* and *Tilted Arc,* say. Those are simple, open curves that had more of a real-time presence because they embraced the contingencies of their sites. As the single *Ellipses* developed into the double *Ellipses* and then into the *Spirals,* and the configuration of the interiors became more complex, so did the experience of time. Once I placed a smaller ellipse inside a larger, it became evident that if I connected one to the other the connection would form a spiral. As you follow the given path in the *Spirals,* everything on both sides—right and left, up and down—changes as you walk, and that either condenses your sense of time or expands it, making you feel anxious or relaxed, as you try to anticipate what will happen next or attempt to reconstruct the path you've already walked. It can be a disorienting experience. Internal time is even more intensely registered in the *Spirals* than in the *Ellipses.* It's not time on the clock, not literal time. This different temporality—it's subliminal—distinguishes the experience of the sculpture from everyday experience.

**HF**: But you once insisted on the continuity between the two.

**RS**: You're still grounded in the concrete place of everyday experience in the recent work. That hasn't changed.

**HF**: Do you still want the viewer to be able to figure out how the sculpture is made? Given this play with temporal and other effects, doing so seems more difficult.

**RS**: In the earlier work the structural language could be easily deduced; with the props and pieces like *Strike* the logic of the intervention is apparent. In the later work it's not so self-evident. I don't know what you can deduce from walking inside a *Torqued Spiral.* Not the plan or the elevation. In fact you can't deduce the inside from the outside. On the outside the *Ellipses* and the *Spirals* undulate and change their shape as you walk around them; they elongate and shorten as they lean constantly away from you. When you walk

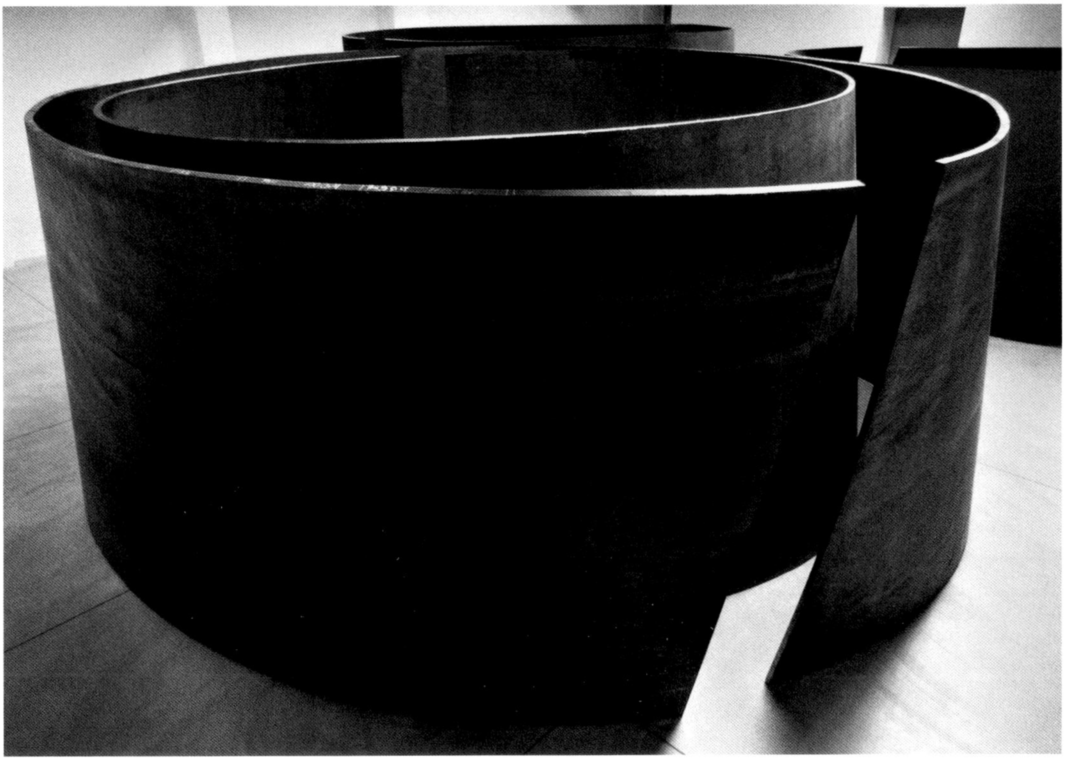

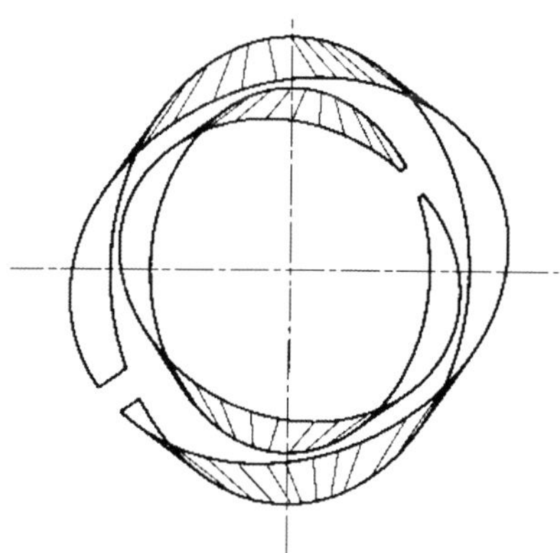

*Double Torqued Ellipse*, 1997. Weatherproof steel, outer ellipse
13 ft. 1 in. × 33 ft. 6 in. × 27 ft. 1 in. (4 × 10.2 × 8.3 m), inner 13 ft. 1 in. × 25 ft.
11 in. × 20 ft. 11 in. (4 × 8 × 2.5 m), plates 2 in. (5 cm). Dia Art Foundation,
New York. Gift of Louise and Leonard Riggio.

Right: Bending diagram for *Double Torqued Ellipse*.

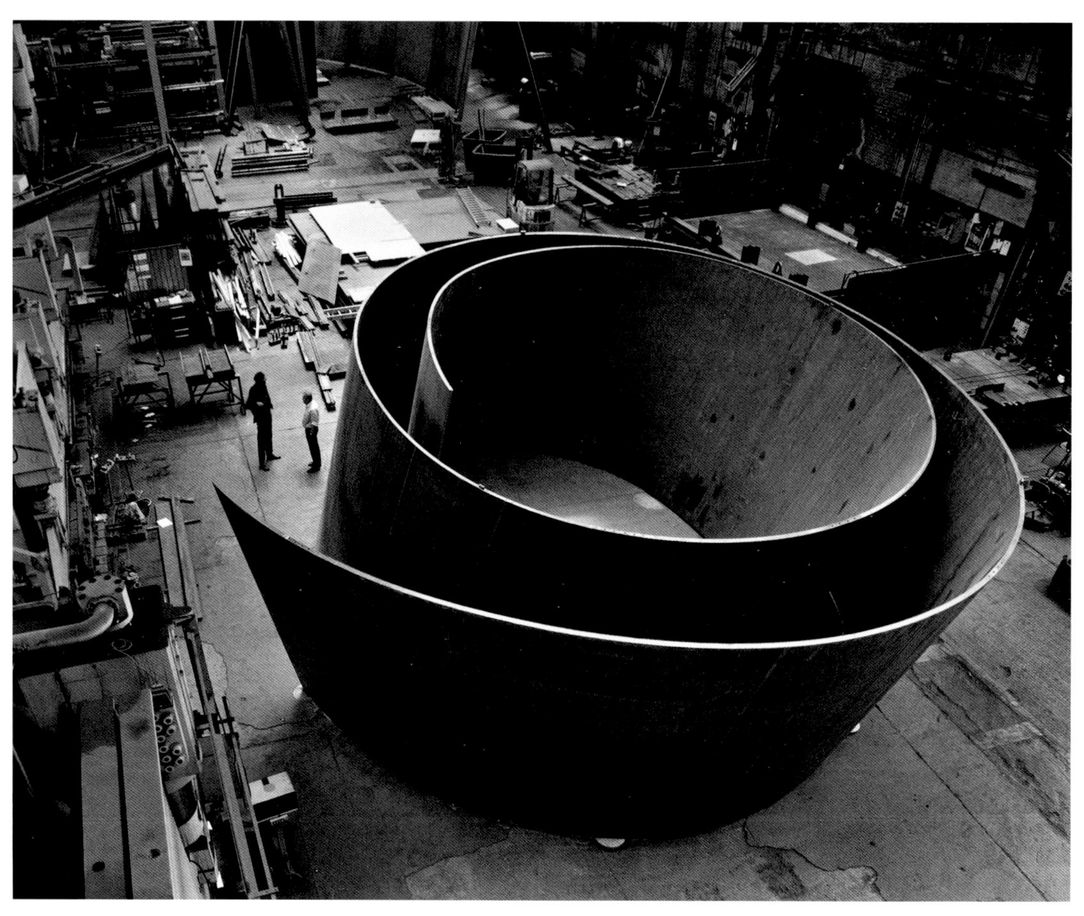

*Bellamy,* 2001. Weatherproof steel, 13 ft. 2 in. × 44 ft. 3 in. × 32 ft. 10 in.
(4 × 13.5 × 10 m), plates 2 in. (5 cm). Private Collection.

inside, the volume rotates from top to bottom; it's the opposite of what you anticipated. Yet the relationship between outside and inside doesn't seem arbitrary. These pieces bear psychologically on the viewer in a more intense way than the earlier pieces.

**HF**: What made you more open to this psychological dimension? Again, you once viewed it with suspicion.

**RS**: Me personally? I came up with Smithson, Nauman, and Hesse, and we never bought into that part of the Minimalist dogma. I've also never written anything against those interpretations.

**HF**: The making of the early work was matter-of-fact; its meanings appeared to be public, not private—that's what I mean. In any case, the psychological dimension is much stronger in the torqued pieces than in your earlier work.

**RS**: Maybe it was always there. It's there, for example, in *Delineator* (1974–75), the piece with the large steel plate flat on the floor and one attached to the ceiling. I think there's also a psychological effect in all the prop pieces.

**HF**: Yes, but that's a physical threat more than a psychological effect. The affective dimension of the *Ellipses* and the *Spirals* is different.

**RS**: Let's approach it another way. If you're splashing lead against the wall, you're throwing molten material into the gutter of the room. Couldn't one infer other things than a formal logic there? No one ever has. It's not very far from Warhol having someone piss on oxidized canvas; it's another way of messing with Pollock. It's also messing with the conventions of casting as well as the givens of architecture.

**HF**: I understand, but that's also different from the effects of the torqued work. In earlier pieces the emotive response of the viewer was always kept in check by a rational analysis— the will to work out the formal logic of the piece. Has that changed?

**RS**: No. Finally, the work is more responsive to its form-making than to anything else. It has to be inventive as form first; if it's not, it's not going to function in any of these other ways, which are attributes. I'll give you an example. If the *Spirals* were Archimedean spirals—that is, if they turned at a consistent rate outward from their centers—they'd be defined by parallel paths, and hence predictable and boring experientially, in terms of both space and time. I had to find a way to transgress forms, to see forms anew. I started out with logarithmic spirals that vary in intervals as they move outward. Here the moves are so unexpected that you can't easily discern the logic of their structure. Did I set out with that goal in mind? Not at all.

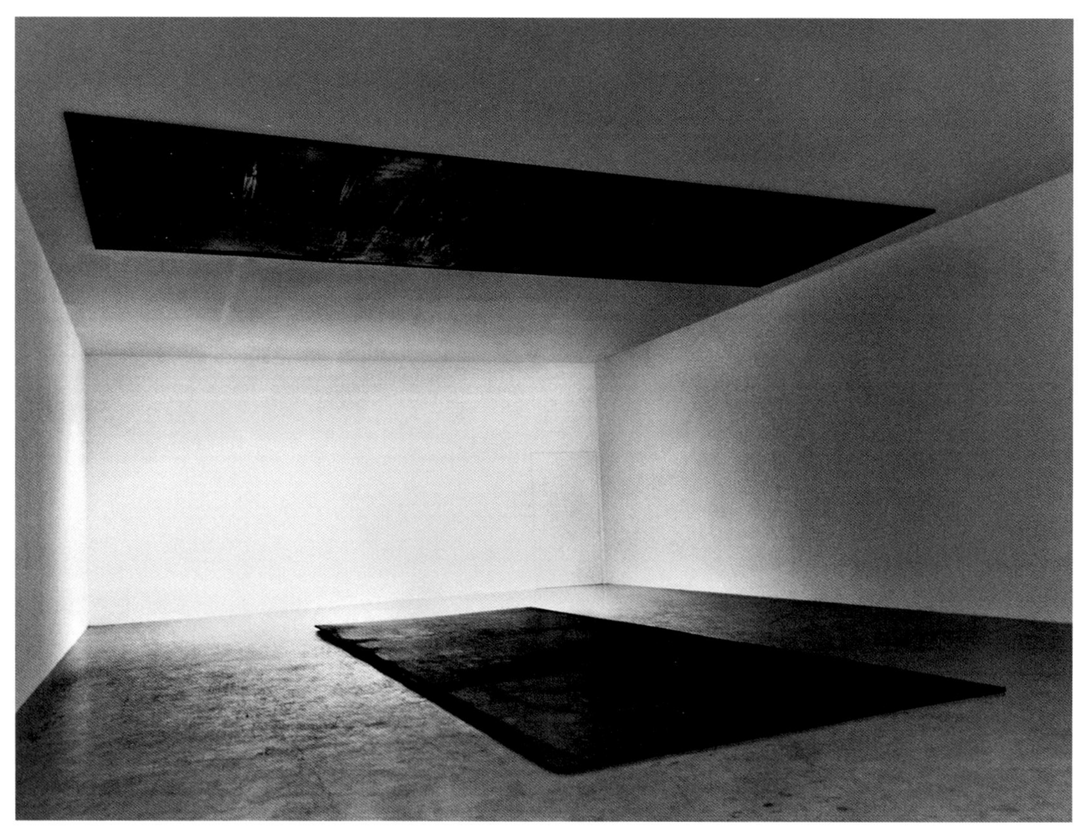

*Delineator,* 1974–75. Hot-rolled steel, two plates, each 1 in. × 10 ft. × 26 ft. (2.5 cm × 3 m × 7.9 m). The Museum of Modern Art, New York. Gift of Edward R. Broida and Gift of Mr. and Mrs. Morton J. Hornick (both by exchange).

**HF**: Maybe the distinction is that the viewer can still intuit the logic, if not know it. There are different kinds of figuring out elicited by your work.

**RS**: That's right. If you see these pieces from overhead, as you can at the installation at the Guggenheim Bilbao (2005–), you can read their structures.

**HF**: Are you now more open to the possibility of reading the work in that way—as an image?

**RS**: I'm still not interested in reading my works as images. When you look at pieces from overhead you can better discern their plan and better understand their structure, but their elevation is always partially masked.

**HF**: The installation at Bilboa is a demonstration of the language of your torqued sculpture. Apart from one serpentine work titled *Snake* (1994–97) there are two *Ellipses,* three *Spirals,* and two pieces with sections of a torus and a sphere. But you also treat the space almost as one field vectored in different ways.

**RS**: In organizing the sculptures in that space I was more concerned with the circulation through the entire space than with any singular image from above. The placement of the work can be easily understood from the balcony that juts out into the space and allows you to overlook the entire field of the gallery. We took *Naples* (2003), the largest and most complex of the *Spirals,* and placed it at the entrance. It has seven plates—all the other *Spirals* have five—and it continues to turn for another quarter rotation, leaning left to right once again. It's placed so you can look directly down into it from the balcony. When you see the pieces from overhead you get a sense of how the single and double *Ellipses* and *Spirals* function. After the most complex *Spiral* comes a single *Ellipse;* I used a new machine to bend this one, which allowed for a much tighter radius. In comparison to earlier singles the angle of the wall in this small *Ellipse* is very acute. Looking down into it from the balcony you see that the oval delineated on the ground and the oval at the top are exactly the same. The oval isn't twisted; it continuously rotates as it rises, and the radius never changes. As with all the *Ellipses,* the continuous rotation makes the steel walls lean inward and outward. The form is constructed through the void. That doesn't exist in nature or in architecture.

**HF**: So that piece functions as a touchstone in this phase of your sculpture. Has this occurred previously when one work signals a qualitative shift?

**RS**: Well, we're back to the question of the prime object, which presents each problem in its greatest simplicity. As I've said, I see *To Lift,* which was generated by simply enacting the verb "to lift" with a sheet of rubber, as a prime object. It was the first piece to deal with surface topology, a concept I reactivated in the *Ellipses.*

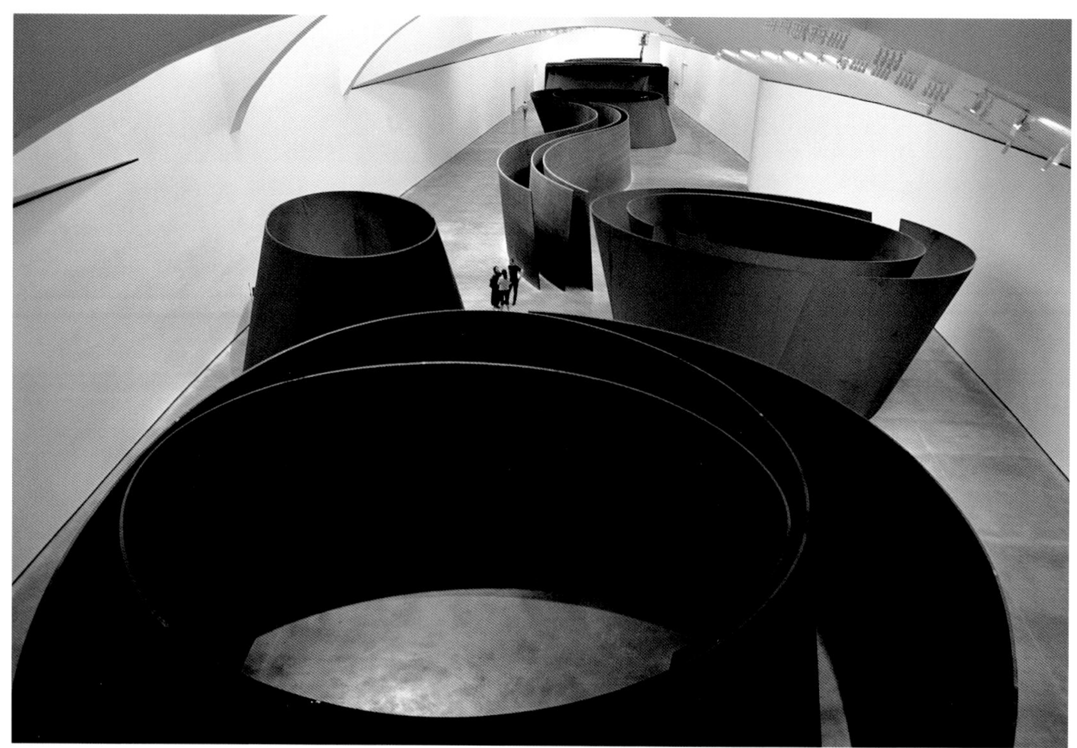

*The Matter of Time*, 1994–2005. Eight sculptures in weatherproof steel of different dimensions installed at Guggenheim Museum Bilbao, Spain, 2005–. Guggenheim Museum Bilbao, Spain.

**HF**: After the complex *Spiral* and the simple *Ellipse,* what comes next in the Bilbao installation?

**RS**: To the right follows a double *Ellipse,* in which the major and minor axes of the inner and outer ellipse are reversed; this offsets the path between the two ellipses so that it's never parallel. After the double *Ellipse* you come to *Snake;* then there are two more *Spirals,* which are significantly different from one another. One is simple: it leans all the way to the right until you get half way around, then there is an abrupt jolt when the curve starts to lean to the left. This spiral creates a broad horizontal interior enclosure. The other *Spiral* is more vertical, moving in and out, compressing you, turning you, releasing you. It's not as elongated, so your stride is not as quick, and the space changes more radically in elevation as it unfolds.

**HF**: How are the torus and sphere pieces related to the *Ellipses* and *Spirals*?

**RS**: After the early *Ellipses* we built the snake piece at Princeton called *The Hedgehog and the Fox* (1999) where the S of the snake is made of elliptical shapes that lean forward and back and are connected by a transitional form. That transitional section led us to consider a form we hadn't dealt with before; it derives from a torus (think of the outside and inside curvature of a doughnut). This new form established the logic for *The Union of the Torus and the Sphere* (2001) at Dia:Beacon. It's of a completely different order from the *Ellipses.*

**HF**: The one that looks like a listing double-ended ship?

**RS**: Yes. The linkage of toruses and spheres is also the basis for *Blind Spot Reversed* (2003–5), which is the last piece in the Bilbao installation. Then there's an open piece with different combinations of toruses and spheres—two toruses, a torus and a sphere, two spheres, a sphere and an inverted torus—all forming different spaces between them, seven passages resulting from the alignment of eight plates. The tension varies in each of the passages. The extreme bending of the steel puts a stress on the material that you register as part of the form-making process. That wouldn't be true of any other material.

**HF**: Excluding the toruses and spheres, is everything at Bilbao still related to the first *Ellipse*?

**RS**: Yes, though the *Spirals* differ somewhat in that there's no stable center—it drifts. But basically this whole group of work is generated by the first *Ellipse.* When I was asked to do the Bilbao installation, I wanted to keep the language contained to one body of work.

**HF**: Do you feel you've exhausted this language of forms, or are there new ones to test out?

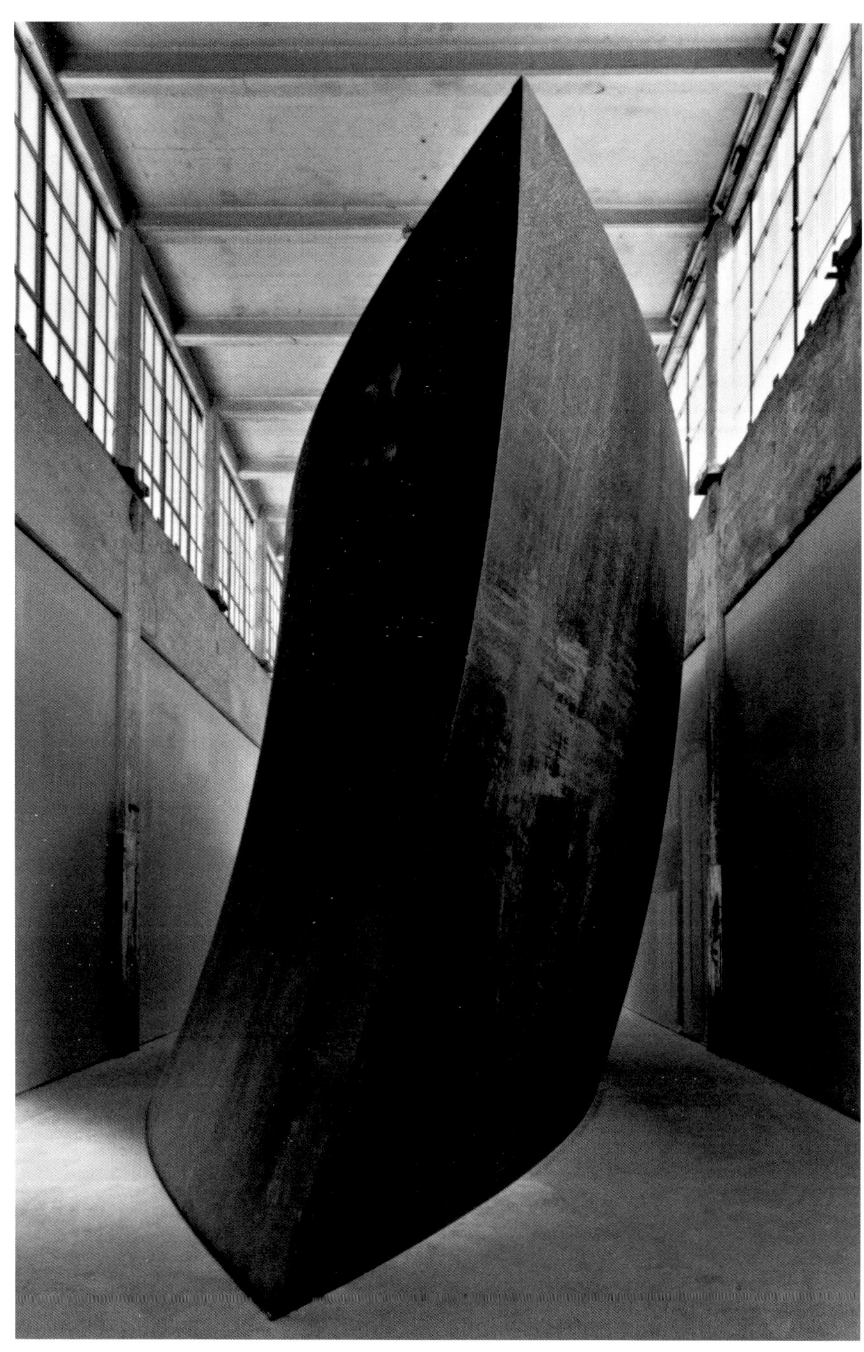

*Union of the Torus and the Sphere*, 2001. Weatherproof steel, a torus section and a spherical section joined, 11 ft. 9 ¾ in. × 37 ft. 9 ½ in. × 13 ft. 2 ½ in. (3.6 × 11.5 × 4 m), plates 2 in. (5 cm) thick. Dia:Beacon, New York. Dia Art Foundation.

**RS**: There are no closed sequences. I go through many permutations to choose the solution that manifests the fullest exploration of a problem—at its most extreme, most abstract, and most consequential. That particular body of work spanned only six or seven years. It's a cohesive language anybody can follow.

**HF**: You opened the catalogue for the Bilbao installation with two pieces: *To Lift,* which established both a primary action and a topological surface; and *To Encircle,* the Bronx piece that established a physical site. How do these signal works relate to the Bilbao installation?

**RS**: I started the catalogue with *To Lift* because, as you say, it's directly related to surface topology, which is played out in each piece in the Bilbao installation. I included the circle in the Bronx to point to the fact that my work is often grounded in urban contexts, and in those cases I want it to be seen as an aesthetic statement in a non-aesthetic place. What runs throughout my work is the need to find a relation to realities other than those codified by art institutions. That need probably stems from my working in steel mills, realizing the potential of steel as a product of the industrial age, a product we all still depend on every day. When I show in galleries or museums I bring industrial procedures into rarefied art spaces. That's very different from showing factory-finished products. The riggers move in to erect the pieces in place. One industry is interfaced with another, the steel industry with the culture industry.

**HF**: But that's a conundrum. A steel town, Bilbao, ages out of its own industrial economy, and decides to retool with the help of a spectacular museum designed and constructed with postindustrial techniques. In this way it aims to shift to a tourist economy with the usual subsidiary service jobs. And that museum then privileges your work, which, to put it unkindly, riffs artistically on industrial materials and means that are more and more outmoded economically.

**RS**: If I had chosen to work in stainless steel, that critique—of using outmoded industrial materials and methods—wouldn't come up. Donald Judd and Ellsworth Kelly sanitized steel by eliminating any trace of the production process, creating immaculate white-glove surfaces, transforming steel into a clean pictorial surface not to be confused with an industrial prod-uct. Before them David Smith glamorized stainless steel by passing a grinder over the surface to create shimmering highlights. Jeff Koons and Anish Kapoor turned steel into bling.

Certainly I'm no longer a member of the working class, but that hasn't changed my responsibility to the production of my work and its context. When I install my work in galleries or museums I attempt to open up the situation. Since my Dia show in 1997 I've noticed a shift in the interest of the audience: more people seem willing to participate in my sculptural language. They couldn't care less about the waning of the Industrial Revolution.

**HF**: Might they be more willing in part because they too have become romantic about the industrial past? There's also your notoriety—that draws people in as well. At the same time others have come to your work because they want to figure it out, to keep abreast of it, to see how it might develop further. And that's because you've used whatever means you have— a catalogue, a lecture, an interview, conversations like these—to show people how the work is conceived and produced. Even as you challenge them, even overwhelm them, you also…

**RS**: Bring them in on it.

**HF**: Literally as part of the work, not only bodily but also…

**RS**: Intellectually. But that sounds like I'm being my own pitchman.

**HF**: Well, a lot of us are interested in your work because we feel it's a way to understand more about our experience, not yours.

**RS**: I hope my private experience isn't being imposed on them. I wouldn't want the Bilbao installation to be seen as simply the aesthetic production of an artist. I'd like any installation to be an open public space where anyone can go—particularly young people. But it can't affect anyone or anything unless the work is inventive formally. It has to be inventive formally to change one's perception, emotions, and experience.

**HF**: Speaking of young people and changed perception, isn't there a new tactility in the torqued pieces? I see kids run their fingers along the surface of the plates as they skip along; it's like a game. Adults also seem to see the surfaces less as walls and more as membranes. How does this haptic dimension affect our spatial experience of the sculptures?

**RS**: I think, as people walk through the torqued pieces, they reach out for balance more than touch.

**HF**: You think it's more cognitive than sensuous? But isn't there a desire to touch here too? This touch isn't aggressive; in fact, my students see it as erotic.

**RS**: That's because they're young! Caress the torqued pieces?

**HF**: Yes—why not?

**RS**: I do talk about the surfaces as skins. I think people have largely lost their sense of touch, and if my work reactivates that need or desire, that's fine with me. I can't deny that people like to touch the work.

**HF**: And here "skin" is not just a borrowing of nomenclature; there's a connection to sensuous architecture. Elsewhere you've mentioned the influence of Baroque architects like

Borromini on this phase of your work, especially his San Carlo alle Quattro Fontane (1665–76) in Rome.

**RS**: This is what I said to the curator Kynaston McShine in the catalogue for my 2007 retrospective at MoMA; it's the best account of my Borromini experience and its impact on the invention of the *Torqued Ellipses:* "That was probably the biggest hit in relation to a misreading of architecture that I have ever had. When I walked into the side aisle of San Carlo, I looked at the central oval of the church and was convinced that the volume was turning. I thought that the void on the ground and the overhead aperture in the ceiling were turned at an angle to each other. When I walked to the center of the room I realized that it was actually a regular oval that rose in elevation, but I was more interested in my misreading…What would happen if the void of the space turned in elevation? Could the volume rotate without changing its radius?"[1]

**HF**: So one origin of the *Ellipses* is a misperception. It's as though "the demons" called the senses, which so worried Descartes, got the better of you, but then you got the better of them, by turning their deception into your truth—I mean, by turning a spatial illusion into a sculptural reality.

Preparing for this conversation, I reread Gilles Deleuze's book on the Baroque, *The Fold*. It was translated into English in 1993, and it had an immediate effect on some architects, who took it as a pretext to explore eccentric shapes. The book also resonates with your torqued pieces, which emerged just a few years later. There is a disconnect between plan and elevation in Baroque architecture too, and Deleuze sees it as a function of "the fold," which is one of your verbs (in fact he believes the fold to be crucial to Baroque sensibility at large). Another characteristic move in the Baroque is to detach the interior from the exterior, Deleuze argues, "but in such conditions that each of the two terms thrusts the other forward." "The matter-fold is a matter-time," he insists.[2] That's cryptic, but it's suggestive in relation to your work, as is his discussion of Baroque architecture as an "operative function" of contraction and dilation, tension and release. In his account of the Baroque the object becomes an "objectile" that "assumes a place in a continuum by variation," and the subject becomes a "superject" whose perspective is not a fixed place of focus so much as a matter of "what comes to the point of view" in movement. That's a little jargonistic, but again it's provocative with respect to your sculpture as an event of continuous parallactic viewing.

**RS**: That's well put.

**HF**: Deleuze is helpful on the disconnect in the torqued pieces between plan and elevation and inside and outside. But, again, how did you get there from your earlier insistence that work be transparent not only in its production but also in its structure?

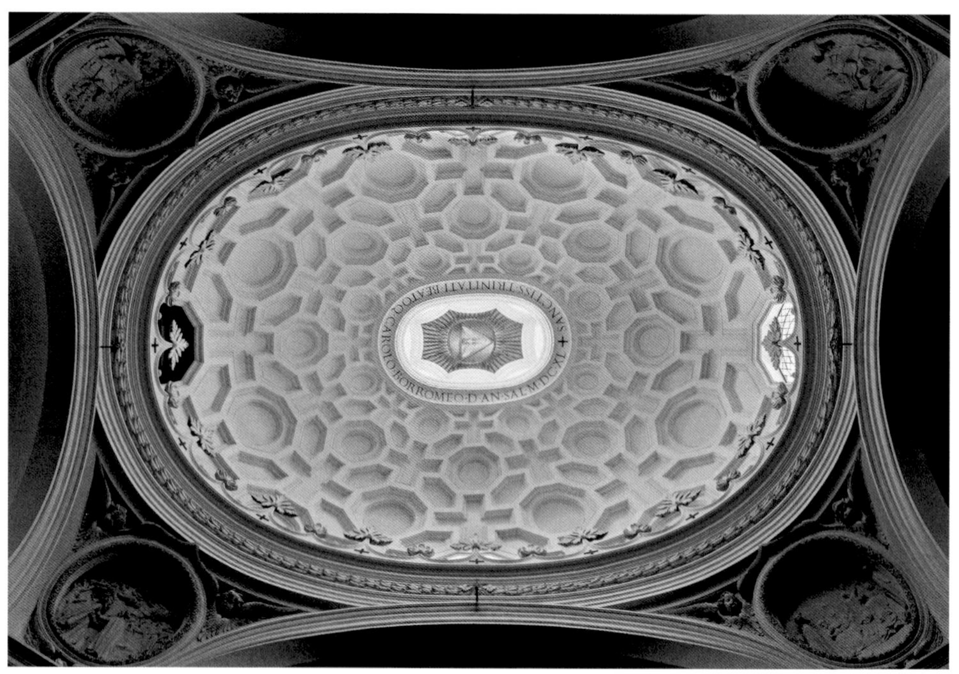

Francesco Borromini, dome of the Church of San Carlo alle Quattro Fontane, 1638–46. San Carolino, Rome.

**RS**: By experimentation. Once I discovered that the tops and the bottoms of the plates move at different rates, implicating you as you walk forward through them, I wanted to pursue the full range of that effect.

**HF**: So it was a complication of the old value of transparency, not a reversal of it?

**RS**: Yes, it was a consequence. Transparency can become a principled kind of constriction, but I got beyond it through an analysis of structure.

**HF**: One more question inspired by Deleuze. "The Baroque world is organized along two vectors," he argues, "a deepening toward the bottom, and a thrust toward the upper regions."[3] The torqued pieces are still very weighty—they still "deepen toward the bottom"—but some also seem almost weightless, at least in places, and often they thrust upward too. Was this weightlessness a new effect?

**RS**: The weightlessness wasn't anticipated.

**HF**: In the Baroque the thrust upward is about the soul aspiring to the divine. What does that effect signify in a sculpture like yours that is adamantly secular?

**RS**: Looking upward or skyward doesn't correlate with aspiring to the divine. It's just another experience of space.

**HF**: Is this distinction between weight and weightlessness a way to typologize your work, with some pieces, some periods, favoring one effect, and others the opposite? Or do the two experiences call out for each other within the same sculpture or body of work? Part of the great pleasure of the torqued pieces—and again I wonder if it's not somehow erotic—is that the two effects or affects are held in tension there.

**RS**: Yes, but that tension can produce a kind of schizophrenia in the work. On the one hand, recent pieces, the forged ones, have favored weight. On the other hand, I've also extended the more weightless path of the torqued pieces, especially as they mutated into sculptures like *Inside Out* (2013). That piece has multiple passages. You can go in and come back, go in and come back: you're forced to make decisions.

**HF**: Let's take up that proposition next.

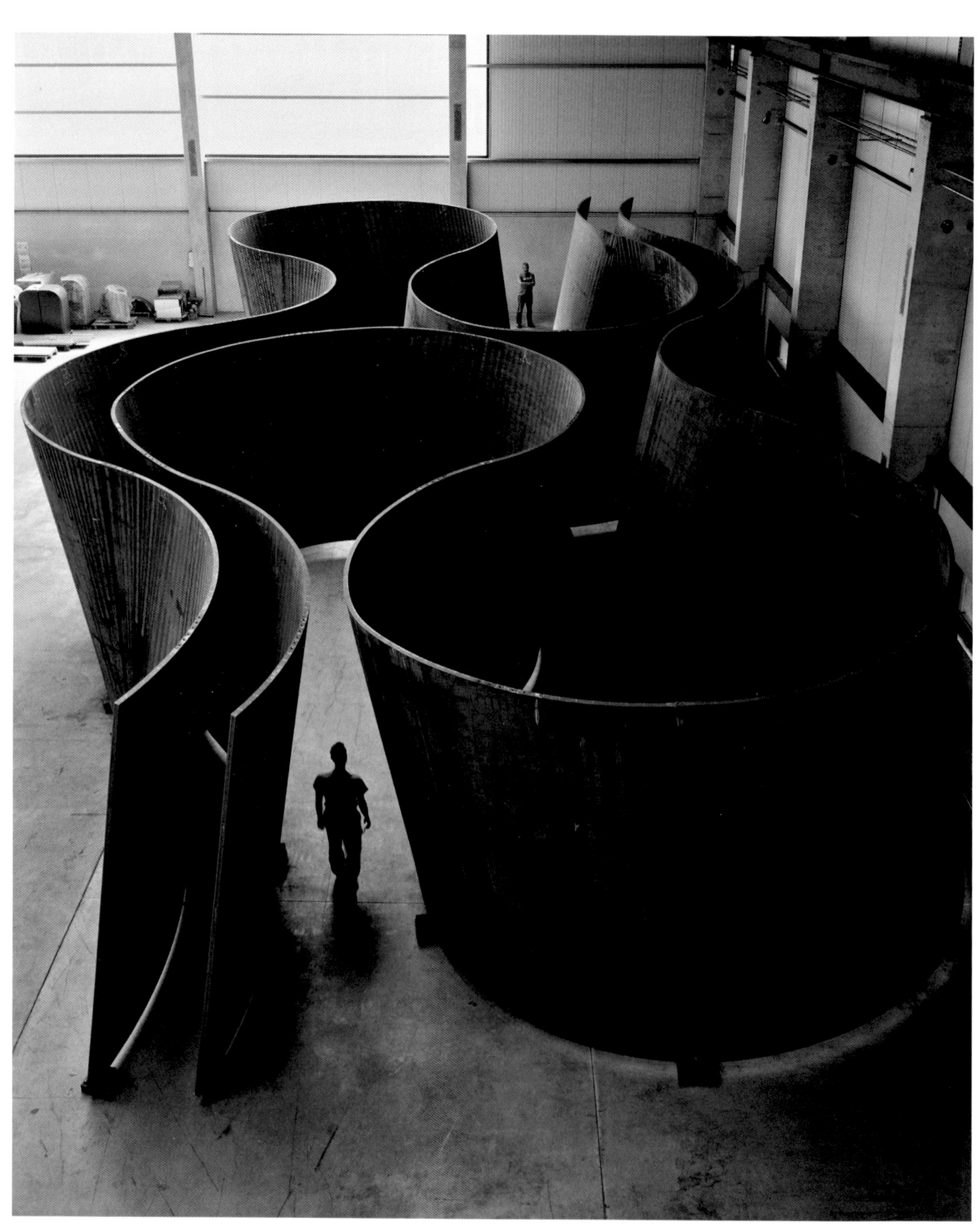

*Inside Out*, 2013. Weatherproof steel, 13 ft. 2 in. × 80 ft. 9 in. × 40 ft. 2 ½ in.
(4 × 24.6 × 12.3 m), plates 2 in. (5 cm). Private Collection.

# Passages and Intervals

**HF**: The Bilbao installation is an overview of a specific language you developed in the torqued pieces, but it's also a proposition about different relations between objects and passages you've elaborated since.

**RS**: In the paths created by the *Ellipses* and *Spirals* the viewer is directed, whereas the passageways in subsequent pieces give you a choice, often more than one. For example, *Inside Out* (2013) has four entrances that are also exits, and you have to choose between multiple directions. Without entering and exiting several times you won't experience the entirety of the work.

**HF**: That's already the effect of the final pieces included in your 2007 retrospective at the Museum of Modern Art.

**RS**: Yes, it's true of *Sequence* (2006) and *Band* (2006), but also of *Open Ended* (2007–8), which wasn't at MoMA.

**HF**: They were the most radical in your disconnection of inside and outside, elevation and plan. Did you reach a limit on that score?

**RS**: No. I stretched it further by focusing on more complex circulations in which the path is driving the void, giving you more options. When you exit *Open Ended,* for instance, you don't know where you are in the room. About halfway through the piece there's a turn, a reversal that disrupts your sense of direction. You have to recalibrate in relation to where you were inside the piece. Yet *Open Ended* isn't a maze; in plan it's quite simple. But it's almost impossible to reconstruct the configuration after you've walked it.

**HF**: Why aim for such extreme disorientation?

**RS**: Being lost throws you back on yourself in terms of anticipation, if not anxiety. That doesn't reflect on how anxiety impinges on your life exactly, but it does force you to deal with decision-making. Decision-making in architectural and urban spaces is almost always prescribed by a given direction. Decision-making in my sculptures brings you to that moment in a pure state—to the here and now where you have to make a choice.

**HF**: Might that help us meet those moments in life more effectively?

**RS**: That's not an assumption I'd make, but sculptures like *Open Ended* might foster awareness of decisions as you're walking. Again, you're not in a situation where there's no way out; it's not a trap. The sculpture offers you a choice of routes, like a roundabout on a highway minus the signage.

**HF**: With the development of GPS technology, it's difficult to get lost. We don't have to navigate much in our lives anymore; our phones tell us where to go, and others can track

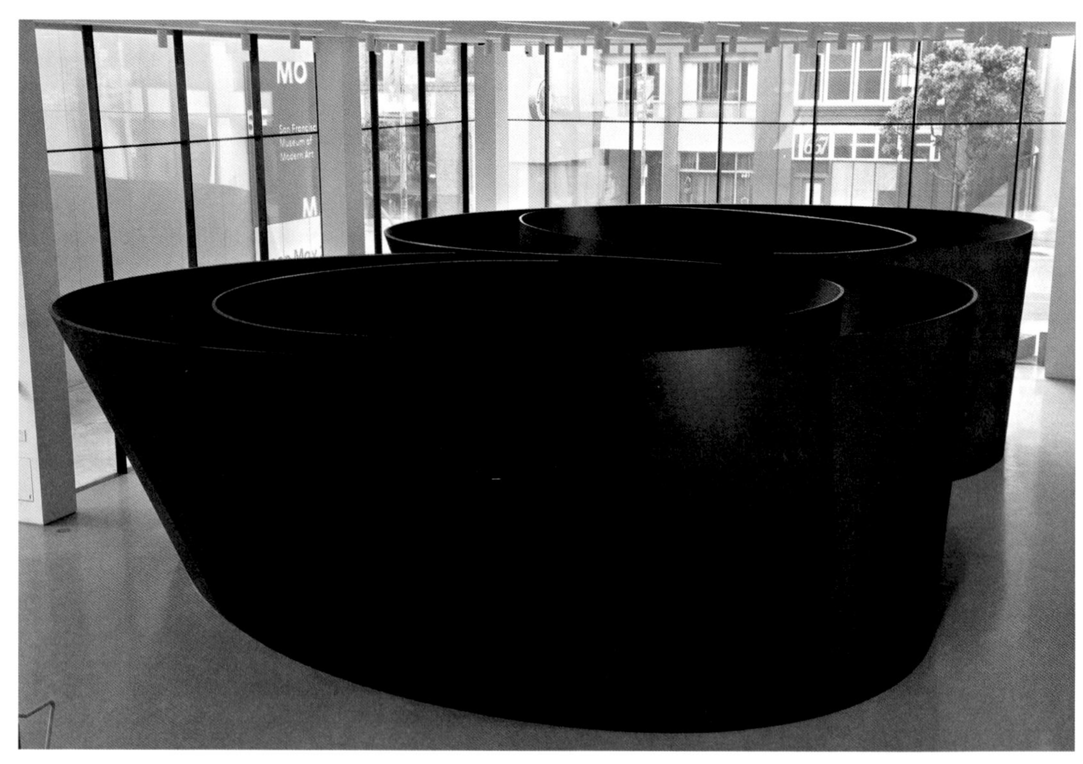


*Sequence*, 2006. Weatherproof steel, 12 ft. 9 in. × 40 ft. 8 in. × 65 ft. 2 in. (3.9 × 12.4 × 19.9 m), plates 2 in. (5 cm). The Doris and Donald Fisher Collection at the San Francisco Museum of Modern Art.

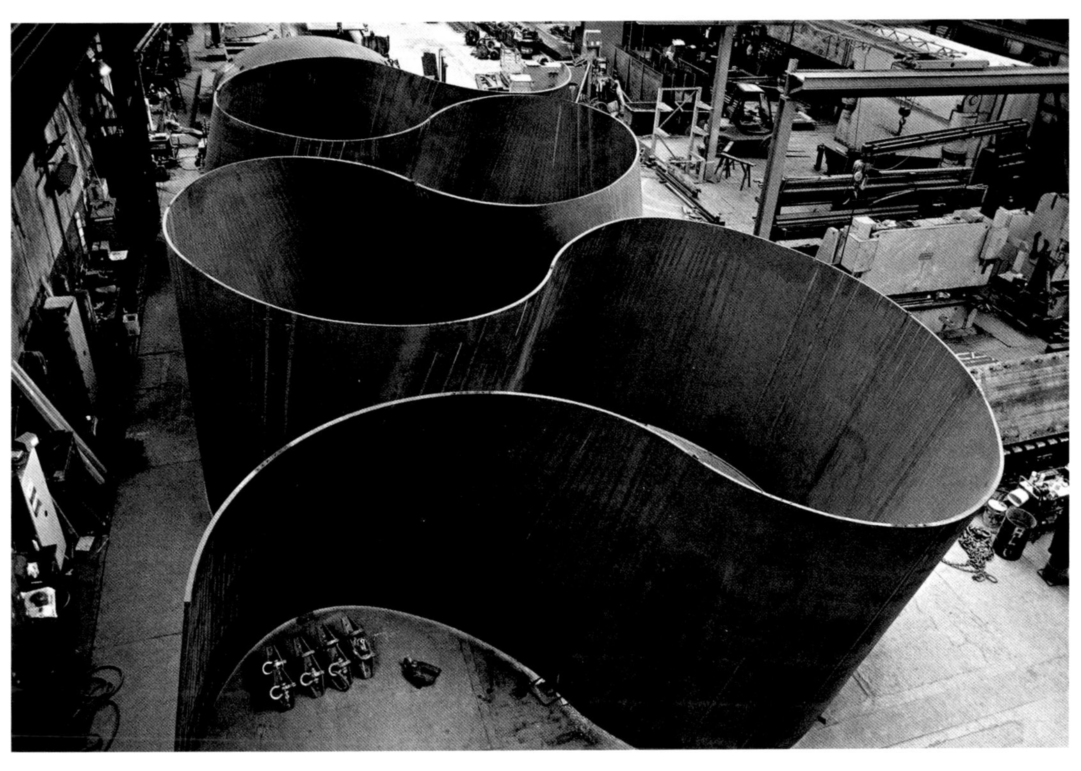

*Band*, 2006. Weatherproof steel, 12 ft. 9 in. × 36 ft. 5 in. × 71 ft. 9 ½ in. (3.9 × 11.1 × 21.9 m), plates 2 in. (5 cm).
Los Angeles County Museum of Art, California. Purchased with funds provided by Eli and Edythe L. Broad.

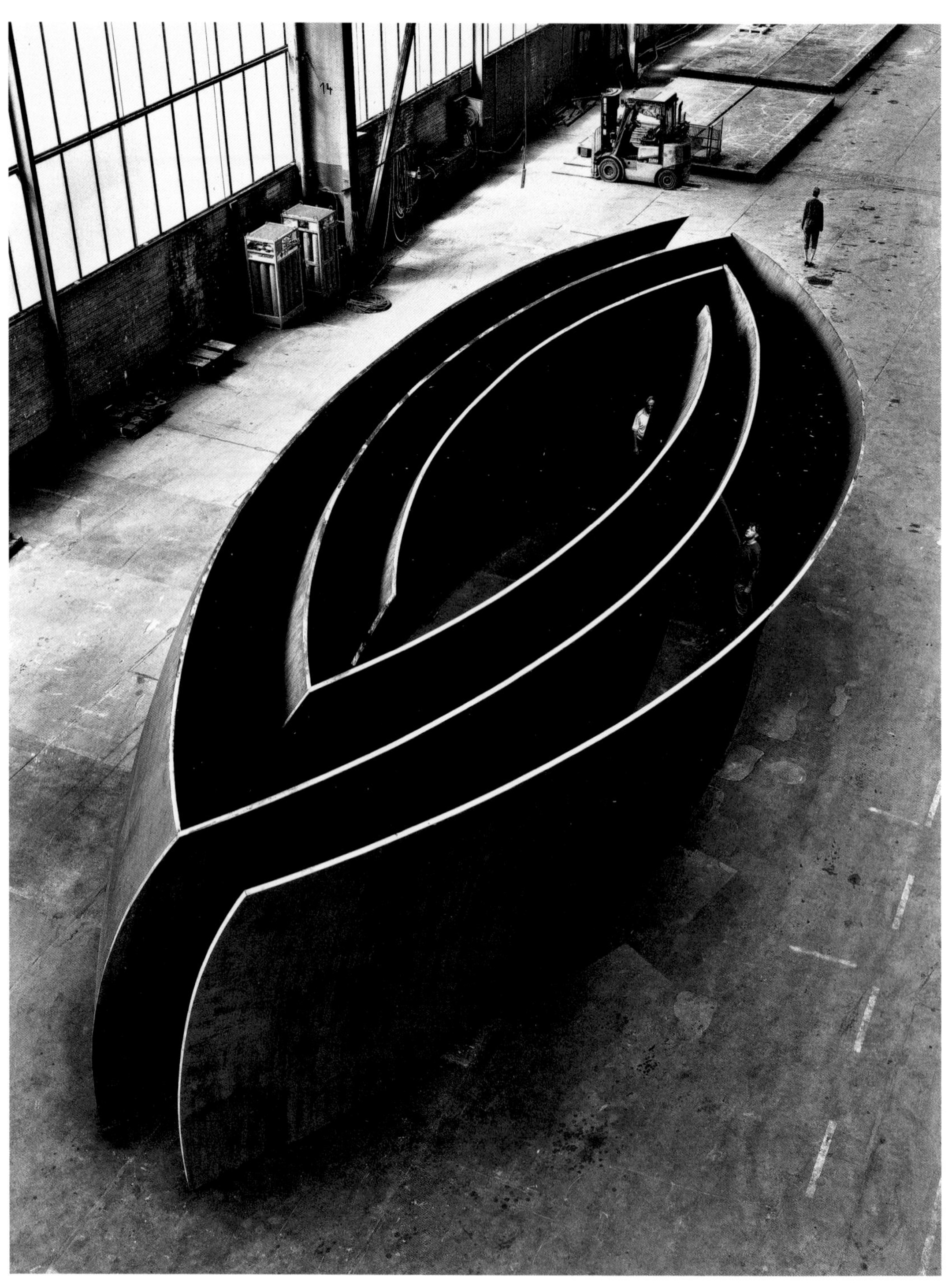

*Open Ended,* 2007–8. Weatherproof steel, three torus sections and three spherical sections,
12 ft. 5 ½ in. × 59 ft. 9 ½ in. × 24 ft. 2 ¼ in. (3.8 × 18.2 × 7.4 m) overall, plates 2 in. (5 cm).
Museum Voorlinden, Wassenaar, The Netherlands.

us too. Arguably this has resulted in a de-skilling in planning, mapping, wayfinding—
in basic techniques of negotiating space and time.

**RS**: You're directed to your location, but the GPS doesn't engage you with outside realities.
In fact using these apps takes away from social intercourse like asking another pedestrian
or driver for directions.

**HF**: What about recent pieces that don't develop from the torqued ones, and which do
mark out space clearly?

**RS**: The tower constructions made with flat plates continue a series that started with
*Sight Point* (1972–75) in Amsterdam. Think of 7 (2011), located outside the Museum of
Islamic Art in Doha, Qatar. It's almost eighty feet high and consists of seven plates eight
feet wide and four inches thick; it has three triangular openings into a ten-foot space on the
ground that narrows to a nine-foot opening at the top that frames the sky. The shaft of 7
has a quick upward thrust, and its volume is more extreme than any of my other towers.

**HF**: *Promenade* (2008), your piece of five plates fifty-six feet high positioned down the
long axis of the Grand Palais in Paris, was closely connected to its site, to the industrial
structure and immense space of that building.

**RS**: 7 engages the architectural history of a very different context. What comes to mind
with a structure that's high and narrow but still can be entered?

**HF**: Well, various towers with military and civic functions, but some with religious ones.
I assume the primary association here is the minaret.

**RS**: Yes. I looked at minarets from Spain and Tunisia to Yemen. But 7 also has a civic
function; it's a place of gathering as well as contemplation.

**HF**: You aim to play on all those associations but in an abstract way?

**RS**: Yes. To designate a place with a tight space of great height is to collect and to ground
the site. You can see 7 from a great distance; it's a point of destination.

**HF**: How do you respond to criticism that such pieces are too monumental? This struck
me in relation to *Promenade* in particular: for some people it was a piece about looking,
strolling, and gathering, informally and freely, but others saw it as overbearing.

**RS**: Overbearing? That's not my sense of how people experienced *Promenade*. I understood
it to be exactly the opposite. Take a piece like *Vortex* (2002) in Fort Worth: it's sixty-eight
feet high, but people hang out there all the time. Kids are often the first to explore a
new work, and I don't think they're overwhelmed by monumentality. One of the reasons

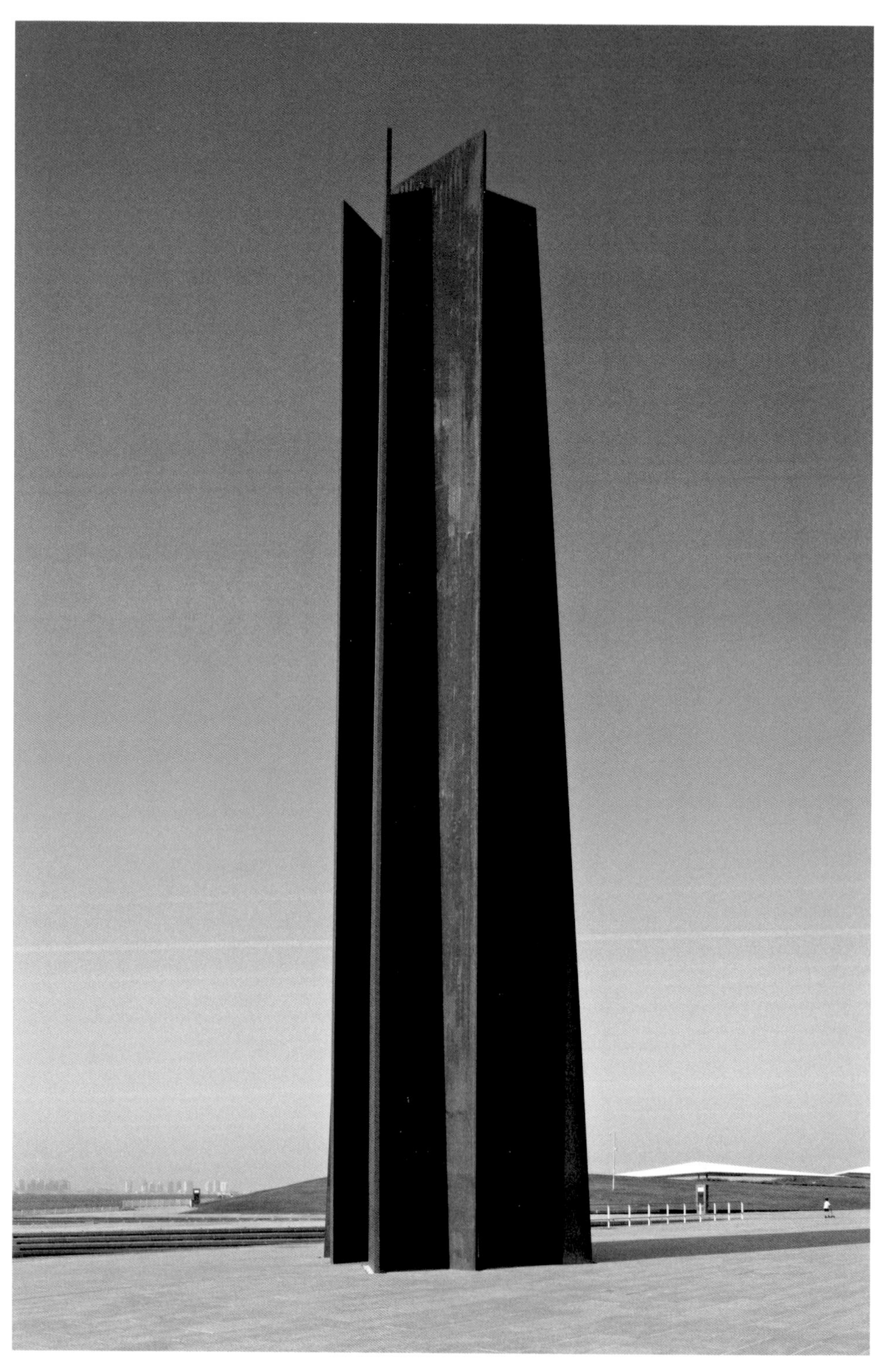

7, 2011. Weatherproof steel, seven plates, each 80 ft. × 8 ft. × 4 in. (24.4 m × 2.4 m × 10.2 cm); 80 × 10 × 10 ft. (24.4 × 3.1 × 3.1 m) overall. Collection Qatar Museums Authority, Doha.

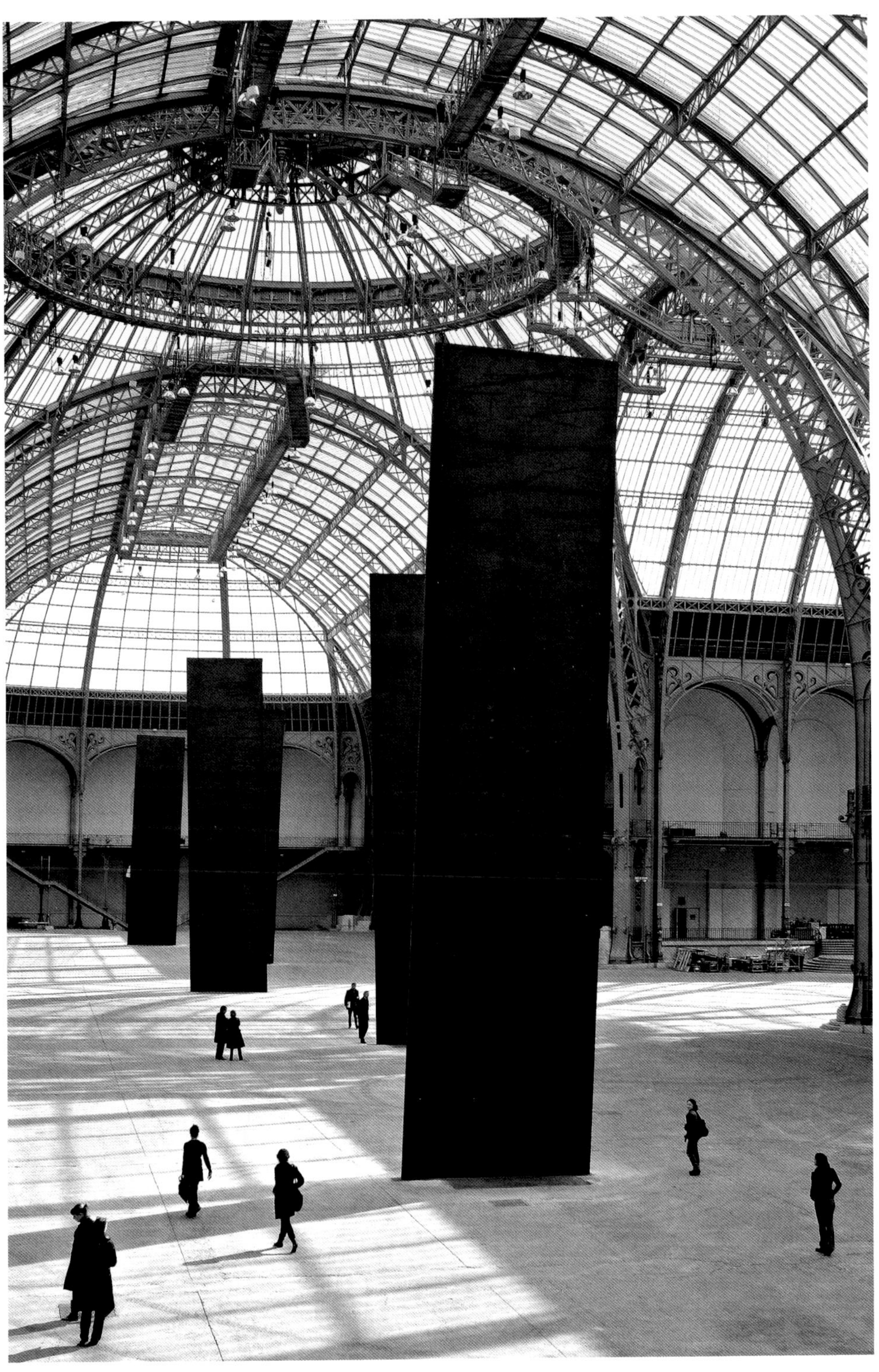

*Promenade*, 2008. Weatherproof steel, five plates, each 55 ft. 9 ¼ in. × 13 ft. 1 ½ in. × 5 in.
(17 m × 4 m × 13 cm). Temporary installation in the Grand Palais, Paris, 2008.

I became interested in the dislocation of paths is to create a more complex matrix for the viewer.

**HF**: I like the notion that the recent work invites us to consider, in a different register, the disorientations we experience in everyday life—not to cope with them exactly, but to see them differently somehow, to play with them even. You don't disorient for the sake of disorientation.

**RS**: No. You have to make choices; you have to decide constantly which direction to take.

**HF**: Do you see pieces like *Promenade* as a synthesis of the vertical pieces and the horizontal pieces?

**RS**: Not consciously. Works like *Junction* (2011), *Cycle* (2011), and *Inside Out* are an extension of *Sequence* and *Band;* they're not as open and transparent as *Promenade.* They deal with curved paths and the circulation they create.

**HF**: 7 looks back to *Sight Point,* as you say, which is a fundamental form in your language. The recent towers seem to pull back from the fast temporalities that the torqued pieces project.

**RS**: No, there are some recent pieces that are even more involved with the speed of the skin.

**HF**: But *Promenade* did call a halt, if only for a time, to the speedy skins of the torqued pieces.

**RS**: The site was very suggestive. The Grand Palais has a powerful central axis, and I wanted to use it to contain the space, to declare the entire space in its measure.

**HF**: How do you decide what new part of your language to push, and what old part to reintroduce?

**RS**: Sequences are open and can be revisited. Depending on the contingencies of a site, a type can be made more abstract, more consequential.

**HF**: Can two types intersect, or are they always discrete?

**RS**: I haven't found a way to bring them together, unless you see the torquing of the vertical plates in towers like *Vortex* or *Connector* (2006) as a combining of two conceptual principles.

**HF**: The art historian Alois Riegl proposed a double spiral as a model of artistic development, the idea being that as an artist delves into the history of his or her work to recover an old type, he or she also pushes it onward and upward, elaborating the type in new ways in the different circumstances of the present.

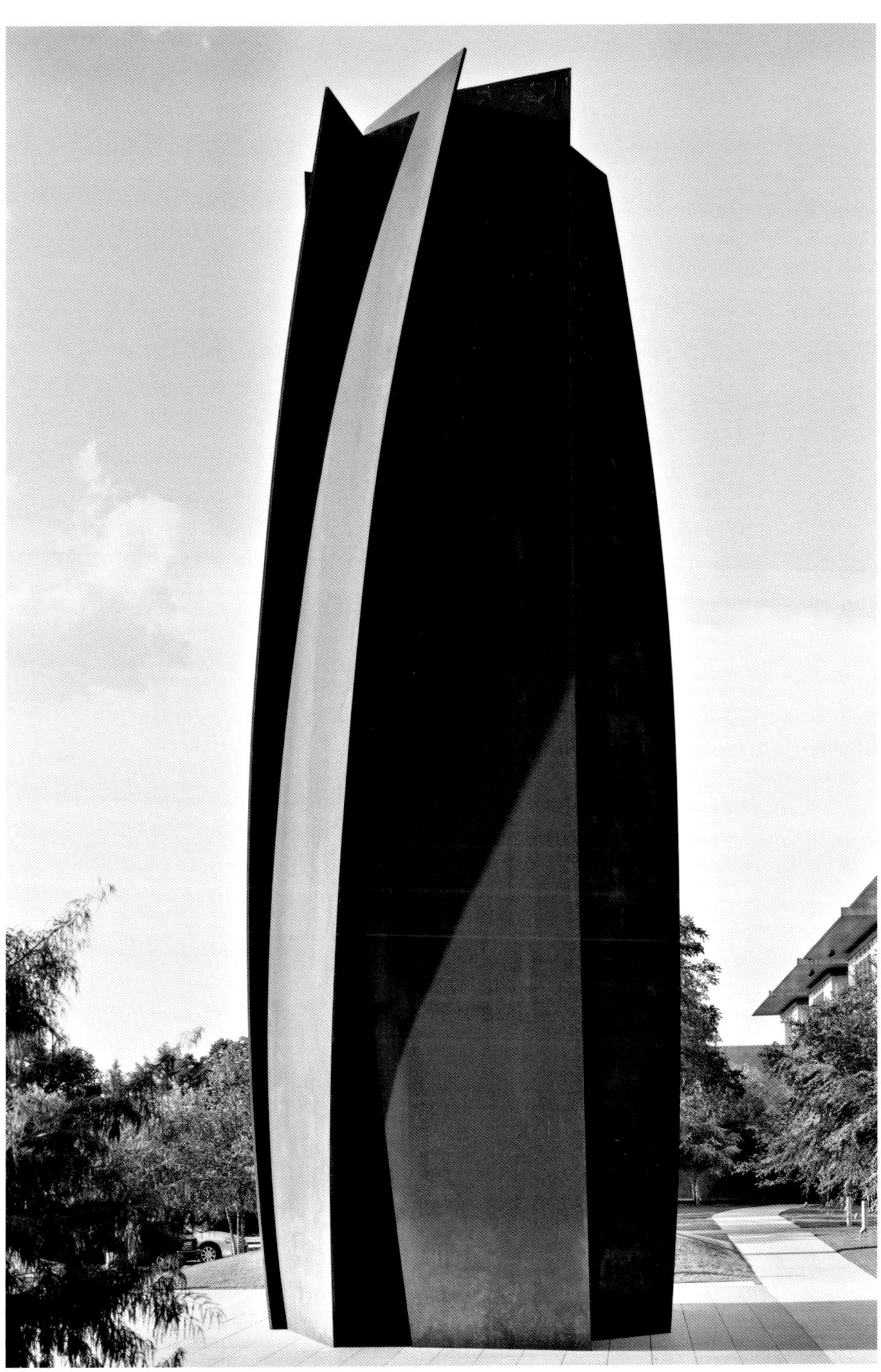

*Vortex*, 2002. Weatherproof steel, seven torqued plates, 67 ft. 9 in. × 11 ft. (20.7 m × 335 cm),
67 ft. 9 in. × 11 ft. 1 in. (20.7 m × 338 cm), 67 ft. 9 in. × 11 ft. 6 in. (20.7 m × 351 cm), 67 ft. 9 in. × 11 ft. 2 in.
(20.7 m × 340 cm), 67 ft. 4 in. × 11 ft. 5 in. (20.5 m × 348 cm), 67 ft. 9 in. × 10 ft. 9 in. (20.7 m × 328 cm),
67 ft. 1 in. × 10 ft. (20.5 m × 305 cm), plates 2 ¼ in. (5.7 cm) thick. The Modern Art Museum of Fort Worth,
Texas. Gift of the Burnett Foundation in honor of Michael Auping.

**RS**: Brancusi did that constantly. So did Picasso, and so does Johns.

**HF**: Do you feel an affinity with that process?

**RS**: No. They saw their work as cumulative, and I don't see my work that way.

**HF**: How do you see it then?

**RS**: It develops mostly by diverging. At times, though, I do go back to points where the work seems to split.

**HF**: What do you see as the main thrust of the recent work?

**RS**: In pieces like *Inside Out* and *Junction* (2011) you have multiple choices—let's call them intervals. With earlier pieces you enter and exit, and there's no real decision to make; your footfalls are propelled by where the path takes you. *Junction* is probably the first example of a curved piece where you arrive at an interval, a point of decision. I'm interested in what that means. Architecture is required to make connections between spaces, which sculpture can forgo or at least suspend. That suspension happens at the interval: it's a break that connects. In architecture you're directed through connections in a way that's predicated on utility. That's the exact opposite of the interval in my recent work; there's no function, only decision. The interval breaks your cadence. How you perceive depends on how you walk; if you change direction, your perception changes. If you have to make a choice about direction, it becomes a thought.

**HF**: An interval is a moment of arrest, then, whereas the passage pieces keep you moving.

**RS**: The arrest is heightened by anxiety, by not knowing which choice to make. Neither *Sequence* nor *Band* has intervals in that sense.

**HF**: Are its effects different from the disorientation we just discussed?

**RS**: You're still being projected forward, and the curves are opening or closing and leaning to the right or to the left. That remains much the same.

**HF**: You've used the phrase "thinking on your feet" to evoke how your sculpture connects and complicates our moving, perceiving, and processing.[1] Is this a new aspect of such thinking?

**RS**: Yes, and it's more complex.

**HF**: Are navigational skills sharpened or appreciated differently somehow? How does the experience of these sculptures relate to everyday spatial experience?

**RS**: Walking down the street or rushing to the subway you often experience a momentary lapse, and you feel lost. Usually people aren't conscious of those moments. The intervals make you aware of them. You realize the lapse isn't simply a blind spot but a moment that asks for a decision. In any case, it brings you back to yourself, to the reality of the moment. The interval breaks your stride, which gives you pause to reflect back or to think ahead.

**HF**: Is there any relation to the interval in temporal arts—in music, say?

**RS**: In music the interval is the space between two tones sounded simultaneously or successively. Steve Reich's music elaborates on that space. That's different.

**HF**: Is this thinking on your feet more in your head or more in your body?

**RS**: It's the rhythm in your body first and the reflection in your head second. I'm not sure how a reflex reaction becomes cognitive.

**HF**: But if it's about decision, it must be cognitive. Maybe the interval is when the cognitive cuts into the perceptual, reflecting on it.

**RS**: That sounds right. The interval is a pause, a brief moment in which you stop to think or act. But it's not a centering moment; there's still no center in these pieces. That's another thing that distinguishes them from most architectural spaces.

**HF**: The interval is an epistemological moment. Most architecture, most urbanism, wants to avoid such moments because they provoke uncertainty, even anxiety. But the result is that they often become "dictatorial" in their directionality, as Walter Benjamin once suggested.[2]

**RS**: Yes, architecture is purposely directional: Go here, go there, walk upstairs, walk downstairs, turn left, turn right, stop, go, no exit.

**HF**: Is there any precedent in your work for this interest in the interval?

**RS**: Elevational pieces like *Interval* (2011), *Ramble* (2014), and *Every Which Way* (2015) have their origin in *Pulitzer Piece* (1970–71), which cuts into the landscape with elevations. *Interval* is involved with the elevation of the plane in relationship to eye level. As the plates open up laterally and shift vertically, you're asked to move across, ahead, and up and down. That effect recurs in *Ramble,* where the clusters of plates are so dense you can get lost. In *Every Which Way* the interval is reinforced by vertical plates that rise several feet above eye level and slow down or even stop your movement, and may cause you to turn sideways or even back.

**HF**: In the 2010s you also developed more sculptures with passages and intervals. How do they differ from previous ones?

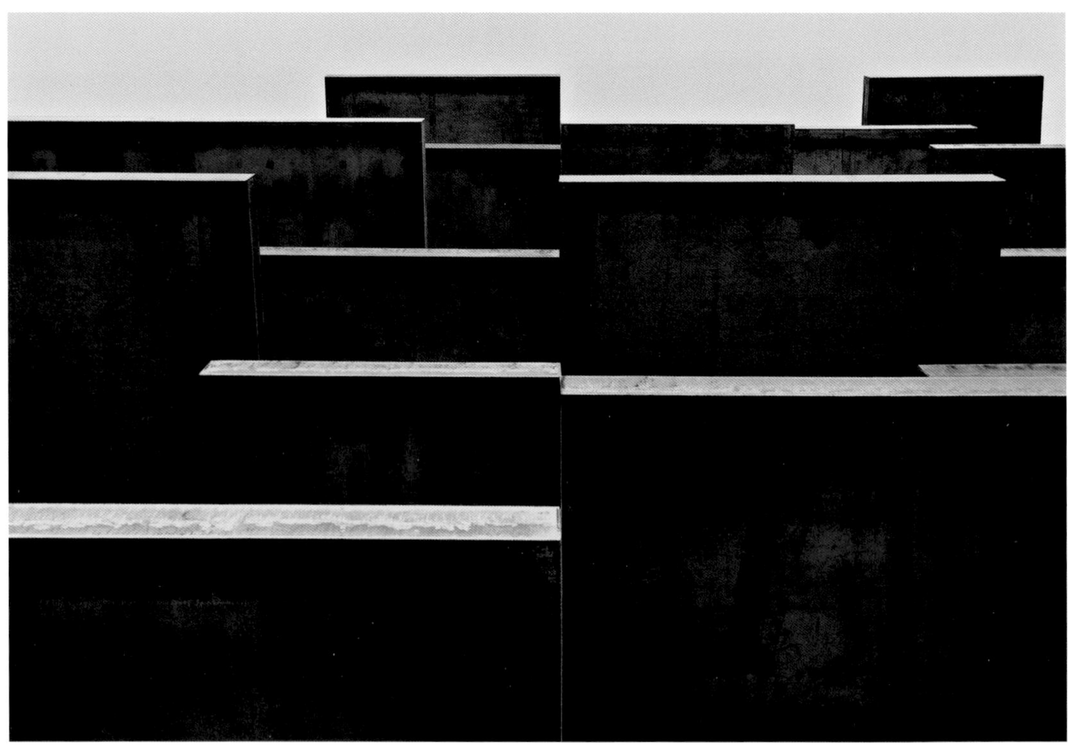

*Ramble,* 2014. Weatherproof steel, twenty-four slabs, two of each: 60 in. × 6 ft. × 9 in.
(152.4 cm × 1.8 m × 22.9 cm), 66 in. × 6 ft. × 9 in. (167.6 cm × 1.8 m × 22.9 cm), 6 ft. × 6 ft. × 9 in.
(1.8 m × 1.8 m × 22.9 cm), 60 in. × 8 ft. 8 in.× 9 in. (152.4 cm × 2.4 m × 22.9 cm), 66 in. × 8 ft. 8 in. × 9 in.
(167.6 cm × 2.4 m × 22.9 cm), 6 ft. × 8 ft. 8 in. × 9 in. (1.8 m × 2.4 m × 22.9 cm), 60 in. × 10 ft. × 9 in.
(152.4 cm × 3 m × 22.9 cm), 66 in. × 10 ft. × 9 in. (167.6 cm × 3 m × 22.9 cm), 6 ft. × 10 ft. × 9 in.
(1.8 m × 3 m × 22.9 cm), 60 in. × 12 ft. × 9 in. (152.4 cm × 3.6 m × 22.9 cm), 66 in. × 12 ft. × 9 in.
(167.6 × 3.6 m × 22.9 cm), 6 ft. × 12 ft. × 9 in. (1.8 m × 3.6 m × 22.9 cm); 6 ft. × 39 ft. 3 in. × 31 ft. 6 in.
(1.8 × 12 × 9.6 m) overall.

**RS**: They present other propositions, each in a self-contained way. For example, the recent curved pieces with pathways are different in kind from earlier ones. In *NJ-1* (2015) and *NJ-2* (2016) I used straight plates in combination with curved plates to create interior pathways. In order to free-stand, the straight plates bend into an acute curvature at one end, like a fish hook.

**HF**: The apparent simplicity of *Through* (2015) also seems new.

**RS**: Yes. I've never made a work where you're invited both to peer down an axis through a narrow gap, which lengthens the distance perceptually, and to walk through an adjacent space of the same length but with a greater width, which compresses both the space and the distance. There's a dichotomy within the work: the same length appears different in viewing than it does in walking. It's the difference between looking down a tight sightline and walking through an open space.

**HF**: In *Through,* the width of the two plates on the one side is the same as the open space that you walk through on the other side, right?

**RS**: Yes. I don't believe that proposition has been considered in sculpture before.

**HF**: The same width and length articulated in very different ways?

**RS**: Yes, looking through a tight sightline and walking through an open space in one contained work. I can point to similar things in architecture, but not as an intention, only as an effect you catch out of the corner of your eye. In the model-making stage I started with two parallel wood plates; the plates were thick and freestanding but didn't do much. It wasn't until I put up the third plate that I realized it added another dimension that's purely visual.

**HF**: There's not a corridor piece in the 1960s or '70s, by you or someone else, that approximates this effect?

**RS**: I don't believe so. The space you're looking through is only six inches wide—you know you can't enter it. And the enormous weight of the plates adds to the sense of constriction.

**HF**: There's a physical disturbance that becomes a psychological agitation, a little like some corridors by Robert Morris or Bruce Nauman. It also made me think about the old tension in Minimalism between the ideal form one knows—a cube, say—and the actual thing one perceives, and how one grapples with that contradiction.

**RS**: You mean you know it conceptually, but that knowledge is overturned perceptually, because the object is actually different from what you project?

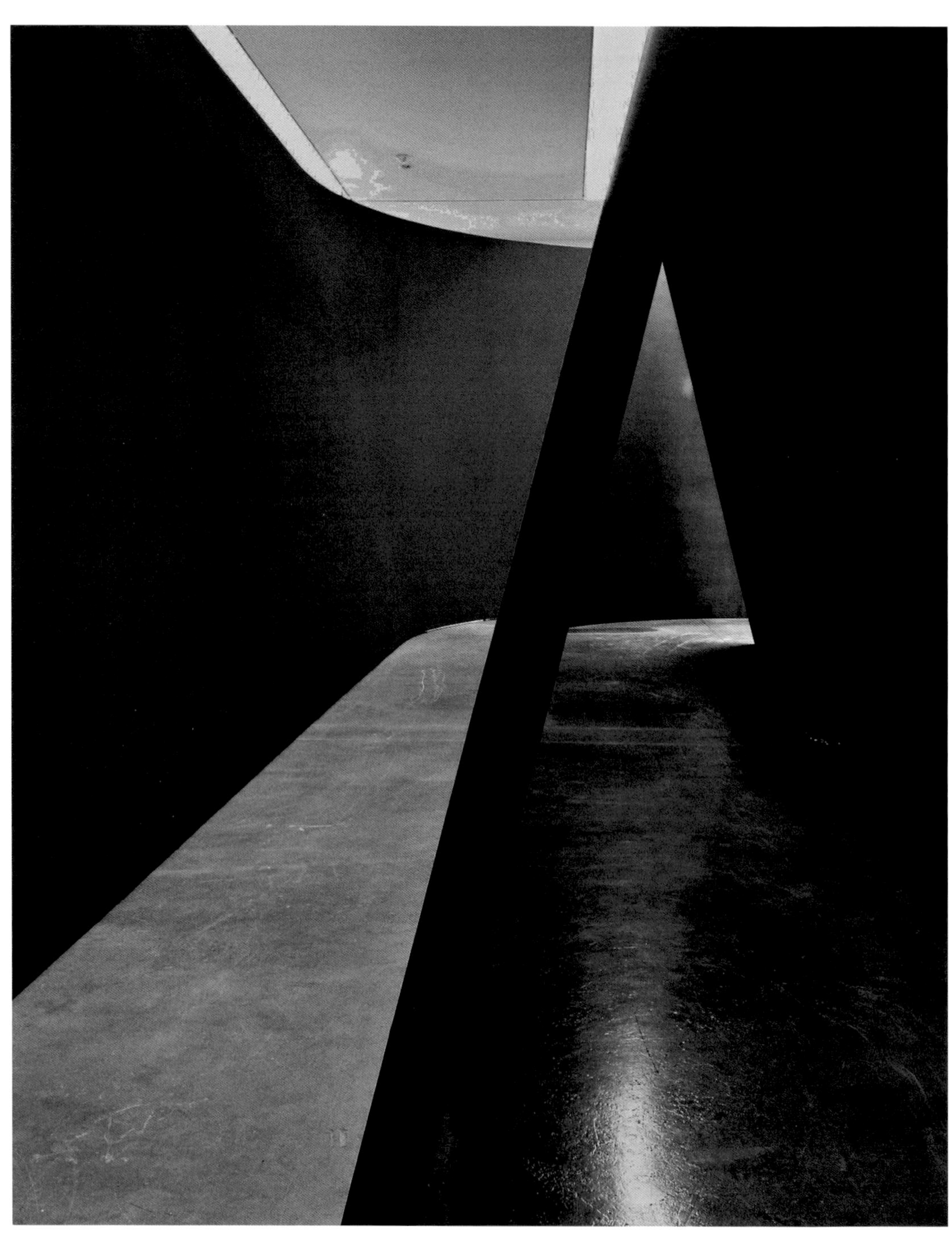

*NJ-1*, 2015. Weatherproof steel, six plates, 13 ft. 9 in. × 51 ft. 6 in. × 24 ft. 6 in.
(4.2 × 15.7 × 7.5 m) overall, plates 2 in. (5 cm). Private Collection.

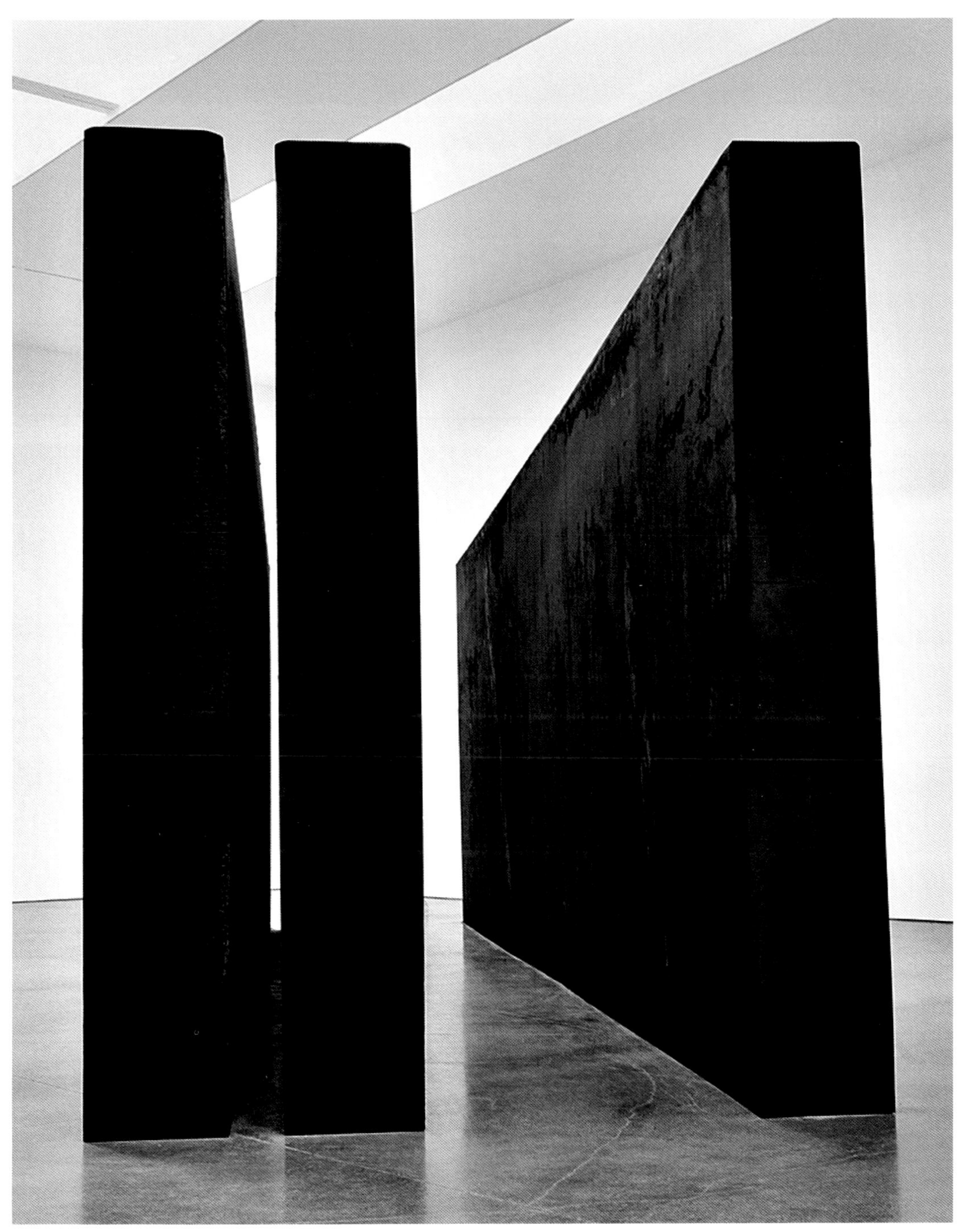

*Through*, 2015. Forged steel, three slabs, each 9 ft. 2 ¼ in. × 29 ft. 6 ½ in. × 16 in. (2.8 m × 9 m × 41.3 cm); overall 9 ft. 2 ¼ in. × 29 ft. 6 ½ in. × 92 ¼ in. (2.8 m × 9 m × 234.3 cm). AMA Collection, France.

**HF**: Yes. For me *Through* reclaims that fundamental tension in your early work—in *House of Cards,* say—but in a different frame. There's the sense of an optical puzzle.

**RS**: If you view all perception as optical, I'll grant the point, but I'm not dealing with the opticality of Minimalism, much less of light-and-space art. *Through* doesn't enter into the kind of illusionism that occurs in Judd's reliefs or Flavin's lights. It doesn't reference the illusionism of painting. It also doesn't fall into the category of an object, which is where most Minimalism remains.

**HF**: I agree. The optical puzzle lies in the fact that you know the two plates in *Through* make a width that is equal to the width opened up by the third plate, but you don't perceive it as such.

**RS**: To me that's more structural than optical.

**HF**: It's both. Take your steel prop pieces called *Counterweights* (2013), where two plates of the same size support each other against a wall. In one piece the long side of the plates is on the horizontal, while in the other it's on the vertical. The optical puzzle is that you know the elements are the same forms but you don't perceive them as such. And then in *Through,* as you say, when you look through the narrow space it seems longer than the space you can walk through.

**Clara Weyergraf-Serra**: There's another optical discrepancy. The outer plate, which frames the space you can walk through, is foreshortened: it looks shorter than the plates to the left.

**RS**: The sightline down the six-inch aperture points directly into the corner of the room, which enforces a perspectival reading of the space and pulls the architecture into the sculpture.

**HF**: It reminded me of *Strike* (1969–71) in that regard. Also, as in *Strike,* you know the plate is a rectangle, but as you walk around, its shape seems to change.

**RS**: If there's a forerunner of *Through* it's *Strike.* When you stand in front of *Through* it reduces itself to a long line that runs into a corner just like *Strike.*

**HF**: There was another piece in your 2016 show that struck me, *Above Below Betwixt Between* (2016), where you put a simple grid of large black and white rectangles on each wall of a tight room, one inverted in relation to the next. Weirdly, I felt my body most intensely in this space. That's because the space was compressive, and you were made very aware of the walls behind you and at your sides as you looked at the one in front of you.

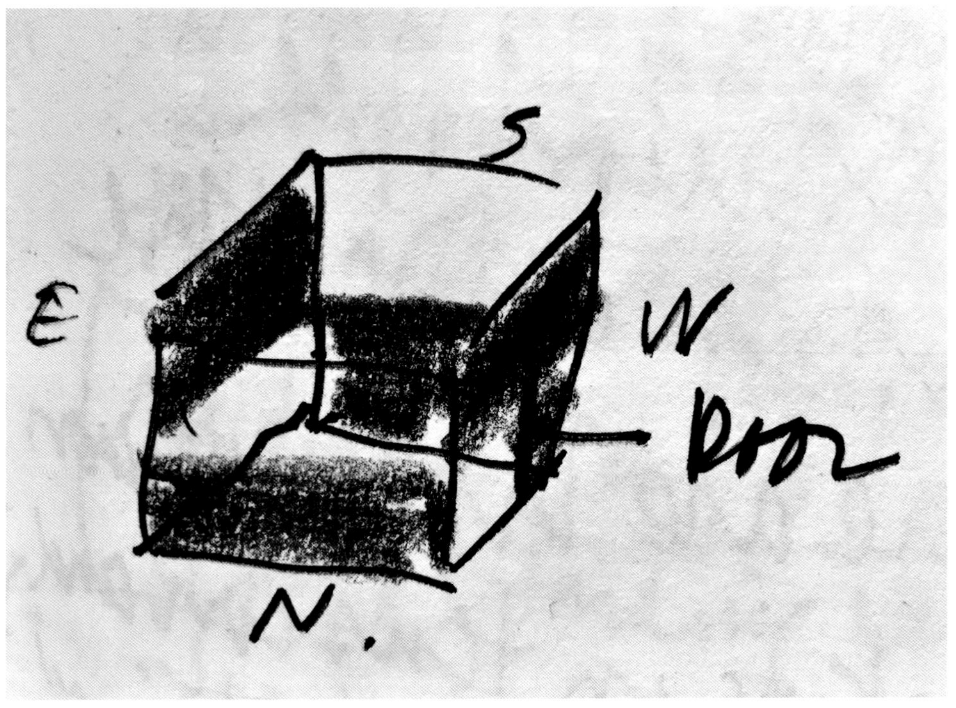

Drawing of *Above Below Betwixt Between,* 2016. Paint stick on handmade Belgian linen, two parts from the ground up, each 9 ft. × 18 ft. 10 in. (2.7 × 5.7 m), two parts from the ceiling down, each 9 ft. × 18 ft. 6 in. (2.7 × 5.6 m).

**RS**: The unexpected effect was that the whiteness of the wall rectangles not covered with black canvas made you rotate your body in the room. That created a strong sense of disequilibrium; you wouldn't think that would happen given the grid structure.

**CW-S**: You kept turning because you wanted to find your center of gravity but couldn't.

**HF**: And because, if you didn't keep turning, the pressure of what was behind you became too intense.

**RS**: And as you turned, you lost the coordinates of which wall you were just looking at. You looked at one wall, then you turned and looked at another wall, and when you turned back you weren't certain as to which wall you were looking at. The dynamics of movement that the installation engendered couldn't be anticipated or organized into an image.

**HF**: It reminded me of El Lissitzky's *Design for an Abstract Cabinet* (1927–28), which also aimed to animate, if not disrupt, the viewer. It was extraordinary to exit *Above Below Betwixt Between* and to enter *Every Which Way,* your arrangement of sixteen steel slabs, because suddenly you were very grounded again—not only by the explicit order of the plates but also by the implicit axis of 11th Avenue, by the grid of Manhattan outside.

**RS**: I was disheartened that some people just walked from one end of *Every Which Way* to the other without taking the time to turn to the right or the left, let alone turn around to look back. If you do look back, what is behind you and what is in front of you are entirely different in terms of elevations.

**HF**: I think the piece asks you to turn again and again as you walk.

**RS**: In *Every Which Way* you confront the frontality of each cluster of plates first, and then turn depending on how much attention you pay. You're led to make a horizontal shift instead of just walking diagonally or straight ahead. Turning around, walking backward, sliding across—that happens a lot in the recent work. Also, due to its verticality—five of the sixteen slabs are eleven feet high—*Every Which Way* has more of an architectural reference than prior pieces.

**HF**: For me it's also urban in the sense that it asks you, as a city does, to look "every which way." I think it was Sartre who said of New York that, even when you're in the midst of it, deep in its caverns, the city seems to be somewhere else, over there somewhere.

**RS**: That's true about *Every Which Way:* it's always there, not here. Even when you're right up against it, it always evades you.

**HF**: That also touches on a basic principle of phenomenology, at least in Merleau-Ponty, who thought that what allows us to see is what lies behind us—that is, what we can never properly see. Even more radically, he held that our ability to see, our cone of vision, emerges out of an invisibility, the opacity of our own bodies.

**RS**: That's very smart. Like the city, *Every Which Way* forces you to make countersteps, twists, and turns continuously. In terms of an orientation to viewing, that experience is the total opposite of *Through.*

**HF**: You're given a specific viewpoint in *Through,* and you never achieve one in *Every Which Way.*

**RS**: They present different propositions as to how to know the rhythm of your body in relation to form, perception, and movement. I don't think I've done two pieces where that's as clearly demarcated.

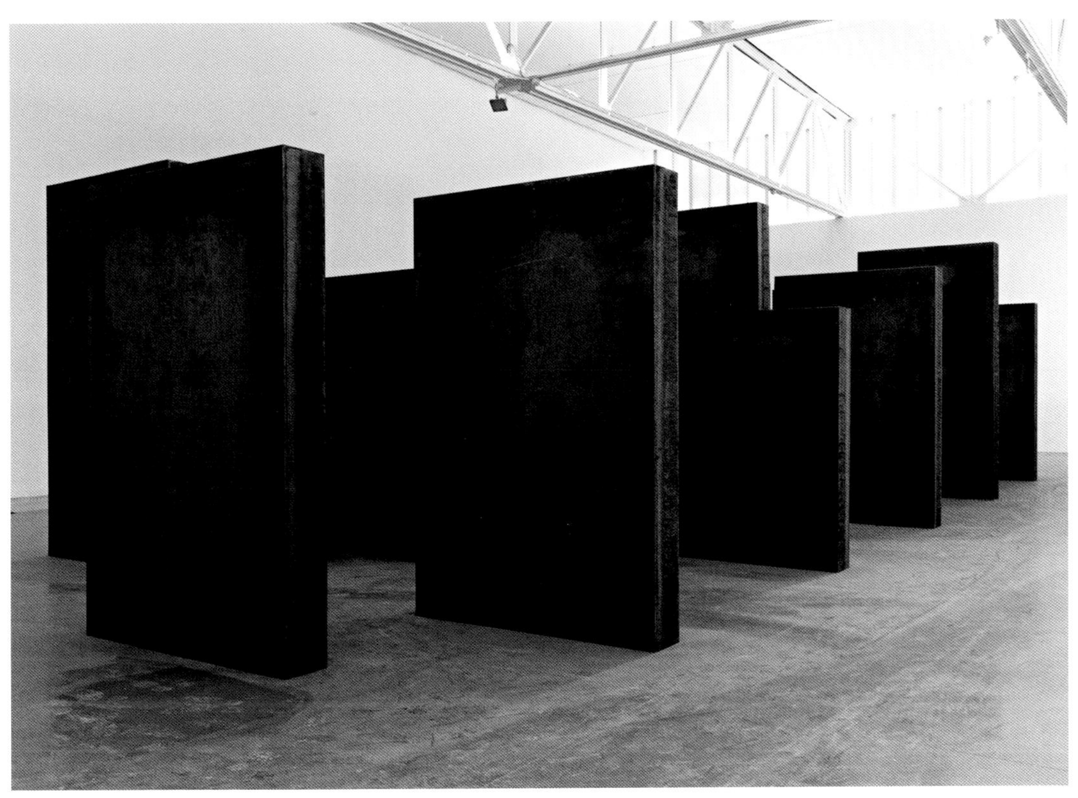

*Every Which Way,* 2015. Weatherproof steel; sixteen slabs, five 11 ft. × 6 ft. × 11 ¾ in. (3.4 m × 1.8 m × 29.9 cm), six 9 ft. × 6 ft. × 11 ¾ in. (2.7 m × 1.8 m × 29.9 cm), five 7 ft. × 6 ft. × 11 ¾ in. (2.1 m × 1.8 m × 29.9 cm); overall 11 ft. × 52 ft. 6 in. × 21 ft. (3.4 × 16.3 × 6.4 m).

**HF**: So in the 2016 show we had a gallery as modernist laboratory in *Above Below Betwixt Between,* a sculptural arrangement in apposition to the urban grid in *Every Which Way,* a classic phenomenological experience in *Through,* and a ceremonial space in *Silence (For John Cage).*

**CW-S**: That show was also about gravity.

**HF**: Yes, it's hard to imagine a more compressive piece than *Silence.*

**RS**: I don't know; maybe it could be pushed further. When we were bringing the plates in, the riggers set two plates horizontally on the floor, right next to each other, and it was astonishing. It reminded me of the Santa Maria cathedral in Burgos, Spain, where there's a slab in brown marble about twenty feet long and a foot high, and next to it lies another slab about six inches lower. There's maybe two feet between them.

**HF**: Are they abstract tombs?

**RS**: No, in Santa Maria the empty slabs were pedestals waiting for the statues of deceased kings and queens to be mounted on top of them. What interested me in *Silence* is very simple. You take a plate with a certain thickness, you lie it down, and it seems twice as heavy as it does when it's standing up. That's something so true, so axiomatic, that no one pays much attention to it. Something lying flat looks much heavier than it does standing up. Also, when you enter the room, the floor seems to tilt. The far end appears to rise up and the near end seems to slope down. The disequilibrium you experience is quite different from that caused by either torqued or vertical pieces. It's the enormous compression of the slab that puts you off balance.

**HF**: What I perceived was a bulging of the plate at its center even though I knew it was flat—it was like a reverse entasis. But what about the tomb association? No visitor I saw took *Silence* to be a platform or a podium.

**RS**: No one stepped on it.

**HF**: No, and it's wasn't simply the taboo of "Don't touch the art." Viewers looked at it in silence; it commanded a distance. That kind of arrest is more definitive than the stop-and-decide effect of the interval, and it's almost the opposite of the propulsion through a passage we experience in the curvilinear pieces. In works like *Silence,* is there a turn away from the emphasis on the movement since your first break into a field condition, a turn away even from the emphasis on action from the very beginning of your practice? And a concomitant turn toward a kind of suspension, even a sort of inanimation?

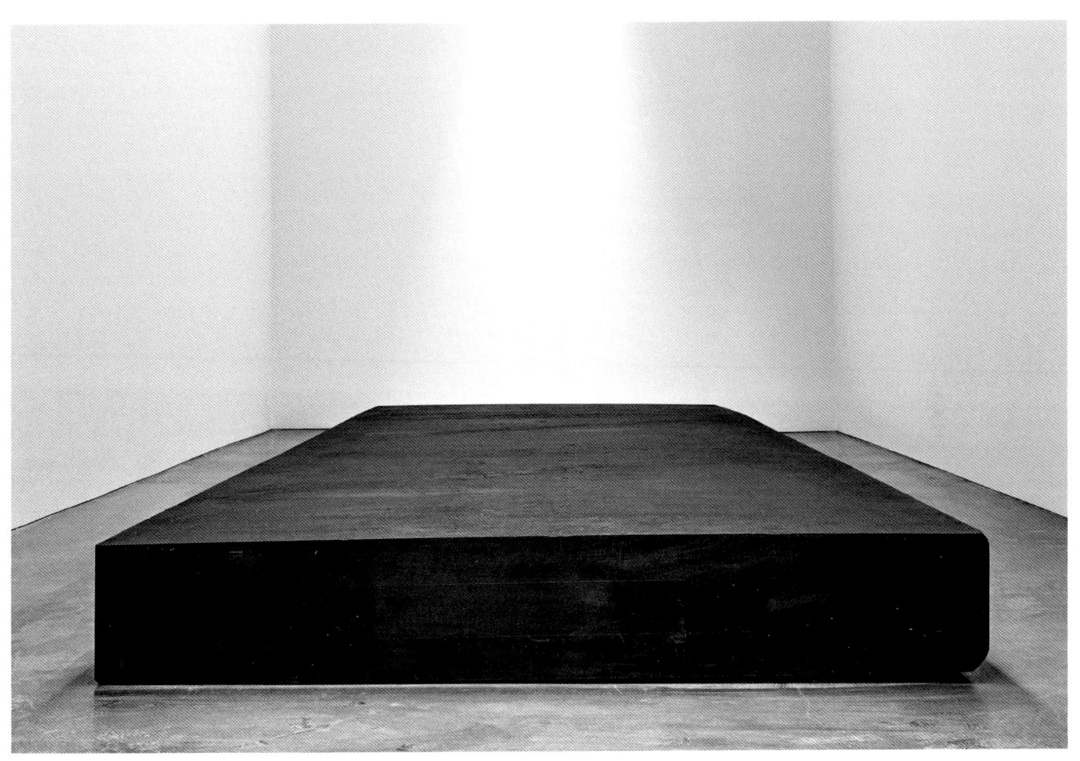

*Silence (For John Cage)*, 2015. Forged steel, 16 in. × 29 ft. 6 ½ in. × 9 ft. 2 ¼ in. (40.6 cm × 9 m × 2.8 m).

**RS:** *Silence* is certainly about stasis.

**HF:** The tomb association brought to mind an old parable told by Adolf Loos over a century ago. Imagine you're alone, deep in a forest, he says, and suddenly you come to a clearing. There's a slight rise in the ground, a mound, and somehow you know the mound is man-made, not natural. And you're hushed; the mound produces a reverence. "Someone is buried here," you think, and Loos says, "*That* is architecture." It's his origin myth of the discipline. Yet why couldn't one say, "*That* is sculpture"? It seems to me that a work like *Silence* revisits that ur-definition of architecture and claims it for sculpture.[3]

**RS:** But Loos's mound has a function. Its purpose is to venerate the person who's buried there.

**HF:** It's not a matter of simple utility. He wants to claim a ritualistic basis for architecture. Why can't sculpture partake of that force too? *Silence* suggests it can.

**RS:** A tomb that's ornamental falls into decorative architecture.

**HF:** A grave stele or a sarcophagus is not sculpture? When Erwin Panofsky called it "tomb sculpture," he was making a category mistake?[4]

**RS:** No. Not at all.

**HF:** You think they hesitate between sculpture and architecture?

**RS:** No. Panofsky's sarcophagi no longer contain bodies. My assumption is that he calls them tomb sculpture because they no longer have a function. They are empty containers. There are really interesting tombs in Panofsky's book on tomb sculpture. I find their scale especially fascinating. Often they're overscaled in relationship to their original function. I've looked at them for years and haven't figured out how to digest them.

**HF:** *Grief and Reason (For Walter)* (2013), which is made up of two big stacks of two heavy blocks, also triggers associations with forms like stelae and sarcophagi. But you seem a little ambivalent about these connections.

**RS:** Not at all.

**HF:** Well, when you presented *Interval,* your arrangement of twenty-four slabs in a staggered grid, all just below or at eye level, you objected when viewers associated it with a graveyard. You told me that connection led them away from the work.

**CW-S:** Richard resisted the simplistic reduction of the sculpture to the image of a cemetery; he didn't resist the evocation of a certain feeling. To me pieces like *Grief and Reason* and *Silence* do elicit an emotional response, but I wouldn't associate them with tombstones.

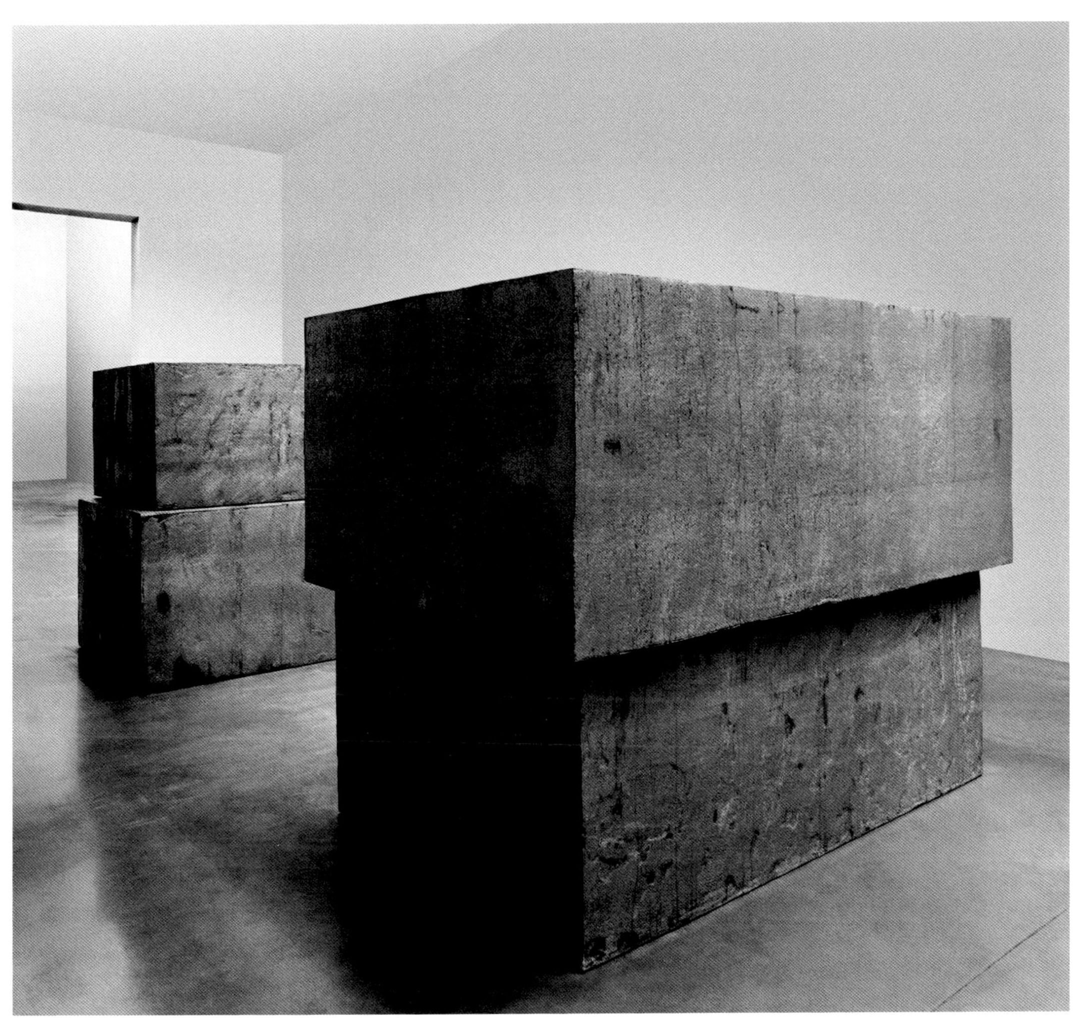

*Grief and Reason (For Walter)*, 2013. Forged steel, four blocks installed in two stacks of two blocks each, 36 × 60 × 84 in. (91.4 × 152.4 × 213.4 cm) and 30 × 54 × 78 in. (76.2 × 137.2 × 198.1 cm); overall each stack 66 × 60 × 84 in. (167.6 × 152.4 × 213.4 cm). Leonard and Louise Riggio, Bridgehampton, New York.

**RS**: You know my text titled "Weight" from 1988? It's all laid out there. Already in the late 1980s I was thinking about those archaic forms. I find them very interesting, particularly the ones that deal with death. Here's the relevant part: "I have more to say about the history of sculpture as a history of weight, more to say about the monuments of death, more to say about weight and density and concreteness of countless sarcophagi, more to say about burial tombs, more to say about Mycenaean and Incan architecture, more to say about the weight of the Olmec heads. We are all restrained and condemned by the weight of gravity."[5]

**HF**: That opens up your relation to the symbolic, which requires a conversation of its own.

# Symbolic Forms

**HF**: There's a symbolic dimension in some of your work that's essential to its effect. Yet, in your resistance to narrative and image, you tend to resist those associations.

**RS**: I push back on narrative and image because people get hung up there. Abstract sculpture has to resist language, resist its metaphorical and imagistic readings. My works aren't abstractions; I'm not like Ellsworth Kelly in that respect. My sculptures are abstract in and of themselves. I'm not advocating to forget, neglect, or dismiss content altogether, but I want to stop its intrusion into the perception of my sculpture. It's my task to push content back, to displace it with new forms.

**HF**: If that's one task, might another be to tap into sculptural forms that have symbolic resonance?

**RS**: That's the trap of postmodern image-making.

**HF**: The symbolic is different from the imagistic.

**RS**: I understand; I'm interested in the symbolic. You don't have to believe in Christianity to see that churches are symbolic. Once, when I brought up archetypes, you asked me if I really believe in them in a way that suggested you don't.

**HF**: The notion of archetypes often depends on a collective unconscious that, at least in Jung, is racial in essence, and that's intolerable. But some forms do seem universal; like Loos's mound, they are often forms that deal with death. Vico argued that the practice of burial was one of the few things that differentiated us as human beings. The vertical stele, the horizontal slab: maybe those are two ur-forms of sculpture that are universal. We could call them symbolic, and I think some of your pieces evoke such forms. It's not because it's called *Silence* (2015) that people are mute in front of it. With its pair of two stacked blocks *Grief and Reason* (2013) also sets up a kind of ceremonial environment. *Equal* (2015) suggests a ritual space even more; its eight blocks evoke a kind of sacred court.

**RS**: Or at least for some people a place of contemplation, of reverence.

**HF**: Yes. So why play down that aspect of your sculpture?

**RS**: I only do when it's a function of content.

**HF**: Is an association with a stele or a sarcophagus a matter of content?

**RS**: It is if the connection is too obvious, if it's overstated. If it's a matter of attributes, then it's tangential.

**HF**: That difference is important to articulate. It's not about abstracting content; it's more about evoking a type.

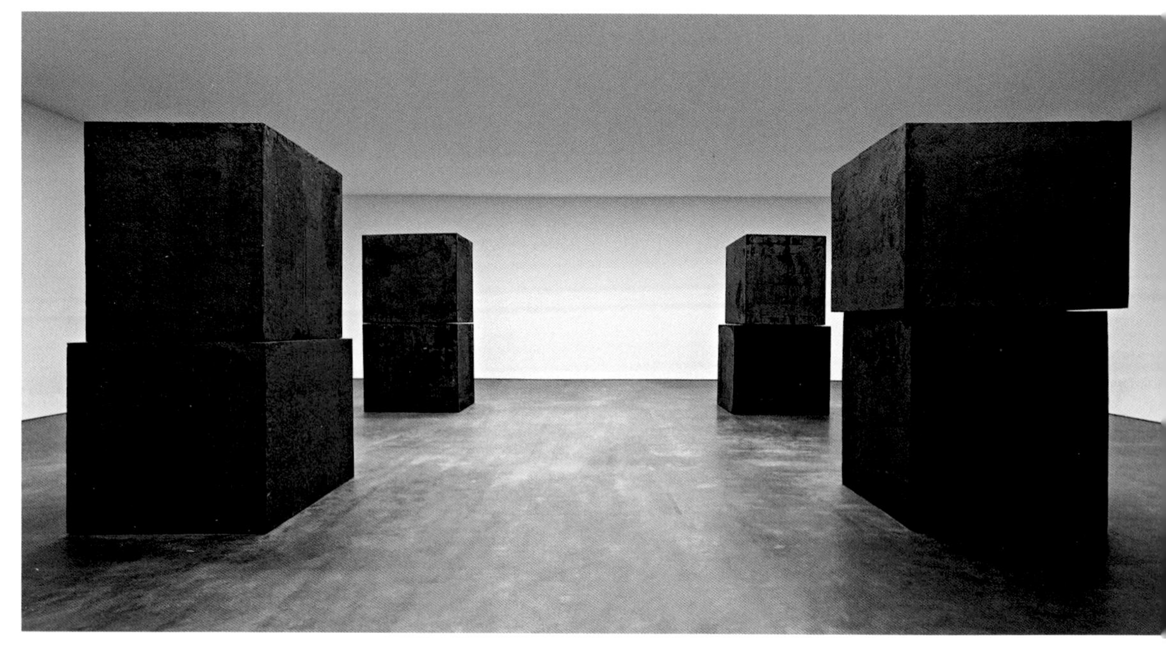

*Equal,* 2015. Forged steel, eight identical blocks, each block 60 × 66 × 72 in. (152.4 × 167.6 × 182.9 cm);
four stacks of two blocks 60 × 66 × 72 in. (152.4 × 167.6 × 182.9 cm), 72 × 60 × 66 in. (182.9 × 152.4 × 167.6 cm),
72 × 66 × 60 in. (182.9 × 167.6 × 153.4 cm), 60 × 72 × 66 in. (152.4 × 182.9 × 167.6 cm), 66 × 60 × 72 in.
(167.6 × 152.4 × 182.9 cm), 66 × 60 × 72 in. (167.6 × 152.4 × 182.9 cm), 66 × 72 × 60 in. (167.6 × 182.9 × 152.4 cm),
66 × 60 × 72 in. (167.6 × 152.4 × 182.9 cm), each stack 11 ft. (3.4 m) high. The Museum of Modern Art, New York.

**RS**: Meaning what?

**HF**: Take *Gravity* (1993), your sculpture in the Holocaust Museum in Washington, D.C. Part of its great force is that one associates it with walls—camp walls, prison walls, border walls, wailing walls, the wall as a barrier or terminus.

**RS**: Those aren't my associations. *Gravity* is a square block impaled in stairs as a form. Everything else is everything else. But the sculpture is in the Holocaust Museum after all; in fact it's on the lowest level in the museum. That's where it belonged; it's the grounding ballast of the museum.

**HF**: But the weight is not merely physical.

**RS**: I understand. Look again at my "Weight" text.

**Clara Weyergraf-Serra**: The gravity in *Gravity* produces gravitas.

**RS**: Probably very few people see it that way, but I agree it evokes a ritual response that might bring death to mind. Am I playing on the edge of those readings? Not consciously, but I accept those accounts.

**HF**: Or take *The Drowned and the Saved* (1992), which was originally sited at the synagogue in Stommeln, Germany. Its two right angles abut and support one another, prop one another up, which leads me to read it as a figure of how survivors can sustain victims, or, conversely, how the dead can support the living. It's all abstract, all in the elements; nothing is imaged.

**CW-S**: Remember the first time you tilted a piece into the ground? You titled it *Tot* (1977), German for "dead."

**RS**: We don't have to go there.

**CW-S**: But you did.

**RS**: *Tot* is a single block impaled in the ground, and it does anticipate *Gravity*. I made *Tot* immediately after my mother's suicide, so it has a commemorative aspect, as *Gravity* does in a different way. But you don't have to know that. Symbols don't deal with particular persons or places.

**HF**: Right. And "subjective" doesn't necessarily mean "private." There's a collective understanding of such forms, and that's what I want to underscore here: along with the rational-constructive and psychological-phenomenological aspects of your work, there's a symbolic-affective dimension.

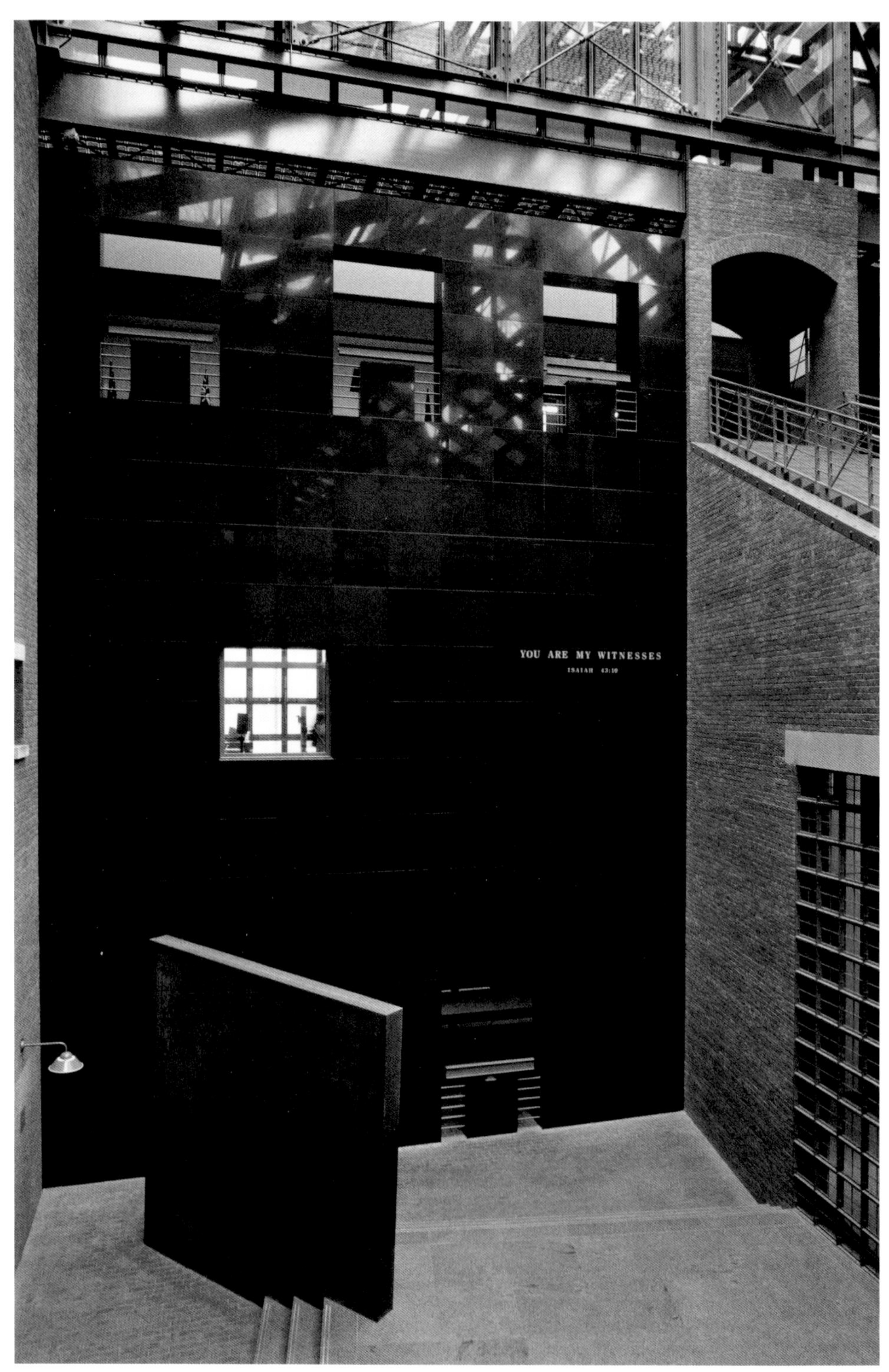


*Gravity,* 1993. Weatherproof steel, 12 ft. × 12 ft. × 10 in. (3.7 m × 3.7 m × 25.4 cm).
U.S. Holocaust Memorial Museum, Washington, D.C.

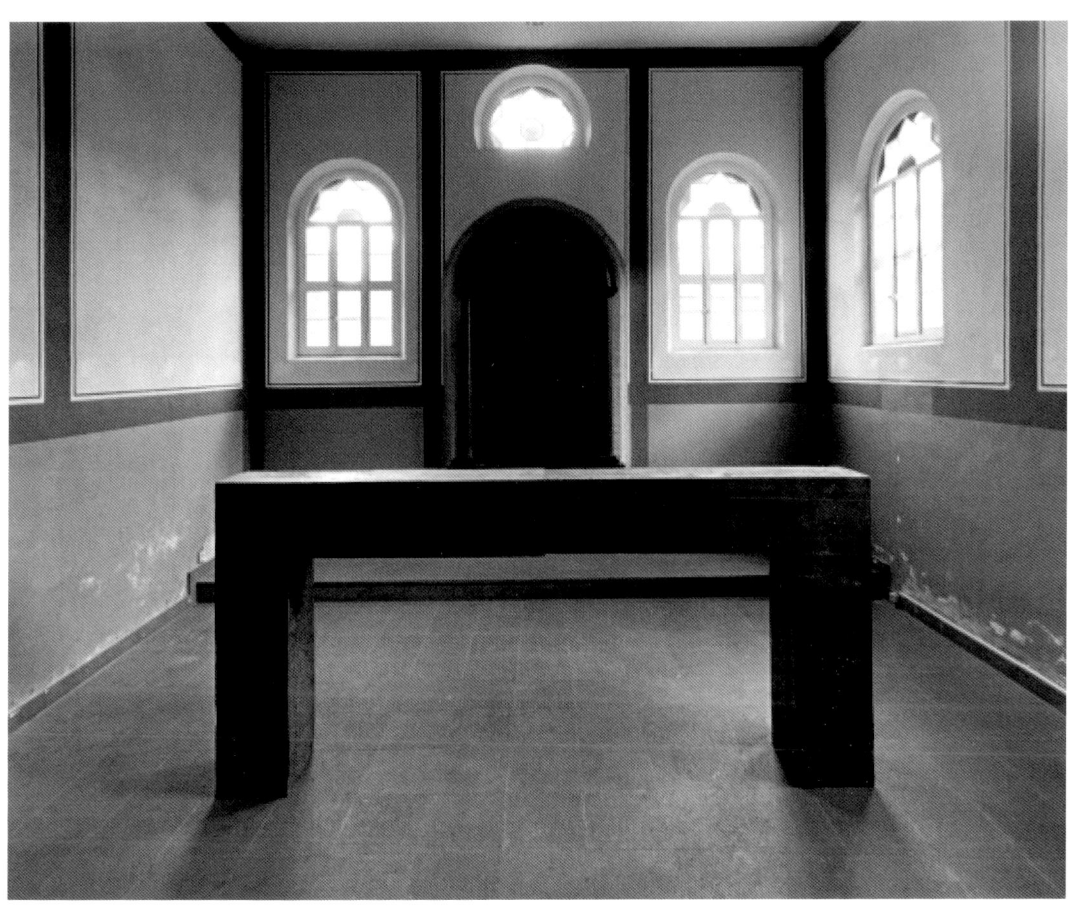

*The Drowned and the Saved,* 1992. Forged steel, two right angles, each 56 ¾ × 61 × 13 ¾ in. (144 × 155 × 35 cm), as installed at Synagoge Stommeln, Pulheim, Germany. Diözesanmuseum, Cologne.

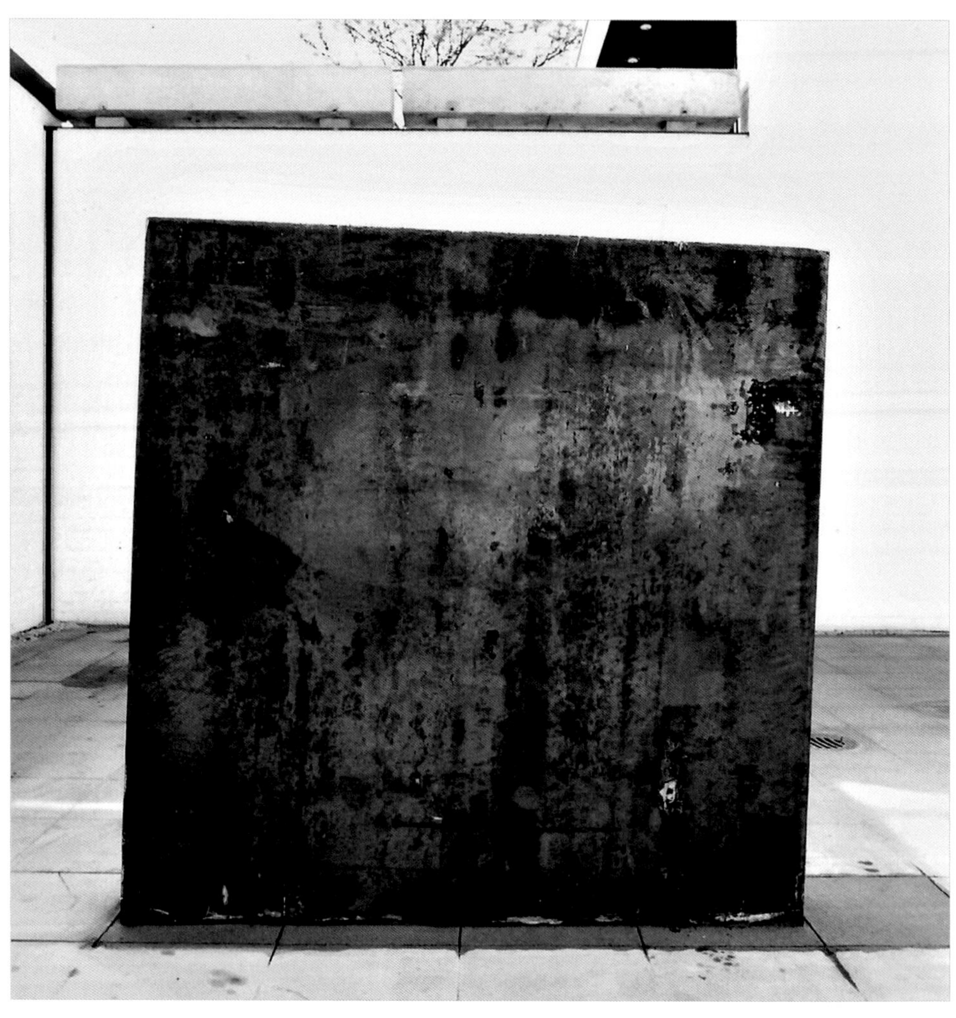

*Tot,* 1977. Weatherproof steel, 6 ft. 8 ¾ in. × 6 ft. 8 ¾ in. × 11 ¾ in. (2 m × 2 m × 30 cm). Stiftung Situation Kunst, Ruhr-Universität, Bochum, Germany. Gift of Alexander and Silke von Berswordt-Wallrabe, Bochum, Germany.

**RS:** Yes, and figuration blocks associations. What I try to do is pare down to the essential. I can't speak for every sculptor, but I don't think many deal with the long history of symbolic forms. Basically they take into consideration the context of their own century, not the history of sculpture as sculpture.

**HF:** What prompted you to open up the chronological purview of sculpture, to look beyond the history of modern sculpture in the West? Some of your peers, like Smithson and Morris, made a similar move.

**RS:** Travel. I went to Machu Picchu, Japan, and Istanbul; I went to Stonehenge; and I took a trip to Sardinia to see the dolmens. Clara and I went to Egypt, Petra, the Aran Islands, and South Korea; we visited Romanesque churches in France. Travel gives you a different acknowledgment of what sculpture has been and could be. You're not constrained by the latest art magazine.

**HF:** What impelled you to travel?

**RS:** Curiosity. I had a need to see what had been made.

**HF:** Also a dissatisfaction with what was given to you as sculpture?

**RS:** That too. It's hard to articulate what to look for in sculpture, or what gives sculpture resonance—what makes for an experience that translates into an emotion. We can use words like "reverence" and "ritual," but even when they're appropriate they're only approximate. What triggers an emotional connection is different for every person.

**HF:** It's different for every person, but every person is capable of that connection. That's basic to aesthetic thought at least since Kant.

**RS:** As you said, people don't walk on *Silence,* and they remain silent—sometimes they barely move.

**HF:** I noticed it especially with *Equal:* people were hushed. They moved through the piece but not at all in the manner they move through your passageways. A touch of the sacred was evoked, but abstractly, in a secular frame.

**RS:** We still end up either with words that are too vague or with words that make an undefinable experience too concrete. *Silence* has a particular aura. That was not intentional. It's an effect I couldn't have predicted.

**HF:** You tend to dismiss such effects as content, while I think they have to do with form— form in a way you can't calculate beforehand and viewers can't grasp in the moment.

RS: I agree; it resides in the form. In any case form is my primary concern. *Silence* is a huge slab lying flat; as I mentioned, that makes it appear much heavier than if it were standing upright.

HF: I wonder if the symbolic dimension is as much in the subject as it is in the object. It's affective. It's also more in your body than in your mind.

RS: I think that's true.

HF: Let me ask about another symbolic form. In a 1981 conversation with Annette Michelson you speak, in relation to your film *Railroad Turnbridge* (1976), about your fascination with bridges:

> I've been on the Golden Gate Bridge and the Bay Bridge all my life. I think,
> if it comes down to little girls liking silk and little boys liking corduroy,
> that little boys like bridges. Later on a bridge becomes more than simply a
> steel artifact spanning two points; it begins to assume symbolic connotations.
> I think if you investigate the notion of a bridge, even if you are a sculptor
> and you are particularly interested in a structural analysis of the bridge,
> you are also investigating an important psychological icon.[1]

RS: I still believe that. When you hear the word "bridge" you don't think only of an industrial structure; you think of bridging, the act of spanning, of connecting two points.

HF: That's not ritualistic; it's not even auratic. It's a different kind of affect.

RS: I don't know. I heard that Jeff Bezos had some Amazon employees stand on the far side of the Golden Gate Bridge for half an hour and stare across.

CW-S: A corporate version of Zen.

HF: Or the latest spirit of capitalism. But isn't bridgeness different in kind from an abstract evocation of a sarcophagus, say, or a stele? And is its effect truly different for little boys and for little girls? Do you see symbolic forms as gendered in that way?

RS: I believe there's a difference, though I don't have any proof—it's just a hunch.

HF: Are there other structures like the bridge, not associated with ritualistic forms, which you've tapped?

RS: Towers.

HF: If a bridge affects us in part because it spans and connects, what is it about a tower?

**RS**: It is grounded in place, and it has an upward drive to the sky.

**HF**: Is that a religious drive?

**RS**: Not necessarily. The tower is a structure that exists across cultures and centuries; it has many different permutations and serves many different purposes.

**HF**: Any other forms or structures?

**RS**: Tunnels and highways. I like how they articulate your perception and movement. When I drive anywhere I look at how the containing walls reinforce the curvature of the road, and I pay particular attention to the elevation of the highway dividers.

**HF**: You've always resisted Tony Smith's epiphany on the New Jersey Turnpike in the 1950s, his experience of driving on the unfinished highway at night, which he took as an exploding of traditional aesthetic limits: "There is no way you can frame it," he says, "you just have to experience it."[2] How is your driving different from his?

**RS**: Smith saw the highway as art.

**HF**: Actually he saw it as an aesthetic experience that exceeded art. How do you see your highway?

**RS**: As syntax.

**HF**: On the one hand you resist language; on the other you rely on its terms, including grammar and syntax. The highway has a syntax you can adapt in your work?

**RS**: When I use the word "syntax" I refer to the syntax of form, not of language. The highway walls help me understand how long a horizontal plane needs to be and, if the topography shifts in elevation, how high it should run over a certain distance.

**HF**: But that's at seventy miles an hour; you're literally speeding by the walking body that you otherwise set as the measure of your work.

**RS**: Nevertheless, I pay attention to highway walls. Also overpasses, especially as trucks drive underneath them: that's a way to gauge height. I look at the flatbeds of trucks for scale. If you do it enough, you can tell if a truck is twenty feet long, thirty feet, forty feet; you can tell how high it is and how much it'll clear an overpass by. I'm also fascinated by the right angle made by truck flatbeds, but I've never figured out how to translate it into sculpture. I like the idea of an elevated and extended right angle that's weightless in the air.

**HF**: This conversation began with symbolic forms, detoured to psychological icons, and somehow ended up on the highway with trucks. What about trains? Were you fascinated by trains, as many kids are, or wasn't that part of your Bay Area experience?

**RS**: Not really. I used to take a train every summer; my mother sent me south to pick beans at my grandmother's farm in Oxnard so I'd stay out of trouble during vacation. That train—it was called the Daylight Special—made a turn near Santa Barbara where I could see the engine and the caboose at the same time, which meant that the curve was extremely acute. That bend fascinated me.

**HF**: I'm a West Coast kid too, and trains were one way to come to terms with the vastness of the landscape, at least east of the mountains.

**RS**: As a kid in San Francisco I traveled mostly by streetcar.

**HF**: That really gives you a sense of the unique topography of that city.

**RS**: When we moved to Ocean Beach we lived in a new tract development. Only four houses had been built, and there wasn't any blacktop road, so we had to walk through the dunes to get to the streetcar line.

**HF**: So every school day you'd go from sand to steel, first trudging along heavily, then clattering along fast?

**RS**: Yes. And as I walked or rode, I'd watch the ships come and go. My room had a back window that faced the ocean, so I'd also watch the ships there.

**HF**: How did they affect you? What's shipness for you? It's a strong psychological icon as well.

**RS**: It's about massive weight displaced in favor of sheer balance. You see a ship in dry dock and you see a ship in the water, and it's hard to put the two together—that transformation from weight to weightlessness.

**HF**: You've described how struck you were as a young child by the precarious launching of a ship. Your father, a pipefitter in the shipyard, took you; it's one of your origin stories as a sculptor, almost a primal scene. You write:

> It was a moment of tremendous anxiety as the oiler en route rattled, swayed, tipped, and bounced into the sea, half submerged, to then raise and lift itself and find its balance. Not only had the tanker collected itself, but the witnessing crowd collected itself as the ship went through a transformation

from an enormous obdurate weight to a buoyant structure, free, afloat,
and adrift. My awe and wonder of that moment remained. All the raw material
that I needed is contained by the reserve of this memory which has become
a recurring dream.[3]

**RS**: Yes, that was intense. I have another memory, a more general one. After a storm at sea Ocean Beach has a very big wave break. My father would go out into it to fish, but my mother was afraid. I remember a lot of fear in relation to the ocean, especially when the wind blew and the surf pounded the beach. When I was very young I went to the beach with my father after a tremendous winter storm. Seven or eight immense sperm whales had been pushed up on the beach and had died. Their huge swollen bodies were way above my eye level. It's another childhood memory I'll never forget.

**HF**: It seems like the inverse of the ship launch—a vision of great mass and weight versus an impression of sudden balance and buoyancy. Would you go fishing with your father?

**RS**: No, that was his sport, his territory.

**HF**: What does the sea mean to you? Are your first associations symbolic, the sea figuring immensity, or phenomenological, the sea representing horizontality?

**RS**: Time.

**HF**: In the human sense of the diurnal, the tides ebbing and flowing, or the inhuman sense of the infinite, as in the endless ocean?

**RS**: Neither. Time in the sense of continuous movement. The ocean is never still.

**HF**: It was still for Mondrian, but I suppose in San Francisco Bay it rarely is. Surge and surf can be very intense there.

**RS**: The Pacific Ocean of Northern California is hardly ever calm.

**HF**: I would've thought it'd be about space for you.

**RS**: It's about time in relation to space, motion in relation to distance.

**HF**: Is that reflected in your work somehow?

**RS**: It is if you see the ocean as one plane in constant movement. I spent countless hours on the beach. In a way I grew up there.

**HF**: Somewhere you speak—it's almost another origin story—about walking down the beach in one direction, seeing the world from that perspective, and then turning around to walk back, only to discover a whole other world opening up for you. A right-handed world first, so to speak, then a left-handed world, sutured together by your body, with the world pivoting on your turning. It's like a tale in Merleau-Ponty demonstrating the phenomenological understanding of perception.

Let's move to a different field of experience. A few minutes ago I asked you about opening up the purview of sculpture, and you pointed to the importance of travel.

**RS**: Again, that was driven by a curiosity as to what sculpture could be beyond the dictates of the art scene. At the time sculpture seemed to me more open than painting. The history and development of sculpture almost seemed to have stopped at a certain point, and I thought more could be done.

**HF**: But to look to other traditions of sculpture, especially ancient ones, is to find an overlap with monuments. At the same time, you deny that your sculpture has anything to do with monumentality. Is there a tension, even a contradiction, there?

**RS**: I'm interested in monuments not because of any sacred vocation or civic function, but simply because they exist and I have to deal with them. I don't know about their iconography, nor do I care.

**HF**: Apart from meanings, do you see effects in monuments that you can develop in your work?

**RS**: Yes. But I'm more curious as to how they continue to function.

**HF**: After their original significance fades away?

**RS**: After their initial purpose is forgotten and their iconography remains interesting only to historians.

**HF**: Is that when a symbolic form emerges for you, after initial meanings and uses drop away? Is the symbolic that which remains in that sense?

**RS**: That's not what historians would say, but it's the case for me. The symbolic arrives after the fact. Certainly that was my experience in Egypt in the early 1980s and in Machu Picchu in the early 1970s.

**HF**: You went to Machu Picchu soon after Japan. What was your experience there?

**RS**: There are sites right around Cuzco and Pissac and along the Urubamba gorge that I mapped—it's in my notebooks—and I made drawings of the walls showing the faceted stones, how they were cut and assembled in place.

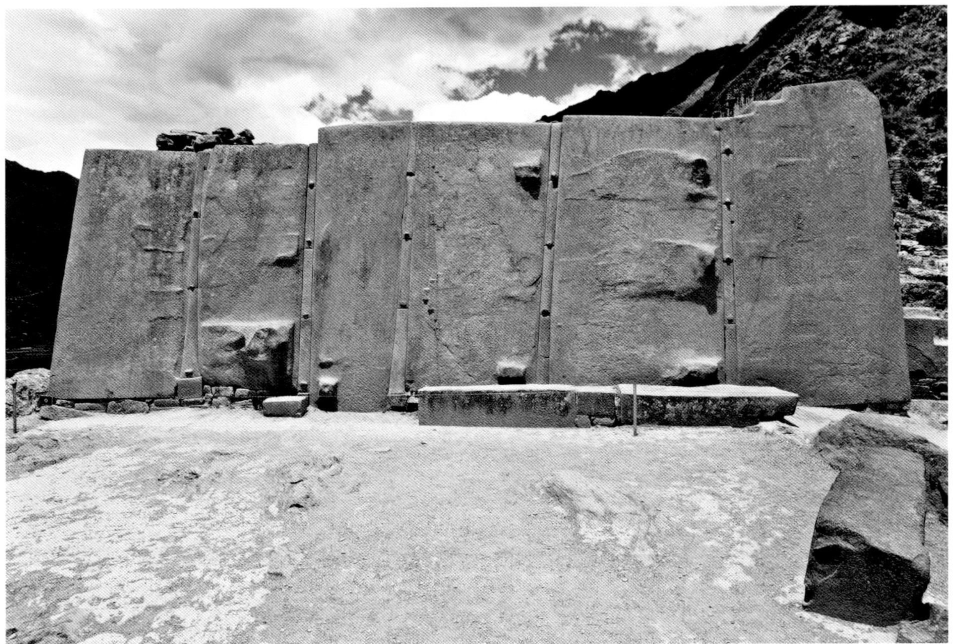

Wall of the Six Monoliths, Ollantaytambo ruins, 15th century. Ollantaytambo, Peru.

**HF**: But that's more structure than symbol.

**RS**: Maybe the two converge. I stopped for a day at a site on the Urubamba River, down the valley from Machu Picchu; it's called Ollantaytambo, where large stones are juxtaposed in a way resembling steles. The scale of *Equal* is connected to that site.

**HF**: What about Machu Picchu itself?

**RS**: That's different; it's about stepped elevations with stairs in between.

**HF**: So more to do with your landscape pieces.

**RS**: Maybe. I dropped acid at Machu Picchu and filled several notebooks with drawings. It was a phenomenal experience. The landscape was different from any I had seen before, and the drawings were different from any I had done before.

**HF**: How different?

**RS**: They were done with a hard lead pencil, and they're very controlled—measured and deliberate and delicate to a degree.

**HF**: What about Egypt? What stood out there?

**RS**: The vastness of it all. The scale, the intense light.

**HF**: The pyramids? The Nile?

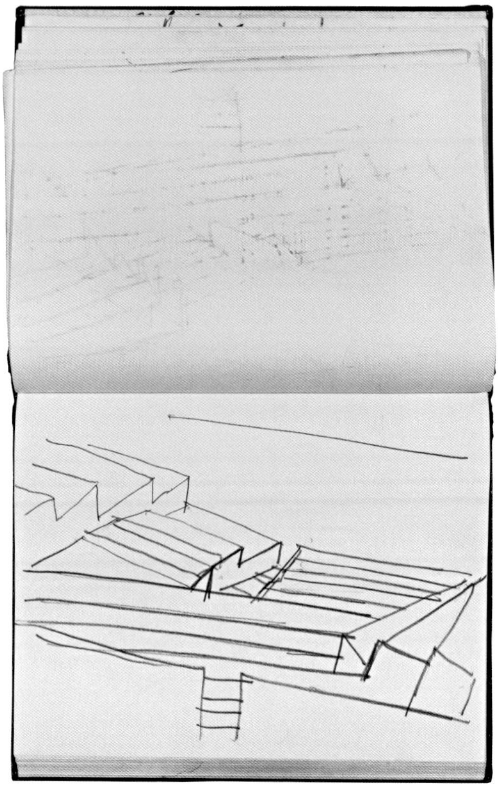

Notebook drawing of Machu Picchu, 1972.
8 × 10 ½ in. (20.3 × 26.7 cm).

**RS:** Yes, and Luxor—the temple, not the tombs.

**HF:** Its structure?

**RS:** Yes, especially the width of its columns, as well as the site and the scale.

**HF:** Did it lead to anything in your work?

**RS:** The columns influenced my forged rounds.

**HF:** You hadn't done any before the trip to Egypt?

**RS:** No; in fact they come much later.

**HF:** So you were led to look to other cultures and other times in part because you weren't satisfied with what was given to you as sculpture. Is that at all aligned with the primitivist turn in Picasso or Giacometti, say, when they took up masks and figures from Africa and Oceania?

**RS:** Maybe, but for completely different reasons.

**HF**: They were interested in particular forms and structures, whether understood abstractly or semiotically, whereas you were interested in different constructions and sites. But it was driven by a similar discontent.

**RS**: I think that's probably true.

**HF**: Is it possible now to see any negative dimension in that impulse? Was this a kind of primitivism or exoticism on your part?

**RS**: No, it came out of a need to educate myself. Most contemporary sculptors go back as far as Rodin, no further.

**CW-S**: Basically, wherever Richard looked, he was interested in tectonics.

**HF**: Is that how you distinguish your investigation of other modes of sculpture from Smithson's and Morris's?

**RS**: Smithson was interested in a multitude of different combinations of high and low culture. He had a range I didn't have—I had little interest in pop culture. Morris was more academic. He worked out of the context of his own art and found ways to support it historically.

**HF**: Let's go back to your resistance to monumentality. It seems to have moderated now—it's more like an ambivalence—but in 1985 you wrote this, and it's categorical: "My large-scale pieces are often referred to as being monumental and oppressive. Neither in form nor in content do they relate to the history of monuments. They do not memorialize any person, place or event. They relate solely as sculpture."[4]

**RS**: No one accused Brancusi, when he went a hundred feet high with *Endless Column* (1938), of making monumental sculpture.

**HF**: I'm not accusing you of monumentality. My question is almost the opposite: Why is the monumental a pejorative for you? What are its negative associations? Is it because people elided it with the oppressive in your case?

**RS**: I think it's a false attribution. It comes in part from Tony Smith's verdict that anything bigger than six feet—the size of his cube *Die* (1962)—is a monument.[5] That became gospel.

**HF**: In that formula Smith also reduces sculpture to the space between an object and a monument. Do you think that definition cut off the potential of size for sculpture?

**RS**: Yes. It became taboo.

**HF**: At the same time you do draw on monuments. I wonder if you protest too much.

**RS**: Maybe I did. But I had to defend myself against a barrage of absurd attacks.

**CW-S**: In the 1980s—remember that was the decade of *Tilted Arc*—"monumental" was used as an insult, and Richard was very sensitive to the label.

**RS**: It still is, and I still am.

**CW-S**: It meant "overwhelming." That's why Richard resisted the confusion of sculpture and monument.

**HF**: Here's a proposition for you. In her influential essay "Sculpture in the Expanded Field" (1979) Rosalind Krauss argued that traditional sculpture in the West was bound up with the logic of monument; that is, it was sited in a particular place, and its figurative language spoke symbolically of that place—of a person, a community, an event, a history. Further, she argued that modernist sculpture broke with that logic as it became abstract, autonomous, and siteless. Her paragon here is Brancusi.

**RS**: I'd contradict Rosalind on one point: I see Brancusi's Târgu Jiu as a site-specific complex.

**HF**: Granted, but here's my question: In your return to site, is there also, in some sense, a return to the logic of the monument—only a monument without monumentality, so to speak, without the symbolical speaking of a people or a place?

**RS**: Hopefully. A monument without monumentality. That sounds okay.

**HF**: So what aspects of the monument do you want to recover? If your site work memorializes anything it might be the lack of a shared history, the lack of a coherent polis.

**RS**: But take *Vortex* (2002), which is the tower between the Kimbell Museum and the Modern Art Museum in Fort Worth: most everyone who visits the museums visits the sculpture. It has become a destination where people meet and gather.

**CW-S**: What returns is the possibility of belonging. When the pieces work, you don't question the placement—they belong.

**HF**: That suggests a different valence of "gathering" from our conversation about sites, one that includes people. Are they invited to feel that they belong as well? I think that's true of some pieces that aren't sited, such as *Grief and Reason* and *Equal*, but also of some towers that are sited like *Vortex* and 7.

**CW-S**: It's true too of the piece in the desert, *East-West West-East*. For me it's most often the landscape pieces that are about belonging.

**HF**: That's a quality of the monumental that doesn't involve the negative associations of ideological persuasion or oppressive scale. And that's what struck me when I watched people encounter *Equal:* it was as if they had a new experience that was, at the same time, an old experience. They couldn't quite understand it, yet it seemed profound.

**RS**: An old experience—what do you mean?

**HF**: Well, they weren't in a church or a synagogue or a mosque or a temple, but that feeling was evoked, and it was unexpected. It's not how you usually feel in a Chelsea gallery.

**RS**: Maybe it triggered an essential recognition but one they hadn't often experienced with sculpture.

**HF**: Despite modern secularization a spiritual life persists. Those sculptures seem to offer a setting for that life, but one free of religious ideology or political manipulation.

**RS**: A spiritual life coded in your DNA?

**HF**: I see it as a cultural inheritance that's very broad but, as a result, fairly diffuse—almost to the point that it's lost.

**RS**: Until it's retrieved.

**HF**: Yes, but it all depends on how; the world is full of religious and political predators who exploit that sense of loss. This leads me to a different question. How do you feel about the adaptation of forms like yours in memorials like the Vietnam Veterans Memorial (1982) by Maya Lin in Washington, D.C.? That became a model for others as well.

**RS**: I think it's perfectly adequate. I have no problem with it at all.

**HF**: Even though it has a function or a purpose you'd reject in your sculpture?

**RS**: People visit for the names of the dead inscribed in the wall, but it might be as interesting without the names—certainly as interesting as sculpture.

**HF**: Do you think Maya Lin and others intuited how you and others had tapped into symbolic forms?

**RS**: Yes, and I'm okay with it—why object? Maya Lin was a student of mine at Yale.

**HF**: I don't object—like many others I'm very moved by the memorial—but I thought you might object. Can you talk about your experience with the Memorial to the Murdered Jews of Europe (2005) in Berlin?

**RS**: Peter Eisenman invited me to collaborate on the proposal. At one point we had the memorial sited below grade, so that the tops of the blocks (there were hundreds of them) were level with the surface of the surroundings. Later we decided to raise the entire field of blocks to street level. We worked out the elevations and the circulation as well as the displacement of the grid, and I thought the result was consequential. Then we were asked to meet with Helmut Kohl to present the project. He took out a red pencil and started to carve up our proposal in a very aggressive manner, reducing it drastically. I told him I once proposed a tower sixty feet high for a site close to the White House, and they said, "Can't you make it forty?" and I said, "No," and they said, "What about thirty?" Kohl leaned forward, with his elbows on the table and his nose right in my face, and said, "But you weren't talking to the Chancellor of Germany!" That's when I pulled out.

**HF**: So it wasn't a disagreement with Eisenman.

**RS**: No, it was because Kohl wanted to reduce the memorial by a third.

**CW-S**: Well, it was a disagreement with Eisenman in the sense that he was willing to go along.

**RS**: Peter will admit as much, and he'll say I had the privilege to walk away and he didn't. I've never seen the piece, but I'm sure the reduction of the scale completely changed how it was supposed to function.

**HF**: I suggested that if your urban pieces represent anything it might be the lack of a coherent public, but that was qualified by your sense that the best pieces gather people. I wonder, as these pieces age, especially the towers, what will they come to memorialize? What value as historical indices might accrue to them? Will they register a certain period in sculpture? Yes. Will they also register a certain transition between an industrial city, an industrial economy, and the postindustrial versions of the same?

**RS**: They might. I think they'll be seen as the last gasp of the Industrial Revolution in terms of sculpture.

**HF**: Not the first breath of another mode that uses postindustrial technologies to transform industrial tectonics?

**RS**: I don't think anybody will follow what I've laid out.

**HF**: You know how modern architecture still looks modern, while everything else—the people, the clothes, the cars—don't? Do you think your sculpture might continue to look modern in a similar way?

**RS**: But much of modern architecture proved to be transitory.

**HF**: That's true, materially, but my point is that it captured the look of the modern in a way that has lasted. When many of us think of that modern spirit, we think of Le Corbusier or Mies, say, or what they offered as machines for living in. I wonder if people will look at your sculpture and see it as a version of what the modern looked like in the late twentieth and early twenty-first centuries.

**RS**: It's a possibility.

**HF**: A last question, perhaps a grim one, certainly another that's difficult to answer: Do you think that, with your recent work, you have entered a "late style"?

**RS**: Yes.

**HF**: What does the term mean for you?

**RS**: More emphasis, more weight, more density, more tension, more introspection.

**HF**: More austerity?

**RS**: Maybe. More emotion.

**CW-S**: More symbolic form?

**RS**: Yes.

**HF**: The classic example of late style is the late quartets of Beethoven. Theodor Adorno and Edward Said wrote of a new asperity in his music, a stripping down, all conventions exposed to the point of dissonance. There's a late style in Yeats too, though it's not so harsh. But then there's the different instance of late Matisse, his "return to fundamentals," which is not so ravaging. In fact he recaptures a pure delight in his late cut-outs. Is a return to fundamentals part of your late style too? Your recent work is often recursive: *Counterweights* looks back to the early props, for example, *Through* looks back to *Strike,* and so on. In this return do you feel more asperity or more delight?

**RS**: In some sense I feel both. I've gone back to forging, and weight has reentered the proposition strongly, with all its symbolic connotations. Some of the heavier pieces make some of the curvilinear work less evocative to me emotionally. The forged works register on a different psychological level. Am I conscious that this is late work? Yes.

**HF**: Can a late style be conscious? It seems Beethoven and Matisse were aware of theirs.

**RS**: I've done a lot of drawings over the last several years. They're a return too.

**HF**: To what? What do you want to reclaim there?

**RS**: The nuance of the experience of making, the sheer pleasure derived from the activity of drawing.

**HF**: Your early commitment to the intersection of material and process?

**RS**: Yes.

**HF**: What's the relation between the sense of austerity in your recent work—you call it "weight"—and the sense of mortality in your life?

**RS**: I think it's one and the same.

**HF**: To what extent is the interest in the fundamental, in the bare…

**RS**: A contemplation of my own death? To a great extent.

**HF**: Different artists respond differently. Picasso became even more manically productive.

**RS**: We don't know what he was thinking; we don't know what Matisse was thinking either. Nor Titian, nor Cézanne. I think late work is very important. It makes you reevaluate the entire body of an artist's work. It's very important for me to make that review as substantial as I can. It's not about repeating; it's about analyzing.

**HF**: It's not necessarily involuted; it can open up a language.

**RS**: Hopefully. Because this is when judgment occurs. If artists fall off in their late work, their earlier work is reevaluated.

**HF**: You talk about weight in your recent work, but there's lightness too. You've long admired Italo Calvino's reflections on lightness in his *Six Memos for this Millennium* (1988).

**RS**: It's the lyricism of lightness. It's there in my recent curves. You don't think of those pieces, which are heavy in tonnage, as being heavy.

**HF**: So you pull the very curvilinear pieces into this period as well? Is there a certain dynamic, then, between light and heavy in your late style?

**RS**: Yes, but right now I'm more interested in the heavy pieces. It's in the drawings where the focus is more on the lyrical.

**HF**: Is there a similar dynamic between heavy and light in your early work? In other words, has that dialectic returned?

**RS**: I suppose so. *Strike* is both weighty and weightless; *Circuit* is too. That tension has always been there.

# Structure, Surface, Speed

**HF**: Here's a paradox: you've made sculpture more specific, more powerful, in large part through a critical engagement with other mediums. Apart from your commitment to contemporaneous forms of dance and music, your work has questioned painting (to the extent that it's pictorial, bound up with the image) on the one hand, and contested architecture (especially in its postmodern incarnation, which privileges scenography) on the other.

**RS**: That's about keeping your mind nimble. Getting caught in your own dictates and polemics doesn't allow you to make new moves. Interest in other fields keeps you flexible (Smithson was a genius at bringing different investigations into his art). You have to keep abreast of a lot of things; you have to be inquisitive.

**HF**: At the same time you're precise about other practices. For example, your work is not about combining sculpture and architecture somehow; it's about understanding what structural principles they might share and then developing them in sculptural terms.

**RS**: Tectonics is implied in the form-making principle of sculpture, first in terms of eradicating the base, which is a convention that's no longer useful, then in terms of how to get a given material off the ground. Here the question becomes: How do weight, mass, and friction work? I have an advantage because I caught rivets and put up trusses as a young person working in steel mills. I knew enough about industrial procedure, and I knew I could bring that knowledge into making art. This gave me confidence. In a similar way— and this goes back to the down and dirty version of Minimalism—Andy Warhol brought the procedures of advertising into art. Later on Barbara Kruger used advertising paste-ups. Importing new models into a conservative practice always gives you an advantage.

**HF**: You've drawn from industrial engineers and modern architects—John and Washington Roebling, Robert Maillart, Mies van der Rohe…

**RS**: Hans Scharoun, too. When I first went to Berlin in 1977, I visited his library and philharmonic hall. He was important when I began to work with volume, in an open field, in relation to a curve. Scharoun was a big influence, as was Frank Lloyd Wright's Guggenheim Museum. Not much had been done with curves in modernism. In fact, when *Tilted Arc* went up, the most startling thing about it was not that it claimed the site for sculpture but that it was a big curve. One reason to build *Tilted Arc* in the Federal Plaza and *St. John's Rotary Arc* at the Holland Tunnel was that I wanted to understand the difference between a concavity and a convexity. When you face the concavity of a curve, the entire breadth of the curvilinear volume opens up in front of you; you see it all at once. However, as you walk around its end and it changes to a convexity, the volume evaporates. It reveals itself only through walking—you can't see the openness of the field or how the volume is sucked into it. Just turning the corner opens up another world: that interested me, and it didn't

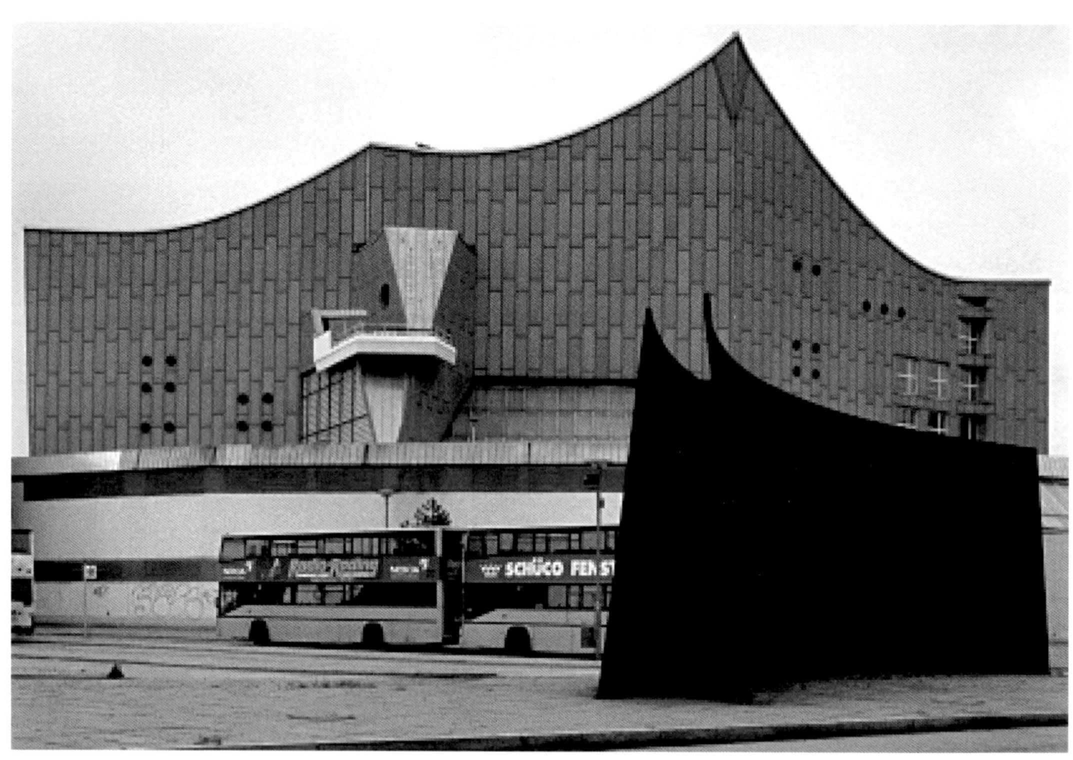

*Berlin Junction,* 1987. Weatherproof steel, two near-identical conical sections inverted relative to each other, 13 ft. 1 ½ in. × 45 ft. 1 ½ in. × 2 ¼ in. (4 m × 13.8 m × 5.7 cm), 13 ft. 1 ½ in. × 44 ft. 3 ½ in. × 2 ¼ in. (4 m × 13.5 m × 5.7 cm). Permanent installation in front of the Berliner Philharmonie, 1960–63, by Hans Scharoun. Collection City of Berlin.

appear to be a central aspect of architecture. There was a concern with curves in the 1930s, but in design more than in architecture.

**HF**: Was this when you became interested in Baroque architects like Borromini?

**RS**: No, that happened later, just before the *Torqued Ellipses*. Alfred Pacquement, who was then a curator at the Centre Pompidou, took Clara and me to visit countless Romanesque churches in France in 1991. Another crucial experience was my first visit the same year to Le Corbusier's Ronchamp; there I filled notebooks with drawings. At Ronchamp the solid and the void are experienced as one and the same. You're in a volume unlike any you've been in; you understand that the space is holding the walls and vice versa, that it's one field, and it affects you physiologically and psychologically. The space is different in kind from anything that has come before. I thought if architecture could have that effect, so could sculpture. Ronchamp is small, but you don't sense or remember it as small. It has enormous volumetric presence, which comes in part from the piercing of the walls that funnels in the light.

In 1966, I hitchhiked from Athens to Istanbul, where I saw the Hagia Sophia. There was a physicality to the light: it was so palpable you could almost touch it. I didn't experience that sensation again until Ronchamp. I made another trip in the mid-1980s with the curator Carmen Giménez to see the Mozarabic architecture around Madrid. They're Christian structures in Moorish Spain built of ponderous stone with small openings letting the light in to illuminate the volume in specific directed shafts. The spaces in Mozarabic architecture are mostly small, dense, compact. The effect is similar to that of Ronchamp, only with Mozarabic architecture the openings in the walls are very narrow and the light is very condensed.

**HF**: What's the relation between the industrial model you brought into sculpture and your interest in these other traditions of building—Hagia Sofia, Romanesque churches, Mozarabic structures, even Ronchamp? Is it all about different tectonic principles?

**RS**: You have the principles, and then you have their effects. What is the effect of a structure whose wall is punctured in a way that illuminates the volume and holds the space, rendering it palpable? The scale, the direction of the light, the lean and curvature of the walls, and the compression all contribute; it's not only tectonics. Basically, what I've always done is ask, "What is it that I'm looking at that I don't understand, and why don't I understand it?" Often I'm very slow to read work, my own and everybody else's. I have to go back and look again and again. Often I don't trust my initial grasp: the immediacy of that first take doesn't allow you to penetrate what you don't already know.

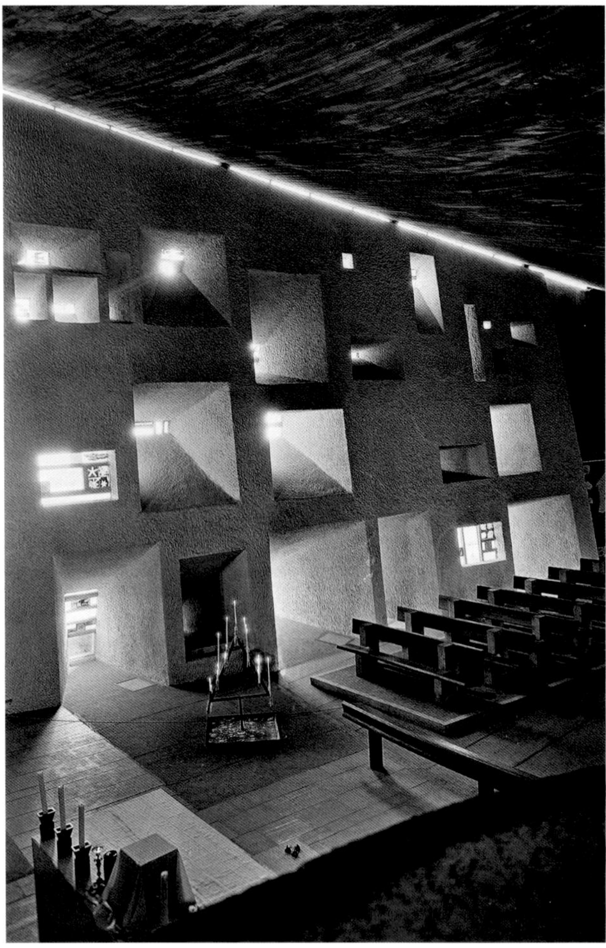

Le Corbusier, Notre Dame du Haut, 1950–55.
Ronchamp, France.

**HF**: What about the framing of your work as it has changed over time? When you, along with others, brought an industrial scale into art, that move tested the architectural context as well. But toward the end of the last century, museums moved to absorb that scale, and there are now many spaces, like Dia:Beacon, that are refurbished factories or warehouses, where the fit between industrial-strength art and architecture becomes almost too perfect. How do you feel about that development?

**RS**: Most Minimalist and Post-Minimalist work was built in loft spaces. Then galleries opened in former industrial spaces in order to accommodate the work (they were surrogates of lofts). Then collectors like Count Panza realized you could take that entire container, package it, and put it up somewhere else. By refining the container you ended up with another container that was transportable and marketable. Galleries and collectors found a way of defusing our first critical thrust. The authenticity of the loft space was lost.

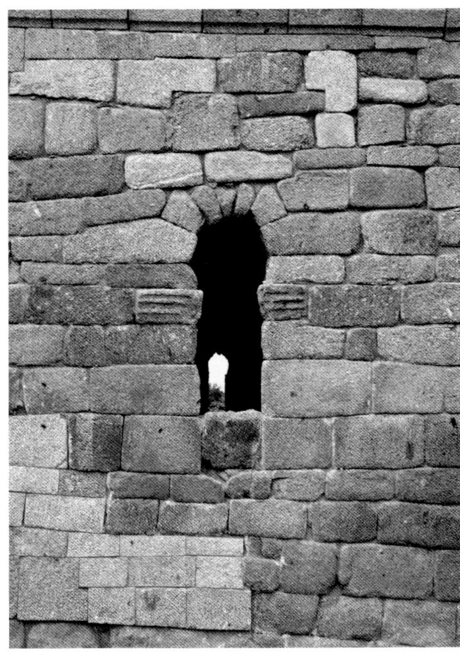

Santa María de Melque, windows, 8th century.
San Martín de Montalbán, Spain.

Are places like Dia:Beacon a cooption of the 1960s? Yes. But if those spaces didn't exist, the work wouldn't be collected or seen.

**HF**: Those settings comply with the industrial units of the work—the module, the grid— in a way that seems almost circular: the work sits neatly inside the space, and it looks great there. First your generation came along to challenge an artisanal idea of art with industrial materials and methods, just at the moment when that industrial order had begun to rust out, at least in this country. Later your industrial work was positioned in old warehouses refitted as art galleries and museums, just at the moment when the postindustrial economy became more important. If your work once broke with the artisanal model of art through industrial means, the residue of those means might now be taken as an aestheticizing, even a romanticizing, of an old mode of production. Or, more generously, they can be seen as resistant precisely because they're old, as a pushing back on a new electronic-digital order. In either case, how do you reconcile your industrial commitments with your use of computer-aided design?

**RS**: We always start with models made of lead. In order to arrive at a decision to build a work we go through a series of models. Once we agree that we have a model for a sculpture we want to build, it is translated to a CAD program on the studio computer. Then that plan is sent to an engineer for evaluation. The engineer's drawings are forwarded to the fabricator. Then there is a back-and-forth between the fabricator and the studio to

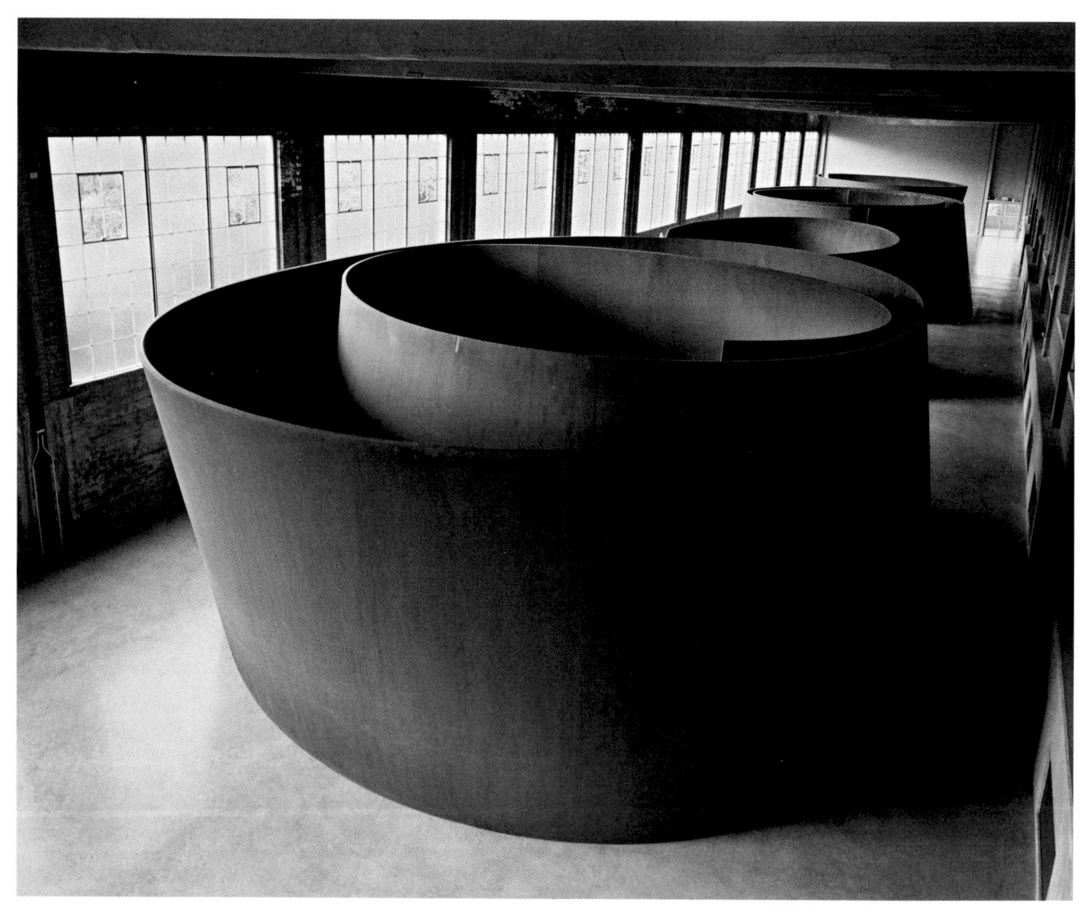

*2000*, 2000 (in foreground). Weatherproof steel, 13 ft. 7 in. × 42 ft. 6 in. × 35 ft. 5 in. (4.1 × 13 × 10.8 m), plates 2 in. (5 cm). Dia Art Foundation, New York.

determine what's possible and what's not—and which changes we are willing to accept. Changes are necessitated mostly by the limitations of the presses and the stability of each plate in a given sculpture. Once the plans fit the criteria of our needs, the fabricator constructs a steel model and ships it to the studio. Often that steel model needs to be adjusted again, so there's another go-around. It can be a long process before we're satisfied, and only then is the steel ordered from the rolling mill and the sculpture fabricated. We seldom work directly from the computer. Inventing forms isn't dependent on software. The computer is just another tool, and it has become part of industrial production anyway.

**HF**: Your work since the *Torqued Ellipses* also speaks to a different kind of spatiality, less rectilinear, more immersive, a spatiality distinct from the clarity of most industrial structures or the transparency of some modernist buildings. This is a spatiality that, however physical, has affinities with virtual space.

**RS**: As you said, industrial structures were largely defined by the grid or at least based on a fairly strict modular frame. Contemporary space is much looser, smoother, and faster; it's concerned with movement more than framing.

**HF**: How faster?

**RS**: It's more related to the surface and its extension. Our first relation to most recent architecture is to its skin. That's a big difference.

**HF**: Spectacular tectonics?

**RS**: Scenographic tectonics, or scenography replacing tectonics.

**HF**: But scenography is what postmodern architecture was about—signs and symbols on a facade. Today, as you suggest, there's a fetishization of the abstract skin. That's what "Minimalism" in architecture has come to mean for many people—not only fast surfaces but also "light construction"—which is almost the opposite of what Minimalism once meant in art.

**RS**: Yes, whereas I'm still interested in the skin as an outgrowth of the volume, in the skin returning you to the space of the void. I want to hold the field by using the speed of the skin. I still want to have the weight, but not as the first manifestation of the piece. The best example—and it might be a step back to go forward—is *Wake* (2003), which is now in the Sculpture Garden of the Seattle Art Museum. Each module is identical and comprises two S-sections that are inverted in relation to each other. As the S-sections lock together, the concavity and convexity of one side lock to the convexity and concavity of the other side.

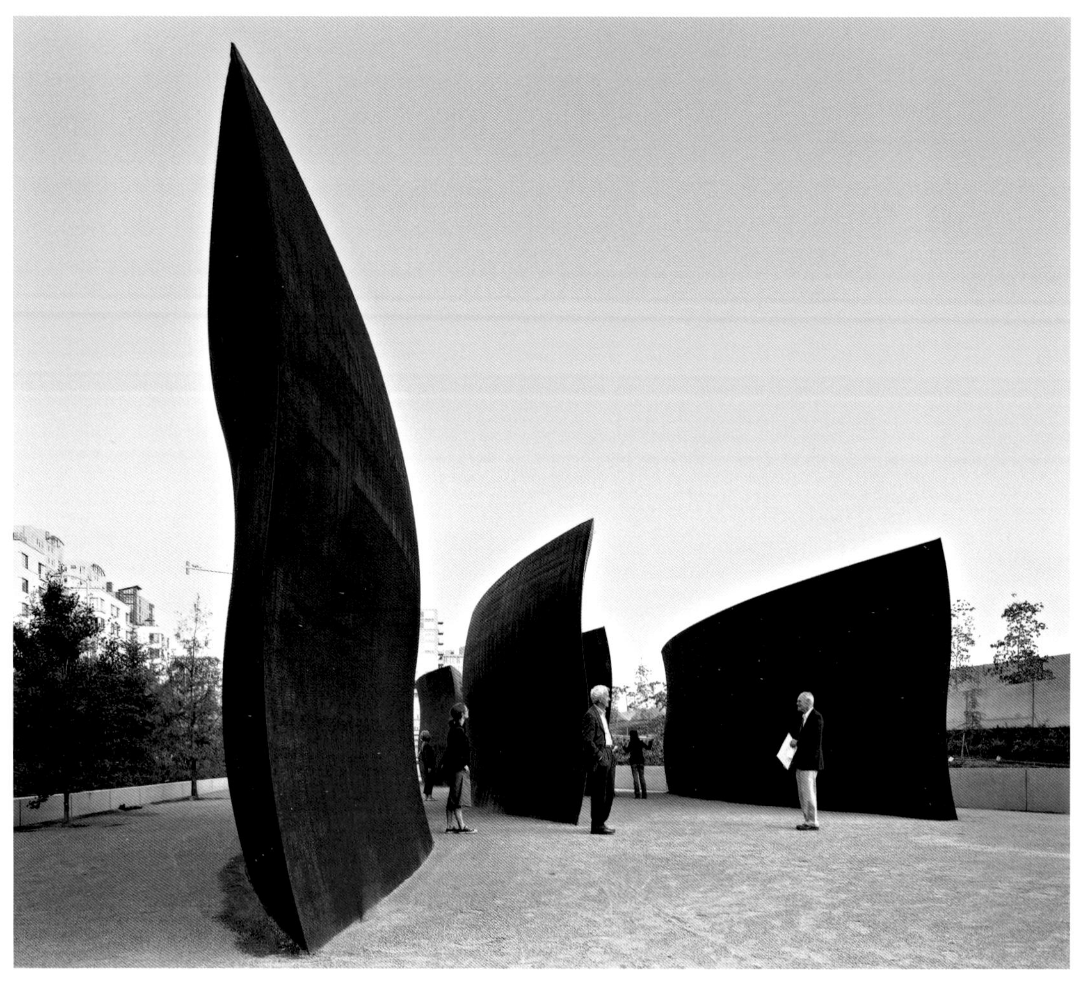

*Wake,* 2003. Weatherproof steel, five units of two torus sections, each 14 ft. 1 ¼ in. × 48 ft. 4 in. × 6 ft. 10 ¼ in. (4.3 m × 14.7 m × 209 cm), plates 2 in. (5 cm); overall 14 ft. 1 ¼ in. × 125 ft. × 46 ft. (4.3 m × 38.1 × 14 m). Permanent installation at the Olympic Sculpture Park, Seattle, Washington.

There are only two prior pieces like it: *Dirk's Pod* (2004) on the Novartis campus
in Basel, and *The Union of the Torus and the Sphere* (2001) at Dia:Beacon. There a sphere
and a torus lock together to create a space that's concealed, not revealed, as you walk.
The work is installed tight in its room, so you are forced against its surface and can't
grasp the room as a whole. The five elements of *Wake* and *Dirk's Pod,* on the other hand,
are set in an open field. What's important is your moving between them, through them,
and around them as they undulate.

You can say that's a return to the Baroque, but whatever it is it takes you into the
field, into the interstices between the pieces. It allows for flow and movement, and it doesn't
reduce to a quick gestalt reading—you never know the configuration.

**HF**: So you've pushed the industrial bases of your work in order to suggest a contemporary
shift in space, but for the most part you still allow us to see, in a modernist way, how
those spatial effects are produced.

**RS**: When I brought the industrial process into my work, I brought in the effects of labor,
not the image. When people in the art world think of industrial structures, they think
of photographs by Hilla and Bernd Becher—they documented the language of industrial
structures. I'm not involved with that language in an imagistic way; I'm involved with
industrial procedures. And sometimes, in seeking to make what I want to make, the
procedures have to be changed, or at least the tools do. Occasionally the fabricators
profit from the change in that it enables them to contract for jobs they weren't equipped
to do before.

**HF**: Even as you've held on to the modernist commitment to transparency whereby you
show your material, structure, and process, you haven't merely reiterated industrial
space: the spatiality of your recent work isn't modular or gridded. But you don't just
plunge us into this new kind of fluid space either, as a lot of installation art has done
with its immersive effects; you don't just rehearse that delirious space. In a way you went
back to the Baroque and other sources to understand what a nonclassical, nonmodern,
nontransparent space is like in order to reflect on its return in the present. But you don't
just leave us there: you provide some distance for us to consider the effects of this new
kind of spatiality.

**RS**: I thought only a sculptural language could do that. My foundation is in industrial
process; in most architecture that process is hidden. Buildings are always more interesting to me before they're clad. I'm not saying structural integrity *is* authenticity—that's
not my polemic—but people can recognize when surface is not coming from structure:
it looks superfluous, ornamental, sometimes even frivolous.

**HF**: As structure becomes more hidden in architecture, your sculpture still exposes it. You've mentioned your relation to modern architects. What about contemporary ones?

**RS**: I think most architects are hostile to my work.

**HF**: Really? Not Peter Eisenman, for example, or Rem Koolhaas or Frank Gehry…

**RS**: Koolhaas has been receptive, but I've never done anything with him. I had a dialogue with Eisenman that was fruitful. My relationship with Gehry is more complicated.

One of the big problems I see in architecture is the division between the structure, the engineering, and the ornamental skin. The architect has become the person who focuses a little on the layout and a lot on the ornament, whether that's glass, titanium that bends, or scenographic surface; the structure is mostly handed over to the engineer. That wasn't the case with, say, Jørn Utzon in his Sydney Opera House: there you still have the architect and the engineer of one mind, and there's a clarity to the building that takes your breath away. Nor was it the case with Louis Kahn, especially at his Salk Institute, where that clarity extends to how the volumes sit on the site.

But the division becomes problematic with recent architecture where more and more architects limit themselves to the design of the skin as ornament. (There are exceptions, such as Koolhaas's library in Seattle where the glass is tectonic.) The difference is that in my work the structure and the skin are one and the same.

**HF**: Do you see your work reflected in contemporary design at all then? There are a lot of young architects who admire your work greatly. What productive elaborations do you see there?

**RS**: I think the curved and torqued pieces have opened up a few generative paths. Some young architects have taken them as cues to move into space with postindustrial means of both fabrication and design.

**HF**: Yet you remain committed to the industrial forging and bending of steel plates in mills, whereas many designers favor newer and lighter materials not produced or assembled in the same ways. What do you make of that difference?

**RS**: My influence on architecture's been perverse, but then influence often is. I'm interested in the potential of material, whereas some architects are interested only in effects. Nevertheless, other designers have dealt with curvilinear structures in ways I appreciate, even when they use materials and forms I find superficial. If anything, the twenty-first century in architecture is marked by the demise of the right angle; there are already more curvilinear spaces, more open spaces, that change velocity, float, or otherwise nuance time. How has my work been assimilated, if at all? Probably by misintepretation. Did some

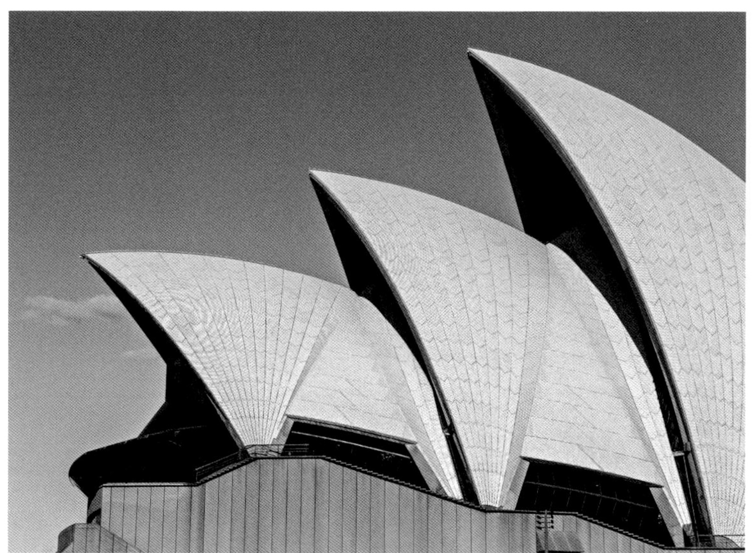

Jørn Utzon, Sydney Opera House, 1973. Sydney, Australia.

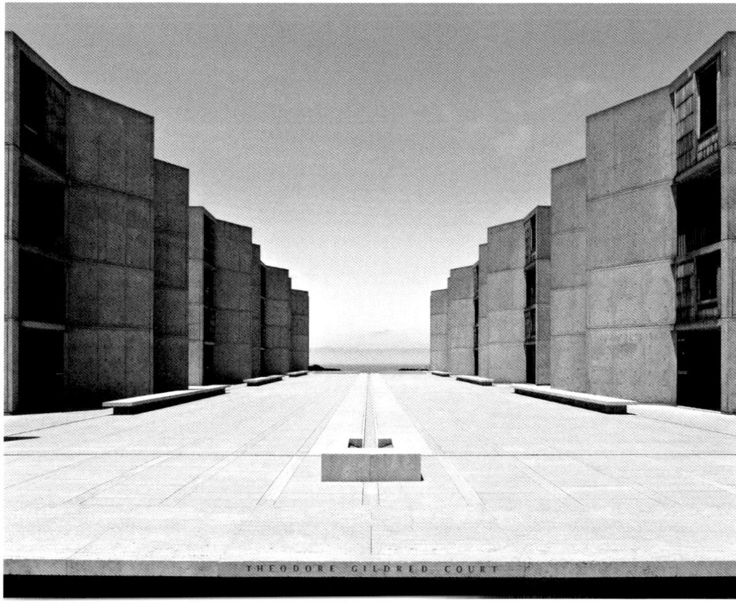

Louis Kahn, Salk Institute courtyard, 1965. Torrey Pines (La Jolla), California.

people take advantage of it in ways I couldn't foresee? Yes. Do I think the work is open enough to allow people to deal with it in a lot of different ways? I hope so. Architects and sculptors will figure it out; some performers, dancers, and others will find it useful— or again that's my hope. Duchamp said that you're lucky if you get thirty or forty years (of course he's had a lot longer). Warhol said all we get is fifteen minutes. Who knows? The fact is you can't know. In the end I still believe that matter imposes its form on form; that's why it's important for me to stick with materials I understand. That wasn't always true of the Minimalists.

**HF**: Personally, I took the Minimalists too much at their own word.

**RS**: You mean you believed the literalist dogma? I think we all did; we all read Minimalism through its rhetoric. But then it became important for my generation to find a way around it.

**HF**: The Minimalist line remains extremely important: it allowed for an entire genealogy of art that opened out to actual space, as in your work, as well as to other notions of space or site—institutional spaces, discursive sites. But what I always took to be a secondary line—an art of light-and-space phenomena à la Robert Irwin and James Turrell—has become more dominant (and here perhaps Dan Flavin returns as a problematic progenitor) as more and more art wants to create an experience of immersive intensity (think of Olafur Eliasson). Your work also speaks to that tendency or, rather, against it.

**RS**: My sculptures don't produce optical effects that engulf the viewer as heightened theatricality. The problem with those fluid spaces is you never feel grounded in them, whereas I'm still interested in grounding the viewer in an experience of place. A lot of those spaces just wash over you.

**HF**: And many people mistake that effect for an ecstatic sort of aesthetic experience. This is a stretch, but do you see any connection between your torqued sculpture and the new cyberspace that emerged about the same time, in particular between the passageways of your pieces and the byways of computer games? I wonder if young people take your work as actualizing that kind of space and delight in it in ways that are foreign to many of us.

**RS**: I don't see the link between kids playing computer games and the experience of my sculpture. It's too much of a leap for me to go from the physical actuality of my sculpture to the virtual world of those games.

**Clara Weyergraf-Serra**: A surfer wrote a delightful text about the torqued pieces comparing them to surfing—to the kind of exhilaration he feels when pushing off on a rising wave.

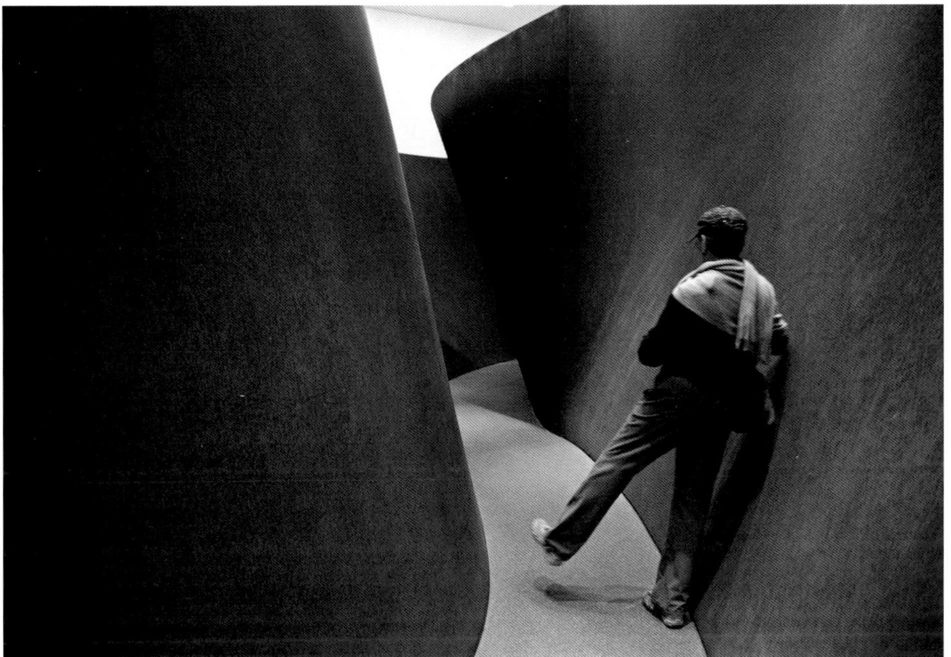

A viewer inside *Sequence,* 2006, at the San Francisco Museum of Art.

**HF:** As people surf the web virtually, some also surf your sculptures physically, especially the serpentine pieces. A bit like boarders, they run up the sides as high as they can go to leave a mark; they make arcs within the arcs.

**RS:** Yes, often you can see the footprints.

**HF:** But those boarder-surfers are actual people, not avatars, and they're not always young. Your outdoor pieces insist on embodiment and movement, placement and context, and in that way they stay clear of two pitfalls of recent architecture—its tendency to indulge in arbitrary forms and to overwhelm viewing subjects—both of which are shared by computer games. In such spaces the subject is not situated; in fact, the apparent auto-generation of forms is almost oblivious to us, with the result that the subject can seem unfixed, almost elided. That's never the case in your sculpture.

# History Doesn't Go Away

**HF**: Where did you start, historically, with sculpture? How did you get your bearings with this art?

**RS**: When I first went to Italy after Yale, what I found most interesting was Etruscan sculpture. For me it has a lyricism and a lightness that doesn't appear in other sculpture. It's obvious to me that Picasso and Giacometti were influenced by Etruscan sculpture. Picasso's early wood sculptures come out of Etruscan sculpture more than African.

**HF**: Art historians say they're more influenced by Gauguin.

**RS**: Influence is almost always synonymous with misreading, but there are Etruscan sculptures that look exactly like those early Picassos. In any case, Etruscan sculpture has a curvilinear line that doesn't occur in Greek sculpture. It's not only light and lyrical; it's also open and extended.

**HF**: "Light and lyrical": those aren't terms often associated with your work. Where's the affinity?

**RS**: What struck me was that Etruscan sculpture is different in kind from anything that came before or after. Every time I go to the Met, I go to the mezzanine to look at the Etruscans. When I first went to Rome I went regularly to the Etruscan Museum.

**HF**: But it wasn't a resource for you.

**RS**: No, but it's something I often think about, not only its lightness but also its curvilinearity. It loops within itself and creates extensions, voids, and volumes. You're often drawn to what you lack.

**HF**: Well, there's an affinity with your torqued pieces. Is it also the sense that it's alien to other traditions that interests you?

**RS**: Yes, its differentiation from what came before and after has continued to hold my attention. Influences are usually not direct; there are delays before they take hold. I have a need to free myself from stifling conventions, the dictates of the moment.

**HF**: Are there other examples of sculpture outside the dominant tradition, or somehow stranded in it, that are compelling to you? When you turned to architecture, it was often to primordial forms of construction, ones that stand at the beginning of a tradition. Is that the case with sculpture as well?

**RS**: Etruscan sculpture is the beginning of a tradition that wasn't continued until centuries later. It was overshadowed by the Greeks.

**HF**: Why are you drawn to sculpture that seems stranded or otherwise stunted?

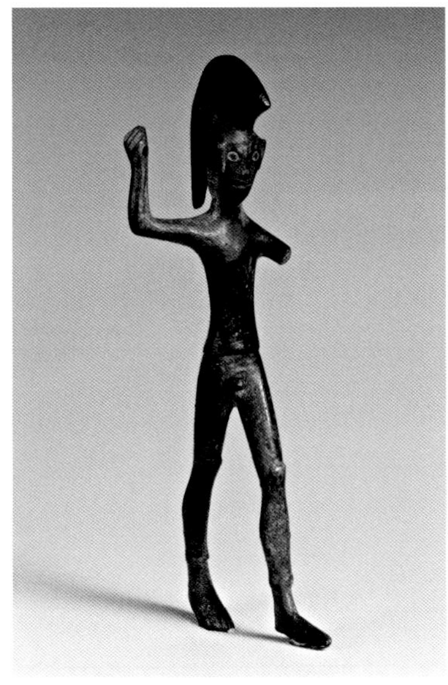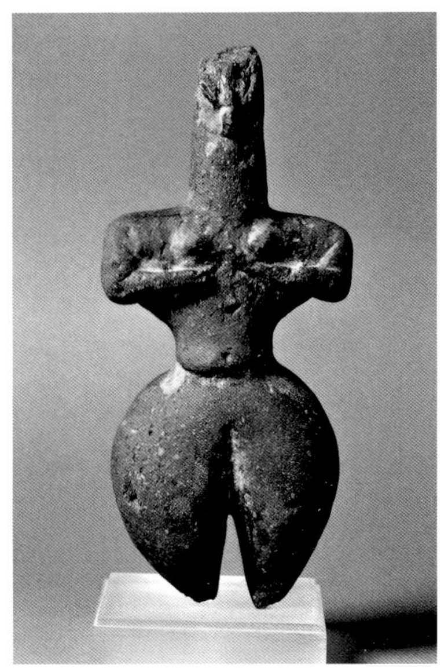

Bronze statuette of a striding warrior,
6th–5th century BCE. Etruscan or
Umbrian. Bronze, 5 11/16 in. (14.5 cm).
Metropolitan Museum of Art, New York.
Gift of George D. Pratt.

Greek idol, 6th–5th millennium BCE.
Thessaly. Terracotta, 7 in. (17.8 cm).
Collection Richard and Clara Serra.

**RS**: What I've always done is look at things I don't understand and ask myself why
it is I don't understand them, including prehistoric sculpture. We have a couple of small
terracotta Venuses.

**HF**: You've been interested in fertility pieces for a while?

**RS**: Forever. We also have a collection of pots, forty at least, from Cambodia. They're
called Ban Chiang. They were buried in a lakebed so they were preserved, and when they
were pulled out of the mud they were absolutely pristine. We collect pots—Chinese,
Japanese, African…

**HF**: You're interested in their volumes?

**RS**: Yes, in their volumes, but also in their balance, their shape, their curvature,
and how they collect and displace space. They're incredibly beautiful.

**HF**: At least originally they're all utilitarian in one way or another, right?

**RS**: I don't think that matters. Like Etruscan sculpture, these objects gnaw at me because
I don't know how to place them or even what to do with them. I've never known how to
incorporate them directly, but I'm convinced I've used them to rethink my work from
time to time. The seepage of influence is hard to pinpoint.

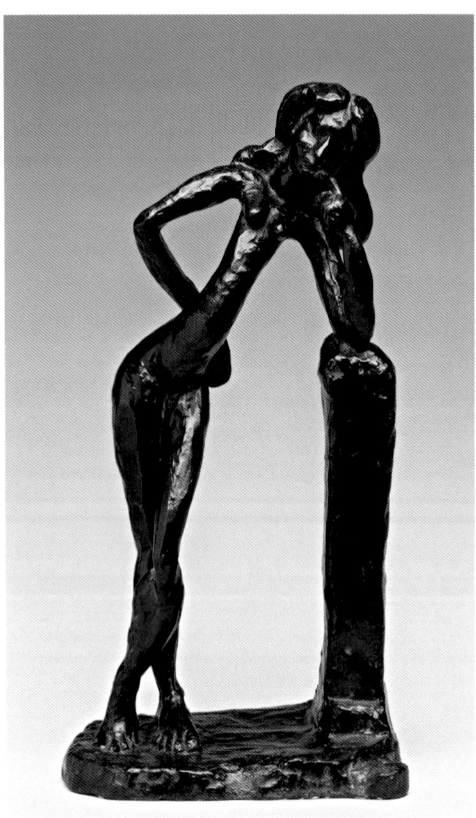

Henri Matisse, *The Serpentine*, 1909. Bronze,
21 ½ × 11 ½ × 7 ½ in. (54.6 × 29.2 × 19 cm).
Philadelphia Museum of Art. Gift of
R. Sturgis and Marion B. F. Ingersoll, 1963.

**HF**: So there are things you simply love and don't want to draw on explicitly?

**RS**: I don't know. There are forms within those traditions that are invaluable, and they might present an opening for me in ways I can't foresee.

**HF**: They're a resource precisely because they remain potential?

**RS**: It's their sheer difference. The only thing I can think of that's comparable to Etruscan sculpture is Matisse's *The Serpentine* (1909)—there's nothing quite like it in modern sculpture.

**HF**: Are there other examples of forms you don't understand but keep in reserve?

**RS**: Yes, there are many. They provide a spiritual fulfillment, and they're stabilizing in the sense that they represent a long history of made things. They show that history doesn't go away, in fact that it's ever present.

**HF**: That's how you see the history of sculpture—as always there, available, not past, or at least not lost?

**RS**: I think it was Emerson who said, "No experience lost." But then he also said, "Write whim on the lintel."

**HF**: Let me ask a different question. Some contemporary philosophers are interested in the time that comes before the human—they call it "ancestral time"—as well as the time that might come after the human, after we cease to exist as a species.[1] Do you think about your sculpture in relation to this deep time, or, less grandly, to the time when everything else will be stripped away from it, when the original circumstances of its making and viewing—its intention, meaning, and context—will disappear? Do you reflect on the deep time of sculpture in that sense?

**RS**: I think my body of work differentiates itself from other sculpture, but that difference might not be discerned in the future. They might just throw it into a big heap called "modern sculpture": Julio González, Picasso, David Smith, etc. Predictions of this sort aren't very useful.

**HF**: When you go to the Met—to the Etruscan gallery, for example—what do you see there exactly? What remains for you when everything else is stripped away?

**RS**: Triggers for thought.

**HF**: Do the intentions of the artist remain? Are they still legible, or can you project them in a way that's valid?

**RS**: What remains is the invention of the artist as he moves away from preexisting forms. What remains is that break with given conventions. That you can still register: the emergence of a new form. And then other new forms follow, and they validate the break.

**HF**: Is that what you mean by "History doesn't go away"?

**RS**: Yes. I'll give you an example. When I first traveled to Europe, I went to Greece, and one of the first things I saw in Athens was *Poseidon* (c. 460 BCE). Some people think it's *Zeus;* it's attributed to Myron, but that's unclear as well. Anyway, it floored me. After looking at Brancusi in Paris, I thought, "Brancusi never opened a form to that extent." He remains contained within the object; he doesn't extend into space horizontally and vertically in that way.

**HF**: Except for *Endless Column,* his forms are usually inward, almost self-involved.

**RS**: *Poseidon* is very advanced, beyond what the Greeks did later, because it opens the horizontal vertical plane. Nothing extends into space like that either before or after.

**HF**: The Greek sculpture that comes first to mind tends to pull the figure around itself,

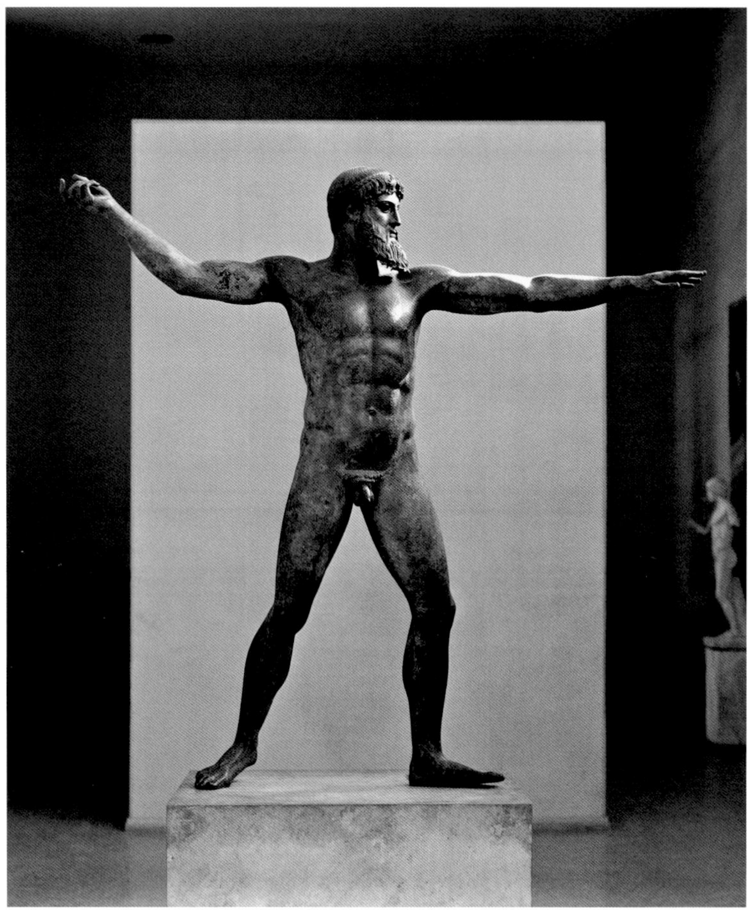

*Zeus* or *Poseidon*, c. 460 BCE. Greek sculpture. Bronze,
6 ft. 6 ¾ in. (2 m). National Archaeological Museum, Athens.

like *Discus Thrower* (c. 460 BCE); it's the same with Hellenistic sculpture, like *Boy with Thorn* (third century BCE). You mean *Poseidon* opens up in such a way that it seems to vector into space?

**RS**: Yes, both horizontally and vertically. He throws a triton into space, and his arms are outstretched, even though the figure's erect. That doesn't happen elsewhere. It returns to the internal structure of the limbs but also extends the volume of those juxtapositions. Figuration hadn't been that open before. Compared to *Poseidon, Discus Thrower* is stiff, and *Boy with Thorn* focuses your attention on the narrative of its figuration rather than the articulation of its form.

**HF**: *Poseidon* is not supported by a tree trunk or any other device.

**RS**: No, it's freestanding.

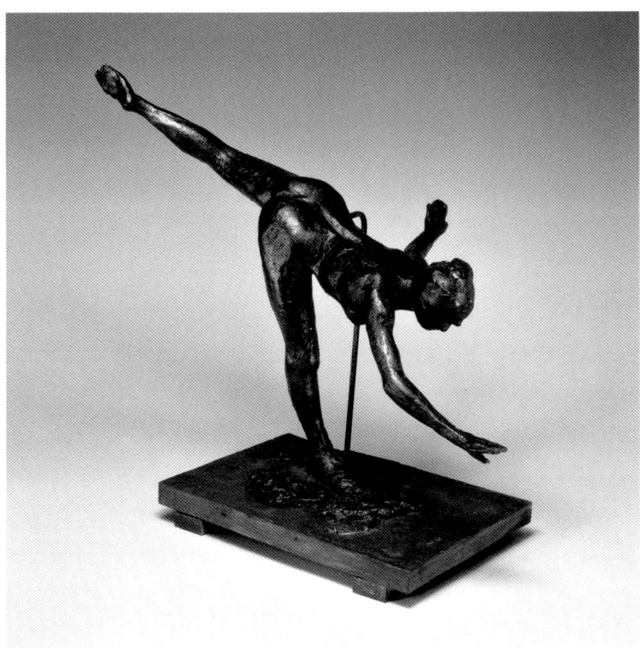

Edgar Degas, *Grande Arabesque, Third Time (First Arabesque Penchée)*, c. 1885/1890. Greenish-brown and black plastiline, overall without base: 16 ⁹⁄₁₆ × 12 ½ × 21 ⅞ in. (42 × 31.8 × 55.5 cm) height of figure: 16 in. (40.6 cm). National Gallery of Art, Washington, D.C. Collection Mr. and Mrs. Paul Mellon.

**HF:** What's also extraordinary is the torsion of the body—it's both frontal and in profile. There are no instances of that extension in related sculpture?

**RS:** It doesn't come up again until Degas.

**HF:** Which Degas do you have in mind?

**RS:** The ballerina with her leg stretched back and her arms forward for balance; it's called *First Arabesque Penchée* (c. 1885/90). In fact there are three or four Degas sculptures of young dancers at the Met that have similar vertical and horizontal extensions.

**HF:** How about Matisse's *The Serf* (1900–1904)? It's a striding figure.

**RS:** I never considered *The Serf* to be of much relevance. I see it as an anatomical study constricted by its own bulk. It looks to be influenced by Rodin without his internal movement within the form. In terms of invention I prefer *Poseidon* over Rodin.

**HF:** What else about the Greeks, or other ancients, that sticks with you?

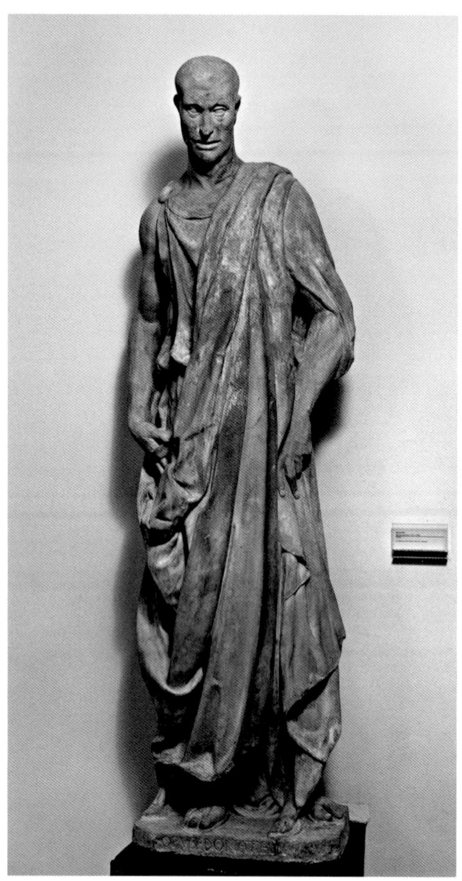

Donatello, *The Prophet Habakkuk*, 1423–35. Marble,
76 ¾ in. (195 cm). Museo dell'Opera del Duomo,
Florence, Italy.

**RS**: When I lived in Florence on a Fulbright I often looked at Donatello. You know his *The Prophet Habakkuk* (1423–35)?

**HF**: Yes. What about it struck you? Why that Donatello rather than others?

**RS**: It's one of the most compelling sculptures I've ever seen. It's imbued with the internal tension of a figure that encapsulates a silent emotion. That's absent from almost every other sculpture I know. You look up at him, and he gazes down at you, though his eyes seem almost blinded. His mouth is open.

**HF**: What does he say? Is he, like most prophets, doomed?

**RS**: I don't know. He speaks with God. If you take Donatello's range, you go from *Habakkuk* to *Gattamelata* (1453), the equestrian statue in Padua. Think of that shift. There's nothing in sculpture, up to that point, that deals with such an expansive volume. Nothing.

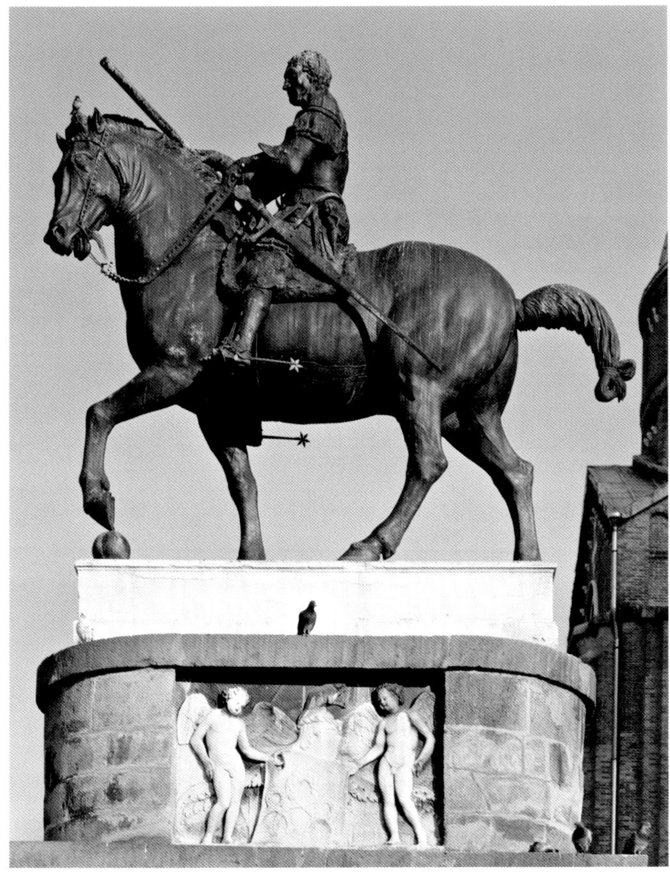

Donatello, *Equestrian Statue of Gattamelata*, 1453.
Bronze, 11 ft. 1 ⅞ in. × 12 ft. 9 ⁷⁄₁₆ in. (340 × 390 cm).
Piazza del Santo, Padua, Italy.

**HF**: What about the *Marcus Aurelius* in Rome, almost thirteen hundred years earlier?

**RS**: You can lift Marcus Aurelius off his horse—horse and rider are separable figures—whereas *Gattamelata* is a unified volume of horse and rider.

**HF**: But the type is an ancient one.

**RS**: I know; there's a whole iconography: one leg up, wounded in battle; two legs up, and so on.

**HF**: So, like the vector of extension in *Poseidon,* it's the force of volume in *Gattamelata* that struck you.

**RS**: Yes, and I'd say both are prime objects (in fact, if I remember right, George Kubler mentions Donatello in his discussion of prime objects), and neither has really been picked up or elaborated on.

**HF**: Anything else about Donatello?

**RS**: The other pieces I really admire are *Saint John the Evangelist* (1410–11) and *Judith and Holofernes* (1455–60). What interests me about *Saint John* is the folds and fall of the drapery from his shoulder to his foot: it's a linear abstraction that contains the posture of the figure. When I was in Florence I passed by *Judith and Holofernes* every day; Judith is static and Holofernes is stricken, and that sets up an internal juxtaposition between an arrested motion pushing upward and a gravitational force pushing downward. At the moment just before decapitation, the figuration rises and falls simultaneously.

**HF**: What about his wood *Mary Magdalene* (1455) with its anguished gouge into the skin of the sculpture?

**RS**: Yes. Even in reproduction it doesn't seem to be a carving; it looks like an emaciated form. In a sense it's a very contemporary work, what today we'd call an anti-formal figuration.

**HF**: It's another rare sculpture that seems to exist somehow out of time.

**RS**: You wouldn't think it's a Donatello. If you consider those five pieces alone, that's an enormous range.

**HF**: Can you talk more about how you look at historical art? On the one hand, you say it's always there, available to you; on the other hand, you're very concerned with innovation, how a new form displaces an old convention, and that displacing would seem to push prior work into an irretrievable past. You're also on the lookout for work you can use in your art—a particular object that can nudge along your practice. The primary criterion seems to be: Is this an invention I can build on?

**RS**: There are forms that replay in your mind's eye, and you ask, "How did that happen?" You think, "I'll find it again, it came before, it'll come again, it fits into an historical context somewhere." But some forms you keep replaying like a loop in your head; they keep coming up, and you don't know how to process them.

**HF**: That's different from the symbolic forms we discussed in another conversation, forms that trigger a set of associations for many people within the same culture. This kind of object seems more like a personal talisman.

**RS**: It becomes a thought you need to translate somehow, to transform in a way that makes sense in relation to your own work, but it's not a conscious process. Certainly I haven't consciously tried to incorporate *Habakkuk* or *Gattamelata* into my work.

**HF**: Any other epiphanies in Florence?

**RS**: I looked at Michelangelo a lot, and I admire his drawings, but I never identified with him, even though I really like many of his pieces. His work seemed overstated. In the Accademia there are four unfinished blocks…

**HF**: The *Slaves* (1513–15).

**RS**: Yes. I paid special attention to them because they give you an idea of his process, how he actually moved into the block. But if you want to find an entrance into sculpture, Donatello is more accessible—accessible in terms of how to think about a path that might be open to you.

**HF**: You mean "entrance" in Kubler's sense—finding a way into a series of preexisting work.

**Clara Weyergraf-Serra**: But you weren't even thinking of making sculpture then, were you?

**RS**: No, but I stopped painting in Florence, and I began to think about the potential for sculpture. In Florence sculpture is all around you, you can't avoid it, it's ever present.

**HF**: What else about the *Slaves*? In part they appeal to a modern sensibility because they're unfinished—you see the process, as you say.

**RS**: Often finished work is resolved to the point that there's no inkling of how it came about. The process is lost.

**HF**: Is that the first sculpture you saw that wore its process on its sleeve? Did that stick with you, the importance of procedural evidence?

**RS**: Not really. While I lived in Paris I looked at Giacometti, and you see his process. There's something else about my time in Florence. Every day I'd eat lunch in the student mensa. It had beautiful Luca della Robbias, and right across the street was the Laurentian Library. Do you know it?

**HF**: You mean Michelangelo's staircase in particular?

**RS**: Yes. I could never figure it out. Why would anybody make that central flowing staircase move down to those irregular oversized ovoids that are stacked so as to break the rhythm of the stairs, and then add two flanking staircases that descend in a very regular pattern? It's a Mannerist artifice. Now, if you go from the *Slaves* to the Laurentian Library, you wonder how this can be the same artist.

**HF**: A break in the work becomes a puzzle for you.

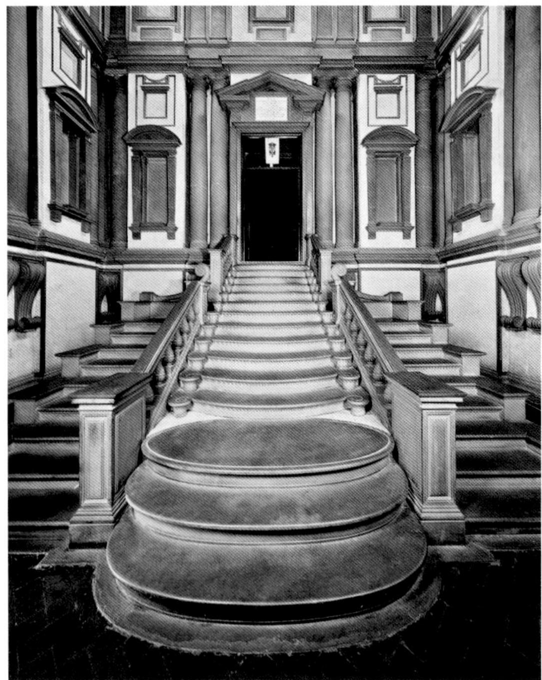

Michelangelo and Bartolomeo Ammannati,
Laurentian Library, 1524–68. Florence, Italy.

**RS:** Yes. Why does Michelangelo move into Mannerism? You can't tell in that building whether the walls are holding up the roof or the columns are, and then you have all these windows that wrap the whole room, many more than necessary. I was completely puzzled. That work ought to have happened decades later. What accounts for those ovoid tongues at the bottom of the staircase that are at a different height from any of the stairs and flow like lava into the vestibule? What was he thinking? Rothko said that the vestibule and the staircase of the library influenced his Seagram murals. Maybe it was the idea of a wall of windows. The connections artists make to historical art aren't necessarily evident in their work.

In Florence I lived in the Piazza Donatello, maybe even in the same studio that Giorgio de Chirico once occupied. There were moments when I'd peer out the window and see spatial configurations and separations that were completely unfamiliar—an opening on to a spatial wonder with a strong undercurrent of Surrealism, far removed from the classical space of the Renaissance. Artists often evoke a perception that we lack and that enables us to catch a glimpse of the world as they saw it.

**HF:** There was an uncanny aspect to Renaissance Florence that de Chirico picked up on?

**RS:** Yes. The fact that I'm interested in de Chirico might surprise some people, but I've always been intrigued by him, especially the spatial displacement in his early metaphysical paintings.

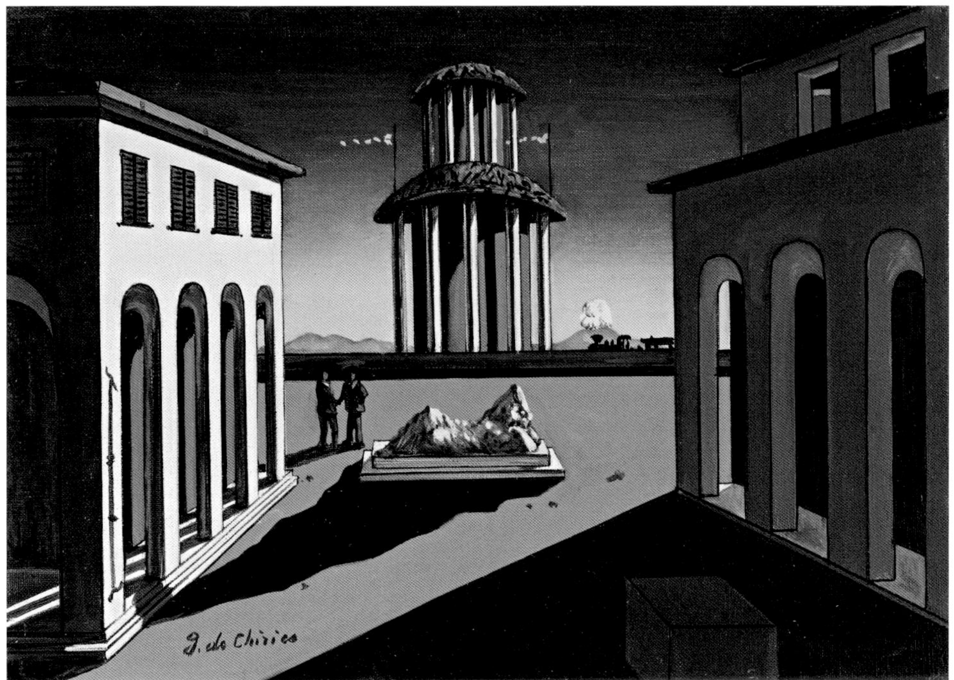

Giorgio de Chirico, *Piazza d'Italia,* c. 1950. Oil on canvas, 9 ¹³⁄₁₆ × 13 ⅞ in. (25 × 35.2 cm). Art Gallery of Ontario. Gift of Sam and Ayala Zacks, 1970.

**HF:** Paintings like *The Anxious Journey* (1913) where the perspective is doubled or otherwise awry?

**RS:** Certainly those, but the very early still lifes too.

**HF:** What about the still lifes—is it the space or the objects, or the objects in the space?

**RS:** The objects in the space on the tilted plane. Once you start looking at de Chirico seriously and you're living in Florence, you see the city through his eyes: the church of Santa Croce, the plazas, the statues in the plazas, the collision of antiquity with contemporary space.

**HF:** For some reason I imagined Florence would be the epitome of rediscovered classicism, and I found the city weirdly estranging when I first visited it. It isn't classical at all in that sense.

**RS:** No, it's not. There's an undercurrent of being lost in the circulation of its streets. Most of the streets are serpentine.

**HF:** Was this another way into your torqued pieces? Did this subliminal experience return much later to be worked out in that line of work?

**RS**: I think that's true. I don't want to get into Tony Smith and his epiphany about the New Jersey Turnpike as a work of art, but I remember walking from the Duomo back to the Piazza Donatello, snaking through the city, and thinking, "This street has a sculptural potential."

**HF**: Your interest in the Laurentian Library anticipates a move from sculpture to architecture. Did that experience have any resonance when you sought out models outside sculpture for the work in sculpture you wanted to produce?

**RS**: No, not at that time.

**HF**: Michelangelo is an artist who worked between sculpture and architecture. Bernini was another, but Bernini doesn't signify for you.

**RS**: Not as much as Borromini. Bernini always looked like licorice sticks to me.

**HF**: You mean he bent his sculpture every which way?

**RS**: Yes. Take a hot-rolled rod of steel, put two Xs on the end, turn it, and you've got a licorice stick you can put in the Vatican.

**HF**: Ouch. Anything else in Michelangelo?

**RS**: No. Again, I found him a little overwhelming. I couldn't find a way in.

**HF**: People say that about your work.

**RS**: With most art, if you're patient, you can find a way into the language, and it will give you some feedback. It's probably true with most people too. If you're patient enough, you can find some opening. It has to do with what you respond to or reach for and your willingness to see.

**HF**: You present sculpture between Michelangelo and Rodin as a desert. It's like John Cage saying that everything between Bach and Schoenberg is uninteresting. I get the point of the hyperbole—it clears space—but is that stretch really so barren for you?

**RS**: You'd have to name the artists you think are relevant, and I'd have to tell you why I think they're not. Who do we go to? Antonio Canova? You'd probably find some relief sculpture.

**HF**: In aesthetic discourse during that entire period there was a bias against sculpture, and relief sculpture became the paradigm of all sculpture because it was most like painting. The problem that the cognoscenti had with sculpture, basically from the Renaissance on, was that it was too material, too embodied, and too ambiguous because it presented too many views. That line was repeated by Diderot, Hegel, and Baudelaire right on down to Greenberg. One solution was the relief. When Adolf von Hildebrand wrote that sculpture should be modeled on the relief, he was advocating pictorial sculpture. To get out of that predicament was one task of twentieth-century sculpture.[2]

**RS**: Meyer Schapiro writes extensively on Romanesque sculpture, and he places it very high up in the canon.

**HF**: That's well before the period we're talking about.

**RS**: He writes about reliefs at the corners of buildings, reliefs that protrude from a right angle, and he goes into raptures over them.

**HF**: That's his early writing—about Moissac and other Romanesque cathedrals in southern France. That's when sculpture was not yet fully independent from architecture.[3]

**RS**: Right, it's an appendage. I don't consider it as sculpture. In fact I don't see any relief as sculpture.

**HF**: So, in order to be considered sculpture, it has to be what?

**RS**: It has to be a volume and a round that deals with space. It has to engage the viewer's body in movement.

**HF**: So we again face this paradox of your work. You're committed to sculpture as a category that's autonomous or at least semi-autonomous. At the same time, as you develop your idea of sculpture, you draw from other disciplines that aren't primarily sculptural, like engineering and architecture. Is that due to the deficit that you saw in the tradition of sculpture from Michelangelo to Rodin and maybe beyond?

**RS**: I didn't want to be limited by existing conventions. I had to find a way to deny them by alternative means.

**HF**: You didn't want to deal with the entire tradition of the figure because it was simply too conventional to you?

**RS**: It was all involved with the replica. Figuration didn't offer any prime objects that were open to elaboration.

**HF**: "Replica" again in Kubler's sense?

**RS**: Yes.

**HF**: I understand that the primary opposition for you remains figuration versus abstraction. But what about your examples of *Poseidon* and *Gattamelata*? You talk about those figurative sculptures as though they were abstract.

**RS**: No, all figurative sculpture is always involved with narrative, and I'm not involved with narrative. If you're involved with narrative, you're involved with the language of narration and representation as well as imagery, and that overrides form—it diverts from the experience of form.

**HF**: So it's not only sculpture understood in pictorial terms that you resist; you also can't abide by sculpture understood in terms of narrative.

**RS**: Yes. I never saw *Gattemelata* as a narrative sculpture. I know it's an equestrian rider, but that's not how I looked at it. I have no idea as to its iconography.

**HF**: So both image, or the idea that sculpture can be reduced to one picture for a static viewer, and narrative, or the idea that experience can be translated into another language, are things to be avoided at all costs.

**RS**: I found them limiting when I started out, and I still find them limiting.

**HF**: A final question or two. In our conversation about your immediate predecessors, you insisted that artists don't "replace" artists that come before.

**RS**: That's right. When Manet looked back to Velázquez, he didn't replace him.

**HF**: In fact you could say he refashioned Velázquez for his own time. That sometimes happens in art history. Vermeer was mostly forgotten until the critic Théophile Thoré-Bürger published his catalogue raisonné in the mid-nineteenth century. And it some-times happens in musical history: Mendelsson reviving Bach is a famous example. Okay, so artists don't replace artists. At the same time you also insist on a Bloomian idea of art history—that art develops by an aggressive displacement in an Oedipal way. How do you reconcile those two notions?

**RS**: Bloom argues you're replacing a father figure, not a historical one, which has to do with your psychic need to open up an immediate space for your work. It's a personal battle, one that doesn't necessarily push out into the path of history.

**HF**: It's a strategic antagonism that's close in time, not a distant affinity. In fact, a distant affinity might be claimed as a way to get around a paternal figure, Manet going to Velázquez to get around Courbet, say. In any case, there's no contradiction between the two for you? History doesn't go away in the long run *and* it's Oedipally antagonistic in the short term?

**RS**: That's right.

**HF**: Okay. Then, in our first conversation about your formation, you began with a testimonial to "self-reliance." We associate the term with Emerson, specifically his idea that Americans must make their own history and not simply "build the sepulchers of the fathers" as he thought Europeans did. Remember the first lines of "Nature" (1836)? "Why should we not also enjoy an original relation to the universe? Why should we not have a poetry and philosophy of insight and not of tradition, and a religion by revelation to us, and not the history of theirs?" How do you reconcile your commitment to that self-reliance with your insistence on historical self-consciousness?

**RS**: Why is that a contradiction? Self-reliance makes you inquisitive. I don't think it excludes history at all.

**HF**: If you don't see a contradiction there, how about the tension between your commitment to the phenomenological here and now of your sculpture on the one hand and your interest in the deep time of sculptural history on the other?

**RS**: You call up the deep time of sculpture in order to make it present.

**HF**: In the phenomenological here and now?

**RS**: Yes. That's the only way it's useful—as experience.

# Sculpture Hadn't Dealt with Steel

**HF**: Can you say more about your resistance to image and narrative? Those aspects of art already came under great pressure a century ago with readymades, assemblages, and constructions. Yet you dismissed readymades from the start and you abandoned assemblages early on.

**RS**: I think assemblages are as narrative as figurative paintings, but I did find a resource in constructions. For me, Picasso's *Guitar* (1912) was enormously important because it opened up the possibility of entering into a space of overlapping planes. In effect it's a three-dimensional Cubist space. *Guitar* is the first sculpture to deconstruct the inertness of sculptural form, though its space remains planar and pictorial and solely visual. The Russians, Tatlin first, understood the implications, and began the Constructivist revolution by inventing constructions you could physically enter. Picasso never realized that potential of his invention. The implications of *Guitar* were greater than those of the *Absinthe Glass* (1914), which is an interesting series and more generative for Picasso himself.

**HF**: He resisted many of his own inventions: he recognized them but didn't carry them forward. Do you remember when and how you came to Tatlin?

**RS**: I started looking at Tatlin when I began propping pieces.

**HF**: Most of the relevant work wasn't known in the West.

**RS**: I saw it in books. I remember one piece with cables across the corner from one wall to the other with pieces of metal in between.

**HF**: One of his corner counter-reliefs. There were publications already in the early 1960s, but not much context, historical or otherwise, for such work. In the early reception of Constructivism in the West, artists like Gabo and Pevsner were privileged because they had emigrated, whereas Tatlin, Rodchenko, and the others weren't well known. What drew you to Constructivism, and what were you able to extrapolate from the illustrations?

**RS**: Working in the context of a room, working from wall to wall, reorganizing the perception of the architecture.

**HF**: What about the treatment of materials? An early Tatlin relief like *Selection of Materials* (1914) presents, almost in a didactic way, how different materials can be manipulated—what iron, glass, and stucco want to be, so to speak. Did that aspect of Constructivism come across?

**RS**: No, I was more interested in the formal aspect of mediating the architectural space, not in the mixing of different materials.

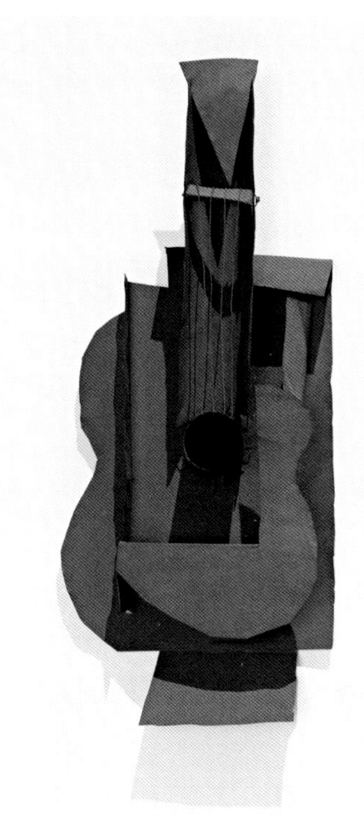

Pablo Picasso, *Guitar,* 1914. Sheet metal and wire,
30 ½ × 13 ¾ × 7 ⅝ in. (77.5 × 35 × 19.3 cm). The Museum
of Modern Art, New York. Gift of the artist.

Vladamir Tatlin, *Corner Counter Relief,* 1915
(reproduction). Iron, copper, wood, 27 ¹⁵⁄₁₆ × 46 ⁷⁄₁₆ in.
(71 × 118 cm). State Russian Museum, St. Petersburg.

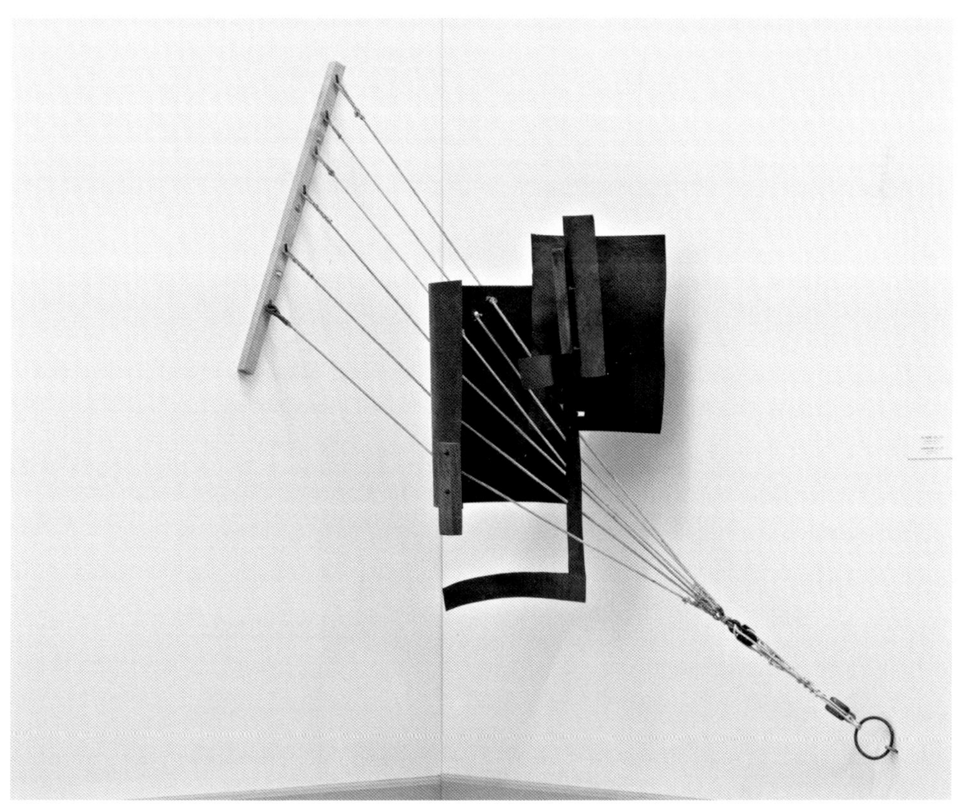

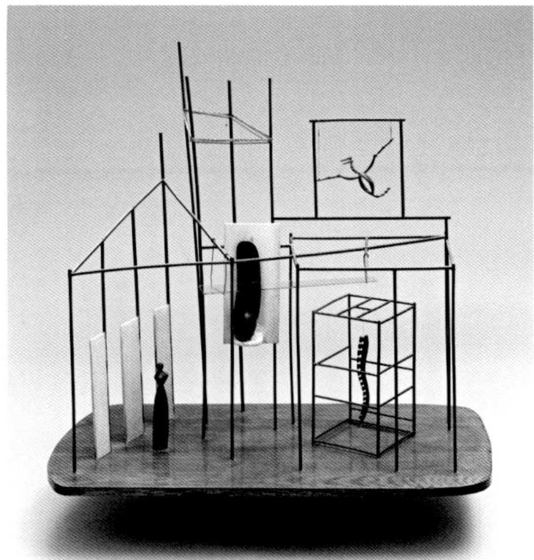

Alberto Giacometti, *The Palace at 4 a.m.*, 1932.
Wood, glass, wire, and string, 25 × 28 ¼ × 15 ¾ in.
(63.5 × 71.8 × 40 cm). The Museum of Modern Art,
New York. Purchase.

**HF:** Did you discuss this work with others at the time? Andre was interested in Rodchenko, and Flavin was interested in Tatlin.

**RS:** I didn't talk with Andre about Constructivism. And Flavin had this high-priest attitude I found disconcerting. But you're playing the art historian drawing up geneaologies. You know who I want to talk about? Giacometti. This might surprise you, but I think his most important pieces are the Surrealist ones.

**HF:** That doesn't surprise me; I agree. But when you talked about how important Giacometti was for you during your time in Paris, it was his figures you had in mind, right?

**RS:** No, it was about seeing the artist who epitomized for me the existential task of confronting work in the studio every day. But the pieces I was most drawn to were his earlier ones.

**HF:** Why?

**RS:** Even though *The Palace at 4 a.m.* (1932) was probably influenced by Picasso's *Monument to Apollinaire* (1928), it opened up a psychological space, a dream space, subliminal and erotic, that wasn't present in other sculpture of the time. And then other pieces intrigued me too—how they claimed the floor.

**HF:** You mean the game board pieces?

**RS:** No. There's a piece called *Project for a Passageway* (1930–31) that's an elongated form on the floor. It has an architectural dimension, but you can also read it as a body stretched out on the floor. Giacometti's *Woman with Her Throat Cut* (1932) is another sprawling

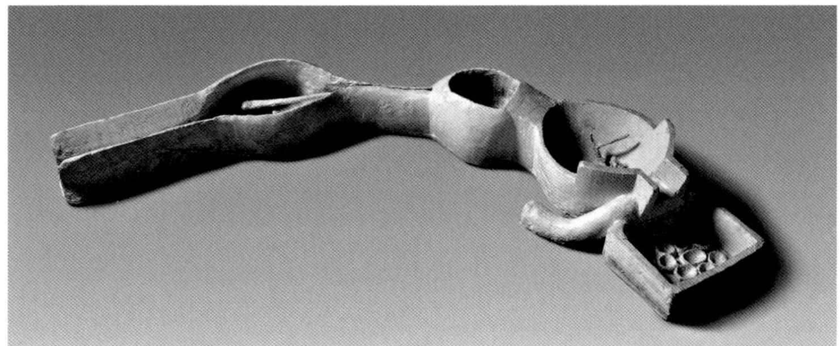

Alberto Giacometti, *Project for a Passageway,* 1930–31. Plaster, 6 ⁵⁄₁₆ × 49 ⅝ × 16 ⁹⁄₁₆ in. (16 × 126 × 42 cm). Kunsthaus Zürich, Alberto Giacometti-Stiftung, 1965.

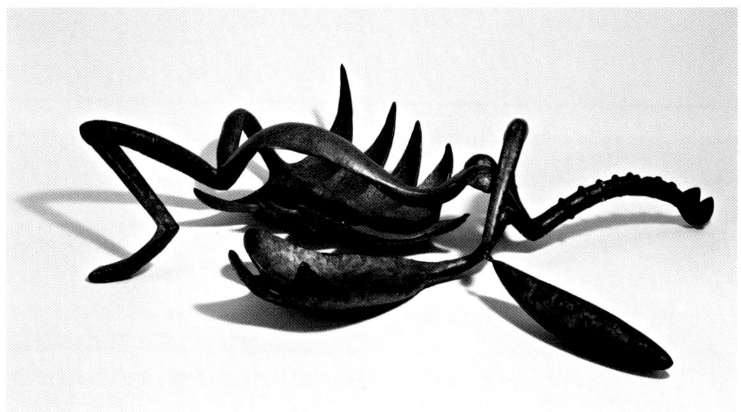

Alberto Giacometti, *Woman with Her Throat Cut,* 1932 (cast 1949). Bronze, 8 × 34 ½ × 25 in. (20.3 × 87.6 × 63.5 cm). The Museum of Modern Art, New York. Purchase.

figuration on the floor. Judd came along later and claimed to be the first to occupy the floor. Not true.

**HF**: Giacometti opened up a psychological space, as you say, whereas Judd was literal in his declaration. Let's stick with Surrealism. You've often criticized it as too figurative, imagistic, narrative—as Greenberg did too, by the way. Why make an exception for Giacometti?

**RS**: When he goes back to the figure, as good as he is, he's still back to modeling, casting, and drawing in space. I'm not going to take anything away from him because I think *Standing Woman* (1948–49) and *Walking Man* (1960) are good in any century. They look like they're deteriorating in front of you.

**HF**: Newman once said they almost seem to be made of spit.

**RS**: They're fragile and vulnerable; it's as though they've been in the Aegean for centuries.

And yet they gather space, even if it's a space that's withered. Still, in terms of the history of sculpture, the little figures and small things he would throw away resonate for me more than the pieces everyone cherishes like *Standing Woman* and *Walking Man*.

**HF**: Which little things?

**RS**: He made small pieces in matchboxes. He'd take them out, roll them around the table, and then put them in his pocket or throw them away. That was during the war.

**HF**: What is it that appealed to you about them?

**RS**: The idea of making something, carrying it in a matchbox like a talisman, and then often discarding it. That's not really Dada. It's about constantly working and constantly disposing, and when he gets to his figures he's doing the same thing—making and disposing, making and disposing. That starts with the little pieces.

**HF**: What about the fetishistic quality of his Surrealist work—did that interest you? His "disagreeable objects" in particular have the ambiguity of the fetish, at once attractive and repulsive.

**RS**: Particularly the one with the hanging ball. That's one of the most erotic sculptures ever made.

**HF**: You mean *Suspended Object* (1930–31), which is a sphere with a cleft suspended above a wedge like a banana. It's hard to know how to identify the objects; they seem gendered, but which is which? It's erotic because it's ambiguous, and it conjures up desire—desire born of lack as Jacques Lacan would have it—because the two parts don't quite touch.

**RS**: I'd take that one, *The Palace at 4 a.m.*, *Project for a Passageway*, *Woman with Her Throat Cut*, and *Hand Caught by the Fingers* (1932), and then I'd take *Cube* (1933–34). You know that bronze piece? It's really a polyhedron.

**HF**: It's a very strange object.

**RS**: It's probably the most abstract sculpture Giacometti ever made. It's as if he lifted the polyhedron out of Dürer's *Melancholia I* (1514).

**HF**: I never saw the connection, but there is a melancholia in Giacometti: his art seems made from a depressive position.

**RS**: There's a similar piece by Picasso called *Death's Head* (c. 1941). I saw it again at the MoMA show in 2015–16, and I can't get it out of my mind. That sculpture gnaws at me; it has enormous weight and mass. It's obviously a death image, and as essential and

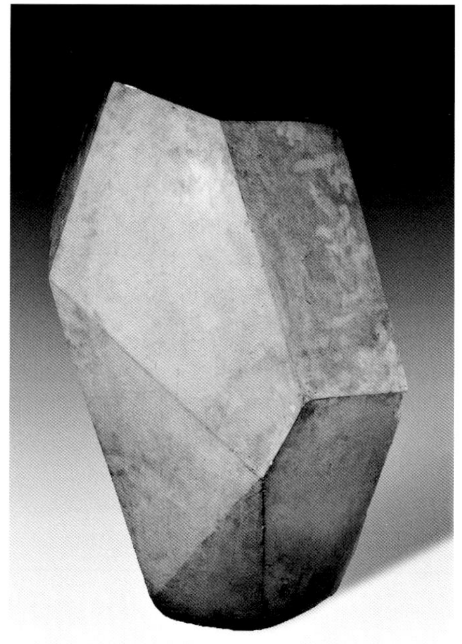

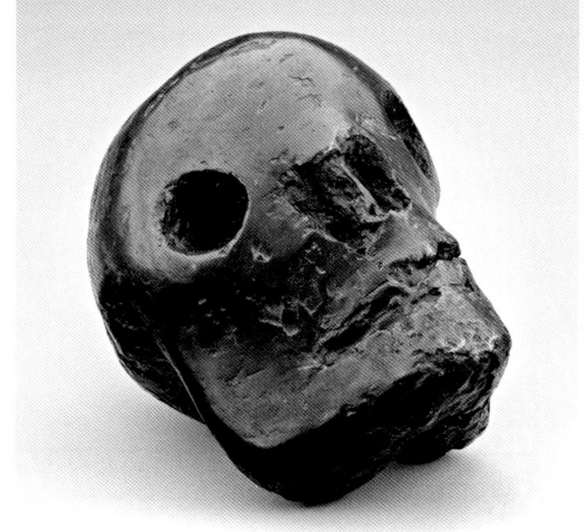

Alberto Giacometti, *Cube,* 1933–34. Plaster, 37 ⅜ × 21 ¼ × 23 ¼ in. (95 × 54 × 59 cm). Kunsthaus Zürich, Alberto Giacometti-Stiftung. Donated by Bruno and Odette Giacometti, 2006.

Pablo Picasso, *Death's Head,* c. 1941. Bronze, 9 ¹³⁄₁₆ × 8 ¼ × 12 ³⁄₁₆ in. (25 × 21 × 31 cm). Musée national Picasso, Paris.

primitive as anything you can imagine. In the photos Brassaï took in Picasso's studio, *Death's Head* is always on the floor.

**HF**: Is that sculptural quality bound up with its skullness, or does it exist apart?

**RS**: I'm not sure, but it was the most grounded work in the show.

**HF**: It has the heaviness of Giacometti's *Cube.*

**RS**: Yet it's figurative, a skull. In fact it's a boulder with a jaw and two holes punched in for eyes. I'd have to step completely out of my own work to do something like that.

**HF**: Well, it has the density of a forged piece, so it wouldn't be completely out of your range.

**RS**: You're saying why not give myself permission to do that?

**HF**: Yes.

**RS**: It'd be a big departure. It's an iconic sculpture.

**HF**: But you always talk about how important it is not to be confined by your work.

**RS**: True. The real problem is that I'm just not interested in figuration.

**HF**: There's a lot of Halloween in Picasso's sculpture. *Death's Head* is one of the few pieces that seems really serious about death, not too maudlin or ghoulish.

**RS**: It makes most everything else look a little frivolous. When you think about Picasso, you never think about weight. That's the only sculpture where weight is the main issue.

**HF**: Let me press you on two other points. One is the occupation of the floor, which you often credit to Brancusi too, at least as your prompt for removing any pedestal or plinth. The other concerns the model of the fetish. Of course, Giacometti, like Picasso and others, was very interested in African sculpture. Did it have any place in your formation?

**RS**: Not until later, when I started collecting Lobi pieces from Burkina Faso. I didn't look at African sculpture seriously until I was in my fifties.

**HF**: Maybe it came to you through osmosis, since those earlier artists had already brought aspects of African art into their work. What about the occupation of the floor? You've said that the removal of the pedestal is the most important move in Brancusi.

**RS**: The wood structures that sometimes hold up the sculpture are part of the work; at the same time they're bases.

**HF**: It's ambiguous. Brancusi liked to pull the base up into the sculpture or pull the sculpture down into the base.

**RS**: As you know, when I was in Paris I went to the Brancusi studio and made a lot of drawings.

**HF**: Did any particular sculptures stand out, or was it the whole ensemble that struck you?

**RS**: Sometimes *The Cock* (1924), but usually different groupings.

**HF**: Did it interest you that he presented his works as a system, a language of forms?

**RS**: Yes, it was there to be read; it was legible and accessible.

**HF**: Was that an insight you didn't get elsewhere—that an artist could produce a grammar, a set of elements, that would generate new arrangements, new works?

**RS**: Any way you wanted to think about sculpture, it was available in Brancusi. If you wanted to go abstract, it was there; if you wanted to go figurative, it was there; if you wanted to go vertical, it was there; if you wanted to go horizontal, it was there. It was all there.

**HF**: There's also the opening to architecture.

**RS**: Yes. Târgu Jiu, his compound of sculptures in Romania.

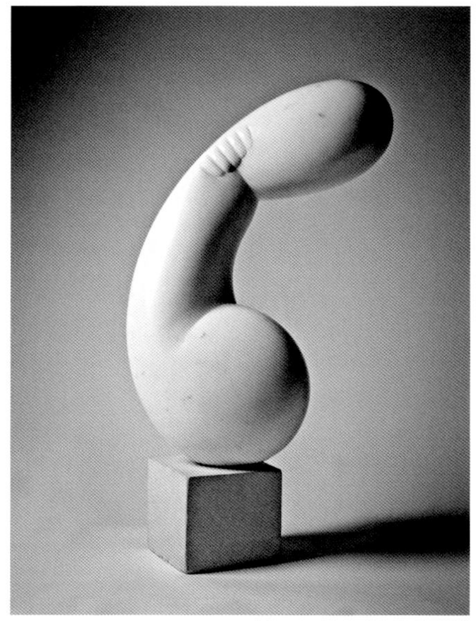

Constantin Brancusi, *Princess X*, c. 1909–16.
Marble with Caen limestone base, 22 × 11 × 9 in.
(55.9 × 27.9 × 22.9 cm). Sheldon Museum of Art,
University of Nebraska–Lincoln. Gift of Mrs.
Olga N. Sheldon in memory of Adams Bromley
Sheldon, 1963.

**HF**: When his work is presented, it's usually as a model of abstraction, like the way he develops *Mademoiselle Pogany* (1913, 1920, 1931), which becomes more and abstract, or the great birds, which do the same thing. But for you the abstract doesn't cancel out the figurative in his work.

**RS**: That's right. Also, when Brancusi makes a modulated column out of wood cut to fit between floor and ceiling, he preempts Judd.

**HF**: But Judd's stacks are shelves, separated, placed at intervals. The column's unbroken.

**RS**: Nevertheless, it's from floor to ceiling, and it functions as a relief, because it's right up against the wall. It's not freestanding; it's not in the middle of the room. What would you say about his *Princess X* (1915)? Don't you think it anticipates Picasso's Boisgeloup heads of the 1930s, which are basically cocks and balls?

**HF**: Brancusi saw *Princess X* as "the eternal feminine." Picasso (some say it was Matisse) replied, "This isn't a woman at all; it's a phallus." A Lacanian would say it's both; it's woman *as* phallus.

**RS**: Don't you think Picasso picked up on that? No one ever puts the two together.

**HF**: Both sculptures also evoke fertility figures. Picasso owned two copies of the *Venus of Lespugue,* which he riffs on in *Venus of Gas* (1945), a piece that is simply an old gas stove burner.

**RS**: *Princess X* and the Boisgeloup series are about the same thing, but Brancusi was there earlier. His sculpture is more erotic, and he wasn't mocking the subject—he didn't turn it into a cartoon like Picasso.

**HF**: Let me ask you a different question about Brancusi. Part of the interest of his work is his equal and opposite commitment to idealism and materialism. On the one hand, there's an idealism in his search for pure, almost Platonic form, the birdness of the bird, the fishness of the fish, and so on. On the other, there's a materialism in his commitment to wood, stone, and bronze. Apart from the abstraction, it's his materialism you develop.

**RS**: You can't separate the two. He reduced his materials to the point of abstraction: the more worked the material, the more pure the form. But I'm not a big fan of the bronzes.

**HF**: Why?

**RS**: I think they border on Art Deco.

**HF**: What you just said—the more worked, the more pure—shows how matter can be sublimated into ideal form, but the reverse can happen too—ideal form can fall back into mundane thingness. It's a famous anecdote: When Duchamp arranged for a Brancusi show in New York in 1926, one of the bird sculptures was held at customs for duty because it was taken to be manufactured object, a utilitarian thing, not an art work.

**RS**: When he polishes his cast bronzes, he strives for effect.

**HF**: Unlike the stone and wood pieces, the bronzes catch light, which tends to dematerialize them. Brancusi seemed to like that effect—the way he photographed them often underscores it. It's also always troubled me a little that he'd do the same piece in different materials; that seems to undermine his own materialism.

**RS**: It's like Cy Twombly going to bronze from his plaster pieces.

**HF**: Where did you get your materialism? What does that word mean to you?

**RS**: I got it from working at factories in the Bay Area.

**HF**: That's a physical relationship to matter. Where do you get your materialism?

**RS**: I don't understand the question.

**HF**: You say matter dictates form; that's a kind of materialism. But you also have a materialist view of history, society, and culture. Where did you get that materialism? Materialism as opposed to idealism.

**RS**: Idealism? I don't even know what the word means.

**HF**: That's telling in its own right.

**RS**: What sculptor is involved with idealism?

**HF**: We just agreed that Brancusi sometimes is.

**RS**: Yes, probably to his deficit. Trying to make a sublime form.

**Clara Weyergraf-Serra**: Giacometti is as well.

**RS**: Giacometti isn't involved with making a perfect form; he's trying to see. You know who might be involved with idealism? Judd.

**HF**: But Judd argued that he wanted to get away from idealism, which he took to mean, in terms of art, that the idea for a work preexists the work, that it is in your head before it is in the world. He thought relational composition was also idealist because it suggested premeditation as well. That was a standard line in his presentation of Minimalism.[1]

**CW-S**: But I don't think Judd worked that way, which might be why I never quite understood where he wanted to go.

**HF**: There's a real gap between what Judd said about Minimalism and what he did as Minimalism.

**CW-S**: I agree. The person who's a materialist in my eyes, which is why I like him so much, is Robert Ryman.

**RS**: And Andre.

**HF**: Is that why you had an affinity for Andre more than for Judd—precisely on the question of materialism?

**RS**: Yes.

**HF**: What about Flavin? A little like Brancusi, he wanted it both ways.

**RS**: I see Flavin and Judd as still involved with painting. Judd had a show at Pace Gallery not long before he died. He had a big plywood box on the floor, and he was there with a can of yellow paint painting the plywood on the bottom of the box. I actually asked him, "Why are you doing that?" In his mind's eye he was still a painter.

**CW-S**: Well, he's interested in surfaces for sure.

**RS**: He's painting it yellow! He could have done it any other way—or not at all.

**HF**: As I've said to you before, I took the Minimalist argument, the literalist argument, too literally, and projected it on to the work. A lot of people did. Rosalind Krauss was on to the illusionistic dimension in Judd early on. For you, then, the Minimalists didn't break with painting enough.

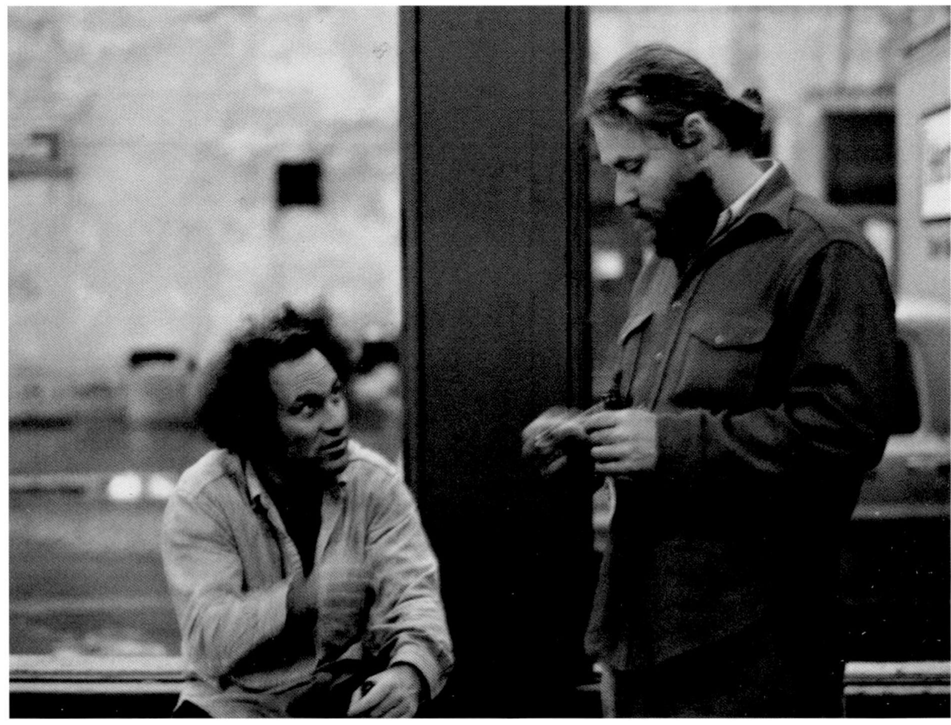

Richard Serra and Donald Judd at Judd's studio, New York, 1972.

**RS**: I don't think any of them was really interested in the history of sculpture.

**HF**: What made your break with painting more emphatic?

**RS**: They wanted to hang on to pictorialism, and I didn't. I wanted to expunge it completely, and they only said they did.

**CW-S**: They also hang on to the object. Space was never the main issue.

**HF**: What about Flavin? He declares a space.

**RS**: More so than the others.

**HF**: What about welded sculpture? Judd said that painting was too part-by-part, too relational, too compositional. You made a similar argument in relation to welded sculpture. Can you talk about that line from Picasso and Julio González to David Smith and its influence on you?

**RS**: They assemble and weld steel parts, then anchor them, in ways that, in terms of gravity and balance, are fake.

**HF**: False to the material?

**RS**: And false to the construction. Basically all my pieces are freestanding. In fact, each part is freestanding in and of itself.

**HF**: So it was the untruth you rejected. That's another materialist commitment.

**RS**: Those artists make-believe something's happening when it's not. I've said to you before that the Minimalist movement—Judd, Sol LeWitt, even Flavin, not Andre—is a neo-Constructivist movement. LeWitt's open cubes are welded steel sculpture painted white.

**HF**: There had to be some resource in welded sculpture for you.

**RS**: I was more attracted to Brancusi. I looked at Picasso's and González's welded sculpture, but I didn't take it very seriously. And I thought Smith was a minor Picasso dealing with assemblage.

**HF**: That's harsh.

**RS**: I understood he was an interesting sculptor, and I liked some of his juxtapositions, but I didn't take him very seriously either. Everyone loves *Australia* (1951). Not me.

**HF**: Too much "drawing in space"?

**RS**: No, too frontal.

**HF**: Smith actually talks about his work as an eidetic image, a mental event; he doesn't stress the purely sculptural aspect as you do.

**CW-S**: He's the three-dimensional equivalent of de Kooning.

**HF**: You mean in terms of gesture?

**CW-S**: No, in being attached to the European tradition and in continuing it.

**RS**: He's attached to assemblage. If you saw him producing a sculpture like *Leda* (1938), he'd lay all the different pieces on the ground, make drawings of the shapes, and then figure out how to put them together. It's straight assemblage.

**HF**: What about the apparent commitment to industrial work—his persona of the sculptor as welder? Did that open up the possibility that you could use industrial processes in sculpture directly, or did it seem like a performance to you?

**RS**: I've never welded anything in my life; I wouldn't know how. That doesn't interest me at all. But bringing the methods of industry into art, as well as the mechanics of building, certainly interested me. The history of sculpture hadn't really dealt with steel; that was my opening. It's like Warhol bringing advertisement and silkscreen into painting, or Cellini bringing goldsmithing into sculpture.

**HF**: That insight didn't come by way of Smith?

**RS**: No.

**HF**: How then?

**RS**: It came after I did the splash piece for Johns where I used a small lead plate bisecting a corner to splash against. After I realized that the corner held the plate in place, I decided to get a large steel plate and shove it into the corner. So the idea came out of my own work; it had nothing to do with the history of welded sculpture. I wasn't interested in stitching metal together with a torch; I was interested in how to open up space. And that's why Judd was interested in me—because I was messing around with space. But I didn't understand Judd. I'd say to him, "You've written about all these artists who are supposedly making 'specific objects.' Why are you casting such a wide net?"

**HF**: What was his response?

**RS**: He'd give me this look that said "young punk." He didn't dismiss me, but Judd wasn't used to people challenging him.

**CW-S**: So why do you think he was interested in those artists?

**RS**: He wanted to gather all of them under his umbrella in order to establish a movement. "Okay, I'm doing 'specific objects,' other people are too, they're all part of my circle." How could he claim H. C. Westermann and Lucas Samaras as part of his movement? If you look at the list of those he anointed, it's pretty absurd.

**HF**: You could also call it generous.

**RS**: Generous? What you're calling generosity I'd call usurpation.

**HF**: It's not like he annexed anyone. "Specific objects" turned out to be a rubric mostly for one artist. Can you say more about how industrial methods supported your opening out into space?

**RS**: It allowed for scale—for putting objects in a field and demarking space between them. I made a series of pieces that had bars on the ground with plates cut into the bars. Then in 1971 there was an accident at the Walker Art Center in Minneapolis, and a worker named Raymond Johnson was killed. After that I decided I was going to set the sculptures on the ground and to place the elements apart. That's when I began working with blocks of different elevations on the floor. I never thought the series with plates and bars was very interesting because the bars were functioning as a surrogate base.

**HF**: Even though the bars are sometimes on top of the plates, they read as a support?

**RS**: You're thinking of earlier lead props where I often set a bar on top. In the steel plate pieces I made in 1970–71 the bars were always on the ground, never on top, and the plates were set into slots cut into the bars. After the accident, I thought, "I'm going to open the cage."

**HF**: You wanted to do that in any case.

**RS**: Yes, but that really kicked it off.

**HF**: I have a question related to the one about industrial methods. You found limited resources in the sculpture that came before you. Is that what prompted your interest in engineers and architects? Was that a programmatic move on your part, or did you feel your way into it? Did the accident reinforce the importance of engineering for you?

**RS**: It was the accident, yes, but I also thought there were very interesting inventions in engineering, particularly in bridge building.

**HF**: You've mentioned the Roeblings and Robert Maillart in particular.

**RS**: And Eiffel.

**HF**: So you took up this field in the mode of research?

**RS**: Yes. But in some ways that interest developed when I was a kid working in steel mills.

**HF**: So it was always already there somehow. That's another aspect of your materialism— the belief that labor produces the world?

**RS**: I believe that totally.

**HF**: That's evident in your work, which is why I see it as Marxist in spirit, even though that's not part of your formation. One aspect of your materialism is your pledge to "demythologize," which is also central to Marxist critique.[2] That's part of the Constructivist legacy of Tatlin and Rodchenko: they called on artists to defetishize the work of art— to expose the process behind the product. In part that's what "truth to materials" meant when Tatlin first uttered the phrase. You've talked about how most sculpture seemed to be untrue to its material and its construction; your imperative was to defetishize as well.

**RS**: To open it up, to expose it.

**HF**: And that's where the work is Marxist—in its testimony to the labor that resides in every product. When you found all that rubber on Thomas and West Broadway…

**RS**: I didn't use it as a found object.

**HF**: You didn't treat it as a product to riff on but as a material to manipulate.

**RS**: Right. I cut it, hung it, folded it, tore it, and flopped it around; I did almost everything I could possibly do with it. Yes, that was a beginning, if not the beginning.

**HF**: Who besides the Constructivists pointed you in that direction? You grew up near Mark di Suvero. What relation does his work have to yours?

**RS**: None other than he lived two doors down in the sandlot and was dragging in timber off the beach and building constructions.

**HF**: Even then?

**RS**: Yes. My mother came to see me once in New York. I took her to the Whitney Museum, and she looked at *Hankchampion* (1960) and said, "Oh, there's a Mark di Suvero." I asked, "How do you know that?" And she said, "He's been doing it all his life."

**HF**: His interest in raw material, balance, and cantilever didn't stick with you?

**RS**: No, it didn't interest me. I found the cantilever too gestural.

**HF**: It wasn't an intermediary between those blurry photographs of Tatlin's counter-reliefs and your own work?

**RS**: When the balance is supported by cables it bothers me. It's the same with some of Frank Stella's sculptures, like the one behind the National Gallery in D.C.; it's tied down by cables.

**HF**: What about Rauschenberg's *Elemental Sculptures*?

**RS**: Those early pieces?

**HF**: Yes, the ones he made in the mid-1950s on Fulton Street, when that neighborhood was in transition, really torn up. Although they're not as elemental as the title makes them sound, they're fairly simple juxtapositions of rocks, scrap wood, twine, and iron pieces. They show a commitment to material as found as well as an interest in construction at its most basic.

**RS**: But they're still put together as compositions.

**HF**: In a way yes, but, again, they're more juxtaposed than composed. He showed some at the Stable Gallery; otherwise I don't think they were around much to be seen. When you arrived in New York in 1966, were you interested in Rauschenberg and Johns?

**RS**: Johns, not Rauschenberg. I saw Rauschenberg as an extension of Schwitters.

**HF**: You saw all his work in terms of collage?

**RS**: Or assemblage.

**HF**: What in particular about Johns?

**RS**: His process, how to invent a mark, how to build a form.

**HF**: You could see, or intuit, the process in his work?

**RS**: Yes, in Johns the image is never as important as the making.

**HF**: Was that due, in part, to his use of encaustic, the way it suspends the gesture, registers the process?

**RS**: Yes, but it happens in his drawing, too: how to invent a mark, how to repeat it, how to make it into a configuration, how to make that configuration into a whole. Johns invented a new way of drawing just as Twombly invented a new kind of calligraphy.

**HF**: And that's what interested you in both those artists.

**RS**: Also, both those artists, but particularly Johns, are unself-conscious in the sense that the impetus of the work is deeper than the result. You sense an unconscious need in the work.

**HF**: People talk about how images return in Johns almost on their own—how they insist.

**RS**: Yes. In his initial entrance into mark-making he almost couldn't care less about the images.

**HF**: There's a compulsive dimension?

**RS**: Yes, and, again, the process is more interesting—for me and, I think, for him—than the image.

**HF**: If Judd was interested in you, in part, because you opened up space, what do you think Johns saw in your work? It's not often that an artist of one generation is so welcoming to an artist of the next.

**RS**: Johns saw the splash piece at the "Anti-Illusion" show at the Whitney in 1969 and thought, "It's coming at me all at once." He was interested in the process of its making, its physicality, how the work looked like the way it happened. He thought it looked like it happened all at once, even though it was built laboriously, ladleful by ladleful, and that's the same with his work: it looks like it happens all at once, almost effortlessly. I think work that's really good can't look too labored.

**HF**: How is that all-at-once-ness different from instantaneity that Greenberg celebrated in modernist painting (Michael Fried famously called it "presentness")?[3] I thought a key criterion for you is that we be able to see the process, which implies a duration, a temporality, in the work—and, again, that we see, or at least intuit, the labor.

**RS**: That's the case in Johns, yes, but it's not true of Judd, Flavin, or LeWitt.

**HF**: Isn't it hard to reconcile the effortless and the processual?

**RS**: It's the result that has to look effortless. When you look at that big Pollock at the Met, *Autumn Rhythm* (1950), it looks effortless. This huge, heavily worked painting looks effortless.

**HF**: For some viewers it comes at them all at once. That's how Greenberg and Fried saw Pollock. For others you can't sublimate the process in that way; you can't forget the materiality of the paint, the physicality of the gesture, the gravity of the drip, and the horizontality of the floor on which it was made. For me it's both at once, and it's that tension between presentness and process, between optical all-at-once-ness and aformal action, that makes the painting great.

**RS**: I don't see a tension between process and presentness. Process constitutes presentness. That's why it looks to me like it happened all at once.

**HF**: And that's important for your work too?

**RS**: It's something I'd like to achieve.

# Controversies

**HF**: Let's talk about the controversies in your career, as you experienced them at the time and as you see them now. Where do you want to begin?

**RS**: I suppose we have to start with *Tilted Arc* (1981). There was one thing I found really disconcerting: while that controversy was raging, there was a lot of criticism not only of my sculpture but of my personality.

**HF**: The one was read in terms of the other?

**RS**: Yes. I was hammered constantly, and I had no access to the press. Just the opposite, in fact. For example, a producer for one of the major evening news programs phoned to say he wanted to explore the concept of site-specificity. So I called different institutions where I had work—in France, Germany, and elsewhere—and arranged for a TV crew to visit the different sites. I thought they'd broadcast a segment that would explain my position.

**HF**: Locate the pieces in their sites, demonstrate the matching of work and setting.

**RS**: Yes. But when the segment aired, the first thing you saw was a pile of burning rubbish under an overpass with a voiceover that said, "New Yorkers have had enough of this." And then it panned to *Tilted Arc*. I was sucker-punched. The producer had me do a tremendous amount of footwork and give him a great deal of information, and he didn't use any of it. He just put his spin on the segment on *Tilted Arc* in order to push his agenda. I realized that if you're an artist going up against the government, you haven't got a chance with the media. None.

**HF**: The attack on *Tilted Arc* was an early salvo in a new cultural politics; it was part of the culture wars of the Reagan years.

**RS**: During the hearing about *Tilted Arc,* Edward Re, who was chief judge of the Court of International Trade, went so far as to say the work was causing a rat problem. That's a fascist tactic. A security inspector testified that the sculpture could be weaponized as a blast wall—that, if you put a bomb in front of it, it could blow up the building. Any claim that could be used to subvert the work, no matter how outrageous, was used.[1]

**HF**: I remember those statements. They presented the public as a mob to be watched and *Tilted Arc* as a wall that hid enemies of the state from government cameras. There was a tenor to the testimony that was paranoid.

**Clara Weyergraf-Serra**: You're right: it was the beginning of a different kind of cultural politics. And Richard's was the case they used to rewrite the guidelines—not only of public art commissions but more generally, too.

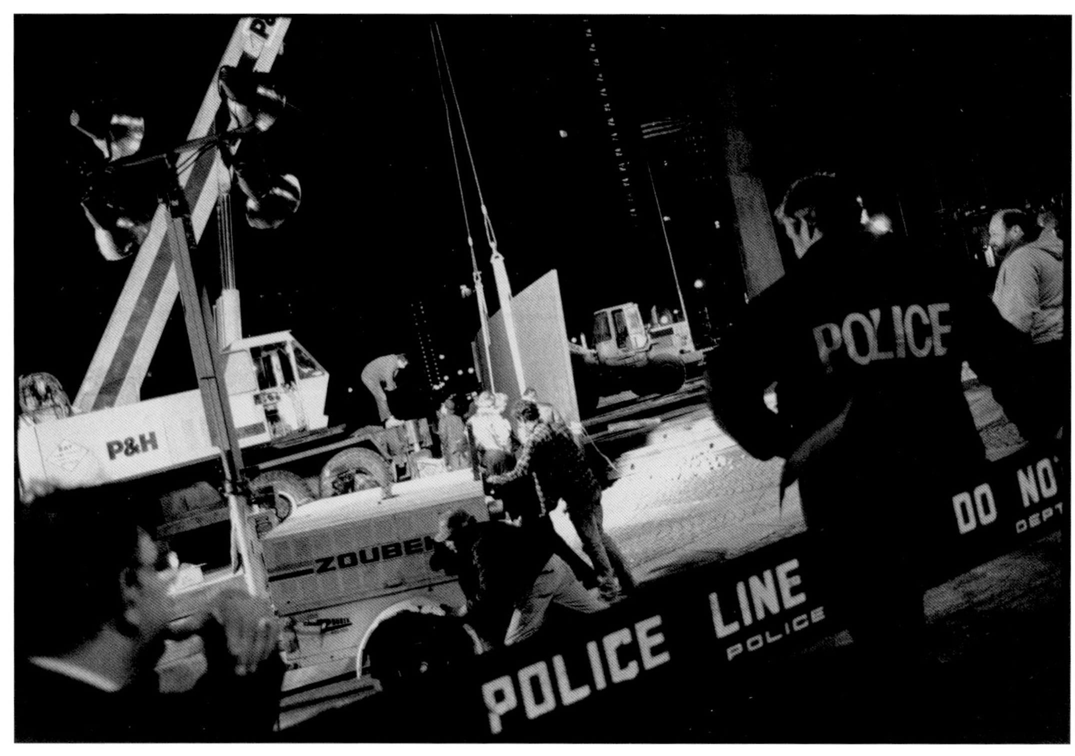


Dismantling of *Tilted Arc*, Federal Plaza, New York, March 15, 1989.

**HF**: With Donald Trump the culture wars are back with a vengeance. Not to romanticize Jackie Kennedy and Joan Mondale as patrons, but there was a dramatic change under Ronald Reagan and George W. Bush (and Bill Clinton didn't do much to alter the situation—he was a populist too). Ed Meese was more a morality czar than an attorney general, and William Bennett, who was head of the National Endowment for the Humanities, essentially wanted to get rid of his own agency (of course that's also back with Trump). *Tilted Arc* was used as a pretext to cut federal support for the arts. If the government can destroy one of its own commissions, that's a good baseline from which to operate.

**RS**: Senator Jacob Javits, for whom the plaza was named, came out in support of *Tilted Arc*. He wanted it to be retained in the plaza, but they completely dismissed him.

**HF**: Re was against the sculpture from the start, but it was only in early 1985—when William Diamond took over the regional office of the General Services Administration, which had commissioned the sculpture in the first place—that things really went south.

**CW-S**: Yes, once Diamond entered the picture, the agenda was clear.

**HF**: Did he come with a brief?

**RS**: My hunch is that he came with an assignment, yes.

**HF**: But then the government, let alone the GSA, didn't come out of it well.

**RS**: We don't know the consequences at that level. Certainly the controversy split the art world.

**HF**: Many people in the art world testified on behalf of the piece, myself included. The great majority of the 180 people who spoke at the hearing in March 1985 supported the sculpture. How was it split?

**RS**: Many people in the art world came out for the piece, but the populist culture that surrounded the art world was totally against it. Grace Glueck led the charge in the *New York Times,* and others wrote attacks in other papers. The preponderance of articles was very negative; it became a media frenzy. And then there were the people who harangued me in the street.

**CW-S**: Richard received death threats over the phone. I went to the police because I was so spooked.

**RS**: Remember the photograph of the Vietcong being shot in the head by the South Vietnamese police chief? They took that photograph, wrote "Kill Serra" under it, and plastered it all over downtown. That came from artists.

**HF**: Was the position against the piece coherent?

**RS**: They said the sculpture blocked the view from the Federal Plaza. I don't know what they wanted to look at.

**HF**: That came from people within the building. What about the populist part of the art world?

**RS**: Some took up the same battle cry.

**HF**: It was unfortunate that the controversy pitted people in support of the sculpture against people who wanted an open plaza for tables and benches. Douglas Crimp pointed out that was an artificial opposition, one that was manipulated by critics of the piece.

**CW-S**: There was talk about benches for people to sit down and have lunch on, and also talk about the fountain, which had been nonfunctional for years.

**HF**: I don't remember the plaza being much used; people tended to hurry across it. But then it wasn't exactly a "leftover" site either, in your sense of the term, like the rotary outside the Holland Tunnel. Did you have any inkling that the sculpture and the site would become so charged?

**RS**: Not before the legal battle.

**CW-S**: That battle dragged on for years, and at that time we didn't have much money. Our first lawyer, Gus Harrow, was determined to win the case, but, sadly, he got cancer, so we turned to Jay Topkis, who was one of the main litigators at the law firm Paul, Weiss. Jay said, "I'll take this case, and I'll take it pro bono. I'll write the best briefs, and I'll do whatever's in my power, but you're not going to win." He put a tremendous amount of work into it, along with an assistant attorney, Leslie Cornfeld, whom I'll always remember. But from the outset Jay said, "I wish you'd come to me when you decided to bring legal action against the government, because I would've told you then, in no uncertain terms, you don't have a chance."

**HF**: So why was Gus Harrow gung-ho?

**CW-S**: He was the lawyer in the Mark Rothko case, which he won.[2] Gus was a one-man office, and he really believed in the cause. But believing in the cause isn't the same as winning the battle.

**HF**: What were the legal consequences? Did Topkis want to make as strong a case as possible in order to set a legal model, if not an actual precedent?

**CW-S**: Yes. Jay thought that, since Richard had started the process and we were so deep into it, it should be concluded in a way that would at least serve as an historical example.

**HF**: And if you pulled out, that wouldn't be so.

**CW-S**: We never contemplated dropping the case.

**HF**: What were the consequences for you personally and for your work?

**RS**: The personal consequences were agonizing, daily, and continuous.

**HF**: Were you able to work otherwise?

**RS**: I continued to work, but the case consumed a tremendous amount of time and energy.

**HF**: Did the world divide for you into two?

**RS**: You mean those against and those for? I didn't see it that way. I thought it was most of the art world against almost all of the media, and the people who knew nothing about art were influenced by the propaganda of the government repeated by the press.

**CW-S**: Richard continued to work. He did more shows with the Castelli Gallery and more pieces in Europe, but every discussion of his sculpture started with a reference to *Tilted Arc*.

**RS**: It was an albatross that wouldn't go away. Even twenty years later people would bring it up. It was the first thing people wanted to talk about.

**HF**: Did it prompt collectors and curators to back away from you?

**RS**: I certainly wasn't getting commissions in the States. On the other hand, as Clara says, I was working a lot in Europe.

**CW-S**: The tide only turned with the show at MoMA that William Rubin did.

**HF**: The retrospective in 1986? But the *Tilted Arc* controversy was still going on.

**CW-S**: Yes. Douglas Crimp wrote an essay for the MoMA catalogue about *Tilted Arc* and site-specificity, which Rubin didn't want to publish.

**RS**: But he did publish it in the end.

**CW-S**: Only because you threatened to cancel the show.

**HF**: It's extraordinary that there'd be an attack from the government at the same time as a retrospective at MoMA. That highlights the cultural divide of the Reagan years.

**RS**: What surprised me was that the retrospective was received very well. I couldn't have anticipated that.

**HF**: Given the controversy?

**RS**: Yes, and the fact that my work wasn't well known in the States then. The reviews were good, and people turned out. That was really gratifying.

**CW-S**: The other immediate result of the *Tilted Arc* fiasco is that we hired John Silberman. Given the character of the work, we needed a good lawyer.

**RS**: After *Tilted Arc* we never again accepted commissions without a contract. We learned how to protect ourselves.

**HF**: What were the consequences of the sculpture for your work at large? Was there any lesson to draw from the reactions to *Tilted Arc*? Did you have any new or changed ideas about site or scale or address?

**RS**: I knew it'd be very difficult, if not impossible, to get commissions for public sites in the States.

**HF**: *Tilted Arc* didn't affect your thinking about any subsequent pieces? It didn't change your language?

**RS**: No. It didn't derail my way of working at all.

**HF**: Any ramifications whatsoever?

**RS**: Again, only personal ones, and they were very upsetting. People yelling at you on the street isn't something you want to experience. It isolated me; it made me defensive and angry. A lot of hostility was directed at me from people I didn't know and who didn't know anything about *Tilted Arc*. I felt smothered day after day.

**HF**: When did the public relation to your work begin to change?

**RS**: With the *Torqued Ellipses.*

**HF**: Yes, there was a dramatic shift in opinion then. Why were they so well received, do you think?

**RS**: In part it was generational. Older people were still disinclined to have any relationship to my work, but then young people found a different expression in the *Torqued Ellipses,* and their parents became interested. That flipped my reputation—I was no longer this hostile outsider. That was a sea change, and it was completely unanticipated.

HF: What was it specifically about the torqued pieces that brought people back to your work?

RS: I think two things primarily. They couldn't anticipate the inside from the outside, and they encountered an interior space that was heretofore unknown to them—it's not in nature, in architecture, or in sculpture. They found it, if not sheltering, at least satisfying. I remember a woman in a wheelchair coming into the gallery. She was so eager to understand a torqued piece that she got up from her wheelchair and walked all around the inside of the ellipse. Particular responses like that: people being startled, becoming curious, trying to come to terms with what they were experiencing.

HF: How did that interest feed back into the media reception of your work?

RS: I have no idea.

HF: But we just agreed there was a dramatic change. How do you explain it?

RS: Yes, in the reception of the work, but I don't know if my media image has ever changed.

HF: Yet somehow you went from "hostile outsider" to central figure. There was an almost begrudging shift in the media: the old story of *Tilted Arc* wilted in the face of the new delight taken in the torqued pieces.

Let's move to other difficult moments in your career. There were two horrible accidents that came before *Tilted Arc*. A rigger was killed at the Walker Art Center in Minneapolis in 1971, and another was badly injured at the Castelli Gallery in New York in 1988.

RS: The worker in Minneapolis was named Raymond Johnson, and the piece consisted of two plates and a pole. He was killed because he was illiterate—he couldn't read the plans. That came out in the trial, which I attended. After the accident the *Village Voice,* which was widely read at the time, ran this headline in bold: "Serra's A Murderer."

HF: Was there any way to respond? After all you were absolved at the trial.

RS: If you're branded a murderer in the *Village Voice,* there's nothing to say. If you try to explain yourself, it only compounds the issue. The most disturbing moment at the trial came when the lawyers showed a file of photographs of the accident itself, with Johnson lying under the plate. That sent me into therapy for eight years.

HF: You say somewhere that your relationship to that event is personal, and that no one can interpret or judge that aspect of it for you.

**RS**: A similar thing happened to Alexander Calder in the same year, 1971. During the installation of a sculpture at Princeton, a worker was killed, but no one said a word. All Calder did in response was paint his sculpture black (I think it was orange to begin with). In my case I was called a murderer. That difference in reception is also political, and it followed through to *Tilted Arc* and beyond. I've had to deal with it since 1971.

**HF**: What other consequences of the accident were there for you? How did it change the production of your subsequent work?

**RS**: I was working with a company called Milgo, and I couldn't work with them any longer. And I wasn't going to continue the series of plate and pole pieces either; the accident ended that. I started separating blocks and plates in a new series of elevational pieces.

**HF**: You pulled your work apart more, opened it out into space more. But it's not as if you gave up on work that was difficult to rig.

**RS**: I didn't give up on rigging, but the separation of space became much more of a driving force.

**HF**: You've argued that rigging is dangerous per se, but that your sculpture is not. Yet many people tend to conflate the two: they believe the danger is in the work, not in the rigging.

**RS**: The work doesn't make the rigging any more dangerous.

**CW-S**: Every piece is engineered by licensed engineers, and there are specific instructions for installation and deinstallation.

**HF**: But the props remain fundamentally precarious, right?

**RS**: Yes, but we take great precaution to cordon them off from the public.

**HF**: You got past *Tilted Arc*. Have you got past the projection of threat in your work, or does that persist?

**RS**: I think it's in for a dime, in for a dollar. If you have a syntax and want to explore it, you can't stop because it's misinterpreted. I pay as much attention as I can to the particularities of every installation, and I try to be directly involved with each one. I have a very close relationship with the riggers, and if something has to be adjusted, reconfigured, or rethought, we close the job down and talk about it.

**HF**: How often does that happen?

**RS**: It happens with every installation. I can always stop the process and ask them to reconsider.

**HF**: The projection of threat or danger—does that persist?

**CW-S**: It's definitely still there. Whenever people talk about the props, they talk about the threat of collapse in a way that assumes that Richard actually plans on it or is actively interested in it.

**HF**: Were there ramifications of the same order from the Castelli accident in 1988?

**CW-S**: I don't think so. It happened as they were deinstalling it.

**HF**: It wasn't in the rigging. What about at the Walker?

**RS**: Deinstallation also.

**HF**: At Castelli it was two big arcs fitted tightly into a large space. I remember that was a major part of the effect of the piece.

**RS**: The sculpture was called *Reading Cones,* and it was supposed to go to the Wacker Building in Chicago. When it fell at Castelli's, a worker named Joe Gallo was injured, and the piece couldn't be removed for a while because there was a lot of contention about what had happened. In the meantime, the building in Chicago was finished with a revolving door at its entrance that made it impossible for the piece to be rigged inside. So it was put out in Grant Park; it was not a site I chose, but it's still there today.

**HF**: So there weren't any significant consequences for your work from that episode? You stayed with the same rigging company?

**RS**: Yes. The company changed its name from Ray La Chappelle and Sons to Budco, but it was the same group of people. Ray La Chapelle's children and his nephew are still running the company.

**HF**: You've told me that the demands of your work have encouraged various steel mills to adjust, even to innovate, their procedures. Did a similar thing happen with the rigging company?

**RS**: We started to work with hydraulic gantries on tracks so that we could bring the material right into the gallery, load it, and lift it, no matter what the weight, and move it with the gantry the entire length of the gallery.

**HF**: When did that begin?

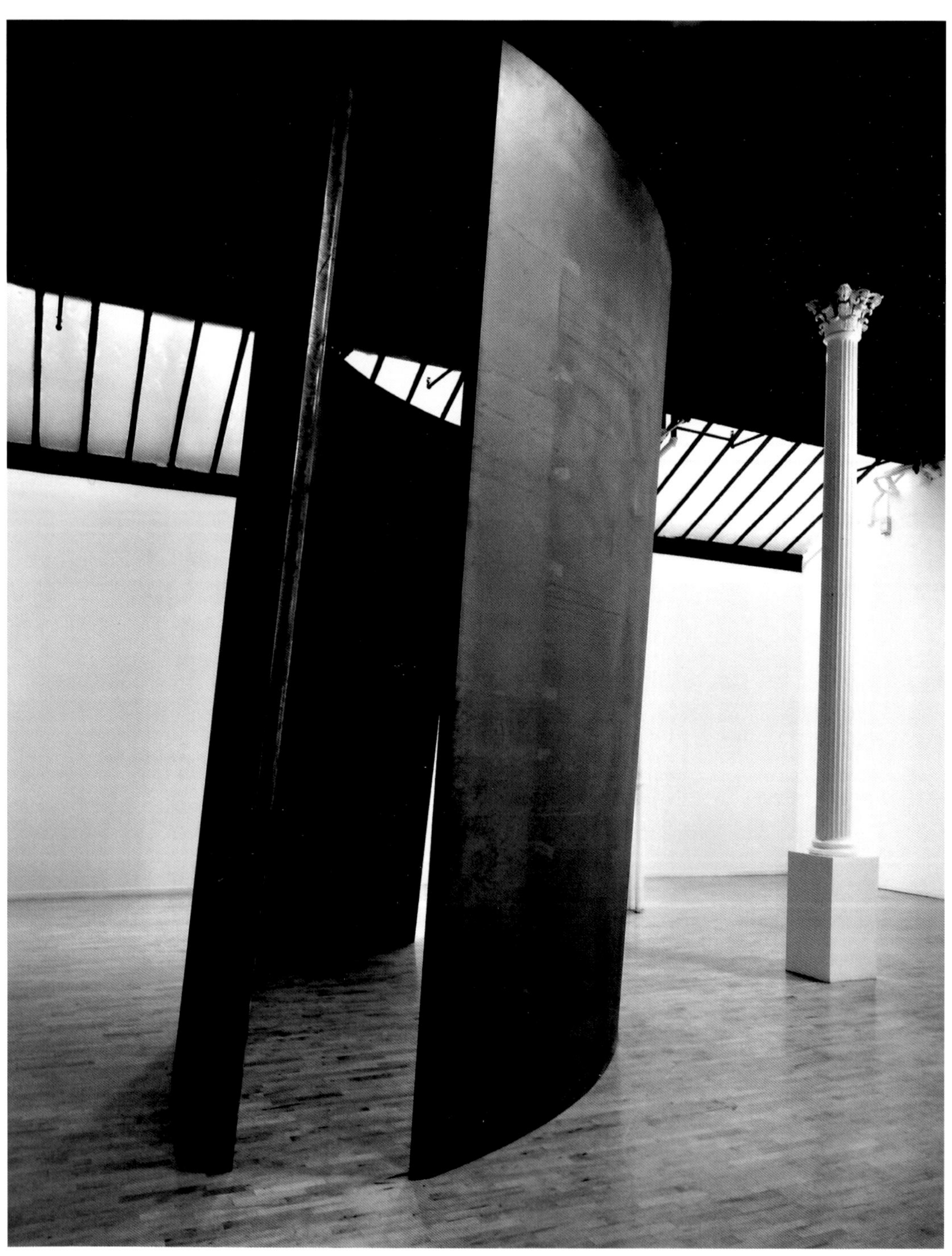

*Reading Cones,* 1988. Weatherproof steel, two identical conical sections inverted relative to each other, 14 ft. 6 in. × 16 ft. 3 in. × 3 in. (4.4 m × 5 m × 7.6 cm), 14ft. 6 in. × 15 ft. 2 in. × 3 in. (4.4 m × 4.6 m × 7.6 cm), as installed at Leo Castelli Gallery, Greene Street, New York, 1988. Acquired by Leo Burnett Company, Chicago, donated to the City of Chicago Public Art Collection.

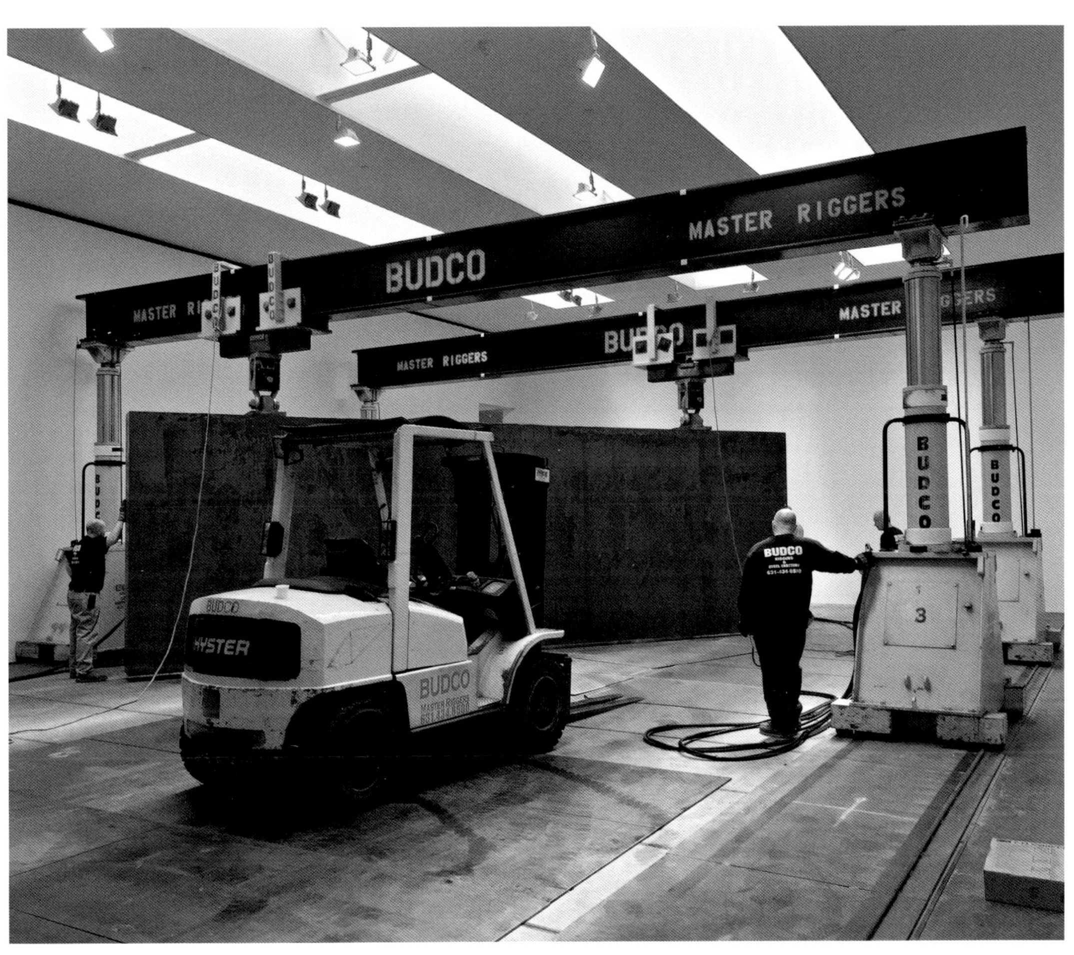

Installing *Through* at the Gagosian Gallery, New York, 2016.

**RS**: The use of gantries to move my work goes back to the 1980s, but the first one with great capacity was used, I think, for an installation at Gagosian Gallery in 2001. It opened up the possibility of installing my work more efficiently and safely.

**HF**: Did it open up the possibility of weight, too?

**RS**: Yes, of weight and size. It changed the potential for large-scale installations.

**HF**: Is this a capability the riggers developed on their own, or did they come to it because of your work?

**RS**: Previously we used heavy-duty dollies. We'd strap a plate down on a dolly and then manhandle it. That was precarious, and we saw we couldn't continue to work that way. We needed a better method of dealing with large-scale works, to move them over significant distances. The riggers did the research and found the hydraulic lift.

**HF**: Was it developed for another job and repurposed for your work?

**RS**: It's used in industry all the time, but it had to be adapted for my sculpture. In Europe, on the other hand, we use air cushions. The pieces are set on inflatable pontoons and slid across the floor. Again, that's a big difference between me and other artists: I've brought the technology of industry into the gallery.

**HF**: Let's move to another controversy. In 1978 an agency called the Pennsylvania Avenue Development Corporation commissioned you to build a work at the western end of Pennsylvania Avenue in Washington, D.C. They also asked the architects Venturi and Rauch and the landscape designers M. Paul Friedberg and Partners to design two plazas. What did you propose?

**RS**: A vertical tower with a very large interior space.

**HF**: What happened then?

**RS**: At one point there was a morning meeting in which Venturi presented his idea of two granite pylons framing the Treasury Building, glorifying it, in effect. Then in the afternoon he came back and said, "Look what I've managed to do over the lunch break," and showed a watercolor with stars in relief on the pylons and flags flying on top of the pylons. I thought it was a big plug for false patriotism, and it really angered me. I told them they might as well add some eagles or some swastikas. I was fired immediately.

**HF**: You and Venturi make an odd couple to begin with. Why did you think collaborating with him would work in the first place?

**RS**: I had no idea Venturi was going to coopt my project.

**HF**: Why was he brought on then?

**RS**: Again, I have no idea. Either he nosed his way in or they wanted to get rid of me by bringing him on.

**HF**: Why do you think that?

**RS**: The person running the PADC took a personal dislike to me. I went into the project with great aspirations and came away feeling I'd been set up.

**HF**: What were your aspirations?

**RS**: To build a piece at the end of Pennsylvania Avenue that could collect people and make a statement that might be worthy of sculpture, without it being coopted by the ideology of the government. That was naïve on my part.

**HF**: This was during the Carter Administration, but it was also the early years of the postmodern architecture championed by Venturi, which took a traditionalist approach to urban planning as well. I can see how it wouldn't go well.

**CW-S**: Venturi's scheme was never built either.

**RS**: His pylons with the flags didn't fly, but they gave him the possibility of doing a miniaturized version of L'Enfant's original plan on the plaza, which was an absolutely silly idea.

**HF**: That's when you delivered your fable about the artist and the architect in a conversation with the French curator Alfred Pacquement: "A chicken and a pig are walking down the street. They pass a sign that says 'Ham and Eggs, 25 Cents.' The chicken says, 'That sounds like a good deal.' The pig says, 'That's easy for you to say. You just have to lay an egg. I lose my ass.'"[3] Would you adjust the moral of the story today, forty years on, or would you hold to it?

**RS**: I think it's still true.

**HF**: There was an earlier controversy we haven't touched on yet, the one surrounding *Terminal* (1977), your tower in Bochum, Germany.

**RS**: *Terminal* is made of four trapezoidal plates, each twelve by forty feet. It was first shown at Documenta 6 in Kassel, but my intention was always to return it to a site in the industrial region where it was produced—the Ruhr Valley. We placed it at the train station in Bochum, in the middle of the street, so it'd be part of the circulation of the city, a point of destination for the train station.

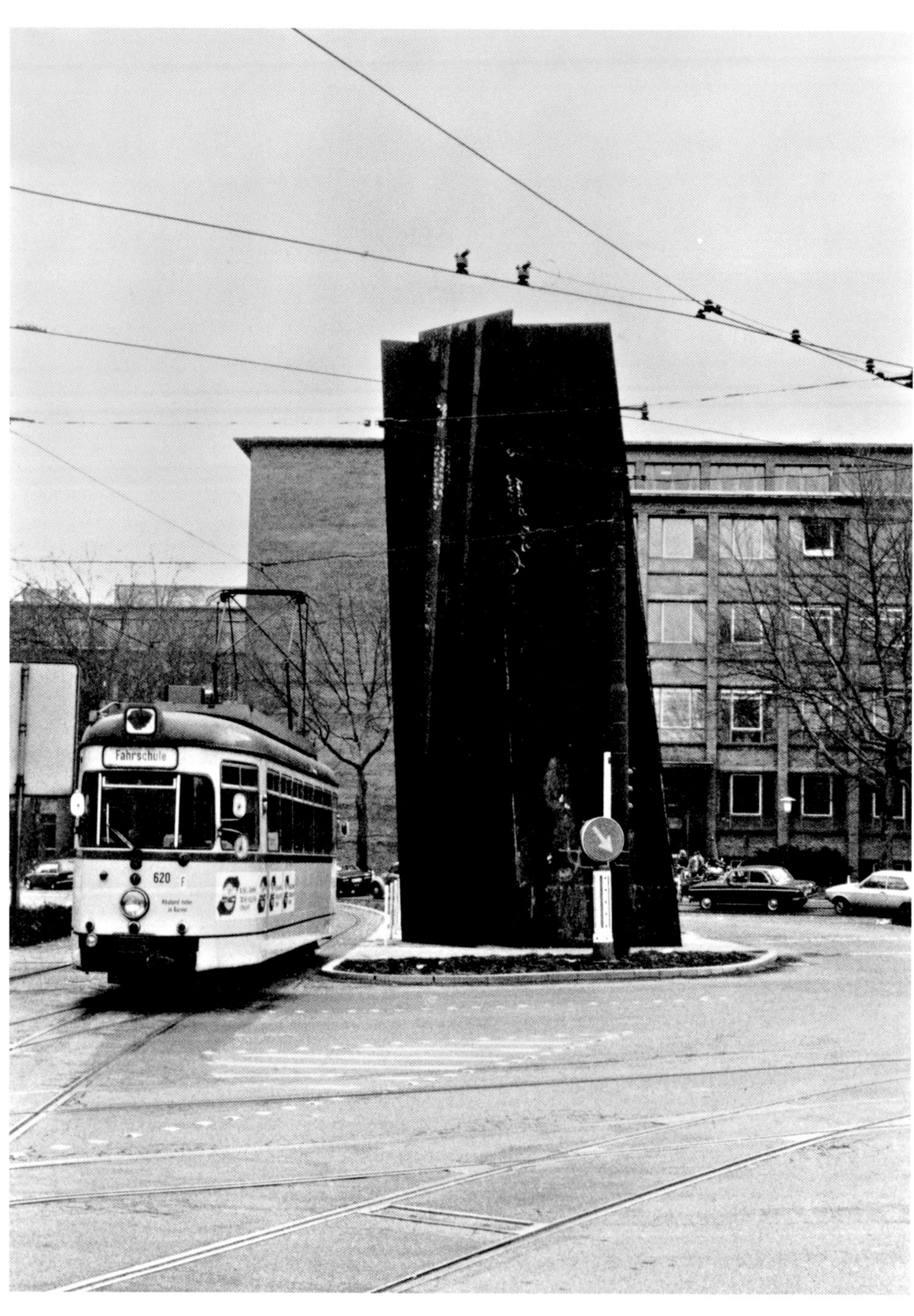

*Terminal*, 1977. Weatherproof steel, four trapezoidal plates, two 41 ft. × 12 ft. to 9 ft. irregular × 2 ½ in. (12.5 m × 3.7 to 2.7 m irregular × 6.4 cm), two 41 ft. × 9 ft. to 12 ft. irregular × 2 ½ in. (12.5 m × 2.7 to 3.7 m irregular × 6.4 cm). Installation at Central Station, Bochum. City of Bochum, Germany.

**HF**: So you saw *Terminal* in some relation to the steel workers who produced it?

**RS**: Yes, but there wasn't any subtext to the piece. I wasn't pandering to them.

**HF**: But it wasn't appreciated by that community.

**RS**: The negative reaction was manufactured by the conservative Christian Democratic Party (CDU), which used it as a political football in an election. The CDU placed thousands of posters throughout the Ruhr Valley denouncing the piece.

**HF**: How did you respond?

**RS**: I didn't.

**HF**: There was nothing you could do?

**RS**: Like what? I don't make political art. I don't make work that propagandizes for a particular position. That's not what I do. Basically my pieces are for any class, any gender, any body.

**HF**: I want to take up that question—how you imagine your viewers—in the next conversation. Let's stick with *Terminal* here. Was this the first time a piece of yours was exploited for political purposes?

**RS**: Probably.

**HF**: So *Terminal* opened a long season of discontent in relation to your work. Was there any reaction to the piece that suggested a different reception, or did the political campaign overwhelm all other accounts?

**RS**: It's hard to analyze reception because it's always filtered through the media and sometimes produced there as well. People are told what to think.

**HF**: Was there any lesson to be learned here? *Tilted Arc* was just a few years away.

**RS**: I think I relearned an old lesson, which is that almost any work can be used for propaganda purposes as soon as you move into public space.

**HF**: You said you're not a political artist, but that's not strictly the case.

**RS**: What are you thinking of?

**HF**: The video *Television Delivers People* (1973) is an early example, the Abu Ghraib drawing *Stop Bush* (2006) a later one.

**RS**: We're getting away from sculpture.

**HF**: Then what do you see as the politics of your sculpture per se?

**RS**: That's a very general question I don't know how to answer. What I do and how the work is received are two completely different things. What I do, my input, isn't dependent on the needs of any group. I don't canvass anyone; I don't take a census and then decide what to make. That's not what I do. On the other hand, I'm fine with what people bring to the work. As soon as you put a piece in a public place, it's going to be judged, and I can't control that. Nor do I want to—I don't want to exclude opinions.

**HF**: That's all on the side of reception.

**RS**: I don't take reception into consideration in terms of my input.

**HF**: I understand, but that's not my question. It's this: Do you see any politics in the very form or structure of your work—in its abstraction, say, or its autonomy?

**RS**: No.

**HF**: Adorno argued that the political value of modernist art lay, first and last, in the autonomy of its form, while Sartre countered that it can be measured only by the engagement of its content.

**RS**: Would Adorno exclude engagement?

**HF**: He would exclude it if engagement meant advocacy of a political position or issue. The dialectical turn in his thought is that it's only through autonomy that you can resist the instrumentalization of politics and assert the independence of what you do, which is a political act. I would've thought you'd be sympathetic to that argument.

**RS**: I agree with that position, and I think engagement is mostly ex post facto—it happens after. I don't direct my work toward engagement, but I think part of its autonomy includes engagement. Why can't it be both?

**HF**: I think it can, but how would you think about your work in that way?

**RS**: You can't have paths that enter into pieces and say you're not engaging a public.

**HF**: That's a different sort of engagement. Adorno meant it in the sense of an ideological commitment, not a physical address.

**RS**: Again, I'm not engaging the public for any ideological agenda.

**HF**: Your practice emerged at a time, the mid-1960s, when the discussion of art and politics for many people was still locked in that old opposition of autonomy versus engagement. Arguably, your work shows that autonomy can be the precondition for a commitment of another kind.

**RS**: That wasn't a concern of the work—I'm not a political philosopher—but it might be a consequence. Give me some examples of autonomy and engagement in art.

**HF**: That's not so clear for those thinkers, but for the purposes of this conversation let's say Piet Mondrian and Diego Rivera.

**RS**: So autonomy is usually associated with abstraction.

**HF**: Often, and that's where your work complicates the question. On the one hand, you insist on your connection to modernist abstraction, which is autonomous in the sense that it's apart from the world; on the other hand, you take abstraction back into the world, often literally plunging it into social space. It's paradoxical to say, but, again arguably, that's where autonomy turns into engagement in your work.

**RS**: Maybe that's because, early on, I was influenced by artists like Rivera, Orozco, and Siqueiros as much as I was by abstract artists. I can't think of many abstractionists who engaged the public.

**HF**: Well, Mondrian saw his Neo-Plastic canvases . . .

**RS**: As a utopian vision of an ideal society.

**HF**: Yes, and Newman believed he could be both abstractionist and anarchist.

**RS**: I always thought that was so much verbiage.

**HF**: You asked for examples; convincing you is another matter.

**RS**: Nor do I think the public engaged the work in that way. It's very different from artists who deal with figuration. Maybe by its very nature abstraction is autonomous.

**HF**: One exception would be revolutionary Russian artists like El Lissitzky who did develop abstraction as a language of political intervention, as in *Beat the Whites with the Red Wedge* (1919). There's also Tatlin, who wanted to push abstraction not only into architectural space but, with his *Monument to the Third International* (1919–20), into political space as well.

**CW-S**: That's in the realm of theory.

**HF**: I understand that it had limited effect. Still, *Red Wedge* circulated widely as an image, and the model for the *Monument* was carried through the streets in political festivals.

**CW-S**: Or it's in the register of utopia—though that version of utopia has always interested Richard more than the Hegelian version that Mondrian was involved with.

**RS**: Do you think that's why abstraction has always sputtered—because it meets resistance from a public that regards it as elitist by its very nature, given that it unfolds according to its internal necessity and doesn't take the public into consideration directly?

**HF**: Yes, by and large. But a strange thing happened with your generation. After you returned abstraction to the world, into the everyday space of real bodies, it was eventually embraced, at least by a lot of people. The old resistance to abstraction was partly overcome.

**RS**: You mean artists like Dan Flavin.

**HF**: Yes, and, for better or worse, artists like James Turrell. In many instances the embrace came at the cost of a spectacularization of abstraction, though—I mean abstraction here as pictorial space or fabricated environment à la Turrell. But abstraction in this expanded sense was also embraced through your work, especially with the *Torqued Ellipses* and after. That was part of the sea change in the reception of your sculpture.

# Contradictions

**HF**: We've talked about some contradictions in your work, but let's bear down on the subject now. I suppose it's difficult for any of us to see our own clearly.

**RS**: When I first met Clara, she told me, "Richard, you have to work with your contradictions." I actually wrote that statement on the wall in the studio.

**HF**: That's a Marxist motto. What does it mean for you?

**RS**: To stay with the direction of my work, while dealing with contradictions that arise, without diminishing the impetus of my aspiration.

**HF**: We've touched on the question of labor in a few conversations. In the 1960s, like some of your peers, you insisted on work: while Judson Dance choreographers stressed everyday tasks, you stressed simple actions, in large part to open up the procedures of art making in a way that others might understand. At that moment some artists preferred the title "art workers." I wonder, though, if the desire to make things transparent to the viewer and to bring together the categories of artist and worker didn't underscore how opaque art had become and how separate artist and worker were. You still emphasize your experience in steel mills and your collaboration with riggers, but what really is your relationship to the working class today?

**RS**: Am I still part of the working class? No. But that doesn't mean I've stopped identifying with it. Is my ethical grounding in the working class? Yes. I get a lot of fulfillment out of my labor: it's always been a resource for me psychologically and spiritually. It's part of my identity. When I was fifteen, I lied about my age to get a work permit so I could roll ball bearings, and I took great pleasure in how many I could do in an hour. I've been working all my life. I wouldn't make that a dictate for other artists, but it's a large part of who I am.

**HF**: When you worked in the steel mills were you a union member?

**RS**: Yes. There were some five thousand workers at Bethlehem Steel, and everybody was required to be in the union.

**HF**: Today only twelve percent of labor is unionized in this country. You say your crucial innovation was to bring industrial materials and methods into sculpture, but you did so at a time when the industrial mode of production was in decline. How does that move appear to you now?

**RS**: It wasn't apparent in the 1960s, but we're the bricoleurs of the Industrial Revolution. We're working at the edge of a scrap heap.

**HF**: "Bricoleur of the Industrial Revolution" isn't the caption that comes to mind when I see photos of you, helmet and gloves on, flinging molten lead. They're as heroic as photos of David Smith welding or Pollock dripping.

**RS**: I didn't heroicize my work. If anyone did, it was the media. I understand that industrial production has a diminished role in our economy, and unions aren't coming back. I also don't see anyone picking up where my work trails off. Certainly they're not going to enter into industrial fabrication in the way I have.

**HF**: Is your identification with workers reciprocated?

**Clara Weyergraf-Serra**: That's what the film *Steel Mill/Stahlwerk* (1979) is about. I had just met Richard at the time, and basically my role in the film was to debunk his over-identification with the workers. Richard gets enormous gratification from working in the steel mills, but the workers don't have that same relationship to the work they do, day after day, week after week.

**RS**: On the other hand, the riggers do. They like some pieces more than others, but they take great pride in the work.

**CW-S**: There's an enormous difference: no great division of labor exists among the riggers. They're seeing the installation of a work through from beginning to end, while production in the mill is totally fragmented.

**HF**: *Steel Mill* is also about the making of *Berlin Block (For Charlie Chaplin)* (1978) sited in front of the Neue Nationalgalerie in Berlin. In one of the interviews in the film Clara asks a worker, "When you forged the seventy-ton cube, a piece of sculpture was being produced. Did that change your relationship to your work?" And he replies, "As far as we were concerned, it was work like any other work." And, strategically, the film doesn't show the full production of the block. In a conversation with Annette Michelson you say you framed and edited the shots so as to convey the fragmentation of labor in the mill. No one has a sense of the totality of the process, not even the worker. So how does one represent labor? It's an age-old question on the Left. Remember the critique of New Objectivity photography delivered by Brecht in the 1930s? "A photograph of the Krupp works or the AEG tells us next to nothing about these institutions. The reification of human relations—the factory, say—means that they are no longer explicit."[1] Benjamin then doubled down on that critique and accused Albert Renger-Patzsch, in his photo book *The World Is Beautiful* (1928), of turning even the poverty created by industrial capitalism into an object of consumption.

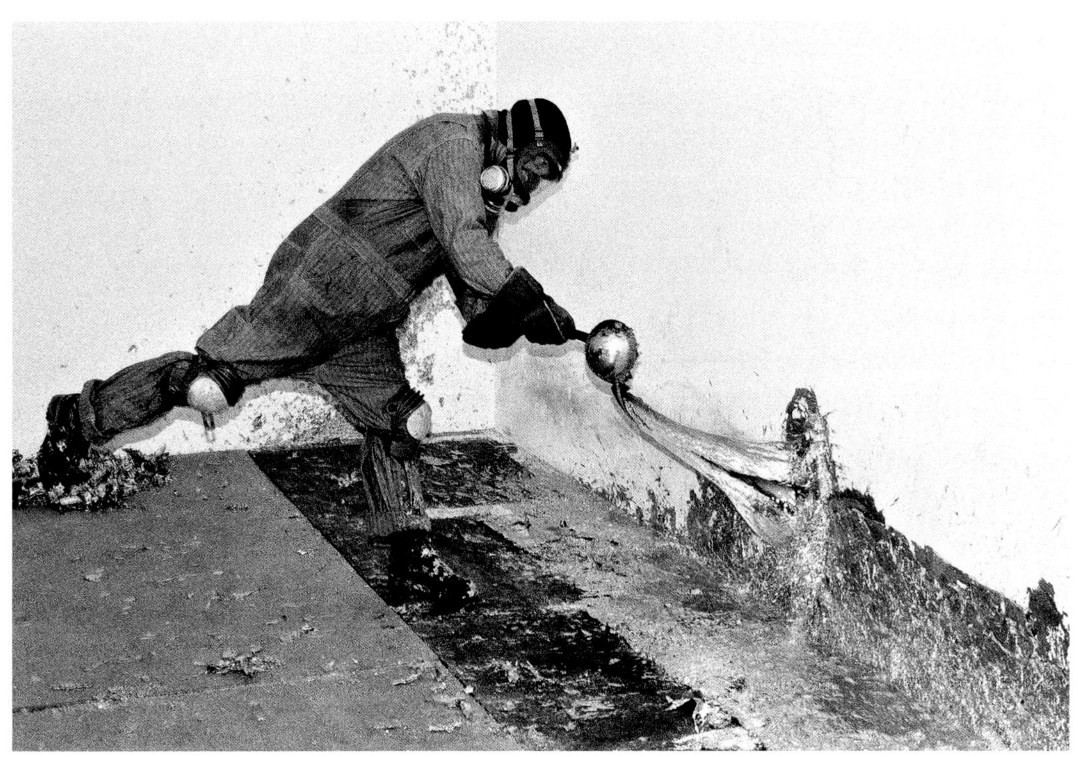

Richard Serra installing *Measurements of Time/Seeing Is Believing* at the Hamburger Kunsthalle, Hamburg, Germany, 1996.

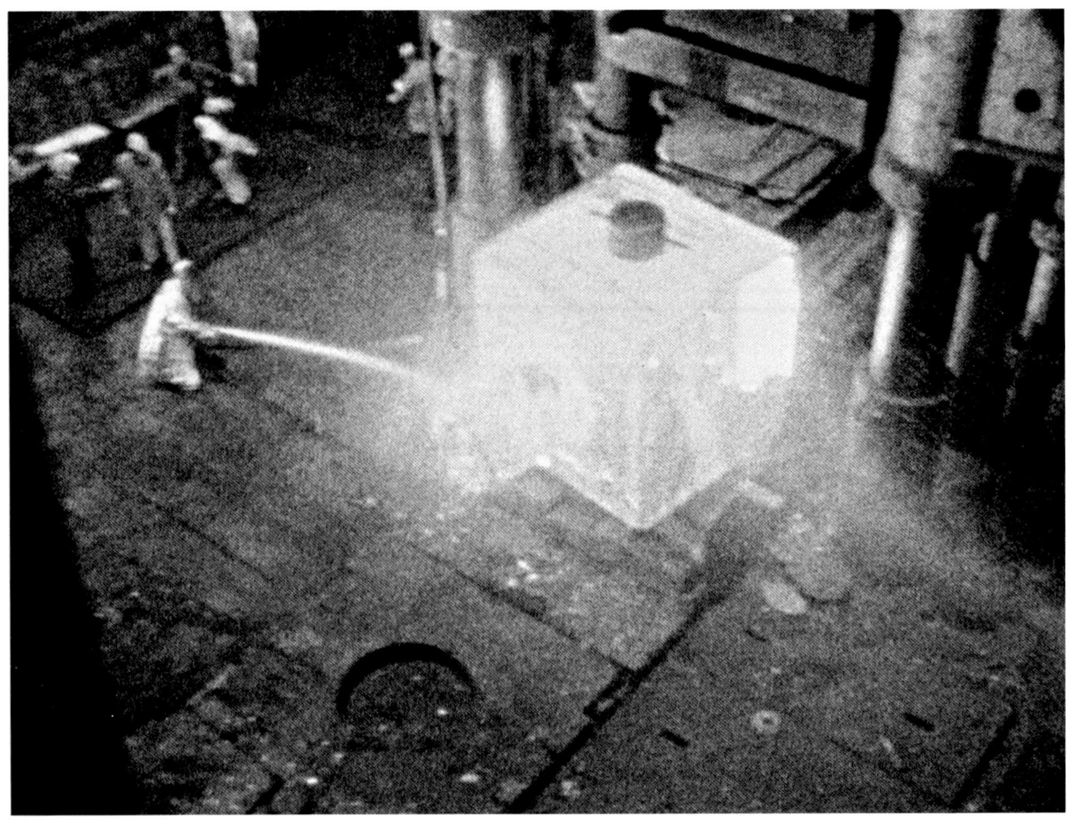

*Steel Mill/Stahlwerk,* 1979, 16 mm film, black and white, sound, 29 min.
(in collaboration with Clara Weyergraf). The Museum of Modern Art, New York.

**RS**: Without getting into the nuances of documentary, I don't know how anyone can represent industrial work adequately. You'd have to investigate the people in relationship to their labor, their living conditions, and society at large. That's very hard to do. I've tried to make industrial procedures evident in my work, but most artists, myself included, are guilty of overlooking the actual labor that produces the materials we use. A lot of artists simply outsource their work. Like most people in this society, they don't make anything anymore; they just order it up, and so it is easy to dismiss the alienation of labor.

**HF**: Jeff Koons is only an extreme example of that far wider phenomenon: as we marvel at the fetishistic production of his work we are blinded to its actual producers. What if I suggested that your *Railroad Turnbridge* (1976), which is my favorite of your films, could be subjected to a critique similar to the one Brecht and Benjamin made of New Objectivity photography—that it aestheticizes an industrial object "and tells us next to nothing…about the reification of human relations"?

**RS**: As I understand the critique of Renger-Patzsch, he showed the exterior of the steel mill and not the labor or the oppression of workers interior to the steel mill. I'm filming a mechanical artifact that's devoid of people from the start. There isn't even a bridge tender; I'm filming a machine.

**HF**: Forty-plus years later there's a real pathos to *Railroad Turnbridge*. You watch this old mechanism open and close, and it seems like a relic of the industrial period. If Joseph Stella could paint *Brooklyn Bridge* (1939) as a hymn, *Railroad Turnbridge* feels like an elegy, and that effect is redoubled by the fact that it's a film, another industrial form in decline, another object of current nostalgia.

This returns us to the present, which is one of deindustrialization, deunionization, and deregulation—in a word, neoliberalism. Can you talk about your work in relation to the neoliberal economy? Your aesthetic, which is also an ethic, is egalitarian in spirit— you've spoken about the fundamental influence of the Mexican muralists and the Russian Constructivists, Communists all—yet your work has prospered at a time of enormous inequality. Put another way, many of your pieces show a deep commitment to public space and public experience, but the art system in which they have emerged is both privatized and privatizing. What about this apparent contradiction between the public nature of your work—the self-evident materials, the transparent construction, the clear presentation—and the private world of super-rich patrons?

**RS**: Most work right now is market-driven, which diminishes the possibility of public art, and museums aren't truly public forums either. Of course I'd prefer a public exchange with my work in situ, without depending on private patrons or, for that matter, without dealing with spectacular settings.

**cw-s**: Richard is trapped in a contradiction. He wants to build his work, and he wants it to be public, but who gets it out there? Putting a piece out in the public today is extremely difficult, and you need public funding. Where does it come from? When he's had a chance to put work in a public place, he's been enormously generous. Often there's just not enough interest. In this system, in order to reach the public, you have to have private support.

**RS**: Also, if I place a piece in a public space, the context is likely to change within a year or a decade, certainly within a few decades. You don't know what's going to happen.

**HF**: "To remove the work," you said of *Tilted Arc,* "is to destroy it." If the site changes drastically, does that mean the work might be altered to the point of destruction?

**RS**: That's an interesting question. A change in context can subvert the work. Take *Terminal* (1977) in Bochum. We sited that tower very close to the streetcar tracks near the train station so it would be part of the circulation of the city, but now those tracks are gone and the content of the piece is changed. It stands isolated on a traffic island.

**HF**: How do you respond to such changes?

**cw-s**: We've never considered that question in Richard's contracts. What can we do?

**HF**: Those contracts must be hard enough for clients to sign in the first place.

**RS**: Yes, and you can't foresee the changes. They do happen, though, both big and small. And they occur not only in urban locations but also in landscape sites, mostly when the clients don't fully understand the placement of the work.

**HF**: Do you have any rights at that point?

**RS**: No.

**HF**: Practically speaking, are semi-public cultural precincts, such as *Berlin Block* (1978) in front of the Neue Nationalgalerie in Berlin, the least compromised of urban sites?

**cw-s**: Probably. That is the reason I was really happy when MoMA bought *Equal* (2015) because I feel a piece like that needs to be seen by a public, not only one patron.

**RS**: Every artist faces the contradictions the market creates, and most are complicit with it. I don't see any way around it, unless you're exceedingly wealthy or make pieces not many people will see.

**cw-s**: It's a problem Richard confronts every time he does a show: he works hard to make his pieces and to place them in a gallery, and then they're gone in two months. It's wishful thinking to imagine they'll be seen by a public for a long time.

**HF**: To put it crudely, a lot of capital is required to support your kind of work, and a lot of capital means a lot of inequality. That's our great political-economic problem. I wonder if there's a way to talk about how your work might be bound up in it.

**RS**: For the most part I've funded my own work. Especially when I started, I didn't live on stipends or at the behest of galleries. Mostly I've generated my own income through my work.

**CW-S**: For years now Richard has financed every piece in every show himself. That has allowed him to experiment without worrying about the market. Being independent from the galleries is very important. If he wants to terminate a relationship with a dealer or work with anybody anywhere, he can. It gives him that freedom.

**RS**: Many of the big pieces don't sell anyway. If I sell one, that usually covers the show and I break even. Many other sculptors do multiples, often selling them out. That's not how I work.

**HF**: I understand that you strive to be independent, but at the same you're embedded in this world of patronage and so partly implicated in its financial operations and their social ramifications. The problem is not only private versus public; it's the domination of cultural institutions—museums, universities, and so on—by neoliberal trustees who, at least in their business affairs, want to privatize almost everything.

**CW-S**: This is a structural issue. It's a system we're all stuck with—it's called finance capitalism.

**HF**: Some younger artists and critics have decided to opt out of this art world. They grew up on institution critique and they think it has reached its limit. They talk about alternative art worlds and institutional liberation, about ways to form groups, collectives, and communities not routed through the market in the same old ways. This comes right out of the Occupy movement.

**RS**: That sounds completely nostalgic, the 1960s redux. Don't you think they'll be coopted sooner than later?

**HF**: Maybe, but some institutions bound up with neoliberalism are headed for irrelevance, at least for these younger artists and critics. There's a strong anti-institutional wind in the land, and it blows from the Left too.

    This might be a good moment to reflect on another institutional complication we've touched on before. Certainly you've tested the limits of production in sculpture, but what about the other side, the parameters of exhibition? I wonder about the unexpected effects of the expanded field of art after Minimalism—about how galleries, museums, and other institutions have moved to encompass this leap in size and increase in spectacle by expanding and spectacularizing themselves. Do you have misgivings about those developments?

**RS**: They all present different problems, and you have to deal with them as they come up, which is to say, continuously.

**HF**: What about the space wars between art and architecture?

**RS**: Give me an example.

**HF**: What I have in mind is how super-sized art and spectacular architecture egg each other on in terms of object-making and space-claiming. How do you feel about museums becoming massive works of sculpture in their own right in a way that can effectively turn artists into installation-makers by default?

**RS**: That's buying into the belief that no artist can match new architecture; we heard that a lot after the Guggenheim Bilbao opened. You can't anticipate what artists will do in relation to the givens of a building. Most artists who understand architecture will find a way to intervene in it, critique it if need be, even transform it. The smart ones know they're part of the arrangement, understand the contradictions, and find a way to override them through the intensity of what they project. That's why they're called artists. Museums want that too, or they should. They can't simply collect collectors. They have to accept art that works the contradictions, that uses them to transgress the given limits, because that's what counts down the road.

**CW-S**: Are you implying that Richard's work has pushed museum directors to expand the size of their buildings?

**HF**: Not Richard's alone, but yes. It's an ambiguous consequence. On the one hand, it has led to extraordinary spaces that challenge artists and audiences alike; on the other, it has produced spectacular effects that can overwhelm both.

**CW-S**: You're talking about a competitiveness between architects and Richard. I don't think he's competitive with them, but some of them are with him.

**HF**: Do you think Frank Gehry is involved in sculptural architecture?

**RS**: No, he's involved in architecture, though sometimes he wants it both ways. There is no such thing as sculptural architecture. They're two different disciplines.

**HF**: What about the tendency to eccentric shape and great size in museum architecture today?

**RS**: Again, artists worth the name will figure out ways to deal with whatever's presented to them. I don't think there's any such thing as too big.

**HF**: What if I claimed that many spaces—the contemporary galleries at MoMA, say, or at LACMA—are out of scale for most work, and that's due in part to the need to deal with very large sculptures and installations?

**RS**: When MoMA did its renovation in the early 2000s, they knew, prior to my retrospective in 2007, that I wanted to show heavy pieces, so one mandate given to the architects was to hang the second floor in a way that would take those loads. So, yes, the second floor was built in part with my exhibition in mind.

**CW-S**: The truth is that, even though museums have grown bigger, hardly any have the floor load or elevator capacity needed to show Richard's work. The new Whitney is a good example: huge spaces, little floor load.

**RS**: On the other hand, the expansion of museums has allowed for more installations, image projections, dance, and performance. The interface between those forms right now is probably a result of these larger spaces.

**HF**: Alternatively, one could say that the larger spaces spectacularize dance and performance in a manner that is directly contrary to their intentions in the 1960s and 1970s.

**RS**: That's not true. Judson Dance and Grand Union performed on large stages and big auditoriums like gyms.

**HF**: There's a great difference between a ratty old gym and a deluxe museum wing. But in sum you'd say the expanded scale of the museum, driven in part by your work, is a good thing.

**RS**: Grand Union didn't perform in ratty old gyms. There's something else to be said in defense of large museum spaces. If you do a comprehensive retrospective—like Sigmar Polke's at MoMA in 2014—you need space to cover the development of the work. What you're questioning is the superfluousness of large-scale work when the work itself doesn't warrant it. In that case the work is trying to match the architecture but ends up diminishing not only its own impact but also the function of the museum.

**HF**: Exactly. And you'd say that's the fault of the art.

**RS**: The fault of the artists—of their aspirations. But there are exceptions. For example, Flavin looks very good in some of those large spaces.

**CW-S**: I think it's the fault less of artists than of planners who try to predict the future.

Nothing looks very good to me in those big spaces. The problem is that architects are asked to design for an undefined future when these large spaces will supposedly be used, but no one seems to analyze carefully what art today requires—which, by the way, sometimes includes load-bearing capacity.

**HF**: There are two related problems here. The first is spectacle carried over from the culture at large into the museum experience. The second is architecture that, in its desire to stay open to the future, defaults on program. What's a library today? Not necessarily a place with books. What's a museum? Not necessarily a place with paintings and sculptures. What's a creative and performing arts center? In the last two decades some colleges and universities have built such centers, but they don't often know what they are. As a result, they default to large spaces that aren't defined, sometimes blobby, sometimes curvy, now sheddy, as if this might compensate somehow for a failure in programmatic thinking.

**RS**: Programmatic thinking changes decade by decade, so it's very hard to plan ahead.

**HF**: In the shed paradigm, as in the huge Culture Shed at Hudson Yards in New York designed by Diller Scofidio + Renfro, will the architecture push back on the sculpture productively, and vice versa? Historically, that dynamic has been very important for your work. For example, at Dia:Beacon you opted for a tight space in the old factory.

**RS**: I knew right away that's where I wanted to be.

**HF**: You sought out the limits of the architecture: you press on the frame and it presses back. So if your work uses that tension, even wants it, and the architecture then expands to the point where that tension thins out, isn't that a problem?

**RS**: Not for me, but it might be for an artist who doesn't know how to deal with a big open field, how to divide it or declare it or otherwise use it. If an artist has his wits about him, he can find a way around the spectacular, and configure a work that deals with his own needs and the open field at the same time. It just requires an ability to analyze the context. As for the dialogue between artists and architects, that's been going on for centuries, and it'll continue.

**HF**: My next topic is also a difficult one. You consistently reject the notion that your work is aggressive. I understand why you do—that accusation often comes before any real experience of your work—and I largely agree with you on this point. But then how do you explain the aggression that is sometimes shown to your sculpture, in the form of graffiti and other markings, if not as a response to an aggression perceived in the work or to an authority projected on to it?

**RS**: Have you ever seen aggression displayed in a museum?

**HF**: So it's about the location of the work rather than the work per se?

**RS**: As soon as you put a piece in the street, you're open to everything that's out there. The reason my pieces are tagged is that they are seen as an intrusion into public space.

**HF**: An intrusion in what way?

**RS**: They probably see my steel as an old industrial material that's out of place in the contemporary city. They don't see form; they see rust.

**HF**: Your work did move into urban space during a time when industrial cities, their manufacturing base and their working class, were falling into decline.

**CW-S**: What about a place like Basel? It's one of the most bourgeois cities you can imagine, yet Richard's piece was graffitied there too.

**RS**: It's not just my pieces that are tagged; there's marking and spray-painting everywhere other than on advertisements. Almost any surface is targeted.

**HF**: If it doesn't matter what the surface is, why aren't outdoor Calders or Caros tagged?

**CW-S**: They're not in the street in the same way.

**RS**: And even if they're nearby, they're not tagged because they cater to a decorative idea of sculpture. They're painted yellow or orange or whatever, so the tagger considers them to be in the realm of art, or at least of urban décor, and gives them a pass.

**CW-S**: We have to think about particular locations. A Calder on 57th Street isn't going to be graffitied, while a Serra in Tribeca is going to be.

**RS**: A Calder in Tribeca isn't going to be tagged either.

**CW-S**: It wouldn't be out there in the first place—that's my point.

**HF**: Or it'd be placed in a special setting like a corporate or governmental plaza that's watched over. Maybe it's a matter not of neighborhood but of precinct—a place that's designated as private or semi-private, which is policed or perceived to be. By and large your sites are different, and again your move into urban space happened at a moment of real distress in the industrial city (we need to think here about "time-specificity" as well). New York was bankrupt, and some communities were hurting from the move away from industrial production. You say you put old industrial material back into an industrial city in decline; maybe that's what elicited the aggression—not against your work alone but against a difficult condition that was social, economic, and political.

**RS**: Are you saying I'm part of the deterioration of the city?

**HF**: Not at all. I'm trying to describe a historical situation that might have affected the reception of your urban sculptures.

**CW-S**: At that time—I'm talking about the early 1980s—Richard was putting pieces in Tribeca, and Tribeca was a community of striving artists.

**HF**: In a broken neighborhood of light industry that was going under.

**CW-S**: And it was in an early phase of gentrification. But the initial aggression came from up-and-coming artists. In a way I understand it: for a time Richard had three big pieces up—*St. John's Rotary Arc, T.W.U., Tilted Arc*—and he had support others didn't have. Of course there was animosity. So the aggression was as site-specific as the pieces. I told you we received death threats from artists who were angry because Richard had the backing to realize large-scale projects in public sites. In a place like Basel the situation was entirely different. It was a city with a rampant drug culture; there the aggression was indiscriminate.

**HF**: Is there a way to see the aggression against your work in a positive light—as an expression of the conflict that lies at the center of any public sphere? For a political philosopher like Chantal Mouffe, conflict is essential to the operation of democracy— democracy not understood, as liberals do, as a process of conciliation ("a more perfect union") but as a negotiation of antagonism that can't be reduced out, an antagonism that is productive as such.

**RS**: You mean that it generates a dialogue.

**HF**: More radically, that it exposes contradictions that can't be resolved away through dialogue, and thus leaves a space open for new groups of people to articulate who they are and what they want. I mean democracy at its best might do this, not that your sculpture on its own does, but its opening to conflict might be an opening to such democracy. From this perspective the aggression against your sculpture highlights a social space that's conflictual, and paradoxically that's a good thing for all of us (at least all of us who still support democracy!).

**RS**: That's not an intent of the work, but it might be an effect.

**CW-S**: I've always thought that if you put work in the street you have to deal with the street. You might not like the reaction, but I've always thought it was worth the risk.

**RS**: There are many pieces in public sites that have not been graffitied, like *Fulcrum* (1986–87) in London; it's been up over thirty years and never graffitied. The tower in Amsterdam, *Sight Point* (1972–75), has been up even longer and never graffitied. How do

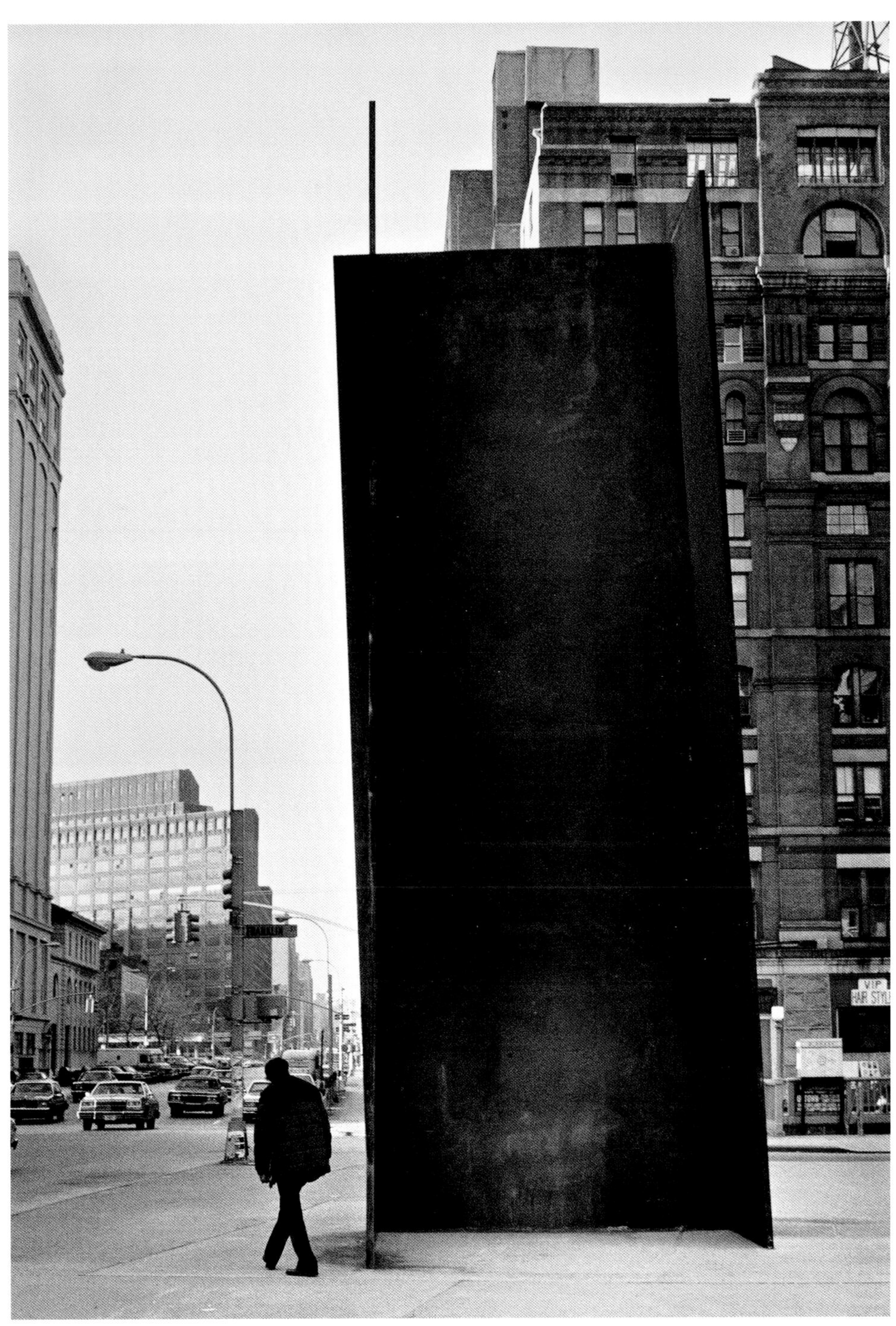

*T.W.U.*, 1980. Weatherproof steel, three plates, each 36 ft. × 12 ft. × 2 ¾ in. (11 m × 3.7 m × 7 cm),
as installed as installed in Tribeca, New York, 1981–88. Acquired by City of Hamburg, 1991,
permanently installed at the Deichtorhallen, Hamburg, Germany.

you explain that? My hope for any urban work is that it'll become part of the syntax of the city and so be accepted over time.

**HF**: I agree with Clara that the problem is site-specific also in a social sense. So there's the question of different locations—gallery, museum, urban site, estate landscape—setting up different expectations, inviting different comportments. In one space viewers might be contemplative, in another not at all. To what degree do the various settings influence how you think about your audience?

**RS**: It's hard for me to anticipate because I don't know who the viewers are before the fact. I don't know anything about their backgrounds. All I imagine—or hope for—is a more perceptive viewer. If I'm ever disappointed, it's when people don't take sufficient time to look.

**HF**: In my experience people take a lot more time with your work, on the whole, than with other work. Let me try another angle on the social dimension of your sculpture. A student of mine speaks about the different activities performed in relation to your sculpture in terms of "social choreographies." On the one hand, there are aggressive acts like the graffiti; on the other…

**RS**: People get married in my pieces. Music is played, dancers perform…

**HF**: And there are also acts that aren't scripted. We talked about how kids run up the sides of your open curvilinear pieces to see how high they can go. That's a spontaneous kind of social dance, more like boarding than tagging, more like surfing than defacing.

**RS**: People have suddenly started singing in the pieces. They also go in and simply sit down.

**HF**: Do you have any anecdotal information about spontaneous encounters between people in the sculptures?

**RS**: In the towers, like *Vortex* (2002) in Fort Worth, people go in and test the echo. There's often shouting as well as singing, and there's clanging on the plates.

**CW-S**: Emmy Pulitzer had a program at her museum in Saint Louis that invited people who had spent time in prison to visit the museum. One man wrote about his experience walking through *Joe* (2000), the torqued spiral in the courtyard. He said it clarified his experience of getting out of prison.

**RS**: He talked about going step by step through a confined space and then coming out into an open one. It was simply written but heartfelt. That kind of response happens mostly in relation to the curved pieces and the towers, not to the forged ones.

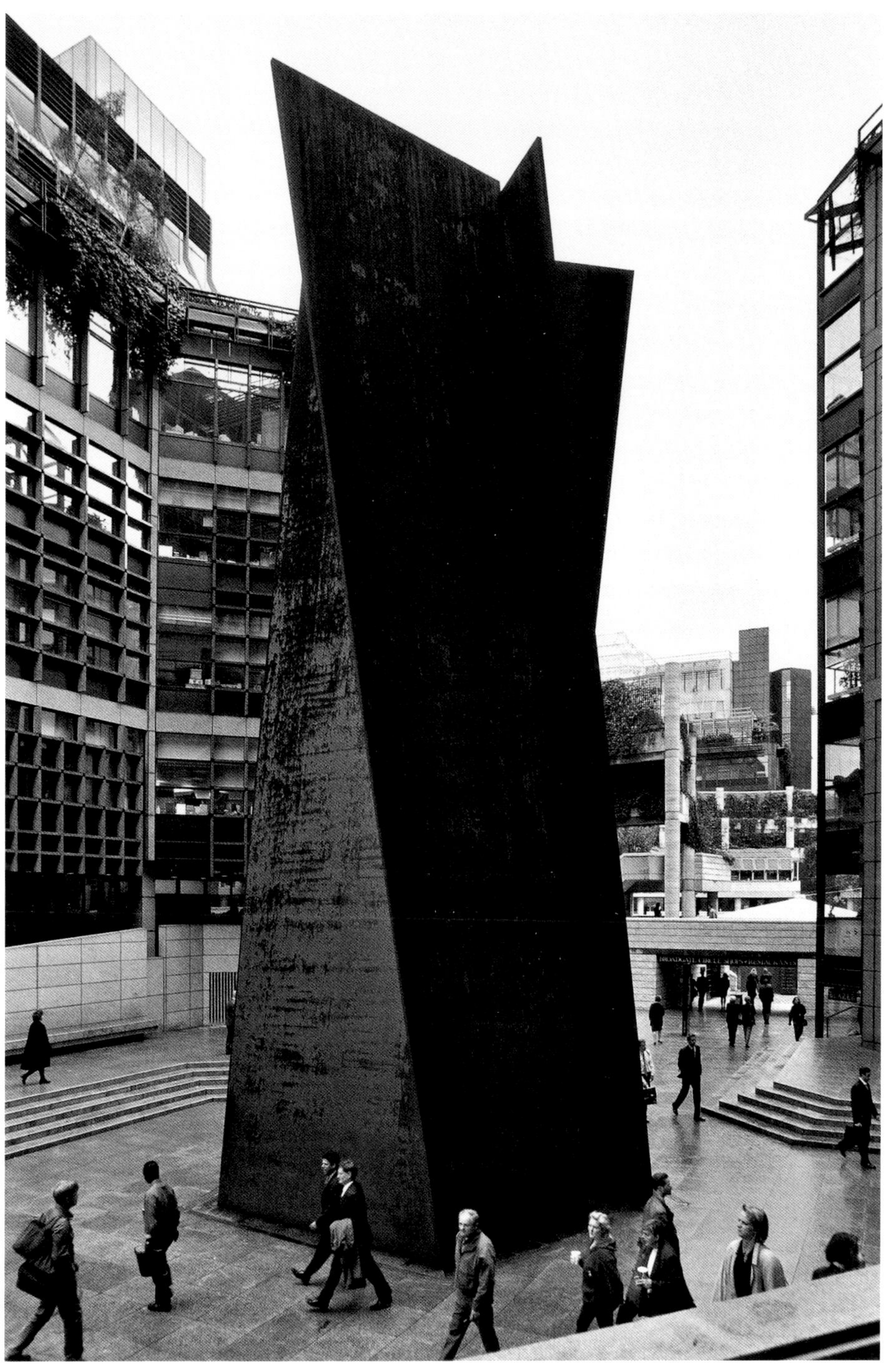

*Fulcrum*, 1986–87. Weatherproof steel, five trapezoidal plates, two 55 ft. × 14 ft. to 9 ft. irregular × 3 in.
(16.8 m × 4.3 to 2.7 m irregular × 7.6 cm), three 55 ft. × 9 ft. to 14 ft. irregular × 3 in. (16.8 m × 2.7 m to 4.3 m
irregular × 7.6 cm). Broadgate, London. Collection Rosehaugh Stanhope Development PLC, London, England.

HF: We talked about "gathering" as a principle of your work—how some pieces seem to call people to assemble, or to invite other kinds of sociability (you mention *Vortex* in particular). Yet there's a different dimension in the work, one that almost asks us to keep a distance. Perhaps the forged pieces have this effect. It's as though the very density of the steel, and the very austerity of the abstraction (a block or a round), induce us to project a special force, a weird authority, on to the sculpture. This was certainly true of some Minimalist objects, like Tony Smith's *Die* or Barnett Newman's *Broken Obelisk,* at least in the public imagination. Stanley Kubrick had played on this effect already in *2001: A Space Odyssey* (1968), in which the silent dark monolith is this dense auratic node of knowledge and power that literally comes from an alien place and speaks to a distant time. And some feminist critics associated this power effect with a patriarchal position, as if "Minimalism" equaled "monolith" equaled "masculinism." Is there a tension or a contradiction between your pieces that seem to gather and your pieces that seem silent, opaque, distant?

RS: I think Kubrick reduced modern sculpture to his monolith, and it happened to coincide with Minimalism. I don't think he was riffing on it consciously.

HF: Nevertheless, that's how Minimalism came to be received in part: a lot of people project a power on to its forms. That's active in the cultural imaginary.

RS: You mean it's built into the iconography?

HF: Or that iconography is projected on to it. Has that inflected the reception of your work at all? If so, might it explain some of the aggression shown toward the sculpture? It's really an authority projected on to the work, which is then seen as oppressive and attacked as such.

RS: That's far-fetched. I can't control the effects of the mediocrity of popular culture. As to the monolith, we have to distinguish between pieces. I don't think I've done a single forged piece that's a monolith in that sense.

HF: Let's move to another question. Just as you have a materialist relation to the physical making of your work, you have a phenomenological understanding of the viewing experience. The beholder modeled by modern aesthetics and modernist painting (in shorthand, by Kant and Greenberg) was a subject imagined as contemplative, detached, even disembodied. As opposed to that beholder, you want your viewer to feel physically present and self-aware in a particular place and time. But might your very focus on corporeal experience in this phenomenological sense lead you to treat the viewer as just a body—in fact as just any body? That is, might it obscure the very differences

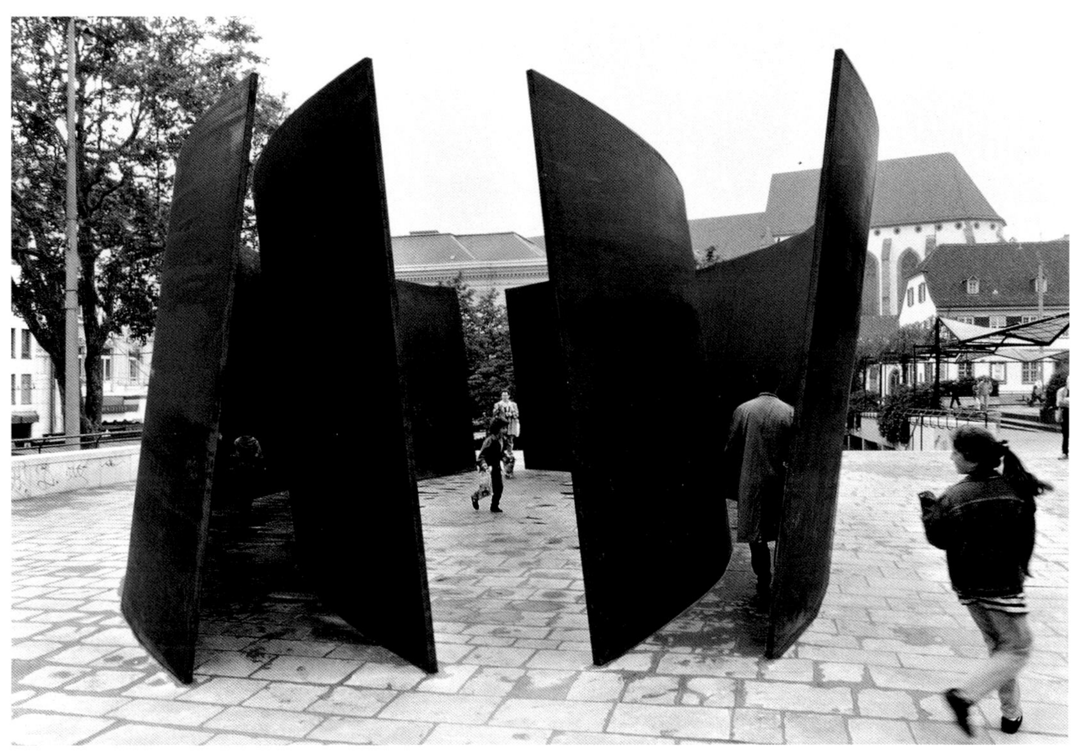

*Intersection,* 1992. Weatherproof steel, four near-identical conical sections inverted relative to each other, two 12 ft. 1 ½ in. × 42 ft. 8 in. × 2 ¼ in. (3.7 m × 13 m × 5.7 cm), two 12 ft. 1 ½ in. × 40 ft. 8 ¼ in. × 2 ¼ in. (3.7 m × 12.4 m × 5.7 cm). Theaterplatz, Basel. Kanton Basel-Stadt, Öffentliche Kunstsammlungen Basel.

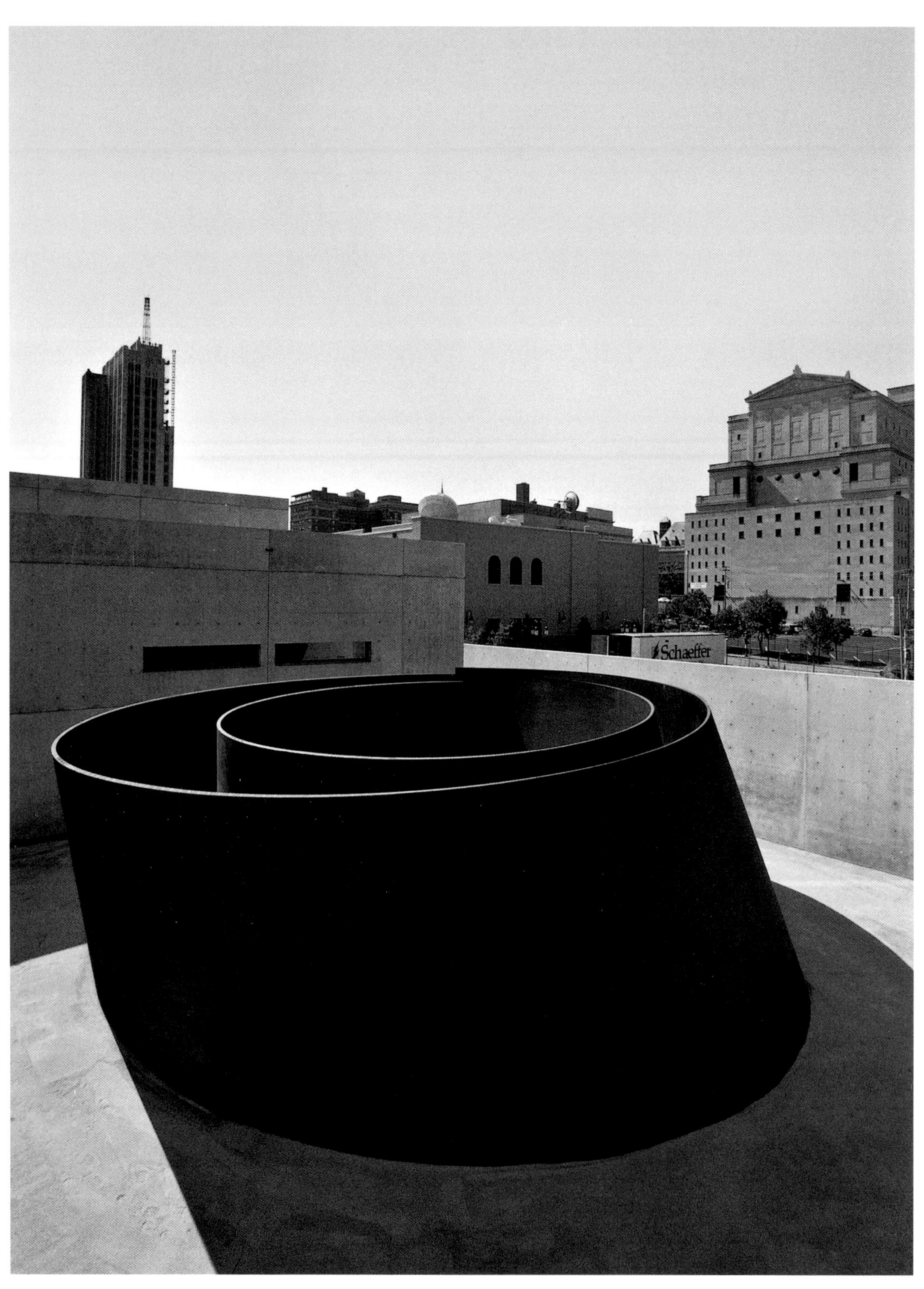

*Joe,* 1999. Weatherproof steel, overall 13 ft. 6 in. × 44 ft. 10 in. × 37 ft. 6 in.(4.1 × 13.7 × 11.4 m), plates 2 in. (5 cm). Pulitzer Foundation for the Arts, Saint Louis, Missouri.

that define us? Certainly you don't differentiate viewers by gender, race, or class. But then we're not all the same; in fact we're not even self-same (I mean we're internally divided by our unconscious). What do you make of that line of questioning?

**RS**: It's simply at odds with my project. I don't want to make any distinctions among viewers. It depends on the work and its context, but my viewer is anybody and everybody. I don't cater to group specificity.

**HF**: But do you see the concern? If your work addresses all people as the same, it might totalize them, or, more precisely, if you frame experience in phenomenological terms alone, you overlook other determinations of subjectivity, those of race, class, and sexuality. As you suggest, that critique could be flipped, and what's taken to be a vice can be understood as a virtue—that you don't differentiate also means that you don't discriminate.

**CW-S**: Richard has to stop at the phenomenological because he wants to leave the experience open. And that's where the work is democratic in a different way. He makes the work available, literally, to anybody and everybody. It's not specific to gender, class, or race. How could it be when, as he's said many times, what the viewer brings to the work is what the viewer brings to the work?

**HF**: So no part of that critique is valid for you?

**RS**: No. Is it for you?

**HF**: Let me suggest how it might be in relation to subsequent art. In a way this is another version of our debate about sites, only here it regards viewers. There I argued that, along with others, you opened up the possibilities of site, but some artists who came after you felt that your definition was limited to site understood as physical space, and they wanted to demonstrate how space, especially in a gallery or a museum, is always institutional as well, always framed by ideological discourses and shot through with socio-economic interests, and often in ways that aren't immediately apparent. That's largely how the investigation of site proceeded in institution critique: first "site" was seen as a physical parameter, then as an institutional frame, then as a discursive apparatus, and so on. And it's roughly the same story with the subjectivity of the viewer. For many artists who came after Minimalism there's no such thing as a phenomenological viewer-in-general. Whether they were influenced by poststructuralist theory, feminist criticism, queer studies, or postcolonial discourse, they all sought to articulate the role of difference—sexual, social, racial, and more—in both production and reception. Of course, this raises the question I asked you in relation to site: Can an artist be questioned according to criteria he or she prepares but doesn't choose to follow up on?

**RS**: What do you mean by "prepares"? I can't foresee the consequence of my actions; nobody can.

**CW-S**: Also, that's where you have to distinguish between the question of site and the question of subjectivity. The site is determined socially, economically, and politically, but the body of the viewer is not determined in the same ways.

**HF**: We might have to agree to disagree on that one. But I take your point that it's democratic to invite everyone in—with the caveat that, practically speaking, not everyone does get in—so that they can differentiate their own experience in relation to the work, to calibrate how it affects them differently. In fact, that's where the student who prompted my question arrived in the end: she now sees the differentiation as happening in the reception of the work, not in its address—that your work is "subject-specific" in the viewing.

**CW-S**: That's exactly right.

**HF**: Okay, a final question, which is also a difficult one (as you say, in for a dime, in for a dollar). In the mid-1980s you remarked that your initial turn, in the mid-1960s, to simple materials like rubber and lead and to everyday processes like rolling, folding, and cutting was undertaken to "demythologize" both the making of art and the role of the artist, and yet fifty years later your work has near-mythic status and you are the most celebrated sculptor in the world.[2] What, if anything, could you have done differently to sustain your initial project of demythologization?

**RS**: You make a leap here that doesn't make sense to me. You go from my own demythologizing of materials to the media's mythologizing of me as an artist.

**HF**: Part of your initial project was also to decenter the artist as origin and end of the work—to give agency to materials and processes as well as to contingencies like accident and forces like gravity.

**RS**: To me those things go into different buckets. How do I reconcile them? How could I? I'm not in control of the reception of my work or the media image of my personality.

**HF**: In your generation at large there was an emphatic move away from the old projection of the artist as master creator, which was still strong in the discourse around Abstract Expressionism. Yet the culture still wants that stereotype of the artist, still demands it even.

**RS**: To quote Carl Andre, "Art is what we do, culture is what is done to us."

**HF**: I love that line, but it's schematic: on the one hand, it tends to absolve us of our own responsibility for culture; on the other, it tends to revive the romantic notion that art is born free.

**CW-S**: Richard doesn't conform to the stereotype of the artist as master creator. It's not anything he aspires to or believes in.

**HF**: It's not about aspiration; it's about what culture does to certain artists. Robert Smithson said forty years ago that every artist has to understand "the apparatus they are threaded through" and figure out a way to deal with it. Today many artists are only too happy to be threaded through—they aspire to it in fact. They take the art world as a game to play and to win, not as an apparatus to resist or to transform.

**RS**: Where the rubber hits the road is where you're part of what's corrupt, and you have to face that contradiction and decide what to do. If you lash out against the institution, you'll be excluded from it. So what you do is keep your counsel, know the context will change eventually, and have some faith that what you're involved with will outlive the moment you're in. Is there a way to make people aware of their contradictions, to involve them in a discussion that opens out to alternative viewpoints? If you throw bombs from the outside you get nowhere; you have to get into the house.

**HF**: "Outlive the moment" suggests that you can somehow transcend your time, or at least that your work can, whereas I expected you to say that the only way for the work to transcend the moment is to dive deeply into it and to express it somehow.

**RS**: You have to be deeply in the moment but with a particular will that individualizes what you do with it. Basically my grounding is in existentialism: it's the will within the moment, drawing on the intensity of that moment, that makes the difference. Sometimes when I look back I wonder how any of it got done. I would've thought everything mitigated against my sculpture—its production, its weight, its scale, its transportation, its rigging. A lot of it has to do with just wanting it to happen and being obstinate. You asked me at the start of this conversation what working through contradictions means to me. It means facing up to whatever problem arises within the making of the work and attempting to turn that problem into a potential for new work. Projecting ideas out of the work, ideas that can't be accomplished at first, is the engine of the work.

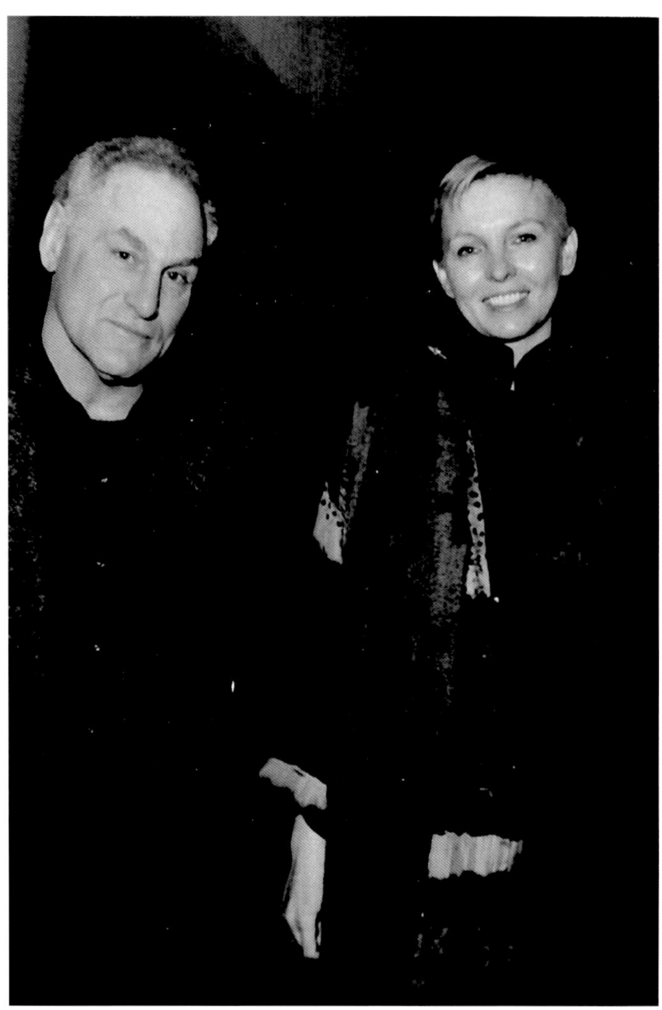

Richard Serra and Clara Weyergraf, 1986.

# Notes

## Preface

1. Serra and I have also discussed his drawing, but we decided to focus on his sculpture for this book.

2. Asked by the *New York Times* about the ten books he would take to a desert island, Serra listed *Self-Reliance and Other Essays* by Emerson first: "I read 'Self-Reliance' when I was seventeen as an undergraduate at UC Berkeley in the 1950s. In this short essay, Emerson takes a stance against conformity and insists on trusting your own judgment, on finding your own path, on living in the present and augmenting what is unique to your own character. These are the principles that have shaped my life and work" (*New York Times,* October 28, 2016).

3. Serra placed *The Anxiety of Influence* tenth in his *New York Times* list: "A young poet who is up against old masters must clear an imaginative space for himself through a creative misunderstanding or misreading of the poets of the past. Bloom defines six categories of overcoming the influence of precursors. He calls these categories 'Revisionary Ratios.' They are useful to all artists."

## Down and Dirty Minimalism

1. Ehrenzweig distinguished unconscious scanning from conscious seeing, or rather he stressed the disruptive persistence of the former in the latter. The influential notion of an "undifferentiated" field of vision (mentioned in "Specific Sites") is also his.

2. Sol LeWitt, "Paragraphs on Conceptual Art," *Artforum* (Summer 1967), 79.

3. Curated by Harald Szeemann, "When Attitudes Become Form," which appeared in both Bern and London, was the first international survey of Post-Minimalist modes of art, as indicated by its subtitle "Works—Concepts—Processes—Situations—Information."

4. *Rose Fractions* (titled after the Billy Rose Theater, where it was first performed) combined prior dances by Rainer; one of these was *Trio A* (1966), in which the grid appeared.

5. See Annette Michelson, "The Films of Richard Serra: An Interview," *October* 10 (Fall 1979).

6. *House of Cards* is dated 1969, when it was first shown; technically, then, *Hand Catching Lead* precedes it. Yet Serra had already begun to experiment with prop pieces, and he wanted to film the assembly of an initial version of *House of Cards* in 1968. When that proved inadequate, he made *Hand Catching Lead.*

## To Lift, To Splash, To Prop…

1. See Donald Judd, "Specific Objects," *Arts Yearbook 8* (1965). On the difference between "quality" and "interest," see "The Crux of Minimalism" (1987), in Hal Foster, *The Return of the Real* (Cambridge, MA: MIT Press, 1996).

## Specific Sites

1. Richard Serra, *Writings Interviews* (Chicago: University of Chicago Press, 1994), 7–8.

2. Ibid., 129.

3. See Robert Smithson, "A Provisional Theory of Non-Sites," in *The Collected Writings,* ed. Jack Flam (Berkeley: University of California Press, 1996).

4. Serra, *Writings Interviews,* 137–38.

5. See ibid., 123. Gestalt readings are also discussed in the Preface.

6. Ibid., 160–61.

7. The city of Paris purchased *Clara-Clara* and placed it in the Parc de Choisy in the 13th arrondissement. In 1993 it was put in storage, where it remains. It was temporarily reinstalled in its original site in 2008 while *Promenade* was at the Grand Palais.

8. Serra discusses this 1932 letter (to the Russian writer Viktor Nekrasov) in *Writings Interviews,* quoting Le Corbusier on Byzantine frescoes in the Kremlin as follows: "I accept the fresco not as something which gives emphasis to the wall, but on the contrary as a means to destroy the wall violently, to remove any notion of its stability, weight, etc." (203).

9. Ibid., 171.

10. Ibid., 175. Here Serra anticipates Rem Koolhaas on "junkspace" by fifteen years or so (see his "Junkspace," *October* 100 [Spring 2002]).

11. Serra, *Writings Interviews,* 126.

12. Ibid., 137, 149–50. "The narrative of seeing" is "not of particular interest to me" (150). For the picturesque in Serra, see Yve-Alain Bois, "A Picturesque Stroll around *Clara-Clara,*" *October* 29 (Summer 1984).

13. Serra, *Writings Interviews,* 120, 170.

14. On this problem see Miwon Kwon, *One Place after Another: Site-Specific Art and Locational Identity* (Cambridge, MA: MIT Press, 2002).

15. See Robert Smithson, "A Sedimentation of the Mind: Earth Projects" (1968), in *Collected Writings,* 85.

16. Serra, *Writings Interviews,* 172.

17. See Hal Foster, "Serra in the Desert," *Artforum* (September 2014).

18. On this development, see Hal Foster, "The Artist as Ethnographer," in *The Return of the Real* (Cambridge, MA: MIT Press, 1996).


**Prime Objects**

1. See George Kubler, *The Shape of Time: Remarks on the History of Things* (New Haven: Yale University Press, 1962).

2. Michael Baxandall, *Painting and Experience in Fifteenth-Century Italy* (Oxford: Oxford University Press, 1972), 86–87, 34.


**Torqued Shapes**

1. Kynaston McShine, "A Conversation about Work with Richard Serra," in *Richard Serra Sculpture: Forty Years,* ed. Kynaston McShine and Lynne Cooke (New York: Museum of Modern Art, 2007), 33.

2. Gilles Deleuze, *The Fold: Leibniz and the Baroque,* trans. Tom Conley (Minneapolis: University of Minnesota Press, 1992), 28, 7. Deleuze takes up Minimalism briefly (123–24).

3. Ibid., 29.


**Passages and Intervals**

1. On this notion, see in particular Lynne Cooke, "Thinking on Your Feet: Richard Serra's Sculptures in Landscape," in *Richard Serra Sculpture: Forty Years,* ed. Kynaston McShine and Lynne Cooke (New York: Museum of Modern Art, 2007).

2. Walter Benjamin, "One-Way Street" (1928), in *Selected Writings Volume 1: 1913–1926* (Cambridge, MA: Harvard University Press, 1996), 456.

3. Adolf Loos, "Architecture," in Wilfried Wang, ed., *The Architecture of Adolf Loos* (London: Arts Council, 1985), 108.

4. Erwin Panofsky, *Tomb Sculpture* (New York: Harry N. Abrams, 1964).

5. Richard Serra, *Writings Interviews* (Chicago: University of Chicago Press, 1994), 184.


**Symbolic Forms**

1. Richard Serra, *Writings Interviews* (Chicago: University of Chicago Press, 1994), 69.

2. See Tony Smith in Samuel Wagstaff, "Talking with Tony Smith," *Artforum* (December 1966), reprinted in Gregory Battcock, ed., *Minimal Art* (New York: Dutton, 1968), 386.

3. Serra, *Writings Interviews,* 184.

4. Ibid., 170.

5. Tony Smith as quoted by Robert Morris in the epigraph to his "Notes on Sculpture, Part 2," *Artforum* (October 1966), reprinted in *Continuous Project Altered Daily* (Cambridge, MA: MIT Press, 1993), 11.

**History Doesn't Go Away**

1. See Quentin Meillassoux, *After Finitude: An Essay on the Necessity of Contingency* (London: Continuum, 2008).

2. See Rosalind Krauss, *Passages in Modern Sculpture* (Cambridge, MA: MIT Press, 1977).

3. See Meyer Schapiro, *Romanesque Art: Selected Papers* (New York: Thames and Hudson, 1993).


**Sculpture Hadn't Dealt with Steel**

1. See Bruce Glaser, "Questions to Stella and Judd," *Artnews* (September 1966).

2. In "Extended Notes from Sight Point Road" (1985) Serra wrote the following: "In all my work the construction process is revealed. Material, formal, contextual decisions are self-evident. The fact that the technological process is revealed depersonalizes and demythologizes the idealization of the sculptor's craft" (*Writings Interviews* [Chicago: University of Chicago Press, 1994], 169).

3. See Michael Fried, "Art and Objecthood," *Artforum* (June 1967).


**Controversies**

1. See Clara Weyergraf-Serra and Martha Buskirk, eds., *The Destruction of* Tilted Arc*: Documents* (Cambridge, MA: MIT Press, 1991).

2. The legal dispute over the Mark Rothko estate is detailed in Lee Seldes, *The Legacy of Mark Rothko* (New York: Holt, Rinehart and Winston, 1978).

3. Richard Serra, *Writings Interviews* (Chicago: University of Chicago Press, 1994), 163.


**Contradictions**

1. Bertolt Brecht as quoted in Walter Benjamin, "Little History of Photography" (1931), in Michael W. Jennings et al., eds., *Selected Writings, Volume 2, Part 2: 1931–1934* (Cambridge, MA: Belknap, 1999), 526. Benjamin doubles down on this attack in "The Author as Producer" (1934). Krupp was a huge steel manufacturer and AEG a vast electric utility in Germany.

2. "Extended Notes from Sight Point Road" (1985), *Writings Interviews* (Chicago: University of Chicago Press, 1994), 169.

# Acknowledgments

The authors thank, at Yale University Press, Patricia Fidler, for her enthusiastic response to our proposal, Amy Canonico, for her astute guidance of the manuscript, and Heidi Downey for her benevolent copyediting; in the Serra studio, Trina McKeever, for her expert assistance; and at Princeton, Lee Colón, for her careful transcription, Hannah Yohalem, for her savvy photo research, and all the students in the spring 2017 seminar "Rethinking Modern Sculpture with Richard Serra" for their critical engagement. Many thanks also to Mark Nelson and David Zaza of McCall Associates for their thoughtful design, and to Chris Calhoun of the Chris Calhoun Agency for his publishing wisdom. This book received a generous subvention from the Barr Ferree Foundation Fund at Princeton, for which we are grateful. It would not have existed at all without the commitment of Clara Weyergraf-Serra and the support of Sandy Tait. Once again we are in their debt.

# Index

Page numbers in *italics* indicate illustrations.

# Illustration Credits

The photographers and the sources of visual material other than the owners indicated in the captions are as follows. Every effort has been made to supply complete and correct credits; if there are errors or omissions, please contact Yale University Press so that corrections can be made in any subsequent edition.

Page 14. Image © CNAC/MNAM/DIST. RMN-Grand Palais/Art Resource, NY. Art © Succession Brancusi—All rights reserved (ARS) 2017.

Page 20 (bottom). Reproduced with permission from The University of Iowa. Art © 2018 The Pollock-Krasner Foundation/Artists Rights Society (ARS), New York.

Page 22 (bottom). Image © The Museum of Modern Art/Licensed by SCALA/Art Resource, NY. Art © 2017 Judd Foundation/Artists Rights Society (ARS), New York.

Page 26 (top). Art © 2017 Stephen Flavin/Artists Rights Society (ARS), New York.

Page 26 (bottom). Image © National Gallery of Canada. Art © Carl Andre/Licensed by VAGA, New York, NY.

Page 29. Photo © Boyd Hagen.

Page 32. Photo © Barbara Moore/Licensed by VAGA, New York, NY. Courtesy Paula Cooper Gallery, New York.

Page 36. Camera: Robert Fiore.

Page 45. Photo Richard Landry.

Page 53. Photo Harry Shunk.

Pages 55, 59, 64, 68, 247. Photo Gianfranco Gorgoni.

Page 61. Photo Balthasar Burkhard.

Pages 69, 71, 72, 96, 118, 126, 129, 130, 133, 135, 176, 178. Photo Lorenz Kienzle.

Pages 73, 80, 83, 84, 94, 113, 114, 120, 154, 172, 237, 249, 252. Photo Dirk Reinartz.

Pages 85, 109, 110, 128, 132, 138, 140, 141, 147, 152. Photo Cristiano Mascaro.

Page 100. Photo Shunk-Kender. © Roy Lichtenstein Foundation.

Page 103. Photo Ann Chauvet.

Page 105. Photo Reiner Friedrich.

Page 116. Photo Gordon Matta-Clark.

Page 124. imageBROKER/Alamy Stock Photo.

Pages 145, 149. Photo Rob McKeever.

Page 155. Photo Werner Hannappel.

Page 156. Photo Rudolf Wakonigg.

Page 163. Jason Langley/Alamy Stock Photo.

Page 174. Photo Lucien Herve. Getty Research Institute, Los Angeles (2002.R.41). Photo © J. Paul Getty Trust. Architecture © F.L.C./ADAGP, Paris/Artists Rights Society (ARS), New York 2017.

Page 175. akg-images/Album/Oronoz.

Page 181 (top). Photo Richard Sharrocks/Alamy Stock Photo.

Page 181 (bottom). Photo courtesy of the Salk Institute for Biological Studies.

Page 186. Photo Credit: The Philadelphia Museum of Art/Art Resource, NY. Art © 2018 Succession H. Matisse/Artists Rights Society (ARS), New York.

Page 188. Photo Credit: Scala/Art Resource, NY. © Hellenic Ministry of Culture and Sports/Archaeological Receipts Fund.

Page 189. Courtesy National Gallery of Art, Washington.

Page 190. Photo Credit: Scala/Art Resource, NY.

Page 191. Photo Credit: Cameraphoto Arte, Venice/Art Resource, NY.

Page 194. Art © 2014. Anrea Jemolo/Scala, Florence Biblioteca Laurenziana. Photo Credit: Scala/Art Resource, NY.

Page 195. Art © 2017 Artists Rights Society (ARS), New York/SIAE, Rome.

Page 201, top. Digital Image © The Museum of Modern Art/Licensed by SCALA/Art Resource, NY. Art © 2017 Estate of Pablo Picasso/Artists Rights Society (ARS), New York.

Page 201 (bottom). Art © 2018, State Russian Museum, St. Petersburg.

Pages 202, 203 (bottom). Art © Alberto Giacometti Estate/Licensed by VAGA and ARS, New York, NY. Digital Image © The Museum of Modern Art/Licensed by SCALA/Art Resource, NY.

Pages 203 (top), 205 (left). Photo credit: Kunsthaus Zürich. Art © Alberto Giacometti Estate/Licensed by VAGA and ARS, New York, NY.

Page 205 (right). Photo Mathieu Rabeau. © RMN-Grand Palais/Art Resource, NY. Art © 2017 Estate of Pablo Picasso/Artists Rights Society (ARS), New York.

Page 207. Photo © Sheldon Museum of Art. Art © Succession Brancusi—All rights reserved (ARS) 2017.

Page 218. Photo Jennifer Kotter.

Page 226. Photo Bill Jacobson Studio.

Page 227. Photo Allison Smith.

Page 230. Photo Alexander von Berswordt-Wallrabe.

Page 256. Photo Jeanne Trudeau.

Page 251. Photo Stephan Nyeffeler.